"Young Bob" La Follette

"Young Bob" La Follette
A Biography of Robert M. La Follette, Jr., 1895–1953

Patrick J. Maney

University of Missouri Press
Columbia & London, 1978

Library of Congress Cataloging in Publication Data

Maney, Patrick J   1946–
  "Young Bob" La Follette.

  Bibliography: p. 315
  Includes index.
    1. La Follette, Robert Marion, 1895–1953.
2. Legislators—United States—Biography. 3. Social
reformers—United States—Biography. 4. Progressivism
(United States politics) I. Title.
E748.L22M36   973.91′092′4 [B]   77–24991
ISBN 0–8262–0230–6

To my mother and father
Blanche and Thomas Maney

Acknowledgments

Many persons aided me in the preparation of this biography. I am especially indebted to Professor Horace Samuel Merrill of the University of Maryland, who first suggested the topic and who guided the study through every stage of preparation. His wise counsel, his patience, and his and Mrs. Merrill's encouragement and friendship were invaluable. Professor Wayne S. Cole of the University of Maryland read the manuscript and generously gave me the benefit of his own deep knowledge of the agrarian progressives and of foreign policy. Professor Robert H. Zieger of Wayne State University not only made numerous suggestions that strengthened the final product but also offered timely encouragement. Others who read the manuscript and offered helpful suggestions were Professors Keith W. Olson and David Grimsted of the University of Maryland; Miles McMillin of the *Capital Times* of Madison, Wisconsin; and Wisconsin Attorney General Bronson C. La Follette. I am particularly grateful to Miss Mary La Follette for sharing with me memories of her remarkable family and for many other kindnesses. The many persons who generously gave of their time to talk with me about La Follette also earned my deep appreciation.

The staffs of many libraries gave me essential help, especially the staffs of the Manuscript Division of the Library of Congress and of the State Historical Society of Wisconsin. In addition, U. S. Senate Historian Richard A. Baker furnished valuable materials.

I also wish to acknowledge a long-standing debt to Professor Frank Crow of the University of Wisconsin—Stevens Point and to thank my parents for so many things. To my wife, Elaine Cowie Maney, I owe more than I can express, for this was truly a joint project. She spent many Saturdays sifting through La Follette papers at the Library of Congress; she typed and proofread innumerable drafts; and she offered incisive criticisms. Through it all she was a constant source of understanding and encouragement.

Contents

Abbreviations used in the footnotes

Belle Case La Follette	Belle
Fola La Follette	Fola
Isabel "Isen" Bacon La Follette	Mrs. PFL
Mary La Follette	Mary
La Follette Family Papers, Library of Congress, Washington, D.C.	Family Papers, with appropriate box and series numbers
Philip F. La Follette	PFL
Philip La Follette Papers, State Historical Society of Wisconsin, Madison	PFL Papers, with appropriate box and series numbers
Rachel La Follette	Rachel
Robert M. La Follette, Jr.	RML
Robert M. La Follette, Sr.	RML Sr.
U. S. *Congressional Record*	*CR*, with appropriate Congress and session numbers

Introduction

Robert M. La Follette, Jr., was a major representative of the famous La Follette dynasty that for many decades wielded great political influence and power, both in Wisconsin and on the national scene. His father, Robert M. La Follette, Sr., working closely with his wife, Belle, launched the dynasty at the beginning of the twentieth century. The elder La Follette died in 1925, after having served as governor of Wisconsin for six years and as United States senator for twenty years. La Follette, Jr., known as Young Bob, inherited the headship of the dynasty. Having served as secretary to his father, he now replaced him in the United States Senate. His younger brother Philip soon became governor of Wisconsin.

In the Senate, where he served for the next twenty one years, Young Bob carried on the family crusade for progressive reform. During his first few years in the Senate, La Follette proved to be an able but rather unimaginative successor to his father. Beginning in 1928, however, he began to rely on his own instincts, to venture into new areas, and to apply his and his father's principles to new problems. A transitional figure in the history of modern reform movements, he linked progressivism, which had flourished during the first decades of the century, with urban liberalism, which took root in the 1920s and flowered during the 1930s and the succeeding decades.

La Follette achieved national prominence during the Great Depression of the 1930s. He was one of the earliest public figures to identify declining purchasing power as the root cause of the depression and to formulate a coherent plan for combating it. His plan included demands for federal relief to the unemployed, massive expansion of public works, a modest degree of national economic planning, and tax reform. A harsh critic of the Hoover administration, La Follette found the New Deal more to his liking. Yet, he was also one of the New Deal's most penetrating critics. La Follette reached the height of his national prominence between 1936 and 1940, when, as chairman of the Senate Civil Liberties Committee, he helped expose the heavy-handed, often brutal manner in which many employers tried to prevent their workers from organizing. The committee conducted an extensive, productive, and generally fair inquiry.

Before Pearl Harbor, La Follette was an isolationist who wanted the United States to avoid involvement in European affairs. During and after World War II he became a cautious internationalist who urged the United States to use its power and influence to check the expansionist tendencies of the Soviet Union. Despite the seeming contradiction, both positions derived from basically the same set of assumptions.

World War II was the most frustrating period of La Follette's career. His progressive philosophy, which had sustained him well to that time, provided no answers to the new and complex problems of wartime. Caught in a cross fire between farmers and organized labor in Wisconsin, he inadvertently alienated important segments of organized labor and thereby weakened his base of electoral support. Following the war, however, he experienced one final success. Seeking to restore to Congress the power and prestige that had shifted to the presidency during the war, he sponsored and steered through Congress the Legislative Reorganization Act of 1946.

Despite his marked superiority as a senator, La Follette possessed striking weaknesses as a political leader. In 1934 he reluctantly abandoned the Republican party to help create the Progressive party of Wisconsin. But he never gave the party the consistent, firm leadership it needed to survive, and he began to devote less and less time to Wisconsin affairs. His defeat in 1946 at the hands of Joseph R. McCarthy was largely due to that neglect. Paradoxically, during his last campaign La Follette placed far more emphasis on the so-called red menace than did McCarthy, whose name would later become synonymous with it.

An exceedingly complex man, La Follette had always regarded public life as something to be endured rather than enjoyed. Yet, following his defeat in 1946 he sadly discovered that private life was less congenial than public life. But just how unhappy La Follette had become, no one realized until February 1953 when, at age fifty-eight, he committed suicide.

CHAPTER 1

The Early Years, 1895–1916

In 1895, Wisconsin, like the nation, was struggling through the third year of the most severe and prolonged depression it had ever experienced. What had started as a bankers' panic two years earlier had spread so rapidly that the wounds of hard times were visible almost everywhere. In the cities, where about one-third of the population lived, many banks and businesses remained closed, and major industries continued to curtail production, thus keeping employment and wage levels low. Perhaps as many as 20 or even 30 percent of urban workers were jobless. Conditions were at least as severe in the state's rural areas, where farm prices plummeted to new lows. For many, the promise of abundance and prosperity made in better days by the proponents of uncontrolled industrialization was now proving to be a mere sham. But even while the depression dragged on, individuals and groups throughout Wisconsin were coming together in a common cause; they were beginning to search for ways not only to end the depression but also to secure permanent control over the system that had brought so much hardship and suffering. From the depression soil was growing a modern reform movement.[1]

Curiously, the family that would play so prominent a role in that movement was escaping the hardships of the depression. There was always work for a lawyer, it seemed, and Robert Marion La Follette was a good one. The reputation he had earned during the 1880s as district attorney and United States congressman attracted a steady stream of clients to his office in Madison, the state capital. With his wife, Belle, and twelve-year-old daughter, Fola, he lived comfortably in a home on the corner of West Wilson and Broom streets in southeast Madison. The La Follette home reflected the family's good fortune. The spacious frame dwelling, with cupola, mansard roof, high French windows, and wide veranda, rested atop a high bluff on the shore of Lake Monona. Although modestly furnished and not nearly so elegant

---

1. David P. Thelen, *The New Citizenship: Origins of Progressivisim in Wisconsin, 1885–1900* (Columbia, Mo., 1972), pp. 57–60.

as the William F. Vilas home or the governor's mansion across town, it was still an imposing structure.[2]

Here, on 6 February 1895, Belle gave birth to her first boy. Robert had long wanted a son, so without hesitation they named him Robert Marion, Jr. Bobbie, as everyone called him, was a healthy, normal child—"a beautiful sturdy little boy with golden curls and big blue eyes with long curling lashes," his proud mother later recalled. Robert, Belle, and sister Fola lavished him with attention. Even after the births of Philip in 1897 and Mary in 1899, Bobbie remained his parents' and his older sister's favorite. For a while at least, life was safe and secure.[3]

The most important influences on Bob, Jr., were his remarkable parents. While growing up and throughout his life, they were the standards against which he measured himself and others. Robert, Sr., thirty-nine years old when Bobbie was born, was slight of build and short, though his thick brown hair, swept back in pompadour style, made him look much taller. When he cocked his head forward, as he did when speaking or listening intently, his furrowed brow and piercing eyes made the nickname of "Fighting Bob" seem fully appropriate; but when he smiled or laughed, that rather harsh image easily gave way to one more warm and friendly.

Born in 1855, La Follette, Sr., grew up in and around Primrose, Wisconsin, a tiny agrarian community about twenty-five miles southwest of Madison. His father, Josiah, whose French Huguenot ancestors had immigrated to America in the middle of the eighteenth century, and his mother, Mary Fergeson, whose Scottish ancestors had arrived about the same time, had come to Primrose from Indiana in 1850. Josiah died only eight months after Robert's birth, leaving Mary with four children and a sizable farm to care for. For Mary this was the second great tragedy in her life; her first husband had died within a year of their marriage. When Robert was seven, his mother married again. Her third husband, John Saxton, was a seventy-year-old man whose harsh discipline and severe Baptist beliefs quickly alienated young Robert.

When Saxton died in 1872, much of the family burden passed to Robert. Yet, despite economic hardships, he and his mother managed to earn enough to cover his expenses at the University of Wisconsin,

2. Belle Case La Follette and Fola La Follette, *Robert M. La Follette* (New York, 1953), 1:91–95; Gwyneth King Roe, "Two Views of the La Follettes: I. Madison, the '90's," *Wisconsin Magazine of History* 42 (Winter 1958–1959): 130–39.

3. Belle and Fola, *La Follette*, 1:110; Belle to RML, 15 February 1915, box 17-A, Family Papers (see list of abbreviations p. x).

which he entered in the fall of 1875. At the university he excelled, not in scholarship, but in extracurricular activities. He owned and edited the school newspaper; extroverted and engaging, he made himself the center of attraction at parties and dances; but most of all, he excelled in public speaking. The high point of his college career came during his senior year when he bested opponents from six states to win the annual collegiate oratorical contest. His winning performance, an analysis of the character Iago from Shakespeare's *Othello*, helped convince the faculty that he deserved a degree, for with all his outside activities he had woefully neglected his studies. While at the university, Robert also met Belle Case. He proposed to her at the end of their junior year, and they were married in 1881, a year after graduation.

For a time La Follette considered a career in the theater, but he chose instead the wider audience that law and politics offered. In 1880 he was admitted to the bar, and a year later, at age twenty-six, he won his first election, becoming district attorney of Dane County. The courtroom provided him ample opportunity to display his dramatic skills, and during the next four years he attracted wide attention throughout both the county and the state.[4] But the ambitious young prosecutor had his sights set on bigger things. In 1884 he ran as a Republican for a seat in the United States House of Representatives. He was elected and, at the age of thirty, became the youngest member of Congress.

While in Washington, La Follette impressed his colleagues with his hard work, thorough preparation, gift for speaking, and loyalty to the Republican party. Despite a few scraps with other members of the Wisconsin delegation, his standing within the party grew, and the leadership eventually rewarded him with a seat on the powerful Ways and Means Committee. During his three terms in the House he played important roles in the formulation and passage of the Interstate Commerce Act of 1887 and the McKinley Tariff of 1890. He also struck up friendships with such congressional powers as "Czar" Thomas Reed, Speaker of the House, and William McKinley of Ohio.[5] Obviously, insurgency had not yet become a La Follette trait.

The Democratic landslide in the election of 1890 temporarily halted La Follette's budding political career. In March 1891 he returned unhappily to Madison, to West Wilson Street, and to the practice of law. But seven months later there occurred an incident that became

---

4. For detailed accounts of RML Sr.'s early life see Belle and Fola, *La Follette*, 1:1–57; David P. Thelen, *The Early Life of Robert M. La Follette, 1855–1884* (Chicago, 1966).

5. Belle and Fola, *La Follette*, 1:52–88.

legend in Wisconsin history. According to La Follette's account, Philetus Sawyer, a United States senator, a millionaire lumberman, and a leader of the state's Republican machine, offered him a bribe. Robert Siebecker, La Follette's brother-in-law and former law partner, who had become a judge, was presiding over a case in which Sawyer and several other prominent Republicans were defendants. The bribe, claimed La Follette, was Sawyer's attempt to buy influence on the court. "Nothing else ever came into my life that exerted such a powerful influence upon me as that affair," he said years later. "I had been subjected to a terrible shock that opened my eyes, and I began to see really for the first time." But "out of this awful ordeal came understanding; and out of understanding came resolution. I determined that the power of this corrupt influence, which was undermining and destroying every semblance of representative government in Wisconsin, should be broken."[6]

Although La Follette may have exaggerated the impact of the Sawyer affair—then and later some said that he longed to get back into politics and seized upon the incident as a handy excuse—it did bring him back into public life. During the next eight years he maintained his law office but rearranged his schedule to allow maximum time for campaigning. In 1894 he managed the unsuccessful gubernatorial challenge of fellow insurgent Nils P. Haugen. Then in 1896, and again in 1898, he himself ran for governor, but both times he failed to get the Republican nomination. The depression of the 1890s, however, had a profound effect on Wisconsin voters. It shattered many of the ethnic, class, and social barriers and the economic assumptions that had hindered previous reform efforts. In 1900 a new social consciousness, combined with La Follette's organizational skills and the internal decay of the old Republican machine, helped to pave the way for his nomination and election to the governorship.

Contrary to the impression La Follette later gave, during his rise to the statehouse he had been slow in proposing concrete reforms. He had advocated a state-wide direct primary for all elective offices and increased taxation of the railroads, both much needed reforms; but in 1896, and again in 1900, he had also supported his old friend William McKinley for the presidency and had warned of the dangers of William Jennings Bryan, free silver, and a lower tariff. Upon becoming governor, however, La Follette vigorously pursued reform. His stated objectives were to make government more responsive to the will of the people and to utilize government to make big business more re-

6. Robert M. La Follette, *La Follette's Autobiography: A Personal Narrative of Political Experiences* (Madison, 1960 [1911, 1913]), pp. 65–72.

sponsive to the needs of the consumer. To these ends, he successfully fought for direct primaries, legislation to control corrupt practices, increased taxation and regulation of the railroads and other industries, and a variety of other reforms.[7]

During his governorship, and later after he was elected to the Senate, La Follette owed much of his success to his mastery of the art of politics. During the 1890s and in his first years as governor, he constructed a powerful political machine, which he supported with such traditional devices as patronage and skillful appeals to diverse interests and ethnic groups. A perceptive judge of character and talent, he attracted devoted and capable assistants to aid in the administration of state affairs. But La Follette was his own best man. An energetic campaigner, he canvassed the state many times over, sometimes working to the point of physical exhaustion or nervous collapse. His most effective asset was his skill on the platform. He "prepared for a speech like a man writing a book," muckraker Lincoln Steffens commented. And his wife, Belle, complained that the preparation of an important address would hang "over the household like a nightmare for months." On paper his speeches read like carefully constructed legal briefs: they were tightly reasoned, full of facts, and a bit boring; yet when he read them before an audience he gave them life. La Follette had charisma. His audiences would sit in rapt attention for hours, laughing when he laughed, hissing and booing when he denounced the villain, and erupting in wild applause and pleading for more when he concluded.[8]

While La Follette had great strengths as a politician, he also had great weaknesses. Although outgoing and sociable by nature, he tended to lose friends as easily as he made them. Too often he translated political differences into personal differences, attributing lack of character or morals to those who disagreed with him. During his first term as governor, for example, he implied that the opponents of his railroad-taxation bill had accepted bribes from the railroad lobby. Some legislators undoubtedly were "on the take," but his blanket accusation permanently alienated others who had opposed the bill out of honest conviction. By this and similar actions, La Follette often solidified the opposition and added to its ranks individuals who might have supported him on other issues. Another liability was his inability

7. See: Thelen, *New Citizenship*; Herbert F. Margulies, *The Decline of the Progressive Movement in Wisconsin, 1890–1920* (Madison, 1968), chaps. 1–2; Robert S. Maxwell, *La Follette and the Rise of the Progressives in Wisconsin* (Madison, 1956).

8. Lincoln Steffens, *The Autobiography of Lincoln Steffens* (New York, 1931), 2:458; Belle to RML Sr., 27 September 1909, box 7-A, Family Papers.

to work consistently well with others. Even some of his close friends and associates believed that he would not join a particular effort or movement unless he could dominate it.[9]

Publicly, La Follette conveyed the image of a serious, almost humorless man, consumed with the passion of his cause. His family knew this side of him, but they knew another side as well. Although politics dominated his life at home as well as at work, he was an openly affectionate husband and father who took great interest in all the little activities of family life. Perhaps because of the loss of his father and the strained relationship with his stepfather, a stable and happy home life was especially important to him. Mary, the youngest member of the family, remembered seeing her father really angry only once, and that was much later in life. Instead of anger, he expressed disappointment or hurt when the children did something that displeased him, and instead of punishment, he relied on the force of example and on moral suasion as incentives for his children to improve themselves. Yet, he still expected much from his children, especially from son Bob.[10]

"I am proud of our Kiddies Mamma," La Follette once wrote to Belle. "They are a rare combination of rare qualities. They could not be otherwise with such a great woman for [a] mother. It is the mother that makes the children what they are."[11] La Follette was being overly modest, for he too exerted a profound influence on them. People later agreed, however, that in physical appearance and temperament Bobbie more closely resembled his mother.

Four years younger than her husband, Belle Case was a hearty, handsome woman with fair hair piled on her head and blue eyes. She was born and raised on farms near Baraboo, a small town about forty miles northwest of Madison. Her parents, Anson and Mary Nesbit Case, had high ambitions for their daughter, and they scrimped and saved enough to send her to the University of Wisconsin. In the same class as Robert, Belle compiled an impressive record. While he barely managed to earn a degree, she finished near the top of the class. While he earned the right to be considered class orator, she too had her triumphs; at graduation she won the Lewis Prize for the best commencement oration. In 1885, at the age of twenty-six, Belle also

9. Margulies, *The Decline of the Progressive Movement*, pp. 53–55; James Holt, *Congressional Insurgents and the Party System, 1909–1916* (Cambridge, Mass., 1967), pp. 142–43, 150.

10. Interview, Mary La Follette, 22 February 1973; see, for example, RML Sr. to RML, 29 July, 20 August 1911, box 11-A, RML Sr. to RML, 5 February 1907, box 6-A, RML Sr. to family, 20 June 1917, box 21–A, Family Papers.

11. RML Sr. to family, 13 December 1916, box 19-A, Family Papers.

became the first woman to graduate from the University of Wisconsin Law School.[12]

When in his *Autobiography* Robert described his wife as his "wisest and best counsellor," he was not merely bowing to a conventional courtesy. Audiences would roar with laughter when they saw Belle tug at Robert's coattails or slip him a note when she thought him too long-winded on the platform. But she went much further than that. She took part in almost all important political conferences, offering her advice freely and frequently. Throughout the years, Belle was both her husband's most severe critic and his most unwavering supporter.[13]

Belle possessed an independent spirit. Before her wedding she asked the minister to delete the command *to obey* from the marriage vows. In public affairs she shared most of her husband's political beliefs, but she did so out of conviction rather than out of any sense of wifely obligation. Occasionally she allowed her highly imaginative and speculative mind to drift into areas where Robert was unwilling to venture. Once she expressed the opinion that the nation could never "return to the old order of personal competition in the business world," an opinion that her husband, the nation's foremost advocate of trust busting, could never endorse. After the Russian Revolution in 1917 she commented that "Communism seems to be the forward step in the solution of economic conditions at this stage of society."[14] And in religion, although a Unitarian most of her life, she eventually became an agnostic. Robert also displayed liberal religious attitudes; but he was never that liberal. Although not a churchgoer himself, he required the children to attend Sunday school and to recite prayers at bedtime.[15]

Belle further exhibited her independence by embracing certain social causes, like the black civil rights movement, that only remotely interested her husband. Although she believed that blacks were inferior to whites, she publicly denounced lynching, segregation, and the disfranchisement of black voters in the South. In addition to civil rights, Belle championed numerous other causes, from reform of

12. Belle and Fola, *La Follette*, 1:36–41, 51; Ann J. Brickfield, "Belle Case La Follette: Progressive Woman" (M.A. thesis, University of Maryland, 1976), pp. 1–4.

13. RML Sr., *Autobiography*, pp. 30, 134–35; see, for example, Belle to RML Sr., 27 September 1909, box 7-A, Belle to RML Sr., 3 August 1903, box 2-A, Family Papers.

14. Belle and Fola, *La Follette*, 1:53; Belle to RML Sr., 16 April 1919, box 24-A, Family Papers.

15. Interview, Mary La Follette.

women's dress habits to world disarmament. Closest to her heart, however, was the woman suffrage movement. In 1914, on one of her frequent speaking tours, she addressed audiences on behalf of suffrage for sixty-four consecutive days. While Belle considered the right to vote vitally important, she believed it only the first step toward women's full participation in society; she urged wives and mothers to free themselves from their "parasitic" dependence on their husbands, develop their talents, and be of service to humanity.[16]

With an active career of her own and with her continuing participation in her husband's career, Belle seemed perfectly suited to public life. Surprisingly, however, she always approached its demands with mixed emotions. Although she gave the appearance of being outgoing and self-confident, she was basically shy. "Even now after all my experience," she once confessed, "I suffer with anxiety" when standing before an audience. Another time, while on the stump in Wisconsin, she told her daughter Mary how she had almost forced her way into the campaign: "I could not endure just to look on." "But," she said, "I do dread to go on the train and be obliged to talk to people."[17] Given her choice, Belle would have preferred a behind-the-scenes role with only occasional appearances on center stage, a preference that her son Bob would later share.

Like her husband, Belle tended to blow some things out of proportion. The normal ups and downs that the children experienced often became great tragedies or triumphs in her mind. As the children grew older, Belle continued to play the role of parent, and her motherly advice sometimes seemed more like outright meddling. When her oldest daughter, Fola, at age twenty-nine, announced her intention to marry George Middleton, a New York playwright whom she had met during her career as an actress, Belle was vehemently opposed and did everything in her power to persuade Fola to reconsider. Years later, when Mary became engaged, Belle repeated the pattern. Belle lost both times, and though reluctantly, she welcomed the outsiders into the sacred family circle.[18]

The children loved, even adored Belle. "The only person that I read of in history that compares with you, is Christ," Phil once told her. And Bob wrote, "Oh! my Mummsie I wish I could tell you all you mean to me; tell you how I appreciate what a wonderful woman you

16. Belle, speech and article files, box 40-D, Family Papers; *Progressive,* 7 November 1931.

17. Belle to Mary, 26 March 1917, box 20-A, Belle to family, 20 October 1920, box 28-A, Family Papers.

18. Belle, letter files, boxes 10-A, 29-A, Family Papers.

are and how proud I am to be your boy. May the good Lord make me somewhat worthy, for I fear even he could not make me wholly so!"[19]

Bob was nearly seven years old when in January 1901 his father became governor and the family moved from West Wilson Street to the stately, sandstone governor's mansion on the shore of Lake Mendota. In 1903, at the age of eight, Bob suffered the first of many illnesses that would plague him the rest of his life. He was confined to bed for many months, and although the doctors were unable to diagnose the illness, the symptoms sounded suspiciously like rheumatic fever. Except for that incident, however, he experienced a normal childhood, or at least as normal a childhood as was possible for the son of a famous politician. He enjoyed swimming in summer, skating and sledding in winter, and riding his horse. When he was a little older his father gave him a pistol and a rifle for hunting. One summer he and his brother, Phil, put on a circus. They rented a tent and performed in front of fifty paying customers. Bob, Phil later recalled, "broke his arm falling off a trapeze in practice, but he was still there and took part in the show."[20]

From the beginning, politics was the center of the family's activities. Bob and Phil, who was two years younger than he, frequently accompanied Belle to the capitol to hear their father address the legislature and to witness important debates between La Follette's supporters, who called themselves progressives, and their opponents, the stalwarts. Occasionally the boys traveled along on campaign trips. At night the governor would bring visitors home to dinner, and the children would listen attentively as the elders discussed politics. The children, recalled Belle, "were present at the councils of the grown-ups if they cared to be, and those who participated for the first time would be surprised to find them listening to the most solemn and confidential political matters." Even though Bob was still too young to comprehend fully all that was going on around him, he did understand that his father was engaged in a long, drawn-out battle with the stalwarts over the enactment of a series of important reforms. He also understood the intense feelings that his father aroused: "I am wearing a black eye that Philip Sanborn gave me in a football game at school," he proudly reported to his sister Fola when he was nine. "But

19. PFL to Belle, 11 March 1916, box 19-A, RML to Belle, 18 February 1917, box 21-A, Family Papers.
20. RML medical history, "Summary in the Case of Mr. Robert M. La Follette," June 1949, box 26-C, Family Papers; PFL to Mrs. PFL, 16 August 1944, box 142-2, PFL Papers.

you know that I am a fair football player, and would not slug back. Philip is a Stalwart, you know."[21]

In 1905 the state legislature elected La Follette to the United States Senate, thus giving him a chance to apply his progressive ideas to national problems. He delayed taking his seat for a year, however, in order to complete the program he had promised Wisconsin voters in the last election. Before leaving for Washington, Robert and Belle looked around for a permanent home in Wisconsin where they could return between sessions of Congress. Having grown up on farms, they had always wanted one of their own, and after a long search they purchased the Maple Bluff Farm for thirty thousand dollars. The sixty-acre estate was located on the northern shore of Lake Mendota, the shore across from the governor's mansion and the city. At the center of the estate was a vine-covered, spacious brick house, dating from the 1850s. Although the La Follettes never intended to make a profit, they ran the place as a farm and purchased a dairy herd, horses, and ponies. In the years to come, the family divided its time between Washington and Maple Bluff. While at the farm, Bob, Phil, and Mary performed their share of the chores, fulfilling their parents' hopes that a taste of farm life would endow them with the trusted agrarian virtues of responsibility and self-reliance. For several summers, Bob also managed the farm and thereby acquired an understanding of farm problems and a good grasp of business matters.[22]

When the elder La Follette entered the Senate, Bob became even more involved in politics. When in Washington, he continued to sit in on important strategy sessions. When at Maple Bluff, his father's almost daily letters kept him and the family abreast of the latest developments. Phil later recalled that "in politics and in public affairs" the senator "had no secrets from us. We opened and read his mail that came to the house, and when we called for him to drive him home at the end of the day we pored over the mail that came to his office." Among the frequent visitors to the La Follette home in Washington were congressional insurgents George W. Norris, William E. Borah, Moses E. Clapp; muckraker Lincoln Steffens; and a particularly close friend, a lawyer who was later to become a Supreme Court justice, Louis Brandeis. To the children, Norris was "Uncle George," Brandeis was "Uncle Louis," and Steffens, "Steff."[23]

21. Belle and Fola, *La Follette*, 1:111; RML to Fola, 12 November 1904, box 3-A, Family Papers.

22. Belle and Fola, *La Follette*, 1:196–97; RML to Belle and RML Sr., 25 July 1912, box 12-A, Family Papers.

23. Philip F. La Follette, *Adventure in Politics: The Memoirs of Philip La Follette* (New York, 1970), p. 21.

Although political affairs occupied much of his time, Bob had other interests as well. In 1909 he entered Western High School in Washington and joined the dramatic club, began to date, and frequently attended parties and dances. Often he devoted his spare time to tinkering with the family car or riding his Harley-Davidson motorcycle, which he had purchased with his share of Grandmother Case's inheritance.[24]

Toward the end of high school, life began to get more complicated for Bob. Up to that time he had enjoyed a relatively carefree, pressure-free existence. But now things began to change. His parents were talking about his future, and the immediate future meant college, at least as far as they were concerned. After all, both of them had earned college degrees, and Fola had graduated with honors and a Phi Beta Kappa key from the University of Wisconsin. So, despite the fact that Bob was only an indifferent student, his parents expected him to follow in their footsteps and attend the university.

College figured prominently in the ambitious plans the elder La Follette had for his son. Even though he himself had compiled a mediocre record at the university, he lectured his son, "Your *success in life* depends on the *thoroughness* and *character* of your work in the University." Old Bob believed that his son was capable of achieving great things in life: "You have the brain and the constitution and the courage to take high rank in any company and to be a leader of power for good as a man." But for Bob to bring out his "splendid powers" and fulfill his promise, his father believed, he had to acquire the habits of industry and self-discipline, and this he could best do at the university.[25]

In 1913, at the age of eighteen, Bob entered the University of Wisconsin, which had changed considerably since his parents' college days. Not only had it grown in size—the enrollment was over four thousand, as compared with three hundred and fifty in the 1870s—but it had also grown in stature. Many people now considered it one of the nation's leading universities. Much of the enhanced reputation of the university was due to the efforts of the elder La Follette. During his years as governor, he had continually fought for increased appropriations for the school and had encouraged high academic standards. Moreover, he had initiated the "Wisconsin Idea," which called upon university personnel to take an active role in government. As a result, many of the professors, besides attending to their class-

24. Ibid., pp. 15–29; RML Sr. to Belle, 29 July 1909, box 8-A, Family Papers; interview, Mary La Follette.
25. RML Sr. to RML, 29 July 1911, box 11-A, Family Papers.

room duties, sat on one or more of the regulatory commissions that La Follette had helped create. Many of the professors had also been a part of La Follette's inner circle when he was governor, and they continued to advise him now that he was in the Senate.[26]

Old Bob viewed his son's entrance into the university as a momentous event, the beginning of a time that would "tell the story" of his life to follow. But Young Bob was less in awe. His first letters home were typical of any incoming freshman: "I have a Sat. eight o'clock which is the devil"; "I have been to a few dances and everybody is doing the grapevine it sure does look funny"; "How are all the Wash. girls. I sure do miss them"; "Please get me a couple of classy ties at the Young Men's Shop"; "I miss you all so"; "Please tell everybody not to forget to drop me a line when they get the time." And he concluded with the usual request for money.[27]

Bob immediately plunged into extracurricular activities and campus politics. Within a month he was running for the presidency of the freshman class. "It will be a stiff scrap," he told his father, "but your name will help tremendously." His platform promised "merit and efficiency in appointments to committees; a democratic administration, devoid of clique or class politics; representation for women on committees"; and doubtless the biggest attraction, "a fine freshman party and two cost-mixers." During the campaign, young La Follette employed his father's style and charged that the opposition had secured the help of conservative businessmen in town. To him, the election meant more than the class presidency; it was a small part of the struggle in which his father was engaged. When he won by eight votes, his father telegraphed congratulations and urged his son to "be nice to the fellows who were beaten and now remember what your real job is."[28]

His real job was to study, but Bob found his courses either boring or too difficult. At the end of the first semester he complained that he missed home: "I don't think I will ever be contented except at home! I miss the politics and the big men that come to the house. I got more out of one conference with Mr. Brandise[sic] and John Commons than I will ever get out of a years work in geology." And he added, "I

26. Merle Curti and Vernon Carstensen, *The University of Wisconsin* (Madison, 1949), 2:15, 108–9, 497.
27. RML Sr. to RML, 29 July 1911, box 11-A, RML to PFL, 24 September 1913, RML to Belle, 2 October 1913, box 13-A, Family Papers.
28. RML to RML Sr., October 1913, " 'Bob' La Follette, Jr. Has His First Political Campaign," *Milwaukee Journal*, 24 October 1913, clipping, RML to Belle, 12 November 1913, telegram, RML Sr. to RML, 7–8 November 1913, box 13-A, Family Papers.

don't care if England has to import most of her food stuffs. And the fact that Norway has more ship's tonnage per capita than any other country is not spell binding. I'd even rather talk with the French ambassadors wife!"[29]

Although he may have been homesick, he refused to sit around and brood about it. He went out almost every night, not to the library, but to parties, dances, and to play cards. He also became an ardent football fan. In the fall of 1914, against his parents' advice, he joined the Beta Theta Pi fraternity. The senator and Belle believed that fraternities were undemocratic. But not Bob. Beta Theta Pi, he said, "stands for all that is fine and good in life and stands for it hard and strong not only in the virtual but in the daily actions and thoughts of all that are true Betas." Two years later, when Phil became a member of the same fraternity, Bob was overjoyed: "I just say that I too thank God that you are a Beta."[30]

Bob's active social life naturally took a toll on his grades. At the end of the first year he was on probation and failed to advance to the sophomore level. At the beginning of his second year, his parents received a letter from the university informing them that his "scholarship record in the immediate past" was "so poor as to occasion unfavorable criticism on the part of the faculty."[31] Because he had not fully revealed to his parents the extent of his failure, the news fell like a bombshell. His father immediately prepared self-addressed, stamped postcards and instructed Bob to report daily on any class recitations or examinations. A few weeks later, Belle traveled to Madison to investigate the situation. She talked with all of his teachers, the dean of the School of Arts and Letters, and the president of the university. She even had lunch with his fraternity brothers and sat in on one of his classes. Doubtless to Bob's chagrin, she learned about his going out every night, about his frequent absences from class, and about his apparent lack of interest in his studies. When the senator received Belle's report, he sent out another batch of postcards, but this time to Bob's teachers. Then he scolded his son: "Oh Bobbie, Bobbie! If you have no interest, no zeal, no ambition for yourself, no pride to make good with the faculty and your student friends, do it for your mother,—if you have to work eighteen hours out of every twenty-four for the balance of the year." "Everybody loves you," he

29. RML to family, 23 February 1914, box 16-A, Family Papers.

30. Belle to RML, 16 May 1914, box 13-A, RML Sr. to RML, 15 May 1914, box 15-A, telegram, RML Sr. to RML, 1 October 1914, box 16-A, RML to PFL, April 1916, box 19-A, Family Papers.

31. Quoted in RML Sr. to RML, 13 March 1915, box 18-A, Family Papers.

reassured him. "Everybody knows that you have the ability. Everyone wants to help you. But *you* have got to do *this thing* for *yourself* and *you can't put it off an hour.*" Another time he wrote: "Now Bobbie, you must not think me hard or driving. This thing is very close to my heart. It has cost me much pain and suffering. It has cost your mother more." Belle in turn urged Bob to do better for his father's sake: "But oh, Bobbie this is a critical time and *you just must come out right.* When papa got those discouraging reports, it seemed to take the gimp out of him."[32]

These and other letters provided insight into the La Follette family relationship. It was a loving relationship, but also one in which the parents placed very great demands on their son. In this case Old Bob and Belle were claiming that their own physical and emotional well-being was dependent on Bob's academic success.

There were many reasons the elder La Follette was so upset over his son's performance at the university. Obviously, Bob was not working up to capacity; he was brighter than his grade point indicated, and his father knew it. Then too, Bob was not acquiring the "discipline," "self-reliance," and "power to concentrate" that the senator believed were the real benefits of a college education.[33]

But there was more to his concern than that. Almost certainly he had political ambitions for his son. Bob's poor performance, he feared, might jeopardize any future political career. For a time the senator considered asking Bob to start organizing university students for the 1916 senatorial campaign. Such an organization, he felt, would aid his own political success and also "lay a foundation" on which Bob "could build for life." And there were other allusions to a life in politics for Bob. Once, after a visit to Madison, he wrote Bob that "if you get on your pins . . . soon enough you would make a great candidate for Governor. You seem to have more friends than I ever had —It almost makes me jealous."[34]

Throughout 1915, Bob's parents kept a close watch on him. They suffered with him through examinations, Belle writing, "my heart aches for my bonny boy and I wish I could do something for his hurts and bruises." His grades improved markedly, and by the second semester of his third year he was finally off probation. But at the same

32. RML Sr. to RML, 1 October 1914, box 16-A, Belle to family, 22 October 1914, Belle's memorandum, "Points not Covered in Letter," October 1914, Belle to RML, 29 October 1914, box 14-A, RML Sr. to RML, 15 October, 9 November 1914, box 16-A, Belle to RML, 11 November 1914, box 14-A, Family Papers.

33. RML Sr. to RML, 13 March 1915, box 18-A, Family Papers.

34. RML Sr. to RML, 15 October 1915, box 16-A, RML Sr. to RML, 14 October 1915, box 18-A, Family Papers.

time, he became ill with a serious viral infection. Recovery was slow, and in January 1916 he withdrew from the university upon doctor's orders.[35]

Although Bob expressed disappointment over having to withdraw and frequently talked about returning, he never finished college. Despite his protests to the contrary, this probably suited him fine. For one thing, the separation from home and family was just too much for him to bear. "It seems that there is something wrong with a system of education that requires a sacrifice as big as that," he said.[36] For another thing, even after his grades had improved he was still bored with his studies. Although he was interested in politics, history, economics, and a broad range of other subjects, he preferred to learn about them firsthand rather than to read about them in books. What reading he did was usually in the newspaper or in journals of politics and current events. Then and always, he was a doer who disliked the confines of formal learning.

But something even more important kept him from returning to the university: his new involvement in his father's career. After leaving Madison, he went to work as an assistant clerk in the senator's office. The job entailed many routine chores like answering the telephone and sorting out the mail; but at least he was back at his father's side, meeting interesting people. Occasionally when the chief secretary was out of town, Bob even got to run the office by himself. "I like the chance to get my hand in and I am sure it is good training," he told his sister Mary.[37]

Bob was content. At twenty-one, the age when most young men were leaving home to begin lives of their own, he was drawn back to his home and family. He knew that sometime he would have to make a decision about the future. But that could wait, for there were more exciting things to do now.

35. Belle to RML, 5 February 1915, box 17-A, RML to family, 16 February 1915, box 18-A, John S. Evans to Dr. Cuthbert, 10 April 1915, box 1-C, RML to PFL, 26 January 1916, box 19-A, Family Papers.

36. RML to family, 16 January 1915, box 18-A, Family Papers.

37. RML to Mary, 12 July 1916, box 19-A, Family Papers.

CHAPTER 2

The Crisis Years

The news was discouraging. It was early February 1917 at the Maple Bluff Farm, and Bob La Follette was reading the latest letter from his father in Washington. War, the senator wrote, appeared more and more likely every day. He added, "One cannot shake off the feeling that an awful crisis [is] impending."[1]

For Young Bob, his father, and his family, the crisis was not long in coming. In April the United States joined Great Britain and France in their fight against Germany, which had been raging since 1914. Shortly thereafter, Senator La Follette, the leading opponent of American intervention in the war, became the target of a nationwide movement that branded him a traitor and sought to expel him from the Senate. Longtime friends and associates shunned the senator and his family, and the La Follettes spent the war years in social isolation. So intense was the feeling against them that at times they feared for their physical safety. Early in 1918 Young Bob experienced a crisis of another sort. Possibly as a result of the emotional strain of the war, he fell critically ill and was bedridden for many months. Finally, in 1919, the crisis ended, but the bitter memories of those years of war and of illness remained with Bob throughout his life.

When Bob arrived in Washington late in February 1917, he found his father working frantically to keep the United States out of war. The elder La Follette was not a pacifist, but he did believe that the current war was strictly a European affair. To him it was just one more of the seemingly endless struggles between imperialistic nations of the Old World, and neither national security nor violations of international law required American intervention. He believed that if the United States did enter the war, the only victor would be the nation's already swollen business and financial elite; and he feared that, in addition to the countless thousands who would sacrifice their lives, the progressive movement and even democracy itself might be casualties. Never before had La Follette been so convinced of the rightness of his cause. Adding to his determination was his belief that

1. RML Sr. to family, 2 February 1917, box 20-A, Family Papers (see list of abbreviations p. x).

the "people," especially the people of Wisconsin, nearly half of whom were of German ancestry, opposed intervention.[2]

Bob shared his father's convictions, and during his first days in Washington he watched with dismay as the nation moved toward war. On 20 February the Senate debated the administration's request for an appropriation of one-half billion dollars to expand the army and navy. "In getting ready to suppress German militarism," Bob complained, "we are out germaning the Germans." The next day he reported that the Senate was considering a revenue bill "which intends to make the small businessman of the country pay for our military establishments; of course he will pass it all along to poor Mr. Consumer and as usual he will pay the price."[3]

The preparedness drive reached a climax a week later when President Woodrow Wilson, seeking to defend American commercial vessels from German submarine attack, asked Congress for the power to arm merchant ships. Convinced that such an action made war certain, Senator La Follette leaped to the attack. He believed that if he could delay passage of the bill, he might still have time to arouse enough public sentiment to avert war. Although a majority in Congress supported the armed-ship bill, La Follette had time on his side, for Congress was set to adjourn in just nine days.

Although the House passed the armed-ship bill, a week went by without the Senate taking any action. Then, on Saturday, 3 March, twenty-four hours before adjournment, the supporters of the administration decided to hold the Senate in continuous session until they could force a vote. Just as determined to prevent a roll call, La Follette and a handful of like-minded senators launched a filibuster. Throughout Saturday evening and early Sunday morning, opponents of the bill held the floor. La Follette, planning to speak last, stayed in his office and worked on his address. Bob, Jr., remained on the Senate floor to help manage the filibuster.

At eight-thirty on Sunday morning, Senator La Follette entered the chamber with the intention of holding the floor until adjournment. But the presiding officer of the Senate refused to recognize him. Enraged, the Wisconsin senator jumped out of his seat, moved into the center aisle, and shouted for recognition. In reaction, a group of Democrats rushed into the aisle toward La Follette, trying to shout him down. Sen. Harry Lane of Oregon, a close friend of La Follette, believed that La Follette was in danger of physical attack, for he later

2. Belle Case La Follette and Fola La Follette, *Robert M. La Follette* (New York, 1953), 1:537–602.

3. RML to Belle, 20, 21 February 1917, box 21-A, Family Papers.

claimed that one of the Democrats, Ollie James of Kentucky, had a pistol under his coat. To protect La Follette, Lane followed James up the aisle, ready to plunge a knife into his neck should he draw the gun. Although the shouting continued, no fight actually broke out.[4]

Bob, standing just inside the door of the Senate chamber, watched all this with alarm. When things momentarily quieted down, he dashed off a short note to his father: "Please, Please, be calm—you know what the press will do—remember Mother." When the debate heated up again, and Senator La Follette angrily declared, "I will continue on this floor until somebody carries me off, and I should like to see the man who will do it," Bob again warned his father: "You are noticeably & extremely excited. For god's sake make your protest & prevent passage of bill if you like but . . . do not try to fight senate physically. I am almost crazy with strain." The wrangling continued for hours, with La Follette constantly trying to secure the floor. Finally, at noon, the Senate adjourned without taking a vote on the armed-ship bill.[5]

The successful filibuster brought a barrage of criticism. The next day, newspapers throughout the country carried Woodrow Wilson's denunciation of the "little group of willful men, representing no opinion but their own," who had "rendered the great government of the United States helpless and contemptible." Editorials followed suit: one called the willful men "Knaves who betrayed the nation in the interest of Germany," another referred to "La Follette and his little group of perverts." Cartoonist Rollin Kirby, in the *New York World*, pictured the hand of Germany pinning the Iron Cross on La Follette. The senator also suffered personal abuse. He and Bob were forced to stop riding the streetcar in order to avoid the hateful stares of fellow passengers, some of whom even spat upon the senator. Throught it all, Bob echoed his father's determination. "Whatever the press or the people may say or do I am satisfied that the course taken was one that had delayed war . . . ; and delay is always possible of a turn which may help to bring us thru the madness."[6]

Yet, however much Bob supported his father's opposition to war, he was somewhat skeptical of his means of expressing it. During the armed-ship debate, Bob had urged restraint and caution. Then, in

4. Belle and Fola, *La Follette*, 1:603–15.

5. Ibid., 1:616–25; RML to RML Sr., n.d., box 20, Family Papers.

6. Wilson quoted in *New York Times*, 5 March 1917, editorials from *Toledo Blade*, 8 March 1917, *Cincinnati Times-Star*, 5 March 1917, *New York World*, 7 March 1917, all cited by Belle and Fola, *La Follette*, 1:626–29; RML to Belle, 16 March 1917, box 21-A, Family Papers.

the wake of the public outcry, he advised his father to draft a detailed public statement explaining his opposition to the bill. Bob felt that if people understood the senator's reasoning, they might be less inclined to criticize him. When the senator ignored his son's plea, Bob telegraphed his mother in Wisconsin and asked her to appeal to him.[7] Thus, Bob revealed a difference between himself and his father, not one of principle, but one of personality and temperament. Bob was more cautious than the senator, more sensitive to criticism, and more concerned about the political consequences of actions.

On 2 April 1917, Woodrow Wilson called for a declaration of war. On 4 April, after a three-hour speech, which Bob described as "one of the greatest, if not the greatest thing he has done in the Senate," the elder La Follette joined five other senators and fifty representatives in voting against the declaration of war. "Henceforth," declared the *Boston Evening Transcript*, "he is the Man without a Country."[8]

Undaunted, Senator La Follette kept up the attack. He opposed conscription, introduced legislation to ensure the rights of conscientious objectors, and worked for a tax system that would prevent any person or corporation from profiting from the war. He also fought the suppression of free speech by opposing the Espionage Act and other measures that he believed to be repressive.[9]

"Things have been moving along here so rapidly," Bob wrote to Phil and Mary, "that it just takes one's breath away.... It is indeed sad to be here and see all the cherished institutions of our beloved country thrown away on the scrap heap all in the name of democracy. Democracy thy name is not war and alas most assuredly not the Democracy of Wilson." Forced conscription particularly upset him. It was, he believed, an absolute "reversal of the history of this and every other democracy."[10]

Principle aside, Bob had a more compelling reason to be concerned about conscription. At age twenty-two, and with a lottery number of 2117, he expected to receive a draft notice by the end of the summer. Although he believed the war to be morally wrong, he, like his father, was not a pacifist. He therefore never gave serious consideration to declaring himself a conscientious objector. But he did, for a time, think of joining the National Guard; his father, after soliciting advice

7. RML to Belle, 10 March 1917, box 21-A, Family Papers.
8. RML to PFL and Mary, 4 April 1917, box 21-A, Family Papers; *Boston Evening Transcript*, 5 April 1917, cited by Belle and Fola, *La Follette*, 1:667.
9. Belle and Fola, *La Follette*, 2:733–45.
10. RML to Mary and PFL, 1 May 1917, box 21-A, Family Papers.

from legal experts, had concluded that the Guard could not lawfully leave the country to fight overseas. But Bob rejected this option and placed his hopes on a medical deferment. Early in June he filled out the registration form and applied for an exemption on the grounds of "poor physical condition caused by a protracted illness." Although his personal physician assured Bob that any examiner who passed him "would be a fit inmate for an insane asylum," the family spent an anxious summer waiting for the time Bob would have to appear for his physical examination. But on 24 August, the examining doctor declared him unfit for military service.[11]

Bob's brother, Phil, who had just turned twenty-one, also faced the draft. But Phil was more adventurous than Bob, and although he opposed the war, the excitement of battle attracted him. Even before the United States had entered, he had considered joining the American Ambulance Corps in France. "This kind of thing is what I need," he said. "It would make a man out of me. In a great many ways, I am weak and childish, I need something to bracen me up—to make me stronger morally and physically—something that will give me assurance in myself physically—assurance that I have the real stuff in me." Phil eventually abandoned the idea of the ambulance corps, deciding instead to enroll in the army's officer training school. As he told his hesitant mother, he believed that having experienced war firsthand, he would later command more respect for his views and thus become a more effective leader for peace. Curiously, he also seemed almost to relish the hysterical outcries against his father. Now, he said, "I have to fight my own way—something I didn't do before. It is a great opportunity—rather than a hardship." Phil believed that adversity bred greatness, and he was forever in search of greatness.[12]

With the threat of the draft behind him, Bob avidly plunged into the work of his father's office. His main duty was to handle the large volume of mail, on some days as many as five hundred letters. "Bobbie," the senator proudly reported, "has the run of this old correspondence and can handle it more rapidly than anyone else—He writes or dictates a splendid letter terse—well phrased—and with the political point." Occasionally Bob helped with the preparation of reports and speeches. Working for his father gave Bob valuable experience in

11. Belle to family, 18 August 1917, RML Sr. to RML, n.d., RML Sr. to family, 2 June 1917, RML to family, 28 May, 2 June, 7 June, 24 August 1917, box 21, Family Papers.

12. PFL to RML Sr., 2 April 1917, box 133-2, PFL Papers; PFL to Belle, 14 April, 15 October 1917, box 20-A, Family Papers.

politics. He knew his way around Washington and the federal bureaucracy. When friends or acquaintances from back home came to
Washington in search of a job, he knew whom to contact and where
to send them.[13]

In his spare time he wrote a weekly column entitled "The Week in
Washington," which he sent out to forty-five small-town, labor, and
Socialist newspapers throughout the country. "In some ways," began
a typical column, "the most significant news of the week is being completely ignored by the metropolitan press. Or perhaps they don't
know it. At any rate I am able to give you a piece of exclusive information. . . . My informant—who is distinctly on the inside—tells me. . . ."
After such a big buildup, the actual news story was usually rather
disappointing, but at least the column was interesting, well written,
and humorous, demonstrating Bob's characteristic blend of understatement and irony.[14]

Bob's performance, on the job and in the column, so impressed his
father that he considered making Bob business manager and editor
of La Follette's Magazine, a weekly publication that the senator had
founded in 1909. The magazine was in serious trouble; sales were
down, and the threat of government censorship posed a constant worry. Bob, his father believed, would get it back on its feet. But Belle
had less confidence in her son's abilities, and pointing to his inexperience, she vetoed the plan.[15]

Bob probably would have been happy to return to Madison and
assume management of the magaine, since life in Washington was
becoming more depressing by the day. The attacks on his father continued, and although Bob could take consolation in the numerous
letters of support, the hate mail was also increasing. But all of this
was minor in comparison to the outcry that followed his father's
famous speech, on 20 September 1917, to the Non-Partisan League
in St. Paul, Minnesota. In the course of his extemporaneous remarks,
the senator said that although the United States had had "serious
grievances against Germany," those grievances did not warrant a
declaration of war. In its account of the speech, the Associated Press
misquoted La Follette as having said that the United States had "no
grievances against Germany." The next day, newspapers throughout

13. RML Sr. to PFL and Mary, 17 July 1917, RML to PFL and Mary, 8
August, 25 June 1917, box 21-A, Family Papers.
14. Copies of "The Week in Washington," box 659–C, Family Papers.
15. RML Sr. to Belle, 13 July 1917, Belle to RML Sr., 13 July 1917, box 21-A,
Family Papers.

the nation carried the story under blazing headlines. But even an accurate account of the speech probably would have meant trouble for La Follette, since it was decidedly antiwar and questioned Wilson's integrity. For many the misquotation provided concrete evidence that the senator from Wisconsin was serving the enemy. One newspaper called him "the most sinister, forbidding figure in later day American history," adding that "his very name has come to spell sedition and speak treason." Former President Theodore Roosevelt termed him one of the "Huns within our gates." Petitions calling for La Follette's expulsion from the Senate flooded the Congress. In response, the Senate Committee on Elections and Privileges began a formal investigation into the grounds for expulsion.[16]

What most distressed Bob was the outcry against his father that arose in Wisconsin. Long-standing political enemies viewed the loyalty issue as a godsend that they might exploit to finally rid the state of La Follette's influence. Because Wisconsin had the largest German population of any state, other people probably felt the state had to prove its patriotism to the nation. In any event, former friends joined old enemies in denouncing the senator. The University of Wisconsin became a hotbed of anti-La Follette fervor. In December students and faculty gathered behind the library to burn La Follette in effigy. The president of the university, Charles Van Hise, who had gone to school with the senator and Belle and who had become president through La Follette's influence, charged him with "aiding and abetting the enemy." Professor of Economics John R. Commons, of whom the senator had said only a year earlier, "Thank God for such good friends," joined the chorus of denunciation. In January 1918, all but four members of the faculty signed a petition demanding La Follette's expulsion from the Senate. "Damn that faculty to hell," said Bob angrily. "I hope that I may live to see each one . . . get what is coming to him if there is any justice in this damn world."[17]

Because he defended his father and continued to take jabs at the Wilson administration in his weekly column, Bob, too, came in for heated criticism. In January, several newspapers refused to accept any further installments. "You need not trouble yourself about sending any more . . . Non-American propaganda," wrote one editor, adding,

16. *Seattle Post-Intelligencer*, 26 September 1917, Roosevelt quoted in *Chicago Daily Tribune*, 27 September 1917, both cited by Belle and Fola, *La Follette*, 2:770–72.

17. Herbert F. Margulies, *The Decline of the Progressive Movement in Wisconsin, 1890–1920* (Madison, 1968), pp. 193–220; RML Sr. to family, 10 December 1916, box 19-A, RML to PFL, 16 January 1918, box 24-A, Family Papers.

"Shame on the man so lacking in patriotic impulse, that he lends aid to the one man power of an enemy nation." Another wrote him, " 'Either you are an American—Or You are Not,' is the slogan of this office." One column even brought a stern reprimand from George Creel, head of the government's Committee on Public Information.[18]

Other members of the La Follette family also suffered abuse. One day, as Bob's eighteen-year-old sister Mary walked along a street in Madison, a passerby spotted her, stopped, and yelled out, "There goes the daughter of a traitor." Phil later recalled an unpleasant encounter with Professor John R. Commons. During the course of a rather strained conversation, Phil pulled a five-dollar gold piece out of his pocket, upon which Commons "pointed at it as if I had a snake in my hand, saying: 'Where did you get *that*?' I replied: 'From Dad for Christmas.' He snarled: 'No patriotic citizen would have gold in his possession in a time of war.' " These and similar incidents caused Belle to worry about the physical safety of her children. Both she and Bob frequently cautioned the rest of the family to avoid any rash statement or action that might provoke authorities into arresting them. As far back as April, Bob had warned Phil and Mary, "Again I say be careful of what you say. One silent but determined pacifist out of jail is worth twenty in."[19]

The stress-filled months after the senator's St. Paul speech were hard on all the La Follettes, especially on Bob. During the days, he struggled to keep up with his office chores. In the evenings, after a hurried dinner, he trudged back to the Capitol to help his father, his mother, and the staff prepare the legal defense that the senator planned to present to the committee investigating the possibility of expulsion. "I am so tired," Bob complained, "that I could sleep" standing "on the toes of one foot."[20]

Then, late in January 1918, he became critically ill with what doctors diagnosed as streptococcal pneumonia. Among his symptoms were swelling of his face and limbs, a high temperature, and the appearance of painful, inflamed nodules scattered over his body. Sparing no expense, his parents called in several physicians, including the famous Mayo brothers from Minnesota. On 7 February, the day after

18. Ward L. Swift to RML, 3 January 1918, D. C. Menfee to RML, 17 January 1918, box 659–C, Family Papers; Belle and Fola, *La Follette*, 2:854.
19. Interview, Mary La Follette, 22 February 1973; Commons quoted in Philip F. La Follette, *Adventure in Politics: The Memoirs of Philip La Follette* (New York, 1970), p. 52; Belle to family, 15 November 1917, Fola to RML, 7 April 1917, RML to Mary and PFL, 4 April 1917, box 21–A, Family Papers.
20. RML to PFL and Mary, 10 October 1917, box 21–A, Family Papers.

his twenty-third birthday, Bob underwent surgery to drain pus from the cavity behind his right lung. After the operation, doctors could offer little more in the way of treatment than rest and proper diet.[21]

Only a few days after Bob came home from the hospital, he suffered a relapse. And so it went through the spring and summer: one day he would seem better; the next day his temperature would shoot up again, and he would seem worse than ever. At times, his condition was so bad that he feared he might die. Belle dropped her outside activities to care for her son. At night, after coming home from the Capitol, the senator would relieve her. "Papa," said Belle, "has had almost as hard a time as Bobbie. He has been so wrought up over him he will not go to bed nights and hovers about his room."[22]

By July, although Bob remained bedridden, the worst was finally over. His doctors now recommended a full year of rest and recuperation, preferably in some place other than Washington. In August the family moved to Hot Springs, Virginia. Then in September, Bob, his mother, and Mary rented a cottage on the Pacific Ocean, near La Jolla, California, where they remained almost a year.

Bob's prolonged illness drained him emotionally as well as physically by reinforcing his latent sense of failure and inadequacy. When Phil left for the army, Bob confided to his sister Fola: "Phil has such a wonderful future before him. I wanted to go in his place. He will amount to so much & I shall never amount to anything." When his father tried to convince him that he would still be able to achieve great things in life, Bob responded, "You have accomplished so very much . . . that I sometimes think you have blazed too straight and steep a trail for one as unfit as I to follow." John Clifford Folger, Bob's closest friend outside of the family, later recalled Bob telling him that, during the months of illness and recuperation, he at times wondered whether life was really worth living.[23]

Late in November 1918, encouraging news from Europe temporarily lifted Bob's spirits. "God what a relief to once more dwell in a peaceful world," he said when he heard of the armistice. The political situation in Washington also improved. In the November elections, the Republicans gained a majority in both houses of Congress. Their majority in the Senate was slim, however, and to the dismay of both Democrats and Republicans it appeared that Senator La Follette held

21. RML, RML Sr., and Belle letter files, boxes 21–24-A, Family Papers.

22. Interview, Mary La Follette; RML Sr. to Josephine Siebecker, 10 February 1918, box 23-A, Belle to PFL, 5 April 1918, box 22-A, Family Papers.

23. RML quoted in Fola to PFL, 31 July 1918, box 22-A, RML to RML Sr., 12 February 1919, box 28-A, Family Papers; interview, John Clifford Folger, 5 June 1973.

the balance of power. Not surprisingly, the committee considering his expulsion rapidly concluded its investigation without taking action.[24]

The diplomatic events following the war, however, were not as encouraging. As President Wilson prepared to leave for the Paris peace conference, Bob predicted that the conference would turn into a "tragic fiasco," a scramble for the spoils of war. Yet he characteristically cautioned his father to "lie low" and "let some one else point out the betrayal." After hearing of the proposed league of nations, he denounced Wilson: "I wish the long faced fraud would stay over there for good and all." In May 1919, he wrote that Wilson, "the past master of hypocrisy," had "sold us out so completely that a few more rotten trades seem not to matter."[25]

By the end of June, Bob had recovered and was ready to leave California. Except for a slight limp—the tendons in the backs of his legs had contracted during the long period of bedrest and inactivity —he showed no physical signs of the long ordeal. Yet, the events of the last two years, especially the war, had profoundly affected him, as he realized, perhaps for the first time, when he stopped off in Madison on the way back to Washington.

It had been over a year since his last visit, and things had changed. But nothing had changed more than his attitude. "I was surprised at how little attachment I have left for this town," he wrote his mother. "I have always felt a thrill on coming in on the train but not this time. I am glad of course to see my old friends and they were all very cordial but the 'patriots' killed the home feeling for me and I do not think I will ever have it again." His father tried to talk him out of it: "I would not let a few cheap skates drive me from the most beautiful place in the world—where I had made my home, reared my family, buried my dead. . . . Eighty percent are our real friends— they have been bound hand and foot & gagged there as they have everywhere in this country & in the world." The elder La Follette could forget, but Bob could not. In the years to come, he would spend considerable time in Wisconsin. One day he would represent it in the United States Senate. Still, he would never be able to shake off the feeling that many people in the state, including some of the family's closest friends, had betrayed his father.[26]

24. RML to PFL, "Monday night," box 24-A, Family Papers; Belle and Fola, *La Follette*, 2:909–12.

25. RML to RML Sr., 19 November, 12, 23 December 1918, 11 May 1919, box 24-A, Family Papers.

26. RML to Belle, 30 July 1919, box 27-A, RML Sr. to RML, 6 August 1919, box 28-A, Family Papers.

The war years also permanently shaped young La Follette's views on foreign policy. By 1919 he was more convinced than ever that America's entry into the war had been a tragic mistake, and he believed that the only possible good that could ever come out of the whole dreadful experience would be a resolution never to repeat the same mistake.

CHAPTER 3

Apprenticeship and Succession

Bob La Follette did not realize it at the time, but in the fall of 1919 he made the most important decision of his life. His father's secretary and chief assistant of many years, John Hannan, had recently resigned, and Bob agreed to replace him. Having ruled out a political career for himself, he fully intended to work for his father only until he found a suitable nonpolitical job. But for the next six years, circumstances, some of which were probably contrived by his father, and a sense of obligation prevented him from leaving the senator's side. As one family member later described it, every time that Bob "made up his mind to break away some crisis—illness or political— seemed to make it impossible for him to leave his father at that particular moment."[1] Then, in 1925, the elder La Follette died, and Young Bob, because of his name, his political experience, and his availability, was the logical successor. By winning a special election in September 1925, he became what he had never wanted to become, a United States senator.

La Follette was twenty-four years old in 1919, but he still had made no definite plans for the future. "With all his force and individuality," his mother observed, "his problem seems to be—to take the initiative—to assume the big responsibility of shaping his own career —of deciding what he shall do and be."[2] He considered law school for a time, but he leaned more toward a career in business or journalism. Of one thing he was certain: he never would seek elective office. Any political ambitions he may have had probably died during the war years, when he saw the terrible price his father had to pay for being a principled public servant. La Follette accepted the job as his father's secretary not because he sought political advancement but because he felt obliged to serve his father. Moreover, it was the safest thing to do. Uncertain about the future, unsure of himself, still very

1. Mrs. PFL, "Isen's Magnum Opus," second draft, pp. 4–5, box 165–3, PFL Papers (see list of abbreviations p. x). Mrs. PFL was known to everyone as "Isen," and she will be referred to by that name in the text.
2. Belle to RML Sr., 6 February 1919, box 24-A, Family Papers.

dependent on his parents, he was thereby able to postpone the day when he would have to venture out on his own.[3]

The elder La Follette had more confidence in Bob than Bob had in himself. Although the senator never said it in so many words, he wanted his son to follow in his footsteps, to pursue a career in politics. Early in 1919, in a letter to Bob and Belle, the senator compared Bob "as he is today with myself at 24." Bob, he wrote, "has better book training than I had at the time. And he has a knowledge of affairs— a grasp of national and world conditions and problems and men equal to that of the men who are called the mature and profound statesmen of our time—of *today*." Addressing himself to his son, the senator continued: "You will start life as a man . . . standing on my shoulders. You have your mother's brain my boy—the best brain in the world. With established health, what a service you can be to your community—your country and humanity." Clearly, it was not Bob the businessman or Bob the journalist that the senator pictured in his mind when he wrote these words, but rather Bob the political leader.[4]

In addition to believing that his son possessed the talents necessary for succeeding in public service, the elder La Follette had another reason for wanting Bob to enter politics. At sixty-four years of age, the senator was obsessed with the thought of dying before he completed his mission in life. "When the last night comes and I go to the land of Never Return," he wrote his family, "what an awful account of *things undone* I shall leave *behind*."[5] Probably he had come to see Young Bob as his successor, as the one who could carry on the crusade after he died.

Belle, who understood her son's personality and needs better than anyone, seemed to sense that her husband was trying to draw Bob into politics, and she tried to put a stop to it. Bob, she subtly cautioned the senator, should be allowed to decide his future without interference from them or from anyone else. To her daughter Fola she reiterated: "Not only for the physical good, but . . . for Bobbie's

3. RML's career plans are discussed throughout letters in boxes 24–31-A, Family Papers. See especially: Belle to RML Sr., 6 February 1919, box 24-A, Belle to Fola and George Middleton (Fola's husband), 4 November 1922, box 29-A, RML to PFL, 21 March 1923, Belle to RML Sr., 26 June 1923, box 30-A, RML to family, 22 February 1924, box 31-A, Family Papers. See also PFL to Mrs. PFL, 3 January 1923, RML to PFL, 19 February 1923, box 132-2, PFL Papers.

4. RML Sr. to RML and Belle, 6 February 1919, quoted in Belle Case La Follette and Fola La Follette, *Robert M. La Follette* (New York, 1953), 2:935.

5. RML Sr. to Belle, RML, and Mary, 26 January 1919, quoted in ibid.

highest development, he should be vested with the responsibility and the privilege of the man at the wheel."[6]

But Old Bob was unable to restrain himself; he could not help but try to plant in his son's mind the idea of a political career. One time, for example, he informed Bob that another Wisconsin family had named a newborn son "Robert La Follette" in honor of the senator. "Say Bob," the senator remarked probably only partly in jest, "you will have a constituency of 'Bobs' strong enough to carry the state by the time you are ready to run for Governor."[7]

Curiously, the elder La Follette focused his ambitions on an unwilling son when he had another son, Phil, who was more than willing to pursue a political career. Phil's wife, Isen, later recalled that he "breathed, ate and slept politics although what future form it would take . . . was still hazy." Phil closely resembled his father. He was extroverted, intelligent, imaginative, somewhat impulsive, a promising orator, and above all, ambitious. Entering law school in 1919, he intended to use the legal profession as a stepping-stone to elective office. Bob expressed the opinion of most people when he predicted a "brilliant career" for his younger brother. "The only thing you have to take care of is your health," Bob told Phil, "The people of Wisconsin will do the rest."[8] Perhaps because the senator and Phil were so much alike, the senator was never as close to him as he was to Bob.

La Follette's duties as secretary to the senator included arranging his father's schedule, researching and writing speeches, and advising the senator, especially on matters of strategy and tactics. He also wrote a humorous column for *La Follette's Magazine* entitled "Facts and Fable from Washington," frequently contributed editorials to the same magazine, and for a time wrote an anonymous, weekly column for the *Capital Times* of Madison. La Follette had a modest flair for writing, and it was not surprising that he was considering a career in journalism. More than anything else, however, he spent these years learning—about political history, domestic and foreign affairs, economics, parliamentary procedure, and practical politics. He never completed college, but under the tutelage of his father, a skilled,

6. Belle to RML Sr., 6 February 1919, Belle to Fola, 28 March 1919, box 24-A, Family Papers.

7. RML Sr. to RML and Belle, 2 May 1919, box 27-A, Family Papers.

8. Mrs. PFL, "Isen's Magnum Opus," second draft, entry of May 1947, pp. 4–5, box 165–3, PFL Papers; RML to PFL, 21 March 1923, box 30-A, Family Papers.

if highly partisan, teacher, he was becoming an educated man.[9]

La Follette enjoyed his job, for the political atmosphere of the capital was both exciting and gratifying. People were becoming disillusioned with the government's postwar policies, and many of those who had condemned Senator La Follette during the war began to have a change of heart. Senator Bob, they said, may have been right after all. With the help of Young Bob, the senator was also making headway in the Senate. He helped lead the successful battles against ratification of the Treaty of Versailles and against United States participation in the League of Nations. A few years later the senator initiated the investigation that eventually exposed the Teapot Dome scandal and the other misdeeds that marred the presidency of Warren G. Harding.[10]

In 1922 La Follette received his first major assignment outside Washington: to manage the reelection campaigns of his father and of other progressive Republicans in Wisconsin. In the September primary and in the November election the progressives swept the state. The senator was elected to a fourth term by the largest margin in the state's history. Although the senator would have won easily even without his son's help, Bob could still take satisfaction in the outcome. He had skillfully managed the campaign and had proved himself a highly efficient organizer and administrator.[11]

In 1923 La Follette undertook an even more difficult assignment. A tax-reform measure was hopelessly bogged down in the Wisconsin legislature. Senator La Follette, who in addition to his Senate duties tried to run the state legislature, dispatched his son to the scene. Bob spent several weeks trying to unite the warring factions in the legislature. He almost succeeded. A compromise tax bill easily cleared the assembly and came within a few votes of passage in the senate. The elder La Follette was ecstatic over his son's performance. He thought that Bob had faced "the *highest* test of *generalship*" and had succeeded brilliantly.[12]

9. Robert M. La Follette, Jr., "Facts and Fable From Washington," *La Follette's Magazine*, February 1922; Robert M. La Follette, Jr., "Roll Call," *La Follette's Magazine*, December 1921; RML to PFL, 2 May 1921, box 29-A, Family Papers. On RML's duties as secretary see RML letter files, boxes 28–31-A, Family Papers.

10. Belle to family, 25 January 1921, RML to PFL, 24 June 1921, box 29-A, Family Papers; Belle and Fola, *La Follette*, 2:974–84, 1041–54.

11. For RML's role in campaign see RML letter files, box 29-A, Family Papers; RML correspondence, boxes 20–24, Herman L. Ekern Papers, State Historical Society of Wisconsin, Madison.

12. RML to RML Sr., 5, 14, 26, 28 June 1923, RML Sr. to RML, 16 June 1923, box 30-A, Family Papers.

Senator La Follette was obviously grooming his son for public service. And thus far almost everything had proceeded according to plan. By 1923 Young Bob knew far more about government and politics than his father had known when he first ran for office. There was only one flaw in the senator's plan: Bob still lacked the necessary ambition. "Please remember," Bob wrote Phil, who was pursuing a job lead for him, "that I have no political ambitions and . . . therefore the matter of location has no bearing."[13]

The senator refused to concede defeat. At times it seemed as though, consciously or unconsciously, he was contriving situations that made it difficult for his son to leave him. For instance, in 1923 Bob was seriously considering several job offers; but he put off a decision, apparently because his father sent him to Madison on the tax matter.[14] In this and other situations he was unable to say no to his father. Clearly, he lacked the independence of mind that would have allowed him to break away, and his father knew it.

In the late summer and fall of 1923, Young Bob La Follette had an experience that made a lasting impression on him and reinforced his views on American foreign policy. He accompanied his parents and a few family friends to Europe. For three months they traveled through England, Germany, Russia, Poland, Austria, Italy, Denmark, and France. This was the first time any of them had been to Europe, and they enjoyed the people, the scenery, and the historic sites. From Paris, Bob wrote Fola and her husband Mid, "What I would give to live here as you did for a year and let politics go its way without me."[15]

Bob and his family were less favorably impressed with European political and social conditions. In the Soviet Union, Bob heard his father tell Russian leaders that they had pushed the revolution too far. Condescendingly, the senator invited them to Wisconsin to learn how to conduct the business of government and reform. In Italy the La Follettes met privately with dictator Benito Mussolini. As Mussolini extolled the virtues of his regime, the senator interrupted. "Yes, but do you have a free press?" he asked.[16]

13. RML to PFL, 21 March 1923, box 30-A, Family Papers.

14. RML to PFL, 21 March 1923, RML to Belle and RML Sr., 26 June 1923, box 30-A, Family Papers; PFL to Mrs. PFL, 3 January 1923, RML to PFL, 19 February 1923, box 132-2, PFL Papers.

15. Belle and Fola, *La Follette*, 2:1074–87; RML to Fola and George Middleton, 11 October 1923, box 30-A, Family Papers.

16. Lincoln Steffens, *The Autobiography of Lincoln Steffens* (New York, 1931), 2:806; Belle and Fola, *La Follette*, 2:1083.

Germany, with the scars left by the war visible everywhere, provided the real shock. One morning in Berlin the La Follettes ordered eggs and milk for breakfast. "There is not even milk for the children or for the mothers with babies," the waiter informed them. Bob and his father spent several days motoring through the industrialized Rhur Valley, which French troops had occupied since the war. Bob described the occupation as "probably one of the most interesting attempts in history and at the same time one of the most cruel. It is attended by the most wholesale suffering of not only the strong but also the weak. Women and children and especially the old and infirm are being crushed in the process." The French, he believed, intended "to starve the population into abject submission" and would be "satisfied with nothing less." For Bob, the trip through Germany dramatically confirmed everything his father had said about the war. It had not been a war involving principle and lofty ideals; rather it had been, especially on the part of France and England, a greedy scramble for the spoils of victory. He had never doubted his father, of course; but now he had seen it for himself. And he would never forget it.[17]

Upon his return from Europe, Bob found himself in another one of those situations that made it impossible for him to leave his father. The senator, suffering from a serious heart condition and from bronchial pneumonia, was forced into a long period of inactivity.[18] Once again Bob felt that duty demanded he stay on as secretary and look after his father's affairs in Washington and in Wisconsin.

So visible was he in and around the Senate that political reporters began to take notice of him. "No gallery of political portraits is complete without one of 'Young Bob,'" wrote columnist Clinton W. Gilbert of the *Philadelphia Public Ledger*, "Most of the session, on account of his father's illness, he has been a whole bloc in Congress by himself without having a seat there." Describing him as a "smiling, friendly, likeable young man, who is incessantly on the alert where his father's interests are concerned," Gilbert concluded that Young Bob had more political experience and occupied a position of greater political importance than any other man his age.[19]

Meanwhile, Senator La Follette was preparing to run for president in the 1924 election as a Progressive. Because of his poor health, his

17. Belle to family, 25 September 1923, box 30-A, RML to "Dear Friend," 5 October 1923, box 1-C, Family Papers.
18. Belle and Fola, *La Follette*, 2:1089, 1094–95.
19. Clinton W. Gilbert, "The Daily Mirror of Washington," 20 June 1924, typed copy, box 132-2, PFL Papers.

doctors, Belle, and Bob all pleaded with him not to make the race. But no one could change his mind. He was convinced that "reactionaries" had a stranglehold on the two major parties and that a third party offered the only hope for reform. Moreover, he had wanted to be president for many years, and in 1924, at age sixty-nine and in failing health, he doubtless realized that the upcoming election was probably the last chance he would have to achieve his goal.[20]

When the campaign began, Young Bob intended to play only a minor role. But his father would assign him one task and then another, and before long he was deeply involved in every aspect of the campaign. He became vice-chairman of the newly formed Progressive party, the vehicle for his father's candidacy. In that position he had a hand in everything from fund raising, to scheduling the senator's appearances, to making policy decisions.[21]

The campaign got off to a promising start. At first it appeared as though Old Bob would do what no recent presidential candidate had been able to do: unite the diverse elements of the nation's Left. The senator received endorsements from prominent labor and farm leaders, old agrarian progressives, urban reformers, socialists, and reform-minded intellectuals and writers. Barring any "bad breaks," the senator said in September, "we have a splendid chance to win complete victory."[22]

Before long, however, the campaign was experiencing almost every imaginable problem. It took months and many costly court battles simply to get the senator's name printed on state ballots. It soon became clear that the prominent leaders who backed La Follette were finding it impossible to bring their followers into line behind the senator. The Progressive party experienced numerous internal problems as well. It had no state or local organizations except in Wisconsin. The high command, including Young Bob, had no previous experience conducting a national campaign, and it showed. The senator managed to raise only $200,000, as compared to $4 million for the Republican candidate, Calvin Coolidge, and $1 million for the Democratic candidate, John W. Davis. Frequently the senator would arrive in one city and have to raise money there in order to finance his trip to the next city. And, although Old Bob more directly addressed himself to the problems of the day than did his rivals, his main theme,

20. RML to family, 17 November 1923, box 30-A, Family Papers; Mrs. PFL, "Magnum Opus," miscellaneous draft, p. 9, box 165–3, PFL Papers.

21. *New York Times*, 26 July 1924. For RML's role in the campaign, see RML letter file, box 31-A, Family Papers.

22. RML Sr. to PFL, 8 September 1924, box 31-A, Family Papers. An unsigned, typed copy of this letter in same file is mistakenly attributed to RML.

the menace of monopoly, did not work for him as it had in the past.

During the campaign Davis and Coolidge all but ignored one another, concentrating their attack instead on the Wisconsin senator. Davis took the high road. He criticized the Progressive platform on its merits. Coolidge supporters took the low road. They accused La Follette of being disloyal because of his opposition to the war, of being in league with the communists, and of accepting campaign money from Moscow.[23]

Despite all the obstacles, there was something rather noble about the La Follette campaign. As one reporter put it, "The spectacle of a man nearly seventy years old with little organization and no money of his own, relying largely for assistance upon his two youthful sons, setting out to lick both the great national parties, is alone sufficient to command respect."[24]

Although Young Bob hoped for a miracle, he knew that his father would lose by a landslide. Shortly before the election he predicted that the senator would carry only one state, faithful Wisconsin. The outcome confirmed his prediction. The final returns gave Coolidge 54 percent of the vote, Davis 29 percent, and La Follette 17 percent. But the anticipation of defeat did not make the actual event any easier to accept. Although his father remained characteristically optimistic about the future, Bob was discouraged. He probably agreed with Fola, who wrote, "I can't see much consolation in it from any angle. It seems to me quite completely disillusioning as to the capacity of 'the people' to stand by anything or anyone who works in their behalf."[25] In any event, the whole experience made Bob forever wary of third-party ventures.

During the nine months following the election, the elder La Follette's health deteriorated steadily. Bob again postponed his own plans in order to manage his father's affairs in Washington, Madison, and elsewhere. In the spring of 1925 he got away long enough to travel with a friend to Europe. He returned in May to find his father in serious condition. A month later, on 18 June, the senator suffered a massive heart attack and died. Bob and the rest of the family were

23. Belle and Fola, *La Follette*, 2:1120–47; Russel B. Nye, *Midwestern Progressive Politics: A Historical Study of Its Origin and Development, 1870–1950* (New York, 1965), pp. 308–19.

24. Paul Y. Anderson, in *St. Louis Post Dispatch*, 1 November 1924, quoted in Belle and Fola, *La Follette*, 2:1145.

25. Ernest Gruening, *Many Battles: The Autobiography of Ernest Gruening* (New York, 1973), p. 124; Mrs. PFL, "Magnum Opus," second draft, May 1947, p. 13, box 165-3, PFL Papers; Fola to Mary, 7 November 1924, box 31-A, Family Papers.

with him at the end, and one by one they silently went to the head of the bed, leaned down, and kissed him on the forehead. The next day they took the body by train back to Madison. Fifty thousand persons filed by the open casket in the east rotunda of the state capitol. On Monday, 22 June, La Follette was buried in Madison's Forest Hill Cemetery.[26]

Since the turn of the century, Fighting Bob La Follette had dominated Wisconsin politics. Now that he was gone, the future seemed uncertain. During the weeks after the funeral, people throughout the state discussed the obvious questions: How would his death affect state politics? Who would succeed him in the Senate?

In 1925, as during most of its history, Wisconsin was virtually a one-party state, and the one party was the GOP. But the Republicans were divided into two warring camps, the stalwarts and the progressives. In general, the stalwarts were conservative. They had close ties to the business community; they frowned on government intervention in the economy, except to help business along a bit; they supported the Coolidge administration; and the majority of them was pretty well satisfied with the status quo. The average stalwart more likely than not had vigorously supported World War I and denounced the elder La Follette for his "traitorous" activities. Not all stalwarts, however, were conservative on domestic issues. Some of them were former progressives who had defected to the stalwart camp because of personal disagreements with La Follette or because they had opposed his antiwar stand.

The progressive faction was a broad coalition of numerous groups and individuals, including organized labor and militant farm organizations. Dissatisfied with the status quo, most progressives were willing to use government to curb the power of big business and to redress the grievances of farmers, workers, and other disadvantaged groups. Most progressives had either opposed American entry into the war or had later concluded that American involvement was a mistake. Just as not all stalwarts were conservative, not all progressives were liberal. Some of them, especially persons of German ancestry, believed in a conservative philosophy but had aligned themselves with the La Follette progressives because of the senator's condemnation of the war.

There was also a highly personal dimension to GOP factionalism. The progressives, because they were such a broad coalition, disagreed among themselves on any number of issues; but they were united in

26. Belle and Fola, La Follette, 2:1148–74.

support of the elder La Follette. Similarly, the stalwarts frequently quarreled among themselves but were united in their opposition to Old Bob.[27]

La Follette's death intensified the progressive-stalwart struggle. The immediate objective of both sides was to capture the vacant Senate seat. A special election to fill the seat was scheduled for September, with a primary on the fifteenth and a general election two weeks later. Since Wisconsin was a one-party state, the crucial battle would take place in the primary, with the winner facing only token opposition in the general election. Stalwart leaders selected as their candidate Roy P. Wilcox, a former state senator and an enthusiastic supporter of the Coolidge administration. Wilcox had first made a name for himself in 1918, when he introduced into the state senate a resolution condemning the elder La Follette for his criticism of the war.[28]

At first it appeared that there might be a fierce struggle within progressive ranks to succeed Old Bob, as spokesmen for various elements of the progressive coalition expressed interest in entering the primary. Upon reflection, however, most progressives realized that a wild scramble after the nomination would splinter the coalition and thereby ensure the nomination of a stalwart. Upon further reflection, most progressives concluded that they would have to unite behind a single candidate and that the candidate most likely to appeal to all elements of the coalition would be another La Follette.[29]

Many progressives looked first to Belle. True, no woman had ever been elected to the United States Senate. But then Belle was no ordinary woman. She was a lawyer, a writer, a public lecturer, a champion of many causes; her husband had described her as his "wisest and best counsellor"; and she understood public questions and practical politics as well as, or better than, any public official. Belle, however, was also sixty-six years old, and she wanted no part of it. "At no time in my life," she announced, "would I ever have chosen a public career for myself. It would be against nature for me to undertake the responsibilities of political leadership." Belle, incidentally, could have said precisely the same thing on behalf of Young Bob. The progressives next thought of Phil, not because he was better qualified than Bob, but because he had the ability and, unlike Bob, he had

27. For a discussion of the stalwart and progressive factions in the 1920s, see Herbert F. Margulies, *The Decline of the Progressive Movement in Wisconsin, 1890–1920* (Madison, 1968), chap. 7 and conclusion.

28. Roger T. Johnson, *Robert M. La Follette, Jr. and the Decline of the Progressive Party in Wisconsin* (Madison, 1964), p. 12.

29. Ibid., pp. 3–6.

political ambitions. But Phil, at the age of twenty-eight, was two years short of fulfilling the constitutional age requirement for a senator.[30]

So that left Bob, who met the constitutional requirement by seven months. And on 30 July, six weeks after his father's death, he announced his candidacy. It was never entirely clear why La Follette, who had repeatedly ruled out a political career for himself, decided to run. Probably it was for the same reason that he had stayed with his father all those years, because of a sense of obligation.

La Follette campaigned for four weeks. He traveled throughout the state and delivered up to four speeches a day. Most of the people who turned out at his rallies were seeing him for the first time, and as he took his place on the platform, they looked him over carefully. He was five feet, seven inches tall, weighed about 145 pounds, and although not overweight, he looked slightly pudgy. He had thick, wavy, black hair, which he parted in the middle; an oval face; slightly protuberant blue eyes; a small mouth; and full lips. People noticed that he looked more like his mother than his father, but he displayed many of his father's mannerisms.

From the start La Follette was a better than average speaker. But compared to his father, one of the great orators of his time, he was disappointing. Prior to the campaign he had addressed a large crowd only once, and that was in 1924 when he read his father's acceptance speech to the convention that nominated the senator for president. He had an excellent voice, deep and resonant, but had not yet learned how to project it properly; as a result, after the first few speeches his voice sounded raspy. At first he appeared ill at ease on the platform, his delivery was mechanical, his gestures awkward and distracting. As the campaign progressed, however, he became more relaxed and his delivery improved. Then and later he was most effective when talking to small groups in informal settings. La Follette was not a dramatic speaker, but he did manage to convey knowledge of the subject matter and convince his listeners that he was utterly sincere.[31]

In his speeches La Follette sounded no new themes and presented no ideas of his own. He based his campaign solely on his father's record, promising more of the same. He advocated economy and efficiency in government, a sharp reduction in military appropriations,

30. Ibid., pp. 5–6; Belle press release, 28 July 1925, box 31-A, Family Papers.
31. Unidentified newspaper clippings, boxes 559–660-C, Belle letter file, box 31-A, RML letter file, box 32-A, Family Papers; Philip F. La Follette, *Adventure in Politics: The Memoirs of Philip La Follette* (New York, 1970), p. 115; interview, Roderick H. Riley, 11 June 1973. Riley, who later served as an aide to RML, heard RML speak during 1925 campaign and recalled details of his awkward delivery.

and speedy payment of the federal debt. He called for the abolition of regressive excise taxes enacted during the war and for the lowering, on a progressive basis, of federal income tax rates. He also favored imposition of a sharply graduated inheritance tax in order to reduce the great fortunes that "imperil the foundations of democratic government." The menace of big business was a constant theme. The government, he declared, should enforce the antitrust laws, and Congress should investigate the Federal Trade Commission in order to discover why it no longer protected the public from the assault of big business. La Follette supported government operation of the electric power and nitrate producing plants at Muscle Shoals in the Tennessee Valley. The Coolidge administration favored turning Muscle Shoals over to private interests. La Follette promised farmers, who had been experiencing hard times since 1921, that he would fight to repeal the Esch-Cummins Railroad Act, a law that many farmers blamed for high freight rates. He promised workers that he would support their right to organize and would support legislation to prevent antiunion judges from issuing injunctions in labor disputes. In the field of foreign affairs, La Follette opposed American participation in the World Court, an adjunct of the League of Nations, but was in favor of the United States entering into treaties that outlawed war.[32]

The outcome of the special election was never seriously in doubt. On 15 September, La Follette easily won the primary, gathering 56 percent of the vote and defeating his nearest opponent, the stalwart Wilcox, by one hundred thousand votes. As expected, he went on to win the general election on 29 September, with 69 percent of the total.[33]

La Follette won the election not because of what he had said during the campaign nor because of how he had said it. He won because he was the son of Fighting Bob. One reporter probably expressed the feelings of most Wisconsin voters when he observed that Young Bob obviously had potential. But, he added, "whether he will develop qualities of leadership remains to be seen."[34] La Follette, who but for loyalty to his father and uncontrollable circumstances would never have become a United States senator, must have been wondering the same thing.

32. *La Follette's Magazine*, September 1925; RML campaign speech, n.d., box 133-2, PFL Papers.
33. Johnson, *La Follette, Jr.*, p. 16.
34. Newspaper clipping, n.d., box 659-C, Family Papers.

CHAPTER 4

The Youngest Senator

There was nothing dramatic or exciting about La Follette's first years in the Senate. Hardworking, energetic, obviously intelligent, he proved himself to be an able, though rather dull, successor to his father. In each situation that arose he tried to do what he thought Old Bob would have done. Consequently, he never really emerged from his father's shadow. As a political leader La Follette experienced two conspicuous failures, though both were due in part to circumstances beyond his control. He was unable to match his father's control over Wisconsin politics, hence during these years the progressive organization in the state deteriorated rapidly. On the national level, his efforts to organize the Senate insurgents into a united bloc ended in frustration.

La Follette took the oath of office on Monday, 7 December 1925, forty years to the day after his father had taken a similar oath upon first entering the House of Representatives. "Bob's voice rang out clear and fine just as Dad's used to on the 'I do,'" reported Fola to absent family members. "I'm sure," she added, "that a goodly number of people must have felt that, though men pass, their work goes on." Not everyone, however, shared her sentiments. When La Follette finished the oath and started for his seat in the rear of the chamber, a visitor in the gallery exclaimed in a loud whisper, "Why he's just a boy! How do they dare trust him?" Others also wondered whether the thirty-year-old senator measured up to the responsibilities of high office. The *New York Times* dismissed him as the "undistinguished son who bears the magic name." Even La Follette expressed doubts. He candidly told a reporter that he hoped to "have a chance to accomplish what actually is in me—if anything."[1]

He was the youngest senator since Henry Clay. But despite his youth and relative inexperience as an active politician, he brought to his new role several very useful advantages. Since childhood he had witnessed hundreds of debates in the Senate; as his father's secre-

---

1. Fola to PFL, 8 December 1925, box 133-2, PFL Papers; *New York Times*, 2 October 1925; newspaper clipping, 12 December 1925, box 660-C, Family Papers (see list of abbreviations p. x).

tary he had helped organize and direct many others. Thus, he was already familiar with the intricacies of parliamentary procedure, senatorial customs, and bill drafting and could immediately play an active role in Senate deliberations. He also inherited a well-trained staff, which had served the elder La Follette for years. Most important, of course, was the "magic name," which automatically attracted a national constituency and widespread publicity, both essential ingredients for a successful political career. During his first months in Washington, dozens of newspapers carried feature articles on "Young Bob." Here, after all, was the dramatic story of a loyal son picking up the banner for his stricken father. Even his appearance and dress, from the "Valentino hairstyle" to the "gray-pearl spats," drew comment.[2]

La Follette had barely taken his seat in the Senate when he became involved in a controversy over his status within the Republican party. In 1924, when the elder La Follette bolted the GOP to run on the Progressive ticket, Republican leaders retaliated by virtually reading him out of the party and by stripping him of his committee assignments. Now they faced the problem of what to do with Young Bob, of whether to continue the injunction or to define him as a Republican and assign him to committees. At first they seemed conciliatory. After conferring with President Coolidge, Senate chieftains James E. Watson and Richard P. Ernst announced that if La Follette would attend the Republican conference, a meeting to map out strategy for the upcoming session, they would not question his "brand of Republicanism" but would treat him as a "regular" and ask for his committee preferences. But La Follette, sensing that some people would interpret his appearance as symbolic submission to the GOP leadership, ignored the invitation.[3]

For its part, the conference avoided the issue and left the final decision to the Committee on Committees. After wrangling for several days over La Follette's status, the eight-man committee voted to a tie. Two days later, however, someone pointed out that one of those who had voted for La Follette, Sen. James W. Wadsworth, Jr., had actually resigned from the committee a year earlier, a fact that he and everyone else had curiously forgotten. Adding to the confusion, there was doubt as to Coolidge's position on the issue since party members on both sides claimed to speak for the president. La Follette, by doing

2. *New York Sun*, 9 January 1926, *Pittsburgh Post*, 23 January 1926, and other clippings, box 660-C, Family Papers.
3. *New York Times*, 2 December 1925; Edward N. Doan, *The La Follettes and the Wisconsin Idea* (New York, 1947), p. 147.

nothing, had already tied the party hierarchy in knots. "It has been rather fun," he wrote his brother, "to sit tight and watch them squirm in and out of the proposition."[4]

Finally, on 14 December, the Republicans acted to stop the growing publicity the affair was receiving; the Committee on Committees, by unanimous vote, recognized the young senator as a Republican and assigned him to the Committees on Manufacturing, Indian Affairs, and Mines and Mining. But La Follette had the last word. In a public letter to Republican Majority Leader Watson, he said that although he would accept the assignments, his first allegiance was not to the party of Coolidge but to the "progressive principles and policies of government as interpreted and applied by the late Robert M. La Follette."[5]

La Follette meant what he said. During the first session of Congress, which ran from December 1925 to July 1926, he spoke from the floor of the Senate on a wide variety of issues. Throughout, his loyalty to the principles and policies of his father was clearly apparent.

On 22 January 1926, he delivered his maiden address in the Senate, assailing the proposed American membership in the World Court. During the speech he sounded a theme that his father had repeated over and over and that he himself would repeat endlessly: "The only way toward peace for the Nation . . . lies in keeping free from the intrigues and imperialism which dominates European diplomacy." The galleries were packed that day, and at one point sympathetic spectators momentarily held their breath. Obviously nervous, La Follette was fumbling with his manuscript when a page slipped out of his hand and floated into the aisle. But he regained his composure, calmly retrieved the page, and continued on. At another point in the speech, he sharply criticized former President Woodrow Wilson. The wife of the late president happened to be in the gallery that day, and when she heard her husband under attack she leaned forward in her seat to catch a glimpse of this brash young upstart.[6]

Two weeks later La Follette joined fellow insurgents in an unsuccessful assault on the Coolidge administration's tax-reduction bill, which eliminated the inheritance tax and in other ways lessened the tax burden of the very wealthy. To La Follette, the measure proved

4. Doan, *Wisconsin Idea*, pp. 147–48; RML to PFL, 7 December 1925, box 32-A, Family Papers.

5. *New York Times*, 15 December 1925; RML to Watson, quoted in Doan, *Wisconsin Idea*, pp. 148–49.

6. *CR* 69:1, 1926, vol. 67, pt. 3, pp. 2577–87; *New York Times*, 23 January 1926; Theodore A. Huntley, in *Pittsburgh Post*, 23 January 1926, and other clippings, box 660-C, Family Papers.

that the administration stood for government "of, by and for great wealth." In March he delivered an impressive, fact-filled defense of public ownership and operation of the electric power complex at Muscle Shoals in the Tennessee Valley. "Before we awake to the danger," he warned, "the power supply will be in the control of a few great corporations, whose ability to hurt and to harm will surpass any trust we have yet known." Throughout the session La Follette also carried on a running battle with the "reactionary majority" of the Federal Trade Commission membership and with the Justice Department for its failure to break up trusts, especially the bread trust.[7]

The tone and substance of Young Bob's early remarks clearly evoked memories of the elder La Follette. There was the same impassioned rhetoric, the same dichotomy between the "special interests" and the "people"; the same sense of impending doom if the Republican leadership persisted in its ways. The Wisconsin senator also displayed his father's boundless energy. He arrived at the Capitol early and left late. After returning to his house on Sixteenth Street, where he lived alone with his mother, he worked past midnight preparing speeches or writing weekly editorials for La Follette's Magazine. "He keeps right on the job as he did when he was a little boy planting potatoes," said Belle with characteristic understatement. "There isn't much glamour about the U.S. Senatorship for him but it is fine experience." Except for an occasional movie, he enjoyed little social life.[8]

Despite the similarities between father and son, Washington observers were quick to notice the marked differences in personality and style. Young Bob was "sedulously staid and reserved, in contrast to the flash that his noted father sparkled before him." He talked "in words of few syllables," was "brief," and knew "when he was through with what he had to say—which could not always be said of Bob the elder." His manner was "confident but unassuming," his speaking style that of "forceful conversation," but his voice lacked "the music and resonance of old Bob's." The son also made "his fights in better nature, devoid of [the] stage settings and spectacular entrances" that had embellished his father's parliamentary battles. With Bob, there were "no dramatic 11th hour appearances to begin a fight just as the final roll call" was about to begin; "no thundering at the presiding officer,

7. RML on tax bill, CR 69:1, 1926, vol. 67, pt. 4, pp. 3616–17, 3677–83; RML on Muscle Shoals, ibid., pp. 4902–16; RML on bread trust, ibid., pp. 12317–26. See also La Follette's Magazine, November 1925, January 1926.

8. Belle to Fola, 9 February 1926, box 33-A, RML letter file, box 33-A, Family Papers.

no thumping of desk tops with clenched fists, no shoving of chairs around and charges up and down the center aisle." Most important, while Fighting Bob "delighted in making enemies," his son "naturally makes friends."[9]

For some people, La Follette's less dramatic style came as a disappointment. But for Senate colleagues, many of whom had grown weary of "stage settings and spectacular entrances" and of sometimes being treated, on and off the floor, like enemies of the Republic, it proved a refreshing change. Sen. Burton K. Wheeler of Montana, who served with both father and son, later recalled that while Old Bob was one of the least popular men in the Senate, Young Bob immediately became one of the most popular. Even the "Old Guard" liked him. James E. Watson, a conservative Republican from Indiana, would often go up to La Follette on the floor or in the cloakroom, throw his arm around him, and relate the latest joke or bit of gossip. George H. Moses of New Hampshire, who later dubbed La Follette one of the "Sons of the Wild Jackass" and whom La Follette considered an "out and out reactionary," personally treated the young senator like a son.[10]

Occasionally La Follette's cordial relationship with his colleagues provided political dividends. For example, he gained a seat on the two most important investigative committees of the Sixty-ninth Congress, the committee that investigated the Tariff Commission and the committee that probed illegalities in primary campaigns. But La Follette was not as successful with the bills and resolutions that he offered during the session. In December 1925 his proposal to update the Seaman's Act, which his father had sponsored in 1915, lapsed and died in committee. In March 1926 his call for a Senate probe into the circumstances surrounding the strike by textile workers in Passaic, New Jersey, met a similar fate. In June, La Follette introduced a far-reaching proposal to limit spending in primary campaigns. His action was prompted by the recently concluded Pennsylvania senatorial primary, in which two candidates, William S. Vare and George Wharton Pepper, had spent a combined total of between $2 million and $5 mil-

9. "Young Bob Seeks No Credit," 12 December 1925, Martin Green in *New York Evening World*, n.d., Mames O'Donnell Bennet in *Chicago Tribune*, 23 January 1926, Theodore A. Huntley in *Pittsburgh Post*, 23 January 1926, J. L. Wright, "Young Bob Good Mixer," n.d., Martin Green in *New York Evening World*, n.d., clippings, box 660-C, Family Papers.

10. Interview, Burton K. Wheeler, 4 December 1973; Clinton W. Gilbert in *Philadelphia Public Ledger*, 25 March 1926, J. L. Wright, "Young Bob Good Mixer," clippings, box 660–C, RML to Gilbert E. Roe, 27 January 1926, box 5-C, Family Papers.

lion. "Such debauchery" of the electoral process, La Follette warned, "means the eventual destruction of representative government in the United States." His proposal, in the form of an amendment to the rules of the Senate, would require complete disclosure of campaign financing and expenditures and place a ceiling on spending. With the primaries only a month away, and with most incumbents not wishing to jeopardize their chances for reelection, the Senate refused even to consider the reform measure.[11]

Like his father, La Follette was determined to play an active role in Wisconsin politics. So, when Congress recessed in July, he rushed back to the state to take part in the upcoming campaigns for the governorship and for the other Senate seat. Although his own reelection was still two years off, the two contests promised to provide an important test of his influence in the state and of his ability to lead the progressive organization.

Earlier in the year, he and Phil, who was now practicing law in Madison, had endorsed Herman L. Ekern for the governorship. Ekern, one of the elder La Follette's closest friends and most trusted advisers, had been a major behind-the-scenes figure in the Wisconsin progressive movement two decades before. As speaker of the assembly, and later as insurance commissioner, he had played a pioneering role in the development of state regulations governing the insurance industry. Before his death, Old Bob had been in the process of grooming Ekern for the governorship. In recognition of his qualifications, but also out of loyalty to their father, the La Follette brothers supported his candidacy. They also endorsed John J. Blaine, who had resigned from the governorship to challenge conservative Republican Irvine L. Lenroot for his Senate seat.[12]

Within the progressive organization, however, some members resented what they thought was an attempt by those "upstart" La Follette brothers and their cohorts to "dictate" who would run for office and who would not. One disgruntled progressive privately declared that although he may have "accepted the dictation of the late Senator La Follette, as did a good many others," he was not now willing "to accept dictation from any other quarter."[13] But the chief dissenter

11. *CR* 69:1, 1926, vol. 67, pts. 5, 9, pp. 5445, 9678; seaman's bill, ibid., p. 609; Passaic probe, ibid., pp. 5938–42, 7569, 7649; campaign spending, ibid., pp. 11461–62.

12. Philip F. La Follette, *Adventure in Politics: The Memoirs of Philip La Follette* (New York, 1970), pp. 123–25.

13. G. M. Sheldon to Charles M. Dow, 30 January 1926, box 133-2, PFL Papers.

was Fred R. Zimmerman, the Wisconsin secretary of state, who challenged the brothers' leadership by entering the Republican primary against Ekern. Throughout the campaign, Zimmerman proclaimed his loyalty to the principles of Fighting Bob but denounced "machine" domination by the "Madison Ring," a reference to the La Follettes, Ekern, and Blaine. Although Bob and Phil waged a vigorous campaign on Ekern's behalf, Zimmerman triumphed in the September primary.

In the Senate race the La Follettes were more successful. Their candidate, Blaine, easily defeated Lenroot. Blaine's victory took on an added, national significance because, during the campaign, President Coolidge had personally appeared in the state to urge Lenroot's reelection.[14]

Still, Ekern's loss was a blow to the La Follette brothers' prestige; moreover it revealed the dissension within progressive ranks. Some observers predicted that the defeat even jeopardized Young Bob's reelection chances in 1928. La Follette recognized the need for a "thorough-going organization" effort, because "many of the leaders upon whom daddy depended have become aged and infirm" and because "so many young voters have become of age since the epoch making fights were made in the state."[15]

If Wisconsin progressives were in need of revitalization and reorganization, so also were the progressives in the United States Senate. "We are drifting along here without much organized effort," La Follette had complained during the first session. Although his liberal colleagues had not "compromised in any way in so far as the record" was concerned, he observed a "lack of punch in their fighting." La Follette cited several reasons for the progressives' plight. "The continued comparative prosperity in industrial centers appears to have completely anesthetized the rank and file," he said, adding that the progressives "have permitted this reaction to dampen their ardor." Then too, "the complete collapse of the Democratic Party as an opposition party" prevented the progressive bloc from effectively wielding the balance of power. La Follette also pointed to the weak leadership of the progressives. After the elder La Follette's death, many insurgents looked to George W. Norris of Nebraska for leadership. But, observed La Follette, Norris was "not in the frame of mind where he is willing to give the necessary time and energy to the or-

14. PFL, *Memoirs*, pp. 124–25; *New York Times*, 3, 9 September 1926.
15. *New York Times*, 9 September 1926; RML to W. T. Rawleigh, 2 February 1927, box 6-C, Family Papers.

ganization of any group activity."[16] The state of the progressives was particularly disturbing for La Follette because he believed that a strong and united insurgent bloc was essential to the reemergence of the progressive movement nationally.

Upon returning to Washington in December 1926 for the last session of Congress, La Follette made his first attempt to organize the Senate progressives. He tried to get them to agree upon "two or three constructive bills dealing with transportation, hydro-electric power and credit." "My idea," he said later, "was that while the legislation probably would not receive consideration at this session of Congress its introduction would outline a constructive position for our group." Until this time, the progressives had primarily played a negative role in the Senate, opposing measures sponsored by the administration; La Follette was trying to persuade them to unite behind a positive program of reform. He also urged them to force an extra session of Congress, which would meet after the short session ended in March. His colleagues, however, rejected both suggestions. Although the progressive bloc did achieve passage of the long-sought McNary-Haugen farm-relief bill, which Coolidge promptly vetoed, the Sixty-ninth Congress adjourned with the progressives still "running a good deal to loose ends."[17]

La Follette spent the next several months in Pinehurst, North Carolina, and in Wisconsin, recovering from a recurrence of his old illness. In his absence, William E. Borah, a progressive Republican from Idaho, tried his hand at organizing the insurgents. Borah succeeded temporarily, and in November 1927 he announced the formation of a united progressive bloc.[18]

This development, it seemed, could not have come at a better time. The Senate, which was to convene in December, would be almost evenly split between the two parties. This was because of the last

16. RML to PFL, 12 February 1926, box 134-2, PFL Papers; RML to Frederic C. Howe, 9 April 1926, box 4-C, RML to PFL, 18 February 1926, box 34-A, Family Papers. In addition to La Follette, the senators who generally called themselves progressives were Republicans William E. Borah of Idaho, Smith W. Brookhart of Iowa, Lynn J. Frazier and Gerald P. Nye of North Dakota, Robert B. Howell and George W. Norris of Nebraska, Hiram Johnson of California, William H. McMaster and Peter Norbeck of South Dakota; Farm-Laborite Henrik Shipstead of Minnesota; and Democrat Burton K. Wheeler of Montana. In 1927 Republicans John J. Blaine of Wisconsin and Bronson Cutting of New Mexico joined the group.

17. RML to W. T. Rawleigh, 12 February 1927, box 6-C, RML to PFL and Mrs. PFL, 25 January 1927, box 35-A, Family Papers.

18. RML letter file, box 35-A, Family Papers; LeRoy Ashby, *The Spearless Leader: Senator William E. Borah and the Progressive Movement in the 1920's* (Urbana, Ill., 1972), pp. 218–21.

election, in which Democrats had picked up seven seats. Hence, the handful of progressive Republicans could wield the balance of power in the Senate. The Republicans even needed progressive support to organize the Senate as the majority party and to retain control of the committees. Presumably the progressives could exact major concessions from the GOP in exchange for their votes for organization. Referring to the progressives, one political commentator said that "seldom if ever, in the history of the Republic have seven men held so powerful a position in the upper branch of Congress." La Follette confidently proclaimed that "we are on the eve of a great development of the Progressive movement."[19]

Nonetheless, the insurgents' ability to take advantage of their supposed balance of power depended on united and forceful action. Aware of this, La Follette, in the weeks before the opening session of Congress, met with fellow progressives to devise strategy and, in particular, to decide what demands to make of the Republican leadership on the issue of organizing the Senate. La Follette urged his colleagues to draw up a list of proposed legislation and then to demand assurance from the GOP that this legislation would at least come to a vote during the first session. The reaction to his plan quickly shattered his hopes for coordinated action. Some senators rejected it outright, wanting instead to trade their votes on organization for better committee assignments. Those who favored his strategy differed over what specific legislation to demand.[20]

In the end only four senators, Lynn J. Frazier and Gerald P. Nye of North Dakota, Henrik Shipstead of Minnesota, and John J. Blaine of Wisconsin, went along with La Follette. On 1 December 1927, they presented their demands to Republican floor leader Charles Curtis. For their votes to organize the Senate as a Republican body, they demanded "definite assurance" that the leadership would not "pigionhole" certain specified proposals in committee, but would advance them to a final vote. These proposals were: the McNary-Haugen farm-relief bill, which Coolidge had previously vetoed; a bill limiting the use of judicial injunctions in labor disputes; and a resolution calling for a thorough investigation of United States policy in Latin America. "The program upon which only five of us were able to agree," La Follette wrote to his brother, "is somewhat attenuated but in my judgment it is better than no action at all."[21]

19. L. C. Speers, "Seven Men Hold the Key to the Senate," *New York Times*, 4 December 1927; RML quoted in *La Follette's Magazine*, 1 December 1927.
20. RML to PFL, 3 December 1927, box 35-A, Family Papers.
21. Senator Frazier et al. to Sen. Charles Curtis, 1 December 1927, box 5-C, RML to PFL, 3 December 1927, box 35-A, Family Papers.

Without the backing of such leading progressives as Borah and Norris, La Follette's challenge posed little threat. On behalf of the Republican leadership, Curtis promised that there would be no unnecessary delays before the Senate considered the three proposals. Although this amounted to much less than the "definite assurance" they had requested, the five senators voted for Republican organization anyway. Curtis mollified those who had held out for better committee assignments by securing passage of a resolution enlarging the committees, thus providing room for more progressives.[22] With relatively minor concessions, the Old Guard had headed off what could have been a major challenge.

On the surface, the Senate progressives presented a picture of harmony. They regularly conferred with one another; and they lunched together at a specially reserved table off the Senate restaurant. At election time they exchanged endorsements and campaigned for one another, each portraying the others as saviors of the Republic. And rightly so, for the "Sons of the Wild Jackass," as Sen. George Moses called them, agreed on most of the basic issues. All were ardent anti-monopolists; all decried the exploitation of the "people" by the "special interests"; and since they came from the Middle West and West, all championed the interests of the farmer. In foreign relations they maintained a united front in opposition to American involvement in European affairs and to imperialistic ventures, especially in Latin America. Yet, when it came down to specific situations like organizing the Senate, too often they were unable to work effectively as a group. This particularly disappointed La Follette, who placed a higher premium on cooperation and unity than did some of his intensely individualistic colleagues, especially the older ones like Borah and Norris. Still he refused to abandon hope that the insurgent bloc would gain a balance of power in the Senate. Nor did he abandon his determination to do everything he could toward that end. At the same time, however, he was not about to permit the progressive bloc's sometimes lackluster performance to injure his own political future. "If I am unsuccessful in securing cooperation," he had written a friend months earlier, "I shall at least make it plain to the public, so far as I am personally concerned, that I am not ready to compromise with the old guard on anything."[23]

During the controversy over the organization of the Senate, an-

22. *New York Times*, 10 December 1927.

23. RML to W. T. Rawleigh, 12 February 1927, box 6-C, Family Papers. For an insightful discussion of the weaknesses of the Senate progressives, see Ashby, *Spearless Leader*, chap. 8.

other, more dramatic story had begun to unfold in Washington. Early in December the Hearst newspaper chain reported that four United States senators—William E. Borah, George W. Norris, Thomas J. Heflin, and Robert La Follette, Jr.—had accepted bribes from the Mexican government. Citing "secret" documents from the Mexican archives, the reports claimed that La Follette had received fifteen thousand dollars for advocating a pro-Mexico policy in the Senate.[24]

The four promptly denied the charges, La Follette calling them "an infamous and cowardly fraud." A special Senate investigating committee, set up to examine the allegations, agreed. It found the "secret" documents to be blatant forgeries and the charges they contained to be absolutely false. For a time La Follette considered bringing a libel suit against Hearst, but because of the time and expense involved, and perhaps also because he did not wish to antagonize the Hearst newspapers in Wisconsin, which had endorsed his candidacy in 1925, he finally dropped the idea of a suit.[25]

Those who had tried to perpetrate the fraud probably chose La Follette as one of their targets because of his persistent opposition to American intervention in the internal affairs of Mexico and other Latin American nations. Since his first months in the Senate, he had criticized the Coolidge administration for using the power of the United States to advance and protect the interests of American businessmen in foreign lands. He was particularly concerned that this policy might lead to war with Mexico, where the reformist regime of Plutarco Calles was attempting to restrict the property rights of American oil producers and landowners. Even when, in the fall of 1927, Coolidge moved toward conciliation by appointing the able Dwight W. Morrow as ambassador to Mexico, La Follette kept up the attack. Noting that Morrow had been a partner in the J. P. Morgan Company, he claimed that his appointment proved that the "great exploiting interests" controlled American foreign policy.[26]

The Wisconsin senator was even more critical of Coolidge's actions in Nicaragua. Early in 1927, when an insurrection threatened to topple the pro-American government of Adolfo Diaz, the president first supplied the regime with guns and then sent the marines to restore order. This "wantonly imperialistic course," said La Follette, endangered friendly relations and healthy economic trade with all of Latin

24. *New York Times*, 16 December 1927.
25. RML quoted in Doan, *Wisconsin Idea*, p. 240; *New York Times*, 20 December 1927; RML to Gilbert Roe, 16 December 1927, box 6-C, Roe to RML, 14 January 1928, box 7-C, PFL to RML and Belle, 16 December 1927, box 35-A, Family Papers.
26. *New York Times*, 17 January 1926; *La Follette's Magazine*, October 1927.

America. Even worse, Coolidge had usurped the war-making power that the Constitution reserved solely to Congress.[27]

Early in 1928, in a nationally broadcast radio address, La Follette outlined what he considered the paramount problems of the time. They sounded familiar: corruption in government, control of electric power by monopolies, the economic plight of the farmer, an inequitable tax structure, and the imperialistic foreign policy of the Coolidge administration. Familiar too was his call for progressives to rededicate themselves to the principles of his father.[28] Thus, after two years in the Senate, he was still focusing on the same issues and offering the same solutions as had the elder La Follette. Only an occasional difference in emphasis, and of course the difference in style distinguished his own career from his father's. Although he had become an able and intelligent spokesman for Old Bob's brand of progressivism, he had not yet shown himself to be conspicuously innovative.

27. *New York Times*, 12 March 1927; *La Follette's Magazine*, January, May, June 1927.
28. RML radio speech, "Dominant Issues in the 1928 Campaign," 14 February 1928, in *CR* 70:1, 1928, vol. 69, pt. 3, pp. 3315–16.

CHAPTER 5

Coming into His Own

Between 1928 and 1930, La Follette began for the first time to follow his own instincts, to venture into new areas, and to apply his and his father's principles to new problems. In the process he became his own man. But this phase of his career was significant for another reason as well. During the late 1920s the nation was sharply divided along rural and urban lines. One manifestation of this division was the inability of agrarian reformers and urban reformers, who had much in common, to forge an alliance. The unfortunate result was that common problems went unsolved. La Follette, however, came as close as any public official to understanding and responding to the needs of both farmers and city dwellers.

One growing problem to which La Follette addressed his attention was the stock market. Since 1924 both the level of trading and the price of stocks on Wall Street, except for a few temporary setbacks, had been mounting steadily. A decade earlier most people had scoffed at the idea of committing their savings to stock-market speculation, but during the 1920s many of them overcame their inhibitions and avidly plunged into what was fast becoming America's favorite sport. Almost everyone, including investors, politicians, economists, and interested spectators, viewed the rise in stock prices as a good thing, a sign of increasing business productivity and of a healthy, expanding economy. And up to 1927 or early 1928, their optimism was probably justified.[1]

In August 1927, the Federal Reserve Board, in order to discourage the excessive incursion of foreign money into Wall Street, lowered the rediscount rate in its New York district, thereby making it cheaper for people to secure loans from their banks. Many people rushed to take advantage of this and then used the money they had borrowed to buy stocks. The Federal Reserve also began to buy government securities on the open market, thus further increasing the amount of money in circulation that could be used for speculation. In September, La Follette became one of the first public officials to sound a warn-

1. John Kenneth Galbraith, *The Great Crash, 1929* (Boston, 1954), pp. 6–7, 16.

ing. Speculation, he said, had now reached "dangerous proportions."[2]

Ensuing developments deepened his apprehension. During the week of 3 December 1927, the level of trading on the New York Stock Exchange was greater than during any other week in history. Year-end reports disclosed another remarkable fact. During 1927 member banks of the Federal Reserve system in New York, as a result of the lower rediscount rate, had increased their loans to investors and to stock brokers by more than a billion dollars over the preceding year, which also was a record.[3]

La Follette neither feared nor predicted a stock-market crash. What did concern him was that too much money was finding its way into the market, thus lessening the amount that banks could and should lend to "legitimate" businesses. By *legitimate*, he doubtless meant small businesses, in contrast to the huge corporations listed on the exchange. Moreover, he argued, the increasing flow of money and credit to Wall Street drained money away from farmers in the West and South. Thus the Federal Reserve Board, by stimulating these trends, was enhancing the power of one part of the country at the expense of the others.[4] La Follette's reasoning reflected the traditional populist-progressive hostility to Wall Street. Nevertheless he had spotted a fundamental weakness in the economic structure underpinning "Coolidge Prosperity."

On 18 January 1928 he introduced into the Senate a resolution that called upon the Federal Reserve Board to curtail the number of loans made by member banks for speculation. Despite the opposition of Federal Reserve Board members, the Senate Banking and Currency Committee recommended passage of the resolution. But when it came up before the Senate, Secretary of the Treasury Andrew Mellon and President Coolidge publicly denied the existence of any problem, and the resolution went down to defeat. Ironically, at this very time the stock market began its fateful leap forward.[5] Had Congress and the Federal Reserve Board heeded La Follette's warning, they might possibly have averted the disaster that befell the nation a year and a half later.

2. Ibid., pp. 6–7, 14–16; Frederick Lewis Allen, *Only Yesterday: An Informal History of the 1920's* (New York, 1964 [1931]), p. 242; *La Follette's Magazine*, September 1927.

3. Allen, *Only Yesterday*, p. 241; CR 70:1, 1928, vol. 69, pt. 2, p. 1644 (see list of abbreviations p. x).

4. *New York Times*, 19 January 1928.

5. Ibid., 1, 8 March 1928; *Atlanta Constitution*, 10 October 1928, clipping, box 660-C, Family Papers; Allen, *Only Yesterday*, p. 242; Galbraith, *Great Crash*, p. 16.

Next, La Follette turned his attention to another sorely neglected problem, unemployment. Despite all the talk about national prosperity emanating from the White House and elsewhere, by 1928 many millions of people were jobless. La Follette called the problem "one of the most serious economic questions confronting the country today." "It is a startling fact," he said, "that there has been practically no consideration of . . . unemployment and the methods of dealing with it by this Government."[6]

He was speaking with the fervor of a recent convert, for until Robert F. Wagner, a freshman Democrat from New York, repeatedly raised the issue on the Senate floor early in 1928, La Follette, like most other progressives, had ignored the problem. But Wagner convinced him that joblessness had reached dangerous proportions and that government action was needed to combat it. On 2 May, La Follette introduced a resolution calling for a thorough Senate investigation of unemployment and of possible measures to relieve it. Two weeks later the Senate approved the resolution and authorized the Education and Labor Committee to conduct the probe during the next session of Congress.[7]

Despite the Senate action, and despite the warnings of La Follette, Wagner, and others, unemployment, like the stock-market boom, failed to arouse much public concern. Leaders in the business community and in the Coolidge administration reinforced this mood of complacency by their continued reassurances that all was still well with the economy. While the Senate was considering La Follette's resolution, Donaldson Brown, vice-president of General Motors, told an assembly of businessmen that the present rate of unemployment resulted from industrial efficiency rather than from overproduction and was therefore a sign of business health. Not to be outdone, Coolidge confidently proclaimed months later that "No Congress of the United States ever assembled, on surveying the state of the Union, has met with a more pleasing prospect than that which appears at the present time."[8]

Even though La Follette was unable to alert the public to the dangers of unemployment, he felt the effort had been worthwhile. He had demonstrated his ability to perceive a serious economic problem that had escaped the gaze of his father and of his fellow Western

6. *CR* 70:1, 1928, vol. 69, pt. 7, pp. 7243, 7591.

7. J. Joseph Huthmacher, *Senator Robert F. Wagner and the Rise of Urban Liberalism* (New York, 1971), pp. 59–61; *CR* 70:1, 1928, vol. 69, pt. 7, p. 7591; *New York Times*, 20 May 1928.

8. *Washington Daily News*, 9 May 1928; Coolidge quoted in William E. Leuchtenburg, *The Perils of Prosperity, 1914–32* (Chicago, 1958), p. 202.

progressives. He had probably enhanced his reputation among urban workers, who were the principal victims of joblessness. And later, when dramatic developments shoved unemployment into the forefront of the nation's consciousness, the study he devoted to the subject in 1928 prepared him to react quickly and authoritatively.

Of all La Follette's activities during the 1928 session of Congress, none attracted more attention, nor did as much to enhance his reputation as an influential senator, than his successful attempt to put the Senate on record as being opposed to another presidential term for Coolidge. He had laid the groundwork a year earlier. In February 1927 he introduced a resolution declaring it "the sense of the Senate that the precedents established by Washington and other Presidents . . . in retiring from the Presidential office after their second term has become, by universal concurrence, a part of our Republican system of government." The resolution further declared that "any departure from this time-honored custom would be unwise, unpatriotic, and fraught with peril to our free institutions."[9] Actually, the resolution as it applied to President Coolidge was of dubious relevance. Coolidge had become president in 1923 as a result of Warren G. Harding's death; then in 1924 he had been elected to his first full term. So, technically, he could run again in 1928 and still not violate the two-term tradition. But if reelected, Coolidge would serve longer than any other president in history, and this was what bothered La Follette. Believing the chief executive to be the "most powerful individual in the world," he warned that "establishment of the precedent that one man may continue to wield this power for longer than eight years would mark a definite step toward the abrogation of popular government." In addition, he feared that any erosion of the two-term custom might allow some future, "unscrupulous" president to perpetuate himself in office. La Follette's personal repugnance for the man he had once called "that codfish in the White House" and for the president's conservative policies was probably another factor that prompted him to offer the resolution.[10] In any event, the Senate declined to act on it during 1927.

Coolidge himself appeared to lay the issue to rest when, in August 1927, he told reporters that he "did not choose to run for President in 1928." La Follette was skeptical. He said privately, "I have had a

9. *CR* 69:2, 1927, vol. 68, pt. 4, p. 4400. La Follette's resolution was almost identical to one passed by the House of Representatives in December 1875 during President Ulysses S. Grant's second term. *Congressional Digest* 7 (April 1928): 141.

10. *CR* 69:2, 1927, vol. 68, pt. 3, pp. 2608–10; *La Follette's Magazine*, July 1927; RML to PFL, 27 January 1925, box 135–2, PFL Papers.

hunch ever since Coolidge issued his . . . statement . . . that he might be renominated. I still believe it within the reaches of possibilities. In the first place, the great financial and industrial interests cannot agree with unanimity and enthusiasm upon any other candidate." His public reaction to the statement was even stronger. He accused Coolidge of engaging in a clever bit of "political maneuvering" and predicted that the president would accept the nomination after a "trumped-up" ground swell of support.[11]

By January 1928 it seemed to La Follette as though the "trumping-up" process were already underway. That month, New York Republicans met and selected a pro-Coolidge delegation for the GOP convention meeting in June. The Wisconsin senator responded by reintroducing his anti-third-term resolution. It read the same as before except for one, clever addition: a paragraph citing the president's "do not choose to run" statement and commending Coolidge for observing the two-term custom.[12]

The resolution created a problem for Senate Republicans. If they voted against it, they would pass up the opportunity to commend their president. Worse yet, they would leave themselves open to charges that they did not believe Coolidge when he said he would not seek another term. If they supported it, they would go on record as opposed to his renomination, and some still hoped he would run again. Obviously the safest course for regular Republicans was to prevent the resolution from coming to a vote. But La Follette, employing his parliamentary skill, caught the GOP leadership off guard and in February maneuvered the resolution onto the floor.

During the spirited debate and floor fight that followed, La Follette again showed impressive acumen by successfully fending off attempts to send the resolution to a committee. He did have to compromise, however. At the insistence of Simeon D. Fess of Ohio, whom most regarded as Coolidge's spokesman on the floor, La Follette agreed to drop the paragraph commending Coolidge for observing the two-term tradition. But even this he turned to his advantage. He said that because Fess and other Coolidge lieutenants could not commend the president, then obviously the president had not ruled out the possibility of a third term. In the end, the Senate voted 56 to 26 for La Follette's resolution.[13]

Although Coolidge supporters were quick to point out that the

11. RML to W. T. Rawleigh, 18 February 1928, box 7-C, Family Papers; *New York Times*, 13 August 1927.
12. *New York Times*, 1 February 1928.
13. Ibid., 8–11 February 1928.

president could still run and not violate the two-term custom, to judge from the press reaction, most people considered the Senate's action a slap at any draft-Coolidge movement.[14] In any event, Coolidge probably had been sincere in saying he did not choose to run, hence the resolution had little effect on the course of presidential politics. Nevertheless, it had been a significant victory for La Follette, one that added markedly to his standing in the Senate.

Encouraged by this success, La Follette further involved himself in presidential politics during the spring. His personal choice for the Republican nomination was George W. Norris. Although often critical of the Nebraska senator in private, he had nothing but praise for him in public: "Able, fearless, and incorruptible—beloved by friend and respected by foe—veteran of a thousand battles for freedom, justice, and clean government, he stands today the acknowledged champion of the rights and interests of the American people." When Norris entered the April presidential primary in Wisconsin, La Follette campaigned for him vigorously. Norris won the primary and Young Bob headed the Wisconsin delegation pledged to him at the GOP convention.[15]

By June, when Republicans gathered in Kansas City, it was clear that Herbert Hoover, the secretary of commerce under Harding and Coolidge, had the nomination already in hand. By almost all accounts, the convention was a boring affair. Surprisingly, Bob La Follette provided one of the few moments of excitement.

On Thursday, 14 June, the delegates met to adopt a platform. Senator Reed Smoot of Oregon led off the proceedings by reading the majority planks. In a dry, monotonous tone he talked on for nearly four hours. Weary spectators periodically nudged one another to keep awake. When Smoot finished, La Follette, wearing a dark grey suit and a bright blue bow tie, stepped up to the podium to present the minority platform of the Wisconsin delegation.

In contrast to Smoot, he delivered a lively address, frequently straying from the text to criticize the Republican policies of the past eight years. He began by recalling that in every GOP convention since 1908 the Wisconsin delegation had presented a minority platform. And "since 1908," he said, "although often met with jeers and hisses in the convention, we have fought it out. Of the thirty-five or more

14. Ibid.
15. RML radio speech, "Dominant Issues in the 1928 Campaign," 14 February 1928, in CR 70:1, 1928, vol. 69, pt. 3, pp. 3315–16; Richard Lowitt, *George W. Norris: The Persistence of a Progressive, 1913–1933* (Urbana, Ill., 1971), p. 403.

proposals suggested in 1908, thirty-two have been written into statute law." As he went on to list the thirteen planks of the platform, he increasingly impressed the delegates, not with the substance of his remarks, since most opposed what he said, but with his manner. He was speaking with confidence and poise, almost as though he were addressing a friendly audience back in Wisconsin rather than an assembly hostile to his views. La Follette twice denounced Secretary of the Treasury Andrew Mellon. Both times he coolly gazed down at Mellon, who was sitting with the Pennsylvania delegation twenty feet in front of the stage. A little later, when he criticized Coolidge for vetoing the McNary-Haugen farm bill, supporters of the veto started a noisy demonstration on the floor. La Follette stepped back from the microphone and waited for the cheering to subside. "Then," one reporter observed, "with arms extended in an attitude of sincerest appreciation, and with the courtliest of bows, he remarked: 'It is so unusual for a representative of Wisconsin to receive applause in a Republican national convention that I thank you from the bottom of my heart.'" Appreciating his good humor, the convention, including Andrew Mellon, laughed and applauded him. At the end of his address, the audience gave him a prolonged ovation, during which La Follette "remained on the platform taking bows like an oldtime vaudevillian, his hand over his heart." But support for the man did not mean support for his platform, and when the chairman put it to a voice vote, the "'noes' shook the building."[16]

La Follette's performance provoked considerable comment, especially from the well-known political pundits who had covered the convention. H. L. Mencken described it as a "pleasant oasis in the desert of blather." Young Bob's theatrics and appearance, however, impressed Mencken less. La Follette, he said, "made his excellent speech and then spoiled it by bowing and smirking like an East Side piano virtuoso. Bob would be a better man if he had a better barber. His haircut beseems Groucho Marx far more than it beseems a statesman, and his sideboards that he affects simply look idiotic." La Follette, incidentally, took the criticism to heart and shortly thereafter began to trim his sideburns well above the earlobe. Damon Runyon called him "one of the rising young permanent professional windjammers of this great nation," adding that "some one has to take the place of William Jennings Bryan and those old boys who have passed along." Will Rogers told his readers that La Follette had made "the only real speech" of the convention: "He spoke in favor of the people.

16. *New York Times*, 15 June 1928; *Boston Herald*, 15 June 1928, Damon Runyon column, and other unidentified clippings, box 660 C, Family Papers.

He was listened to, but his amendments were not adopted. They kept in the Wall Street ones."[17]

Several weeks after the convention, La Follette opened his re-election campaign. A year earlier he had predicted a "bitter battle." But the extremely favorable publicity he had received in Kansas City, plus the fact that many Wisconsin voters had listened to his speech over the radio, brightened the prospects of victory. By the end of June no one had yet arisen in the Republican party to challenge him for the nomination, prompting his mother to comment that his performance at the convention must have "scared all candidates off."[18] But not for long. In July, George Mead, a paper-mill owner, a banker, and the mayor of Wisconsin Rapids, came forward to oppose him.

La Follette conducted his campaign much as he had in 1925, only now he displayed more self-confidence and had a record of service to which he could point. As always, he vowed to continue the work of "our great leader," his father. He directed most of his fire at the Coolidge administration and tried to equate his opponent with its policies. When speaking to farmers, he emphasized his support of the McNary-Haugen bill, Coolidge's vetoes of the measure, and the convention's failure to endorse it. When speaking to workers in the southeastern part of the state, he recalled his unemployment resolution and endorsed labor's rights to organize and bargain collectively. Throughout, he sidestepped the controversial prohibition issue, although his platform called for liberalization of the Volstead Act. In the September primary he defeated Mead easily, by a two-to-one margin.[19]

The primary win almost ensured La Follette's victory in November. Indeed, his Democratic opponent, Michael K. Reilly, withdrew from the race in October, leaving only William H. Markham, a Hoover supporter and conservative Republican running as an independent, to oppose him. La Follette reported no expenditures for the general election campaign and spent much of his time outside Wisconsin, working for progressive candidates in Minnesota, North Dakota, and Montana.[20] He did not, however, involve himself in the presidential

17. H. L. Mencken in *Baltimore Sun*, 22 June 1928; Damon Runyon column and "Will Rogers Says," clippings, box 660-C, Family Papers.

18. RML to W. T. Rawleigh, 12 February 1927, box 6-C, Belle to Mary, 30 June 1928, box 36-A, Family Papers.

19. RML campaign speeches, box 554-C, Family Papers; *New York Times*, 13 July, 17 August, 3, 5, 6 September 1928.

20. Philip F. La Follette, *Adventure in Politics: The Memoirs of Philip La*

contest. Although Charles Curtis, Hoover's running mate, made a surprise endorsement of him, calling him "that brilliant young man," La Follette refused to reciprocate because of the GOP platform. The convention, he said, "was controlled by the great bankers and industrialists of the East. They wrote the platform." Nor did he follow the path of some progressives, like George Norris and even his brother Phil, who endorsed Alfred E. Smith, the Democratic contender.[21]

In the general election, La Follette garnered an impressive 85 percent of the vote, running well ahead of other Republicans on the ticket, including Hoover, who swept Wisconsin and the nation. But even in victory there was disappointment, since Walter J. Kohler, an industrialist and archenemy of the progressives, won the governorship. Kohler's win both in the primary and in the general election again demonstrated that however popular Young Bob might be, his coattails counted for very little.[22]

Despite this setback, voting patterns across the nation encouraged him. His progressive colleagues in the Senate fared remarkably well, and all those for whom he had campaigned won. Moreover, he perceptively noticed that long-standing patterns of voting behavior had broken down. Smith had made inroads into traditionally Republican areas, especially the cities; Hoover had begun to crack the solidly Democratic South. With party loyalties thus giving way, La Follette thought that the chances of a genuine realignment of the party structure, along liberal and conservative lines, had increased significantly.[23]

In the months after the election, La Follette retreated into the Mayo Clinic in Rochester, Minnesota, and then went to Florida in an attempt to regain his health. For the past two years he had persistently suffered from a variety of ailments. Most serious among them were phlebitis, an inflammation of the leg veins that had produced one blood clot and that had the potential to produce others, and what doctors called a streptococcic infection that led to periodic swelling of the fatty tissues around the eyes, nose, and cheeks. La Follette had undergone an exploratory operation, several biopsies, tests of all kinds, and numerous treatments, and still his doctors were unable to discover the cause of the streptococcic infection or to prescribe effective

---

Follette (New York, 1970), p. 127; *New York Times*, 31 October, 20 November 1928.

21. *New York Times*, 8 July, 10, 27 October 1928; PFL, *Memoirs*, p. 127.
22. *New York Times*, 7, 8 November 1928
23. *La Follette's Magazine*, November 1928.

treatment for it. In fact Young Bob had become something of a medical curiosity at Mayo's. Even the "best men on the entire staff" were mystified. One day a visiting physician from Germany looked in on him, declared his symptoms to be "very interesting," but was at a loss to suggest a solution.[24]

La Follette's illnesses took their toll emotionally as well as physically. On the surface he seemed to take his health problems in stride: "I am not discouraged" and "we must have patience" he said repeatedly. But his family feared otherwise. "I worry a great deal about Bob," Phil confided to his wife, Isen. "I sense what you have remarked on before—a sort of inward giving in—or confession of the power of these prolonged illnesses." His mother sensed it too. "Not for a moment," she wrote him early in 1929, "would I yield to the thought that you cannot get *well*."[25]

At the very least, La Follette experienced deep frustration over the uncertainty that poor health brought to his life. Although he had been dating his secretary, Rachel Young, for many years and although he believed that "no one can have a complete existence without attempting to make a home and have children," he was reluctant to marry as long as his health was such "an uncertain quantity." He also worried that his health was impairing his work in public life. Shortly after he turned thirty-four, he wrote his mother: "I thought of Daddie too on my birthday more than ever because I do think of him so much every day and as a living vital force too for he is that in my life. I only hope I can get my health established because I feel quite confident that with it established I can help to carry on in my small way the great work which he did."[26]

After missing most of the winter session of Congress, La Follette returned for the special session in April 1929, which President Hoover had called to deal with farm relief. Despite continued ill health, the Wisconsin senator plunged into battle on several fronts. He immediately joined his agrarian colleagues in pushing for a farm measure similar to the McNary-Haugen bills that Coolidge had twice vetoed. Essentially, La Follette wanted the federal government to help farmers dispose of their surplus crops abroad by paying them subsidies

24. RML to Fola and George Middleton, 27, 28 November 1926, RML to family, 9, 10, 14, 15 November, 13 December 1926, box 34-A, Family Papers; RML to PFL, 4 October 1928, box 134–2, PFL Papers.

25. RML to Belle, 12 February 1929, box 37-A, Family Papers; PFL to Mrs. PFL, 6 August 1927, box 134–2, PFL Papers; Belle to RML, 28 April 1929, box 37-A, Family Papers.

26. RML to Belle, 7 May 1929, RML to Rachel, 26 July 1929, RML to Belle, 12 February 1929, box 37-A, Family Papers.

to export. This, he believed, would raise domestic prices on farm goods and thus increase farm income. Hoover opposed the idea and supported instead the creation of a federal farm board that would help farmers organize and market their products more efficiently; in essence he wanted a plan to help farmers help themselves. In the end, Hoover prevailed and Congress passed the Agricultural Marketing Act. La Follette voted against it, accusing the administration of settling for too little.[27]

In the midst of the debate over farm relief, La Follette became involved in a brief, though highly significant, squabble over the Senate rule that imposed secrecy on its executive sessions. According to the rule, which dated back to the nineteenth century, when the Senate met in executive session to consider presidential nominations for public office, the proceedings, including the roll call on the final vote, were to be kept secret unless the Senate, by majority vote, opened the sessions to the public. Furthermore, no senator, under pain of expulsion, could publicly disclose how he or anyone else had voted. Only the final outcome of confirmation or rejection was to become known to the public. In theory, the Senate was thereby freed from the pressure of public opinion and able to exercise a more detached, objective judgment on the fitness of presidential appointees.[28]

In practice the secrecy rule had proved ineffective. To circumvent it members had only to publicly announce their votes before the final roll call. Some senators privately disclosed the complete details of executive sessions to reporters. Others, like La Follette and his father before him, believed that secrecy violated the spirit of the Constitution and regularly revealed to their constituents how they had voted.[29]

In May, President Hoover nominated Irvine L. Lenroot, a former senator from Wisconsin, for a judgeship on the United States Court of Customs Claims. The Senate met in secret executive session and approved the nomination. Several days later, United Press reporter Paul R. Mallon wrote a story describing the deliberations and naming those senators who had voted for Lenroot. Similar accounts appeared in newspapers throughout the country. Obviously one or more senators or staff members had leaked the information to Mallon and to others.

Even though there had been similar disclosures in the past, this

27. *La Follette's Magazine*, April, May, June 1929; *CR* 71:1, 1929, vol. 71, pt. 3, p. 3396.
28. *La Follette's Magazine*, June 1929.
29. *CR* 71:1, 1929, vol. 71, pt. 2, pp. 1812–17; RML radio speech, 1 June 1929, in ibid., pp. 2218–19.

one incensed the Republican leadership in the Senate, particularly Senators David A. Reed of Pennsylvania, George H. Moses of New Hampshire, and Hiram Bingham of Connecticut. They prodded the Rules Committee into issuing a subpoena to Mallon, requiring him to testify and to reveal the source of the leak. When he refused, Senator Reed moved to cite him for contempt of the Senate.

At this point, La Follette rose to defend Mallon and to attack the secrecy rule. In a democracy, he said, the people must be able to hold their elected representatives accountable for all of their actions. Thus Mallon and other reporters performed a valuable public service by revealing how senators voted in executive sessions. And, since the secrecy rule applied only to senators, any attempt to punish Mallon amounted to suppression of freedom of the press. As for the rule itself, La Follette argued that it violated the Constitution. Moreover, rather than allowing the Senate to reach a more objective judgment, the secrecy rule often served as an excuse to conceal unqualified nominees from public scrutiny. He reminded his colleagues that they had confirmed Harding appointees in secret, including Albert B. Fall, Harry Daugherty, and Charles R. Forbes, whose involvement in the Harding scandals had demonstrated their unfitness for public office. Quoting his father he said, "Evil and corruption thrive best in the dark."

La Follette went on to read an article that Theodore Huntley, a former reporter for the *Pittsburgh Post-Gazette*, had written years earlier. It described in full the executive session that had considered the nomination of John J. Esch to the Interstate Commerce Commission. The article also contained a direct quotation from Senator Reed. Thus, pointed out La Follette, the man who at present "is so sedulous about preserving the complete secrecy of executive sessions" had himself once violated the rule. Not only that, but Reed, instead of threatening Huntley with a contempt citation as he was now doing with Mallon, had later hired Huntley as his personal secretary! La Follette cited other newspaper accounts indicating that many senators had also breached the secrecy rule. By the time he finished, the Senate, including a red-faced Reed, was convulsed with laughter.[30]

La Follette succeeded not only in embarrassing some of his colleagues but also in bringing about a major alteration of the secrecy rule. On 18 June the Senate voted to make secrecy the exception rather than the rule. Thereafter, when it met to consider nominations,

30. *CR* 71:1, 1929, vol. 71, pt. 2, pp. 1814–15; *New York Times*, 22, 23, 24 May, 2 June 1929; Edward N. Doan, *The La Follettes and the Wisconsin Idea* (New York, 1947), pp. 264–65.

the proceedings would automatically be open to the public unless a majority of the Senate voted to close them.[31]

The fight against Senate secrecy, like La Follette's other scattered forays over the previous year and a half, impressed observers, enhanced his national reputation, and earned him the respect, albeit grudging, of his political opponents. By 1929 most people no longer regarded him simply as the son of Fighting Bob, but rather as an established politician in his own right. Conservative columnist Frank Kent wrote: "He is a factor in the Senate, a thorn in the side of the Administration, a clever parliamentarian, a very astute and knowing little guy, indeed, who plays his game intelligently and well." But what most impressed Kent, as it did others, was La Follette's modesty: "He is by no means a great man but the great thing about him is he knows it, which is to say that he is very much smarter than several other senators approximately his age, afflicted with delusions of grandeur."[32]

La Follette had come into his own. But his career was significant for other reasons as well. By 1929 or 1930 it had become apparent that, in contrast to most of his progressive colleagues in the Senate and to Western progressives generally, he was tending toward a new style of progressivism—one more sensitive to the problems of the urban-industrial sections of the country and less constricted by the cultural values of agrarian America.

Most Western progressives seemed oblivious to the profoundly important demographic changes that were taking place during the 1920s. In 1920 the Census Bureau reported that, for the first time in American history, more people lived in cities than in rural areas and on farms. By 1930 the urban population had increased to 56 percent of the total population, and more people worked in manufacturing than in agriculture. Few progressives seemed to have grasped these facts; or perhaps having grasped them, they sought to protect a way of life and a system of values that were rapidly passing. In any event, when most progressives spoke of "the people," they had in mind farmers and inhabitants of small-town America, who were overwhelmingly white and Protestant. They treated city dwellers, industrial workers, ethnics, and racial and religious minorities as outsiders, when they treated them at all. During the 1920s, progressives increasingly concentrated also on cultural issues, like prohibition and immigration restriction, which were dear to the hearts of many agrar-

31. CR 71:1, 1929, vol. 71, pt. 3, pp. 3054–55.
32. Frank Kent, "The Great Game of Politics," *Baltimore Sun*, 3 April 1930.

ians but were anathema to most urbanites. Of course, progressives and their followers had no monopoly on narrow-mindedness; urbanites and their spokesmen were often just as ignorant of, and unsympathetic to, the needs and values of rural America.[33]

Western progressives, including La Follette, agreed with what William Jennings Bryan had said about the economic primacy of agriculture to the 1896 Democratic convention: "Burn down your cities and leave our farms, and your cities will spring up again as if by magic; but destroy our farms and the grass will grow in the streets of every city in the country." In his address to the 1928 Republican convention, La Follette declared, "From 1776 to our own day, agriculture has been the basic industry of this country." A few weeks later he added that "there can be no sound prosperity when agriculture, the nation's basic industry, is being discriminated against and forced to the wall."[34]

But La Follette, almost alone among progressives, also recognized the other side of the coin. If cities could exist and thrive only so long as the farmer supplied food, the farmer could survive and prosper only so long as he had an urban market for his products. Therefore, the relationship between city and farm was not one of dependency, as Bryan had expressed it, but rather one of interdependency. Speaking of the industrial work force, La Follette said, "Here is a group whose incomes have been estimated to approximately forty billion dollars, or . . . sixty percent of the total national income. Upon their employment and purchasing power depends the prosperity of the American people."[35]

The importance La Follette placed in the economic well-being of urban labor was what had prompted him, in May 1928, to call for the Senate investigation into unemployment. The workingman, however,

33. Good discussions of the urban-rural conflict and the progressivism of the 1920s are the following: LeRoy Ashby, *The Spearless Leader: Senator William E. Borah and the Progressive Movement in the 1920's* (Urbana, Ill., 1972); Paul A. Carter, *The Twenties in America* (New York, 1968), chap. 3; Lawrence W. Levine, *Defender of the Faith William Jennings Bryan: The Last Decade, 1915–1925* (London, 1965); William E. Leuchtenburg, *The Perils of Prosperity, 1914–32* (Chicago, 1958), chaps. 7, 11, 12.

34. Bryan quoted in Paul W. Glad, *McKinley, Bryan, and the People* (Philadelphia, 1964), p. 138; RML speech to 1928 GOP convention, box 554-C, Family Papers; *New York Times*, 13 July 1928. For the agrarian orientation of other prominent progressives, see, on Borah: Ashby, *Spearless Leader*, pp. 8, 79, 92–93; on Bryan: Levine, *Defender of the Faith*, p. 197; on Norris: Lowitt, *Norris*, p. 292; on Nye: Wayne S. Cole, *Senator Gerald P. Nye and American Foreign Relations* (Minneapolis, 1962), pp. 3–13.

35. *La Follette's Magazine*, May 1928.

needed more than investigations, and La Follette recognized this. On Labor Day 1928 he told an assembly of Milwaukee workers that "no social and industrial system can be Christian until it is so organized that *every honest* and *willing worker can find work*, and work so remunerative that he cannot only maintain his own working powers in health and efficiency, but shall also be able to give his wife and children a decent, healthy, joyous and honorable life." La Follette was less clear on how society could achieve those goals, although he did believe that organizing workers was a step in the right direction.[36]

Of all the Senate progressives, La Follette was probably the most consistent defender of organized labor. Workers, he believed, had a constitutional right to organize and bargain collectively with their employers. He supported legislation to curtail the power of the judiciary to issue sweeping injunctions in labor disputes. In 1929, when a Pennsylvania judge handed down a sweeping injunction against the Amalgamated Clothing Workers, La Follette charged that there had never been "a more glaring example of the misuse of the injunction power of the courts," and he called for a Senate investigation of the matter.[37]

La Follette even expressed sympathy for some radical labor organizers. Early in 1930, when Mother Jones, the woman who had helped found the Industrial Workers of the World and who had manned many a barricade on behalf of the workers, lay near death at the age of ninety-nine, La Follette called her the "Grand old woman of the American labor movement," "beloved of the oppressed and downtrodden." He also pointed to the inequities of a judicial system that fell most heavily upon the poor and the workers. After a jury acquitted oil magnate Harry F. Sinclair of charges stemming from his involvement in the Teapot Dome scandal, La Follette lamented the fact that Tom Mooney and Warren Billings remained behind bars. Mooney and Billings were labor organizers who faced life imprisonment as a result of their conviction, largely based on perjured testimony, for setting off a bomb during a Preparedness Day parade in San Francisco in 1916. Also while Sinclair escaped prison, members of the Workers' party were in jail for distributing communist literature. "The trouble with American justice," La Follette observed, "is not that punishment for crime is too light and uncertain. Let a

36. RML Labor Day address, 1928, box 554-C, Family Papers.
37. *New York Times*, 17 September 1929. In addition to La Follette, progressive senators Henrik Shipstead and George Norris also strongly supported anti-injunction legislation.

poor man or woman or a heretic go into court and the punishment is swift and sure, often reverting to the jungle in its savagery."[38]

Even though La Follette advanced the interests of workers, he did not believe that the process of organization would, or should, instill them with class consciousness. Like his father and like most progressives, he refused to believe that classes existed in America. He supported labor unions because of the check they placed on business and because of their practical benefits: their ability to achieve higher wages, shorter hours, and better working conditions.

Partly in response to the constituency he served, La Follette displayed a broader social vision than his colleagues. Wisconsin was more urbanized and more industrialized than the home states of other progressives. By 1930, 53 percent of its people lived in cities and towns. Although Wisconsin advertised itself as "America's Dairyland" and agriculture remained the backbone of its economy, more people worked in manufacturing and industry than in agriculture.[39] Organized labor was also active, especially in the populous southeastern section, which included the cities of Milwaukee, Racine, and Kenosha. The Socialist party, under the leadership of Victor Berger, had enjoyed considerable success in Milwaukee for decades. Berger served in Congress through most of the 1920s, and Socialist Daniel Hoan was mayor of Milwaukee during the same decade.[40] From a political standpoint, then, the number of industrial workers in Wisconsin and the strength of organized labor and of the Socialist party all made it necessary for La Follette to speak to the needs of the urban workingman.

But La Follette's broader social vision also derived from his personal background. He had not grown up on a farm. Maple Bluff was more a retreat for him, and the farming chores were more recreation than work. Moreover, since the age of eleven, Young Bob had spent more time in Washington than in Wisconsin. He had also traveled twice to Europe, though like his father, he gave the impression that

38. *Progressive*, 4 January 1930; *La Follette's Magazine*, May 1929. In 1929 *La Follette's Magazine*, a monthly publication, became the *Progressive*, a weekly publication.

39. U.S. Department of Commerce, *Statistical Abstract of the United States* (Washington, D.C., 1940), pp. 8, 58–59. By contrast, in the states of other Senate progressives the percentage of urban dwellers was as follows: Idaho (William E. Borah), 29%; Iowa (Smith Brookhart), 49%; Minnesota (Henrik Shipstead), 42%; Nebraska (George Norris), 35%; North Dakota (Gerald P. Nye), 17%; South Dakota (Peter Norbeck), 19%.

40. Concerning labor, see Thomas W. Gavett, *The Development of the Labor Movement in Milwaukee* (Madison, 1965); on the Socialist movement, see Bayard Still, *Milwaukee: The History of a City* (Madison, 1948), pp. 515–68.

Europe had not much to offer. His sister Fola and her husband, play-wright George Middleton, whom he frequently visited in their Green-wich Village apartment, introduced him to the theater crowd in New York and later in Hollywood. So La Follette was aware of a world wider than Wisconsin and the Middle West. As a result he rarely indulged in the sentimental longing for the farm life and the corner grocery store that so characterized other Western insurgents.[41]

Less imbued with the cultural values of rural America, La Follette felt no need to defend those values by entering two of the most ex-plosive controversies of the 1920s, religion and prohibition. During the decade, the revival of Protestant fundamentalism, which cul-minated in the Scopes trial in 1925, epitomized the effort by rural seg-ments of the population to protect their faith and their way of life from the religious and cultural pluralism of the cities. Although Wil-liam Jennings Bryan's crusade against the teaching of evolution was an extreme example, most progressives regularly employed the rhe-toric of Protestantism, thereby alienating the non-Protestant popula-tion of urban America.

La Follette's attitude toward religion resembled his mother's rather than his father's. After attending Sunday school for a short time as a child, he never again went to church. He rarely discussed religion, but on those occasions when he alluded to it, he gave the impression that he was, like his mother, a skeptic or an agnostic. When his brother was married, he sent his congratulations: "If there was a god and he should love and bless you as I do, your lives would be a rose strewn path through the land of joy."[42] In addition, La Follette's speeches lacked the biblical quotations and references with which his father and fellow progressives frequently punctuated their speeches.

Prohibition proved even more divisive than religion, arraying rural "drys" against urban "wets." It also cut through the ranks of liberalism and rendered impossible any lasting coalition between rural and urban reformers. Most of the Senate progressives supported the "noble experiment," though they varied in the emphasis they placed on it. To Borah, liquor was "a curse of the human family. Whether sold in the open saloon or the brothel, its natural haunt, or secretly purveyed in defiance of the law, the wicked stuff works its demoral-

41. For examples of the sentimental longings of progressives see Ashby, *Spear-less Leader*, p. 93, and Gerald P. Nye mourning the disappearance of the "corner grocery man, the little druggist, the struggling farmer," in *CR* 71:3, 1931, vol. 74, pt. 3, pp. 3059–70.
42. Interviews, Mary La Follette, 22 February 1973; Bronson C. La Follette, 5 July 1973. RML to PFL and Mrs. PFL, 16 April 1923, box 132–2, PFL Papers.

ization and ruin to individuals, communities and states." Sen. Smith W. Brookhart of Iowa denounced the evils of drink with the same fervor with which he castigated the trusts. One day he took the floor of the Senate to reveal the "lurid" details of a party he and several other senators had attended at which liquor was served and gin-filled silver flasks were passed out as souvenirs. Naturally, he made it clear at the outset that he had not known beforehand about the drinking part. As his colleagues listened, some in shocked silence, others trying to suppress grins, Brookhart went on to disclose that several senators, whom he declined to name, had actually imbibed. For the Iowa senator the episode was a blatant example of immorality in high places.[43]

Brookhart might have been equally shocked had he known about the private life of his young Wisconsin colleague. La Follette personally opposed prohibition; and he, his brother, and his sisters all enjoyed an occasional drink, though always in the privacy of their own homes. "We all had plentiful helpings [of liquor], which went to our heads a little," wrote Phil after one family gathering. Political considerations, however, dictated caution in public. In Wisconsin, as elsewhere, prohibition was an explosive issue. Like his father, La Follette took the safest, though not the most honest, course and said as little about the issue as possible. His platform in 1928 called for amending the Volstead Act to permit the manufacture of light beer, a concession to the wet sentiment; but he never came out for full repeal, and during his campaign he completely avoided mention of the subject.[44]

In addition to his broader social vision and to his disinclination to involve himself in the cultural controversies of religion and prohibition, La Follette's political style also set him apart from other progressives. He was much less of an individualist. Although the Senate insurgents managed several notable successes during La Follette's initial years in the Senate, they never achieved unity or came close to realizing their supposed balance of power. Part of the problem was the intense individualism of various members of the progressive group. Borah, unwilling to cooperate with his colleagues except on his own terms, epitomized this trait.[45]

43. Borah speech, 30 May 1926, quoted in Ashby, *Spearless Leader*, p. 241; *New York Times*, 6 November 1929.

44. PFL to Mrs. PFL, 3 January 1923, box 132–2, PFL Papers; PFL, *Memoirs*, pp. 81, 84; Progressive Platform of 1928, box 3-C, Family Papers; *New York Times*, 24 January 1928; Alan Edmond Kent, "Portrait in Isolationism: The La Follettes and Foreign Policy" (Ph.D. diss., University of Wisconsin, 1956), p. 107.

45. Ashby, *Spearless Leader*, chaps. 5, 8.

La Follette, on the other hand, had "a powerful asset that his father never possessed—the will and the ability to cooperate." Throughout his first years in Washington, he consistently worked behind the scenes to organize the progressives. During 1929, for example, when the Senate considered the Smoot-Hawley tariff bill, La Follette took the lead in trying to unite his colleagues by holding frequent meetings, recommending strategy, and coordinating the activities of the outside organizations that were supplying information to the progressives.[46] More often than not, however, his efforts ended in frustration, and the insurgents stalked off in their own separate directions, leaving La Follette to lament over the sad state of the progressives. Although the fiercely independent character of the progressives undoubtedly was the principal reason for La Follette's repeated failures at organization, his youth may also have contributed. Men like Borah and Norris had known him since the days when he accompanied his father into the Senate chamber in short pants. For years they had been known to him as "Uncle George" and "Uncle Bill." Although they liked and respected him, they probably found it hard to regard him as their leader. For his part, La Follette's self-doubts about his own leadership capacity reinforced that attitude. But, however much he might complain about his colleagues in private, he kept his feelings from the public.

While in many respects La Follette tended toward a new style of progressivism, in several other respects he clearly remained a product of the older progressive tradition. For one thing La Follette displayed a streak of self-righteousness that was characteristic of the progressive movement from the turn of the century on. Of course politicians of all political persuasions regularly invoked God and morality to support their positions. But progressives seemed to have exaggerated that tendency. Thomas B. Reed, long-time speaker of the House of Representatives, once said to Theodore Roosevelt, "Theodore, if there is one thing more than another for which I admire you, it is your original discovery of the Ten Commandments." After the Paris Peace Conference in 1919, French Premier Clemenceau described his encounters with Lloyd George of England and President Woodrow Wilson this way: "I had to deal in the peace conference with two men, one of whom thought he was Napoleon and the other Jesus

46. Walter Davenport, "Wisconsin for Smith," *Collier's* 100 (20 October 1928): 8–9, 51; RML to Belle, 18, 21 May 1929, box 38-A, Family Papers; [Drew Pearson and Robert S. Allen], *Washington Merry-Go-Round* (New York, 1931), p. 190.

Christ."[47] Had Reed and Clemenceau sat down with Bryan, Borah, or Old Bob La Follette, they could well have said the same things. They could also have said the same of Young Bob.

And indeed, it was La Follette's self-righteousness and excessive moralism that most annoyed his critics. In 1928, when he refused to endorse wealthy industrialist and stalwart Walter J. Kohler for governor of Wisconsin even though Kohler had won the primary, the *New York Times*, among his most persistent critics, mocked him. It seems, a *Times* editorial said, that the progressives received their campaign money from "the People," while Kohler got his from the special "interests." "The sincere milk of truth flows only from Progressive lips," it sarcastically concluded.[48]

Developments after Kohler's election also showed La Follette's self-righteousness. Because Kohler had spent huge sums of money in his campaign, Phil La Follette and other progressives, with the support of Bob, accused Kohler of violating Wisconsin's Corrupt Practices Act and filed a lawsuit against him, asking the courts to invalidate his election. Kohler admitted to excessive expenditures, but he argued that he could not be held accountable for money that others had spent on his behalf without his knowledge or authorization. The Wisconsin Supreme Court upheld Kohler and dismissed the lawsuit.[49]

Because of the charges against Kohler, a special committee of the Wisconsin legislature undertook an investigation of the Corrupt Practices Act with a view to revising or strengthening it. In January 1930, as part of its investigation, the committee went to Washington to question La Follette about his 1928 campaign. Under tough interrogation, La Follette admitted to several irregularities in the financing of his primary race. According to Wisconsin law, there was a $5,000 ceiling on expenditures for each contestant in the Senate primary. La Follette's campaign committee had reported spending $4,933.46, just under the limit. But another committee, which ran the campaigns for other Republican progressives, had put out literature endorsing the entire state ticket, including La Follette. Taken together, the two committees had spent more on his behalf than he had reported and probably more than the law allowed. Moreover, La Follette claimed to be unaware of contributions that his mother and his brother had made to his campaign. He had been too busy traveling around the

47. Reed and Clemenceau quoted in Leland D. Baldwin, ed., *Flavor of the Past: Readings in American Social and Political Portraiture* (New York, 1969), pp. 251–52.
48. *New York Times*, 28 September, 31 October 1928.
49. PFL, *Memoirs*, p. 128; unidentified clippings, box 661-C, Family Papers.

state, he suggested, to keep a strict record of contributions and expenditures. And, he claimed, he should not be held accountable for spending of which he had no knowledge. Thus he invoked the same argument Kohler had used to defend himself before the Wisconsin Supreme Court.[50]

La Follette's attitude toward immigrants and racial minorities also placed him within the older progressive tradition. In the early 1920s, Congress, with the support of most Western progressives, prescribed a quota system that greatly restricted immigration from southern and eastern Europe. In the late 1920s a movement arose to even further restrict the entry of "undesirable" immigrants. Although La Follette did not speak directly on the issue, he lent his support to the movement by giving space in *La Follette's Magazine* to proponents of restriction. In one issue Sen. Gerald P. Nye of North Dakota, a progressive, complained that under existing law too many Greeks, Italians, Slavs, and Poles and not enough northern and western Europeans could enter the United States. "So long as we permit immigration to our shores," Nye wrote, "we ought to jealously insist upon a continuation of that strain which had come to us down through all the years from those countries of Northern Europe which have contributed so splendidly to our progress and our well-being in America." In a preface to the article La Follette described Nye as a leading expert on the subject of immigration, thus implying that he endorsed Nye's views on the subject. Political considerations doubtless prompted La Follette's stand on this issue, since a majority of Wisconsin's immigrant population came from northern and western Europe.[51]

Similarly, on the issue of race, La Follette sided with the progressives, although he did so quietly. Racial prejudice knew no political, sectional, religious, or even ethnic boundaries. Yet the insensitivity of progressives to the oppression of black people was especially conspicuous because these particular whites so consistently proclaimed themselves to be the champions of the people and of the oppressed. La Follette's prejudices were less blatant than those of some of his colleagues. For example, Sen. Hiram Johnson of California described blacks as lazy and stupid, and Sen. Peter Norbeck of South Dakota wanted to send all blacks back to Africa.[52] Still, the Wisconsin senator accepted the common stereotypes of black inferiority. A year before

50. Transcript of RML testimony, 22 January 1930, enclosed in Arthur F. Stofer to RML, 19 May 1930, box 8-C, Family Papers.

51. Gerald P. Nye, "Evils of the National Origins Clause," *La Follette's Magazine*, June 1929; Robert C. Nesbit, *Wisconsin: A History* (Madison, 1973), p. 478.

52. Ashby, *Spearless Leader*, pp. 249–50.

entering the Senate he wrote to his brother: "Today we got a new maid by the name of Pearl. She is several shades darker than the jewel from which she derives her name but I hope she will prove a prize nevertheless." But it was not so much what he said or did that aligned him with his colleagues, but what he failed to do. He never devoted a major speech or article to the subject of racial injustice. Nor did he ever express the personal anguish that even his mother had experienced over the race problem. In short, his policy was one of neglect rather than one of overt hostility.[53]

An exception to La Follette's relative neglect of minority groups was his effort on behalf of the American Indian. Like his father, he continuously held a seat on the Committee on Indian Affairs, a rather thankless task from a political standpoint, since both press and public paid little attention to the activities of the committee or to Indians in general. In February 1928 La Follette became a member of a special subcommittee that launched an intensive, three-year investigation into Indian problems and that eventually brought about major reforms in government relations with the Indians. La Follette also consistently fought to increase appropriations in the Interior Department's budget for Indian tribes, especially the Menominee tribe of Wisconsin; and he remained ever watchful for schemes that threatened to deprive Indians of their land and mineral rights.[54] Other progressives, too, seemed more concerned with the problems of Indians than with the plight of blacks, perhaps because Indian affairs so often involved the familiar issue of public- and Indian-owned lands being exploited by business interests, but also because there were more unresolved Indian problems in their states than there were black problems.

La Follette also shared with progressives a hypocritical stance on special-interest politics. Progressives, from the beginning of the movement, claimed to speak for all of the people, regardless of region, occupation, or class. At the same time, however, they denounced the self-serving politicians who supported legislation beneficial to a special interest such as big business. In so doing, progressives ignored the fact that they themselves often supported legislation that benefited special interests such as farmers.[55]

The tariff issue was a prime example. After more than a year of

53. RML to PFL and Mrs. PFL, 2 April 1924, box 132–2, PFL Papers.
54. RML to PFL, 9 April 1926, box 133–2, PFL Papers; RML speeches, bills introduced, and miscellaneous material pertaining to Indians, box 140-C, Family Papers.
55. Ashby, *Spearless Leader*, pp. 13–15; Richard Hofstadter, *The Age of Reform: From Bryan to F.D.R.* (New York, 1955), pp. 7–8.

wrangling, Congress, in June 1930, passed the Smoot-Hawley tariff
bill, which imposed the highest tariff rates in American history. Just
before the Senate passed the measure, La Follette rose to denounce it.
"I realize," he admitted "that the votes are here to pass this bill. In my
judgment, we are about to send to conference the worst bill in the
history of the Republic." "As the bill stands today," he continued, "it
is the product of a series of deals, conceived in secret, but executed in
public with a brazen affrontery that is without parallels in the annals
of the Senate." The proposed tariff duties, he said, were "the handiwork of a combination of lobbyists" at a cost to consumers of over a
billion dollars. All this was doubtless true, but as the *New York Times*
pointed out, "Mr. La Follette's sympathy with 'the mass of the consumers' would be more effective if the dairy products of Wisconsin
. . . were not to cost the mass of consumers more." Although La Follette had supported tariff reductions on most items, he voted to raise
the duties on such Wisconsin products as milk, butter, and beef. Other
progressives did the same for products from their states. Also, La
Follette's support of a federal tax of ten cents per pound on oleomargarine greatly benefited Wisconsin dairy interests.[56]

56. *CR* 71:2, 1930, vol. 72, pt. 6, pp. 5974–79; *New York Times*, 26 March
1930; *CR* 71:2, 1930, vol. 72, pt. 9, pp. 9436, 9442, 9559.

CHAPTER 6

Fighting the Depression

It was during the Great Depression of the 1930s that La Follette earned national prominence. During the early years of the depression, 1930 to 1932, the Wisconsin senator emerged as the leading congressional advocate of bold government action to confront the economic crisis and as one of the most penetrating critics of the Hoover administration. Unlike many Hoover critics, La Follette offered concrete alternatives to administration policies. His antidepression plan included measures for direct federal relief to the unemployed, massive expansion of public works, and a modest degree of national economic planning. None of his measures became law during the Hoover years; nonetheless, by 1932 he had forced a hesitant Congress and an even more hesitant administration into accepting a greater share of responsibility for the plight of the unemployed.

The elder La Follette's career offered no clues as to how to combat a depression, so Young Bob was on his own. His initial response to the crisis was not very constructive. After the stock-market crash of October 1929, he tried to fix blame, saying, in essence, "I told you so." Appearing with President Hoover before the Gridiron Club in New York City in December 1929, La Follette reminded the audience of his unsuccessful attempt early in 1928 to curb speculation on the stock market. "If the Federal Reserve Board, the investing public and the country had heeded the braying of the Jackasses in the Senate," he said, the crash might have been averted. "But alas the poor sheep followed the advice of those so-called bellwethers of business sanity in high places, who assured them that there was no ceiling to the Bull Market."[1]

But aside from occasional jabs at the Republican leadership, past and present, for having ignored the warnings of the progressives, La Follette generally supported Hoover's initial actions to combat the depression. Hoover, rejecting the hands-off approach of previous presidents during an economic crisis, moved quickly on several fronts. In November he summoned business leaders to the White House and

1. Gridiron speech, 14 December 1929, box 7-C, Family Papers (see list of abbreviations p. x).

got them to promise to maintain production, employment, and wage levels. Acting through the Federal Farm Board, he took steps to stabilize plummeting farm prices. He also urged Congress to take up the slack in unemployment by expanding public works. The only part of Hoover's plan that La Follette rejected was a proposed tax cut, which he viewed as an unwarranted boon to "great wealth."[2]

Early in 1930, as it became apparent that business leaders were failing to keep their pledges to Hoover, La Follette backed a series of modest unemployment measures proposed by New York Democrat Robert F. Wagner. The first of these bills would expand the government's facilities for gathering unemployment statistics; the second would establish a national system of employment agencies; and the third, aimed more at future depressions than at the existing one, would set up a reserve fund to be collected in times of prosperity in order to provide money for public works projects in times of depression. La Follette accurately described the Wagner package as "only a modest beginning" but "nevertheless an attempt to deal with the most pressing human problem of our time."[3]

In March, during the Senate debate on the first of Wagner's measures, La Follette took note of the increasing number of demonstrations protesting unemployment and of the angry and frightened reactions of many public officials to them. Some people charged that communists were behind the disturbances. In the House of Representatives, Hamilton Fish of New York called for a full-scale investigation of communist activities. La Follette, hoping to avert another "red scare," declared, "It is a grave injustice to the millions of American men and women who are, through no fault of their own, thrown out of employment and are asking for an opportunity to earn their daily bread, to drag across this trail the red herring of another 'red' baiting campaign." He conceded that some "misguided" individuals might seize upon widespread unrest due to unemployment for their own purposes, but he argued that what few communists there were in the country had no real influence. The best way to eliminate unrest, he concluded, was to solve the unemployment problem.[4]

By the time Congress recessed in July, La Follette knew the government had to do much more; but as yet he had no specific plan. Like everyone else, except the president, he seemed confused and adrift.

2. *Progressive*, 28 December 1929, 4 January 1930.
3. Ibid., 24 May 1930.
4. Irving Bernstein, *The Lean Years: A History of the American Worker, 1920–1933* (Boston, 1960), pp. 426–28; CR 71:2, 1930, vol. 72, pt. 5, pp. 4609–12.

During the summer and fall of 1930, he turned his attention to what he considered a more immediate problem, the election of his brother to the Wisconsin governorship. Since 1926, when he completed one term as Dane County district attorney, Phil had practiced law in Madison and had taught night courses in the University of Wisconsin Law School. All the while he anxiously awaited an opportunity to reenter public life. He might have run for governor in 1928 but was unable because of the vehement opposition of John Blaine and other progressive leaders. At that time even his mother opposed his candidacy, fearing that two La Follettes on the ticket would jeopardize Young Bob's chances for reelection. But by 1930, Phil, at age thirty-three, had emerged as the only progressive in the state with a chance to unseat conservative incumbent Walter J. Kohler.[5]

Those who knew and observed the La Follette brothers over the years often found the differences between them more striking than the similarities. Short, slender, his hair swept back in a modified pompadour, Phil resembled their father in appearance, personality, and style more closely than did his brother. Phil, said one observer, "is a dramatic 'chip off the old block' where Bob is a refined splinter." Their sister Mary thought that Phil was more "creative and imaginative," Bob, more "realistic and practical." "Phil had the brains, the imagination," recalled one friend, "Bob had the sense, his feet on the ground."[6] Phil was outgoing and, among intimate friends, open, although initially he often struck people as cold and aloof. Bob, on the other hand, usually impressed people with his warmth and sincerity; yet all agreed that ultimately he was harder "to know." But they differed most in their political attitudes and styles. Phil, doubtless the more ambitious, loved politics and everything about it. A fiery but undisciplined orator, he would march up and down the platform, take his coat off, loosen his tie, wave his arms, and sometimes lose himself and his audience in rhetorical excess. He thrived on campaigning. His boast at the end of the gubernatorial campaign that he had set a record for the number of speeches was typical: "about 275 speeches in all; heretofore the record was 230 in Wisconsin—Bryan made 175 in his famous 1896 campaign."[7]

5. Interview, Isabel B. La Follette, 5 July 1973; Philip F. La Follette, *Adventure in Politics: The Memoirs of Philip La Follette* (New York, 1970), pp. 134–40; PFL to Mrs. PFL, 18 March 1944, box 142–2, PFL Papers.

6. John Franklin Carter [The Unofficial Observer], *American Messiahs* (New York, 1935), p. 111. Interviews, Mary La Follette, 22 February 1973; Roderick H. Riley, 11 June 1973.

7. Interviews, Mary La Follette; Gordon Sinykin, August 1972; Morris H. Rubin, 1, 8 August 1972. Mrs. PFL, "Isen's Political Diary," 13 May 1938, box

Curiously, during the campaign, the brothers avoided discussion of the economic crisis. Back in May, Bob had singled out unemployment as "the most pressing human problem of our time." But on the stump he rarely mentioned it, concentrating instead on the increasing power of the Supreme Court, the Smoot-Hawley tariff, and the evils of chain banks and utility conglomerates. Wisconsin voters seemed not to mind. In the September primary they handed Phil a landslide victory over Kohler and thus assured him of the governorship in November. A cartoonist for the *Chicago Tribune* showed the figure of Old Bob looming in the background and quipped, "When Wisconsin Falls for an Idol, She Does a Thorough Job of It."[8]

The day after the primary Bob married his secretary, Rachel Wilson Young. She was an attractive thirty-six-year-old woman with blue eyes, a fair complexion, and short brown hair with highlights of auburn. The fifth of eight children, she had been born in Falls Church, Virginia, and raised in the District of Columbia, where her father, though trained to be a Methodist minister, worked for the Census Bureau.[9] Rachel could be warm, friendly, and fun loving. At times she also could be stern and aloof, evidence perhaps of the influence of her deeply religious father, who once warned one of his daughters that "vice and immorality abound" and that she should not become "absorbed in this world's vain and unsatisfying momentary, vanishing pleasures."[10] When they were in their teens Bob and Rachel lived in the same northwest Washington neighborhood. Their romance probably began in the summer of 1917, shortly after the United States entered the war. Many evenings that summer Bob would drop his father off at the Capitol and then pick up Rachel, two of her sisters, and other neighborhood friends and drive to a Maryland amusement park. There, for a few short hours, they could dance and forget a world at war. "These were happy and gay evenings," Rachel's sister Louise later recalled. "We 'turkeytrotted,' 'fish-walked,' 'bunny hugged,' 'tangoed,' and waltzed until Bob had to go back to the Capitol to take his father home." About 1924 Bob persuaded Rachel, who had attended business school after high school, to work as a secretary

161–3, PFL Papers; PFL to Fola and George Middleton, 26 September 1930, box 39-A, Family Papers.

8. Speeches and press releases, 1930 campaign, box 555-C, Family Papers; Lyle W. Cooper, "Good News From Wisconsin," *New Republic* 64 (15 October 1930): 228–30; *Chicago Tribune*, 18 September 1930.

9. Louise Young, Rachel's sister, to author, 8 June 1977.

10. Interview, Bronson C. La Follette, 5 July 1973; Ludwick Craven Young to Louise Young, 13 June 1925, a copy of this letter is in the possession of the author.

in his father's office. When the elder La Follette died she stayed on to work for Bob.[11]

Although Bob and Rachel had been dating for many years, the wedding came as a surprise to everyone outside the family. "With 'Young Bob' regarded as distinctly woman shy," wrote one reporter, "this wedding seemed to Washington the news of the day rather than Phil La Follette's success in the primary." At Rachel's request, a simple, Episcopalian ceremony was held in the library of the Maple Bluff Farm, with Phil and his wife, Isen, as the only witnesses. "All in all everything went off beautifully," Bob wrote to his mother who had remained in Washington, "and the fact that we could avoid all the bunk usually associated with a wedding is a source of great satisfaction to both of us."[12]

Rachel doubtless knew that the La Follettes were a close-knit family. But just how closely knit she probably did not realize until the honeymoon, when Phil and Isen, apparently at Bob's request, went along. Not only that, but when the foursome arrived at a resort in northern Wisconsin, Phil promptly invited two other couples to join them for the weekend. In fact, Rachel never managed to penetrate the family circle. Unlike the other La Follette women, she disliked many aspects of politics and did little to conceal it. One time, after spending three days with Bob on a speaking tour through the Middle West, she complained that it was "the hardest work in the world— hard travelling and never getting away from people. Honestly I would rather scrub floors."[13] To some of her politically minded in-laws, especially Phil and Isen, such an attitude bordered on heresy.

In November, after Phil's one-sided victory, Bob La Follette turned his attention to the economic crisis and considered for the first time what he and the progressives should do about it. To Basil Manly, head of the People's Legislative Service, he wrote, "It seems to me . . . that the progressives should have a program of unemployment relief." He mentioned expansion of public works as another possibility but doubted that any action would be "sufficiently immediate to relieve the acute suffering that is already manifest in the large centers and will grow increasingly distressing with the onset of winter." Nor did he think that the "mobilization of the existing relief agencies and public contributions," which he predicted Hoover would advocate,

11. Louise Young to author, 8 June 1977.
12. *New York Evening Post*, n.d., clipping, box 661-C, RML to Belle, 19, 24 September 1930, box 40-A, Family Papers.
13. PFL, *Memoirs*, p. 144; interview, Robert E. Sher (one of persons whom Philip invited on the honeymoon), 30 May 1973; Rachel to Grace Lynch, 1 November 1933, box 11-C, Family Papers.

would relieve the distress of the jobless. So La Follette was inclined toward, though not yet committed to, direct federal relief. But of one thing he was sure, "the progressives should assume the leadership in this crisis."[14]

Before taking a definite stand on the relief issue, La Follette decided to personally investigate the unemployment problem. He was always skeptical of the economic statistics that the administration released, and rightly so, since he suspected that the administration purposely juggled figures in order to put the best possible light on the situation. Administration reports merited skepticism for a less sinister reason as well. In those days the government did not keep an accurate record of employment levels or of most other economic trends. Its procedures for gathering such information were haphazard and unscientific.[15] In December 1930, La Follette and Democrat David I. Walsh of Massachusetts sent questionnaires to the mayors of all cities with populations of five thousand or more. The two senators asked the mayors to estimate the extent of unemployment in their cities and to assess the effectiveness of local relief efforts. At the same time La Follette asked William Green, president of the American Federation of Labor, to submit the results of a similar inquiry he had made among labor leaders in major cities throughout the country.

The replies that poured into La Follette's office over the next several months painted a grim picture of economic conditions. From Pittsburgh came the report of twenty thousand jobless and a "great deal of suffering"; from Detroit, over two hundred thousand unemployed, and the number was increasing by five hundred a day; from New York City, eight hundred thousand jobless. The average unemployment rate in 17 Ohio cities was over 17 percent. The replies also demonstrated the inadequacy of local relief efforts. In 461 cities, a family of four, with the breadwinner out of work, received on the average only $6.07 per week in public-assistance payments. This fell far short of the sum needed to maintain a bare minimum standard of living. Some cities reported that they had gone bankrupt trying to meet relief needs. Of those cities responding to the question, 305 favored federal aid, 215 opposed it. Even though the survey was incomplete—many mayors failed to respond in full or in part—it did cast serious doubt on the optimistic assessments of the Hoover ad-

14. RML to Basil Manly, 13 November 1930, box 507-C, Family Papers.
15. RML to PFL, 25 November 1931, box 135-2, PFL Papers; Albert U. Romasco, *The Poverty of Abundance: Hoover, the Nation, the Depression* (New York, 1965), p. 62.

ministration. Moreover, it convinced La Follette of the need for immediate federal assistance.[16]

By the time the lame-duck session of Congress opened, La Follette was in an aggressive mood, ready to demand bold government action and ready to attack the administration on all fronts. On 9 December he opened fire on the administration by introducing into the Senate a resolution that at first glance seemed harmless enough. It stated, "The relief of human suffering ... should take precedence over the interests of wealthy income-tax payers." A remark made by President Hoover to a reporter the day before had prompted La Follette to offer the resolution. Hoover had said in essence that unnecessary federal relief measures would place too great a burden on taxpayers. At no time, however, had he said anything about "wealthy" taxpayers as La Follette implied. Nevertheless, Hoover blundered into the trap and directed his Senate supporters to block the loaded resolution, which they obediently did. He thus placed himself and his supporters in, as one observer described it, "the incredible position of seeming to object to feeding the hungry and clothing the needy lest the funds required for those worthy purposes be forced from the pockets of the nation's small and relatively rich taxpaying class, already the favorites of much Republican legislative solicitude."[17]

During the session La Follette emerged as an outspoken proponent of federal relief to the unemployed. The administration and its congressional spokesmen, however, staunchly opposed relief and offered a variety of arguments against it. They argued primarily that existing agencies, like the Red Cross, local community chests, and city and state welfare departments, were already providing adequate relief. La Follette effectively countered by disclosing the pessimistic replies to his questionnaire.[18] Opponents of relief also argued that federal aid would erode states' rights. La Follette dismissed that claim outright: "In that splitting of legal hairs and theories I am not the least bit interested." The depression, he said, "was due to causes with which the municipalities and state governments had nothing to do."

16. CR 71:3, 1930–1931, vol. 74, pts. 1, 2, 3, pp. 697–710, 1173–1222, 3087–88. One newspaper, noting that it cost six thousand dollars to print the replies to the questionnaire in the Record, editorialized, "While crying out with a loud voice in behalf of the unemployed, [La Follette] squanders the taxpayers' money in useless and futile procedures." The survey, it concluded, was "useless propaganda." Unidentified clipping, box 663-C, Family Papers.

17. CR 71:3, 1930–1931, vol. 74, pt. 1, p. 426; Frank Kent, in Baltimore Sun, 16 December 1930, New York World, 17 December 1930, clippings, box 662-C, Family Papers.

18. Romasco, Poverty of Abundance, pp. 129, 149; CR 71:3, 1931, vol. 74, pt. 2, pp. 1666–67.

"If any government entity is responsible, or has had any share of responsibility in producing this economic crisis, then surely it is the Federal government." Thus, La Follette argued, the federal government must assume the responsibility for providing relief.[19]

The most frequently heard objection to relief, however, was that it would amount to a dole and would be destructive of the recipients' characters and initiative. "This cry of 'dole' is preposterous," answered La Follette. Speaking to those who thought relief would destroy character he demanded to know, "What do you think is happening to the character of the men, women, and children who are going hungry and cold in the cities during these winter months?" The word *dole*, he thought, could more "properly be used to characterize what the administration has done in the face of the suffering and distress throughout the nation. According to Webster, 'to dole is to deal out in small portions; to deal out scantily or grudgingly.'" More important, La Follette found ample precedent in American history for federal relief. He cited dozens of cases, the earliest in 1827, in which Congress had appropriated funds to aid the victims of famines, floods, earthquakes, and fires, both at home and abroad. He reminded his colleagues that no senator had arisen to denounce the dole in 1919 when Congress appropriated $100 million to relieve the starving people of Europe; nor had anyone cried "dole" in 1928 when Congress spent $1.5 million on the victims of the Mississippi flood. If the government had always aided the victims of natural disasters, why, he asked, should it refuse to help the victims of an "economic catastrophe"?[20]

In advocating relief, La Follette stood almost alone. Even among his liberal colleagues there was little support for it. Norris thought it imperative "to keep the manhood and womanhood of America upon a high standard, by not compelling the men and women of our country to become subjects of charity for food and clothing." Wagner, an acknowledged champion of the unemployed, later admitted that "No one took a more determined stand than I against consigning those out of work to the humiliating experience of charitable relief." In late 1931, Gov. Franklin D. Roosevelt of New York, already the leading contender for the Democratic presidential nomination, announced his opposition to the dole.[21] Instead of relief, most liberals

19. CR 71:3, 1930–1931, vol. 74, pt. 1, pp. 697–710, 1173–1222, 4431–38.
20. Ibid.
21. Norris quoted in Richard Lowitt, *George W. Norris: the Persistence of a Progressive, 1913–1933* (Urbana, Ill., 1971), p. 494; Wagner quoted in J. Joseph Huthmacher, *Senator Robert F. Wagner and the Rise of Urban Liberal-*

supported public works, which they deemed more productive and less debilitating to character. La Follette, on the other hand, supported public works, but argued that it took too long to plan and to implement works projects. He pointed out that although in early 1930 Congress had appropriated $50 million for public construction, by September of that year, fewer than ten thousand had been given work on new projects. Thus, he argued, relief was needed to fill the time lag between the approval and the implementation of public works.[22]

In addition to relief and public works, La Follette, in February 1931, offered the third part of his antidepression plan, asking for the creation of a national economic council. La Follette's proposed council would have fifteen members, three from each sector of the economy: industry, finance, transportation, agriculture, and labor. The president, with the advice and consent of the Senate, would appoint the members from lists submitted by groups representing each economic sector. The council's job would be to keep abreast of general economic and business conditions, to study economic problems, and to recommend solutions to those problems. La Follette's bill would require the council to submit an annual report to the president and Congress and to submit any other reports it deemed necessary. The Senate referred the bill to the Committee on Manufacturing and authorized La Follette, the chairman of the committee, to conduct hearings during the summer recess.[23]

The Seventy-first Congress adjourned on 4 March 1931 without having taken much action to combat the depression. The Republican supporters of Hoover spent most of the session defending the president's approach to the crisis. Democrats, with their eyes already fixed on the 1932 election, had spent their time blaming Hoover for the nation's plight; but with the notable exception of men like Robert F. Wagner and David I. Walsh, the Democrats had offered few alternatives. As usual the progressives had been unorganized, each one, as La Follette's mother observed, "playing a lone hand." La Follette likened the Congress to Nero, "fiddling while Rome burns."[24]

La Follette feared that unless something was done the next Congress would be equally unproductive. The progressives, he thought,

---

ism (New York, 1971), pp. 93–94; Harris Gaylord Warren, *Herbert Hoover and the Great Depression* (New York, 1967), p. 149.

22. CR 71:3, 1930–1931, vol. 74, pt. 2, pp. 1173–1222.

23. Ibid., pp. 1688, 5462–63.

24. Belle to Fola and George Middleton, 17 January 1931, box 40-A, Family Papers; CR 71:3, 1930–1931, vol. 74, pt. 2, p. 1688.

held the key. The 1930 elections had increased their strength in both houses; and if they could unite behind a concrete legislative program, they might force Congress to act.[25] But first it was necessary to organize them and get them to draw up such a program.

To that end he persuaded Senators Norris, Borah, Wheeler, Bronson Cutting of New Mexico, and Senator-elect Edward P. Costigan of Colorado to summon progressive leaders from throughout the country to a March meeting in Washington. The conference, La Follette told his sister, "was my idea and I had to overcome a lot of inertia and resistance among my colleagues to get it called." On the eve of the conference, La Follette went on the radio to explain its purpose. "It is not . . . a political conference in the ordinary sense," he said. "It is to be directed solely toward the formulation of a constructive legislative program to be presented and fought for at the next session of Congress." That program, he stressed, "must be definite and specific for we cannot cope with tremendous economic problems with catchwords or with vague panaceas."[26]

On the morning of 11 March, nearly two hundred men and women gathered at Washington's Carlton Hotel for the opening session of the conference. Among them were some of the best minds and most active leaders in the country: historians Charles and Mary Beard; sociologist Edward A. Ross; journalists Lincoln Steffens and Bruce Bliven; economists Stuart Chase, George Soule, and Leo Wolman; labor leaders Sidney Hillman and William Green; social workers Florence Kelley and Lillian Wald; insurgent farm leader Milo Reno; and many others. With Congress adjourned, the conference held the national spotlight for two days, and the press provided full coverage. The nation was looking desperately for leadership, the progressives had promised to provide it.[27]

After introductory remarks by Senator Norris, whom the sponsors named chairman, the conference broke down into five committees, each to consider respectively the problems of agriculture, the tariff, representative government, public regulation of electric power, and unemployment and industrial stabilization. From the outset the conference lacked focus. The participants spent much of their time considering proposals that were only remotely connected with the immediate problems of the depression. For example, the discussion

25. RML radio speech, 7 March 1931, box 555-C, Family Papers.
26. RML to Fola, 18 April 1931, box 41-A, RML radio speech, 7 March 1931, box 555-C, Family Papers.
27. Transcript, "Proceedings of a Conference of Progressives," box 508-C, Family Papers.

group on representative government considered congressional reform, abolition of the lame-duck session of Congress, and abolition of the Electoral College.[28]

The session on unemployment and industrial stabilization, which La Follette chaired, came more to the point. But each of the scheduled speakers prescribed his own personal antidote to the depression. George Soule and Leo Wolman favored some sort of centralized economic planning. Father John A. Ryan, chairman of the National Catholic Welfare Council, called for a vast expansion of public works. And the president of the AFL, William Green, stressed the importance of a five-day workweek.[29]

On the second and final day, Norris introduced a note of pessimism. As long as Hoover remained president, he said, there was little chance of Congress enacting a substantial program. "What we do need in order to bring prosperity and happiness to the common individual is another Roosevelt in the White House," he concluded with obvious reference to New York's governor, Franklin D. Roosevelt. The remark brought extended applause and sent reporters scurrying for the telephones.[30] But it probably also put a damper on the proceedings. Norris was saying in essence that whatever the results of the conference and whatever the progressives would do in the months ahead, the prospects of success were dim without an ally in the White House.

The conference ended ahead of schedule. Because so many people had left town before it was over, the sponsors called off the final session. Before leaving, the participants had agreed on a series of vague resolutions. The five committees, however, promised to continue their search for a concrete program for presentation to the next session of Congress.[31]

Public response to the conference was mixed. La Follette, recalling the difficulty he had in persuading his colleagues to call it in the first place, was "rather proud of the results," though he admitted that "only the next few months will reveal whether the committees appointed to draft legislation will actually produce constructive and effective measures." Others were less impressed. "The chief significance of the conference," wrote journalist David Lawrence, "was its lack of significance." "It was," he added, "neither radical nor conservative. It followed the philosophy of pussy-footing which has wrecked

28. Ibid.
29. Ibid.; Romasco, *Poverty of Abundance*, pp. 218–19.
30. Transcript, "Proceedings of a Conference of Progressives," box 508-C, Family Papers.
31. Ibid.; *New York Times*, 13, 14 March 1931.

many a conference of middle-of-the-roaders." The *Washington Post* said that "the nucleus of a mighty revolution was in their grasp," but the progressives came up with "an assortment of illogical and warmed-over proposals" instead of a revolutionary program. The *Review of Reviews* castigated the participants for showing "little evidence of having renovated their thinking machinery for at least thirty years." Professor John Dewey, chairman of the League for Independent Political Action, addressed an angry letter to the sponsors of the conference. "What," he asked, "has paralyzed Progressive Senators into acquiesence in the plan of exploiting interests to reduce the American people to a state of industrial feudalism and serfdom?"[32]

Extreme complaints, like Dewey's, were probably unfair. Perhaps, as George Norris thought, people expected too much from the progressives. "We are . . . so often expected to perform the impossible," he wrote a constituent and added, "What the people do not see . . . is that we are not in control. We are . . . in a very small minority. We are plugging along, fighting an entrenched machine." But by and large the critics were right. In the end the conference failed to achieve either progressive unity or a concrete antidepression program, its two main purposes. After the March meeting the sponsoring senators moved off in different directions. Columnists Drew Pearson and Robert S. Allen observed about the progressives: "Individually they are the most righteous and forward-looking men in public office in the capital. . . . Collectively they have been without plan or purpose, unorganized and ineffectual."[33]

Despite the absence of progressive unity, La Follette was prepared to press ahead, alone if necessary. In April he stepped up his attacks on Hoover. "His calloused indifference got under my skin," La Follette told his mother after issuing a particularly stinging denunciation. He added, "I suppose people will think I have an obsession on Hoover but it does seem as though someone should keep after him and no one

32. RML to Fola, 18 April 1931, box 41-A, Family Papers; David Lawrence, "Station USA," *Saturday Evening Post* 203 (16 May 1931): 33, 103; *Washington Post*, 13 March 1931; "Wearing the Progressive Label," *Review of Reviews* 83 (April 1931): 33–34; John Dewey to Senators Norris, La Follette, Cutting, Wheeler, and Costigan, 18 April 1931, box 431-C, Family Papers. However, "The Progressive Conference," *New Republic* 66 (25 March 1931): 137–39, viewed the proceedings more favorably: "Perhaps the most significant note of the conference—that it pointed in the direction of a planned economy for the benefit not of large profits, but of the rank and file of this country—was largely overlooked by the press reports and editorial comment."

33. Norris to J. D. Ream, 24 March 1931, quoted in Romasco, *Poverty of Abundance*, p. 217; [Drew Pearson and Robert S. Allen], *Washington Merry-Go-Round* (New York, 1931), p. 184.

else in Washington appears to feel as keenly as I do about the shameful manner in which he has neglected his responsibilities in this economic crisis."[34]

During the spring of 1931 La Follette went on a speaking tour that took him to Boston, New York, and St. Louis. At every stop his message was the same. Hoover's approach to the depression had failed; a new approach was necessary. "Nation-wide depression," he said, "breeds self-examination, awakens a realization that human institutions cannot be regarded as sacred if they fail to maintain and promote the welfare of the nation as a whole." "It is obvious," he continued, "that we cannot manage our highly developed and intricate machinery upon the basis of ideas of organization and control developed in a predominately agricultural and individualistic society a hundred and fifty years ago." In Boston he outlined a seven-point recovery program: federal aid to the unemployed, unemployment insurance, centralized economic planning to bring industrial stabilization, a shorter workday and a shorter workweek, maintenance of wage levels, rehabilitation of agriculture, and to pay for all this, sharply graduated income and inheritance taxes. Should the nation's leaders fail to adopt such a program, he warned, dire consequences could result: "To the inflamed spirit of a people crushed by hunger and adversity, nothing is impossible, not even revolution." He concluded that as "unpleasant as the suggestion is, we must remember that democracy may be unable to stand the strain and that here, too, there may come dictatorship, either of the people or of the moneyed Fascist interests."[35]

La Follette alarmed and angered conservatives everywhere he spoke. "In the midst of discouragement and depression," said the *Washington Post*, "the senator lifts his eyes to the glorious light of socialism. All that is necessary is for Uncle Sam to stretch forth his magic wand and make the poor rich and the disheartened happy." The *Buffalo Evening News* described his recovery program as "a mere collection of demagogic phrases from which no definite meaning in terms of actual laws can be drawn by anyone." "La Follette," it said, "is affording an example, not of a statesman with a sense of responsibility for governing people, but of a reckless politician concerned only in the results of an election."[36]

Since there was little he could do in Washington, La Follette re-

34. RML to Belle and Mary, 14 April 1931, box 41-A, Family Papers.
35. RML speeches, Boston, 23 April 1931, New York City, 26 April 1931, box 555-C, Family Papers; *New York Times*, 24, 27 April 1931.
36. *Washington Post*, 25 April 1931; *Buffalo Evening News*, 25 April 1931, clipping, box 662-C, Family Papers.

turned to Wisconsin for the summer. While there he and Phil spent long hours discussing their political futures. For years the brothers had toyed with the idea of dropping the Republican label and forming a third party.[37] Believing the time had come to act, Phil presented his brother with a dramatic proposal: They should immediately organize a third party and Bob should be its presidential candidate in 1932. The idea of Young Bob running for the presidency was not entirely new. In recent years several Washington columnists had predicted that if and when a new party arose, the thirty-six-year-old Wisconsin senator was a likely choice to head it.[38]

La Follette, although hesitant, took the proposal seriously enough to appeal for advice from his mother, without whom he never made an important decision. Belle opposed the idea. "Such a course," she wrote Bob, "would be inconsistent with the calm, balanced judgment you have shown since you entered the field of politics." "And," she added, "I think it very important that you and Phil take no hasty ill-considered action that would destroy the confidence your followers have in your leadership."[39]

The brothers heeded their mother's advice and, for the time at least, abandoned plans for a third party. If they had launched a national movement, they probably would have failed to gain the support of many important progressive leaders. Norris, for example, staunchly opposed a third party.[40]

Belle's advice to her sons was her last. In the middle of August she entered a Washington hospital complaining of stomach pains. During an examination a doctor accidentally punctured her intestines, and peritonitis set in. On 18 August, at age seventy-three, she died. Bob and Phil had arrived from Madison only hours before the end. The family then accompanied the body to Madison for the funeral in the library of the State Historical Society and for the burial in Forest Hill Cemetery.[41]

Belle's death was a great blow to Bob. Ever since his father had died, his mother had been his main source of counsel and encouragement. She, more than anyone else, had understood the pressures put on him by public life, having to live up to his father's name, and nagging ill health. She had also sensed his feeling of inadequacy and

37. RML to Fola, 15 May 1931, box 41-A, Family Papers.
38. Belle to RML, 8 August 1931, box 40-A, Family Papers; Frazier Edwards in *Washington Herald*, 23 March 1931.
39. Belle to RML, 8 August 1931, box 40-A, Family Papers.
40. Norris to John Dewey, 27 December 1930, tray 8, box 3, George W. Norris Papers, Library of Congress, Washington, D.C.
41. PFL, *Memoirs*, pp. 155–56.

his need for reassurance. At the same time she had always demanded that he strictly adhere to the incredibly high La Follette standards.[42]

Three months later La Follette suffered another personal tragedy. In November, Rachel gave birth to their first child, a girl. The baby died five hours later. "As I see it," Bob wrote Fola, "life is only a test of one's stamina and it only differs in that some appear to have the thumb screws twisted down a little harder than others. It is this struggle to find the courage to meet the impacts of life which seems in one sense to make it an experience of sufficient magnitude to justify enduring it." If there was any consolation it was in his deepened relationship with Rachel: "I have a sense . . . of our two beings having been fused inseparably in this furnace of torture."[43]

With the onset of winter, millions of people experienced tragedies of their own. Unemployment continued to rise, topping the ten-million mark by year's end. Despite valiant efforts, local relief agencies were failing miserably in the face of mounting need. Some family breadwinners picked through trash cans or scoured garbage dumps for scraps of food. One of the estimated one hundred and thirty-two thousand unemployed in Wisconsin was former Gov. Fred R. Zimmerman. One day Phil La Follette's secretary spotted Zimmerman standing in a long line outside the capitol building. Wearing a tattered coat and looking a bit ashamed, the ex-governor was in search of a job.[44]

In December 1931, in this atmosphere of widespread distress, the Seventy-second Congress convened. With both houses closely divided between Republicans and Democrats, much attention focused on the progressives, and among the progressives on Bob La Follette. Months earlier columnist Frank Kent had predicted that "to a large extent the next Congress will be 'Little Bob's' Congress. It will be interesting to see what he does with it."[45]

Hoover, not La Follette, dominated initially. The president's annual message to Congress contained the usual amount of back patting. Voluntary relief efforts had succeeded, he claimed. No one was going hungry or cold. But in this and subsequent messages Hoover also revealed his newfound belief that the depression was far from over and that stronger action was needed, especially in the area of finance and credit. He therefore urged Congress to liberalize Federal

42. For example, see Belle to RML, 8 August 1931, box 40-A, Family Papers.
43. RML to Fola, 7, 11 November 1931, box 41-A, Family Papers.
44. A. J. Altmeyer to PFL, 12 September 1931, box 11-1, PFL Papers; interview, Gordon Sinykin.
45. Frank R. Kent, "The Great Game of Politics," *Baltimore Sun*, 25 March 1931.

Reserve Board procedures, to create a system of home-loan banks, and most important, to erect a reconstruction finance corporation with the power to make government loans to banks, insurance companies, railroads, and other businesses. Hoover hoped that these measures would stem the tide of bank and business failures, encourage lending and borrowing, stimulate production, and in general restore the confidence of businessmen. In line with his view that "the major forces of the depression now lie outside of the United States," he also asked Congress to extend relief to European nations by declaring a one-year moratorium on the repayment of World War I debts. Above all Hoover wanted stringent economy and a balanced budget, which would require tax increases and certainly no spending for unemployment relief or for further expansion of public works.[46]

La Follette supported some of Hoover's recommendations, though with little expectation that they would accomplish much. After changing his mind several times on the debt moratorium, he finally bolted progressive ranks to vote for it. In January 1932, he again incurred the disfavor of many progressives by going along with the majority of Congress to set up the Reconstruction Finance Corporation.[47] He even gave a sympathetic ear to Hoover's call for a balanced budget, although he disagreed with the president over the means to achieve it. La Follette favored raising the rates on "large incomes and great fortunes" and opposed the administration-backed sales tax, "because it is a scheme to place a heavier tax burden . . . upon those least able to bear it."[48]

In general, La Follette considered Hoover's program inadequate and the philosophy behind it misguided, and he quickly set to work on alternatives. In December 1931, in rapid succession, he introduced measures to create a national economic council, to provide relief to the unemployed, and to expand public works.

The economic-council proposal was slightly different from the version La Follette had offered in May. A group of economists, headed by J. M. Clark of Columbia University, whom La Follette had asked to look into the subject, had suggested some changes. The hearings on the original bill, held from October to December, led to other changes. In final form the bill called for the president, with Senate consent, to appoint nine members to the council. The selection of

46. Warren, *Hoover*, pp. 143, 155, 157–67.
47. Telegram, RML to Herbert Hoover, 24 June 1931, box 9-C, RML statement for Movietone, 29 October 1931, box 555-C, Family Papers; *CR* 72:1, 1931, vol. 75, pt. 1, p. 1126.
48. RML statement for Movietone, 23 November 1931, box 555-C, Family Papers.

members was to be based on each candidate's "acquaintance with and understanding of national economic problems." The council had to include at least one expert from each of six fields: industry, finance, transportation, labor relations, agriculture, and scientific management. No member could serve more than four years. Another provision called for the council to "initiate the organization of councils or associations within the various major branches of production, distribution, and finance." These subcouncils would study economic problems and make recommendations to the main council. The major duties of the council were to keep abreast of "general economic and business conditions," to consider problems affecting the economy, and "to formulate proposals looking to the solution of such problems" for action by Congress and the president. In short, the council was to serve as an economic fact-finding and advisory arm of the federal government.[49]

La Follette's proposed council received mixed reactions. The *New York Times* dismissed it as just "another advisory committee," which would merely duplicate the activities of already existing government agencies and which would only add to the bureaucratic tangle in Washington. Others, however, viewed it as a step toward a planned economy—a view that La Follette reinforced. "This piece of legislation," he said, "is a challenge to the fixed belief that hard times and good times alternate in cycles. I do not believe hard times are necessary provided it is possible to look ahead and plan to meet the emergencies that may arise." He concluded that "the only sound approach to the problem of unemployment and industrial instability is the creation of the necessary public machinery of planning and control."[50]

Yet, compared to other plans circulating around at the time, La Follette's council was only a modest step in the direction of economic planning. In September 1931, Gerard Swope, the president of General Electric, proposed the formation of trade associations within each major industry. These trade associations, composed of businessmen, would have the power to coordinate production and stabilize prices within their industries, thus replacing wasteful competition with cooperation and planning. The associations would also elect representatives to a national coordinating council. In addition, Swope wanted to compel industry to adopt pension and unemployment insurance

49. U.S. Congress, Senate, *A Bill to Establish a National Economic Council*, S. 2390, 72d Cong., 1st sess., 1931, copy in box 348-C, Family Papers.

50. *New York Times*, 2 November 1931; RML quoted in Edward N. Doan, *The La Follettes and the Wisconsin Idea* (New York, 1947), pp. 164–65.

plans. Although La Follette supported both the formation of trade associations and the adoption of unemployment compensation, he rejected Swope's idea of investing the association with the power to stabilize prices. This, he thought, would lead to government-sanctioned price fixing. La Follette likewise rejected economist Stuart Chase's far-reaching plan for the creation of a peace industries board modeled on the War Industries Board of World War I. Chase wanted to invest the board with broad powers over production and distribution.[51]

Basically La Follette's plan was moderate. In fact he never advocated comprehensive national economic planning. Nor did he ever give thought to the economic reorganization of society that real planning would have to entail. In many ways his proposal for an economic council was consistent with older progressive ideas, particularly those of his father. It was enough, he seemed to think, to have an organization of experts to uncover the facts, formulate proposals, and submit them to the president and Congress for appropriate action. Then too, La Follette was realistic enough to realize that no blueprint for a planned economy was likely to make any progress in Congress in the foreseeable future.

La Follette's proposal stimulated considerable discussion on the subject of planning. In addition to Swope and Chase, many others came forth with their own schemes, ranging from historian Charles A. Beard's "five year plan" to the Fraternal Order of Eagles's proposal for a "governmental industrial commission."[52] However, there appeared to be more interest outside Congress than within, and La Follette's bill failed to make any headway.

La Follette next pressed for the expansion of public works. Early in December, Senator Wagner called for a $2 billion public-employment program. La Follette, believing that sum insufficient, countered with the most comprehensive public works proposal introduced in Congress to that time. After consulting with economist Harry Woodhouse, Father John A. Ryan of the National Catholic Welfare Council, and others, he called for an appropriation of $5.5 billion. One-tenth of that sum was for federal projects, the rest for state and municipal projects. La Follette also sought to centralize the administration of

51. R. Alan Lawson, *The Failure of Independent Liberalism, 1930–1941* (New York, 1971), p. 63; Arthur M. Schlesinger, Jr., *The Age of Roosevelt: The Crisis of the Old Order, 1919–1933* (Boston, 1957), pp. 182, 201–2; *New York Times*, 29 October 1931.

52. "Congress Considering National Economic Planning," *Congressional Digest* 11 (April 1932): 97–118.

federal works programs. He recommended creating an administration of public works and gathering under it the many federal boards and commissions, scattered throughout the bureaucracy, that supervised public works projects.[53]

In contrast to many proponents of increased spending, La Follette also presented a plan to pay for his appropriation. He wanted the government to sell "prosperity bonds" just as it had sold Liberty Bonds during World War I. "If we could sell $25 billion worth of bonds during the war for purposes of destruction," he said, "it seems utterly absurd to contend that we could not float a short term issue of government bonds for constructive purposes." He argued that large and small investors would find government bonds a safer investment than the stock market. To finance the retirement of the bonds, La Follette proposed an additional 2 percent surtax on the incomes of persons making five thousand dollars or more, though middle-income groups could make certain deductions.[54]

During the ensuing weeks, La Follette went on the radio and wrote several articles to build public support for his bill. He promised that if enacted the bill would provide paying jobs "directly or indirectly for at least 4.5 million persons." With their purchasing power thus increased the newly employed could buy more goods, which in turn would stimulate production and open new jobs in the consumer industry. The increased demand for goods would also help the farmer, who would see the prices on his products go up. Furthermore, public works projects, like highway and building construction, would increase the demand for iron, steel, lumber, and other materials and therefore get the heavy industries moving again. Finally, he predicted that the bond issue would "bring out of hoarding the billion and a half dollars now idle" and "would put to work part of the twenty-eight billion unemployed dollars in the savings banks." "This program," he concluded, "is the only feasible means of bringing a measure of prosperity in the immediate future."[55]

After outlining his proposal on William Hard's NBC radio program, La Follette received "a splendid response in letters and telegrams." But he admitted privately that he had "not much chance to pass the public works bill." He was right, for the opposition mobilized itself

53. Huthmacher, *Wagner*, p. 89; *CR* 72:1, 1931–1932, vol. 75, pt. 1, p. 1126.
54. RML speech, 26 December 1931, RML article entitled, "We Need Purchasing Power Not Credit," 29 January 1932, box 555-C, Family Papers.
55. RML speeches and articles, boxes 555-C, 556-C, 663-C, Family Papers; *Progressive*, 2 January 1932.

quickly. The *Washington Post* called his plan "fanciful and impractical." The *Chicago Evening Post* warned that "bond panaceas are dangerous" and added that "they may in the end come nearer to killing the civic patient than curing him." Even before La Follette had revealed the details of the bill, the administration had announced its opposition to any massive expansion of public works and any "unorthodox" bond schemes. "The problem of unemployment," reported a subcommittee of the President's Organization for Unemployment Relief, "cannot be solved by any magic appropriation from the public treasury." La Follette responded by denouncing the administration for "counseling the nation to resign itself to a policy of inaction and despair."[56] La Follette's bill fared little better than his proposal for an economic council. He failed even to get it placed on the Senate calendar. And when in June 1932 he offered it as a substitute for another measure, a bipartisan majority soundly defeated it, 56 to 12.[57]

It was the third of La Follette's antidepression measures, an unemployment-relief bill, that stirred the most interest and led to the most dramatic debate of the session. Like nearly all of his proposals, this one was the product of many minds. In November 1931 a group of prominent social workers, distressed by their inability to cope with relief needs, traveled to Washington to appeal for federal assistance. Among them were William Hodson of the New York City Welfare Council; Allen T. Burns, director of the Association of Community Chests; J. Prentice Murphy, director of the Philadelphia Children's Bureau; and Joanne Colcord of the Russell Sage Foundation. The group first approached Senator Wagner and urged him to introduce a relief bill. Wagner declined. The social workers next presented their case to La Follette, Senator-elect Costigan of Colorado, and Rep. David J. Lewis of Maryland. La Follette, having advocated federal relief for almost a year, needed no persuasion; neither did the other two legislators.[58]

On 9 December, La Follette introduced a relief bill that incorporated many of the social workers' suggestions and that also drew details from a draft of a proposal his brother had passed on to him. At the same time, Costigan in the Senate and Lewis in the House offered

56. RML to Fola and George Middleton, 21 January 1932, box 42-A, Family Papers; responses to RML bill and RML's reaction quoted in "That $5,500,000,000 Depression Cure," *Literary Digest* 112 (9 January 1932): 9.
57. *New York Times*, 23 June 1932.
58. Fred Greenbaum, *Fighting Progressive: A Biography of Edward P. Costigan* (Washington, D.C., 1971), pp. 122–24; Huthmacher, *Wagner*, p. 93.

bills similar to La Follette's. Curiously, neither La Follette nor Costigan had been aware of the other's intention to introduce relief legislation, and when they discovered that they were both after the same thing, they combined their bills into one.[59]

The resulting measure provided for a grant of $375 million to the states. The states were then to arrange for the distribution of relief payments to the needy. A particularly controversial provision would create a federal emergency-relief board with broad powers to regulate state relief activities and to establish standards. The bill concluded with a farsighted provision that entrusted the federal board with power to dispense relief to those migratory workers and their families who were not legal residents of any state.[60]

The hearings on the bill before La Follette's Committee on Manufactures produced shocking evidence of the plight of the unemployed and of the inability of public and private welfare agencies to cope with the mounting distress. William Hodson, director of relief activities in New York City and the first of many welfare experts to testify, set the tone for the hearings. Although admitting that statistics were seldom very accurate, he estimated that as many as one hundred and fifty thousand persons who needed relief in his city were not receiving it, even with charity organizations working at full capacity. Those fortunate enough to get some help, he added, were only living at a bare subsistence level. Witnesses from across the country told the same story; only the details differed.[61] The only question the hearings left unresolved concerned not the need for federal aid but whether the La Follette–Costigan bill, with its modest appropriation of $375 million, would be sufficient.

Late in the afternoon of 1 February 1932, the Senate began to debate the relief measure. La Follette spoke first, consuming the better part of two days with a wide-ranging address that drew heavily from all his previous speeches on the subjects of unemployment and relief. Wage earners, he asserted at the outset, had suffered most from the depression. Many of them had lost their jobs, their savings, even their homes. Yet since 1929 the federal government had ignored their plight, concentrating instead on helping corporations, insurance com-

59. CR 72:1, 1931–1932, vol. 75, pt. 1, p. 192; Greenbaum, Costigan, pp. 123–24; PFL to RML, 22 November 1931, box 41-A, Family Papers; Doan, Wisconsin Idea, p. 168.

60. CR 72:1, 1931–1932, vol. 75, pt. 2, p. 1997.

61. U.S. Congress, Senate, Subcommittee of the Committee on Manufactures, Hearings on S. 174 and S. 262, 72d Cong., 1st sess., 1931–1932, p. 12; Schlesinger, Crisis of the Old Order, pp. 173–74.

panies, banks, and persons of wealth. "Two billion one hundred and sixty millions of dollars has already been provided by the Congress and the administration during this depression for the relief of those who own property and securities in the United States," he said, referring to income tax cuts and the Reconstruction Finance Corporation. "Now, when it is proposed that the Congress shall give consideration to a measure providing relief of those ... who, through no fault of their own, find themselves destitute, cold, hungry, and homeless, the contention is raised that there is not sufficient evidence to demonstrate the necessity for Federal action in this crisis."

If the Senate needed evidence, La Follette promised to provide it. He quoted extensively from the testimony of the social workers and relief administrators who had appeared before his committee. He unveiled the results of his latest survey of city mayors showing that a majority of them favored federal aid to help meet the crushing burden of relief. And he presented studies indicating that many children were suffering from malnutrition as a result of the depression. Anticipating the expected objections to relief, La Follette argued, as he had in the past, that federal aid had ample precedent, that relief was not solely the responsibility of state and local governments, and that the bill would not establish a dole. At one point, Millard Tydings of Maryland interrupted, suggesting that the Senate should not act "until there is concrete evidence from the governors themselves that the States will not or can not" handle the problem. "Mr. President," La Follette snapped back, "I am not willing to wait for information from the governors while people starve. The evidence is overwhelming that the relief being afforded is inadequate, that people are suffering. Whether the governors confirm and back up that evidence, or whether they deny it, the evidence from competent witnesses stands on the record." He ended with an emotional appeal: "If we permit this situation to go on, millions of children will be maimed in body, if not warped in mind, by the effects of malnutrition. They will form the citizenship upon which the future of this country must depend. They are the hope of America." [62]

As La Follette turned the floor over to Costigan, even critics of relief, like Tydings, conceded that he had made a strong case. His effective presentation also may have foiled a move planned by Democratic and Republican floor leaders to shut off debate on the bill. When he began his speech, La Follette explained to Fola and Mid, "it was common talk" that Joseph T. Robinson and James E. Watson, the

62. *CR* 72:1, 1931–1932, vol. 75, pt. 3, pp. 3068–95.

minority and majority leaders, "had it all set to send the bill back to the committee" when he concluded. "I was not satisfied with my address," he said further, "but the evidence piled up so that the Coalition of Democrats and Republicans abandoned their idea."[63]

During the ensuing two-week debate, critics of the La Follette–Costigan bill coalesced into two groups. One group, composed of Republican supporters of the administration and a few conservative Democrats, opposed federal aid of any sort. One of their spokesmen was Ohio Republican Simeon D. Fess. "There is no doubt," declared Fess, "that there is not a city in the country which can not take care of its unemployed." Give a dole once, he warned, and people "will come to demand it as their right." And pounding his fists on his desk until they were bloody, Fess concluded that "every American that cares for the history of a great country ought to stand against any proposal so demoralizing, so effective in the breakdown of the moral and mental fiber of our citizenship as this would eventually be."[64]

A majority of the Democrats formed the other opposing faction. Many of them frankly admitted that La Follette and Costigan had proved the need for at least some federal relief; but they objected to the means by which the two senators would make funds available to the states. For one thing, they preferred loans rather than outright grants. More important, Democrats, especially those from the South, were horrified at the prospect of a federal board supervising local relief activities. Should the bill pass, warned Hugo Black of Alabama, the states would be subjected to more "bureaucratic control" than the provinces of the Roman Empire. In one of his first appearances on the floor, Huey Long, the firebrand from Louisiana, concurred. Democrats also predicted, with good reason, that the La Follette–Costigan bill would surely incur a presidential veto.[65]

On 3 February, Democrats Hugo Black, David I. Walsh of Massachusetts, and Robert J. Bulkley of Ohio offered a substitute relief measure, which provided the $375 million in loans rather than in grants for the states. It required the governors to make formal requests for loans and to submit statements saying that "the amount so requested is necessary . . . and can not be obtained either from public or private sources." The states were to have full authority over the disbursement of relief funds with no interference from Washington.

63. RML to Fola and George "Mid" Middleton, 5, 19 February 1932, box 42-A, Family Papers.

64. CR 72:1, 1931–1932, vol. 75, pt. 4, pp. 3666–70; Jordan A. Schwarz, The Interregnum of Despair: Hoover, Congress, and the Depression (Urbana, Ill., 1970), p. 153.

65. CR 72:1, 1931–1932, vol. 75, pt. 3, pp. 3306–25, 3576.

A final provision loaned an additional $375 million to the states for public works projects.[66]

La Follette wrote Fola and Mid that the Democrats had "resorted to political trickery. They proposed a substitute which they knew would not work just to enable them to say that they had proposed *something.*" He joined Costigan in a point-by-point attack on the substitute bill. La Follette argued that the states, with their treasuries already depleted, would be hard pressed to repay interest-bearing federal loans; therefore they would have to increase regressive property taxes. The federal government, on the other hand, could finance relief through income and inheritance taxes and thus place the burden on those best able to pay. Costigan pointed out that thirty-four states would be ineligible for federal loans because of constitutional prohibitions. Both senators were skeptical of the substitute bill's provision requiring the governors to initiate the aid process. The need for relief was obvious, they argued, whether the governors recognized it or not. Moreover, La Follette said, many governors, especially Republicans, out of pride or out of loyalty to the administration's antirelief policy, would refuse to seek aid even though their states desperately needed it. Finally, Costigan criticized the Democrats for failing to provide any national supervision, an omission that he felt might lead to misuse of relief funds. The only feature of the substitute that La Follette and Costigan found meritorious was the grant for public works, and they later incorporated that provision into their own bill.[67]

As the debate moved to a conclusion, Senator Wagner, believing that there were enough votes to pass a relief measure of some sort, tried to persuade the sponsors of the substitute and the La Follette–Costigan forces to agree on a compromise. But neither side would budge. On 15 February, La Follette, Costigan, and their supporters combined with administration-supporting Republicans to reject the Democratic substitute, 48 to 31. The next evening, after a grueling two-week debate, the Senate voted down the LaFollette–Costigan bill, 48 to 35. "I am not depressed as a result of the outcome," La Follette wrote to his sister. "Really we made a much better showing than I expected . . . when I opened the debate."[68]

66. Ibid., pp. 3313–14.

67. RML to Fola and George Middleton, 19 February 1932, box 42-A, Family Papers; Greenbaum, *Costigan*, p. 126; *CR* 72:1, 1931–1932, vol. 75, pt. 4, p. 3801; Huthmacher, *Wagner*, p. 94.

68. Huthmacher, *Wagner*, pp. 94–95; RML to Fola and George Middleton, 9 February 1932, box 42-A, Family Papers. For a view somewhat critical of RML's role in debate, see Schwarz, *Interregnum of Despair*, pp. 154–55.

Although La Follette may not have realized it fully at the time, even in defeat he and Costigan had significantly advanced their cause. During the debate the two senators won over to their side several key figures who had previously opposed federal relief. The most important convert was Wagner. Only months before, the New York Democrat had rejected charity, preferring instead to concentrate on the public-employment approach. But the introduction of the La Follette–Costigan bill forced him to reexamine his position and ultimately to support federal relief. The same was true of Norris and Borah.[69] The addition of these prominent liberals to the ranks greatly strengthened the relief forces. La Follette and Costigan had also forced Senate Democrats to confront the issue for the first time. Most of them backed the weaker substitute, but even that amounted to tacit recognition of the need for relief. Also, the two senators succeeded in placing foes of relief on the defensive. Some continued to argue that the states and municipalities could handle the problem without federal aid; but in the face of overwhelming evidence to the contrary, many others reluctantly began the search for the least objectionable way of implementing a relief program. In the long run, the defeat of the La Follette–Costigan bill proved to be a decisive turning point in the battle for relief.

In late February and March, La Follette tried to maintain the momentum through a series of personal appearances in Washington, Chicago, and Wisconsin. At times he sounded radical. "In a period such as this," he said to an audience of educators, "we are prone to re-evaluate all of our institutions; and, so far as I am concerned, I am ready to accept the doctrine that those which no longer serve the best interests of all people are no longer justified in their existence."[70] Statements like this reflected La Follette's persistent habit of sounding more radical than he was. He declined to specify what institutions were outmoded; and as his other remarks during the tour suggested, he was referring more to policies, especially the policy of laissez-faire, than to institutions. But it was a measure of the changing mood of the country that, whereas such statements a year before brought cries of "socialism" and "demagoguery," now they attracted little notice.

By the spring of 1932 economic conditions had worsened so much that the nation's leaders were inflicted with a sense of impending

69. Huthmacher, *Wagner*, pp. 93–94; Lowitt, *Norris*, pp. 494–95; William E. Borah to H. H. Freedhein, 6 February 1932, box 335, William E. Borah Papers, Library of Congress, Washington, D.C.; Marian C. McKenna, *Borah* (Ann Arbor, Mich., 1961), p. 273.

70. RML speech before National Education Association, 24 February 1932, box 556-C, Family Papers.

doom. After touring Wisconsin, Phil La Follette reported to Bob that "unless something rather drastic is done both in the direction of furnishing employment and inflation, I doubt if things will hold together." He added ominously, "We may be faced with the necessity of action any time to avoid serious conflict." Thomas Amlie, a progressive congressman from Wisconsin, thought it "certain that before we can get out of this thing we are going to see rioting working men led by communists." The progressives, said Amlie, would then find themselves "in the middle of the stream and perhaps without any great degree of influence. On the one hand the reactionaries will seek to control the situation by control of the military forces, while on the other hand those who have become desperate will go clear over to the left wing." The progressives were not alone in fearing for the future. Hoover and his congressional supporters, who had long since stopped issuing optimistic forecasts, were now privately predicting severe crises ahead.[71]

In this mood, and knowing that they would soon have to face the voters, leaders in both parties realized that they could no longer dodge the relief issue. In May, Senate Democrats, spurred on by Wagner, came out for relief and for the expansion of public works. The administration, bowing to the inevitable, set forth counter proposals. By the end of the month it was clear that relief in some form would be forthcoming.

There followed two months of complicated maneuvering and compromising. Under the skillful direction of Senator Wagner, a measure suitable to a majority in Congress and to the administration took shape. Finally, in mid-July, Congress passed, and Hoover signed, the Emergency Relief and Construction Act. The measure authorized the Reconstruction Finance Corporation to loan $300 million to the states for relief purposes and to loan $1.5 billion to states, municipalities, and private corporations for "self-liquidating" public works projects. It also appropriated $324 million for federal employment projects.[72]

La Follette voted for the Emergency Relief Act, but with great reluctance and only after unsuccessfully trying to strengthen it through a series of amendments. He argued that by making loans, rather than outright grants, available to the states, the government was giving with one hand and taking with the other. He predicted, correctly as

71. PFL to RML, 15 May 1932, box 42-A, Family Papers; Thomas R. Amlie to F. B. Fries, 10 May 1932, box 6, Thomas R. Amlie Papers, State Historical Society of Wisconsin, Madison; Schwarz, *Interregnum of Despair*, pp. 158–59.

72. Huthmacher, *Wagner*, pp. 94–101; Schwarz, *Interregnum of Despair*, pp. 160–73; Warren, *Hoover*, pp. 204–8.

it turned out, that the Reconstruction Finance Corporation would be niggardly in its dispensation of relief loans. Finally he considered the amounts appropriated for relief, especially for public works, grossly inadequate.[73]

Still, despite its deficiencies, the measure was at least a partial victory for La Follette. For over a year he had stood almost alone in advocating federal relief; now Congress and the administration, in what one senator described as a "sudden, remarkable somersault," accepted his basic contention that states and municipalities could not cope with relief needs.[74] For the first time, the federal government assumed responsibility for providing relief to the unemployed.

Although the relief fight consumed most of his energies, La Follette played a key role in other important battles during the session. In January he managed to block passage of a secrecy provision in a military-appropriations bill. The provision would have allowed the president to keep secret from the public and Congress the development and manufacture of certain weapons and the establishment of military installations. La Follette's opposition reflected his belief that government secrecy, except in the most extreme cases, was unwarranted and potentially dangerous. In March he introduced a measure to establish a national referendum in which voters could nominate candidates for the presidency. Although the referendum would not be binding on the major parties, he believed that it would pressure them into nominating the people's choice. The measure, however, failed to stir much interest, and it eventually died in the Judiciary Committee. During April and May, La Follette successfully helped lead a coalition of Democrats and progressives in an attack on the administration-backed sales tax. The defeat of the sales tax paved the way for enactment of the Revenue Act of 1932, the most progressive income tax bill since World War I.[75]

The toughest decision La Follette had to make during the session concerned the demands of World War I veterans. In June more than twenty thousand unemployed veterans, calling themselves the Bonus Expeditionary Force, descended upon Washington. They came to

73. Schwarz, *Interregnum of Despair*, pp. 168–73; on the operation of RFC relief activities, see Schlesinger, *Crisis of the Old Order*, p. 241, and Romasco, *Poverty of Abundance*, pp. 224–26.

74. Sen. Hiram Johnson to McClatchy, 14 May 1932, quoted in Schwarz, *Interregnum of Despair*, p. 173.

75. *CR* 72:1, 1931–1932, vol. 75, pt. 3, pp. 2334–35, 5728; Thomas R. Amlie to Fred Kull, 18 April 1932, box 5, Amlie Papers; Schwarz, *Interregnum of Despair*, pp. 137–39.

demand immediate payment of the bonus that Congress had approved in 1924 as compensation for wartime service but that veterans were not to receive until 1945. Since the bonus had already been approved, the veterans argued, they should get it then, when they really needed it, rather than have to wait twenty years. The House of Representatives agreed and promptly passed Wright Patman's $2.4 billion bonus bill.[76]

Since entering the Senate, La Follette had consistently supported legislation favorable to veterans, and he was under considerable pressure from veterans' groups and from others to support the Patman bill. Yet he was skeptical of it for several reasons. For one thing, the bill only benefited one special-interest group, and La Follette thought the government should aid all of the unemployed, not just that minority of them who happened to be veterans. For another thing he feared that payment of the bonus would jeopardize other recovery measures, especially his $5.5 billion public works bill. Having spent billions of dollars on veterans, an economy-minded Congress would be unlikely to appropriate additional billions for public works. La Follette also thought that the government would not be able to afford to fund both programs. This last concern reflected his moderation in fiscal matters. Although both then and later he had the reputation of being Congress's preeminent spender, he always believed that there were very definite limits to how much the government could spend.

As La Follette wrestled with the problem, his brother wrote him a lengthy letter in which he said, "I think if I were in your place, I would vote for it." The bonus, Phil argued, was sound in principle and sound economically; and he cautiously warned of the political consequences of opposing the popular measure. In the end, however, La Follette rejected his brother's advice and joined the Senate majority in defeating the bill. As he explained to Phil, "I prayed over your letter a long time but in the last analysis I could not see my way clear to vote for the bonus. One of the things I regret mostly about it is the fear that the veterans in their anger may take it out on you in the coming campaign."[77]

During the ensuing weeks La Follette received hundreds of letters from disgruntled veterans. Undoubtedly the letters that hurt his feelings the most were those that compared him unfavorably to his father. One ex-serviceman wrote, "The old adage, 'like father, like

76. Schlesinger, *Crisis of the Old Order*, p. 257; Warren, *Hoover*, pp. 224–36.
77. PFL to RML, 14 June 1932, RML to PFL, 24 June 1932, box 40-A, Family Papers.

son' does not apply in this case." Another said, "I am certain that if your great father was living he would vote for the bonus and for humanity. Why didn't you?"[78]

When Congress recessed in mid-July, La Follette immediately left for Wisconsin, where his brother was involved in a difficult reelection campaign. As governor, Phil La Follette had achieved some modest successes but had clearly failed to excite the majority of voters or to rebuild the broad progressive coalition that had brought his father continued success. Moreover, he was an incumbent at the time when economic conditions in Wisconsin and in the nation reached the nadir, causing voters to look desperately for new, or at least different, faces to lead them. Compounding his problems, during 1932 there was a resurgence of the state's long-moribund Democratic party as a result of widespread dissatisfaction with Hoover and the Republican national leadership. This development threatened to siphon progressive votes out of the all-important Republican primary.

The outcome of the September primary confirmed the progressives' worst fears. Former Governor Kohler crushed Phil La Follette by close to one hundred thousand votes. And, in a completely unexpected upset, John B. Chapple, the editor of a northern Wisconsin newspaper who had accused progressives of being socialists and communists, ousted John J. Blaine from his Senate seat.

Most political analysts blamed the La Follette and Blaine losses primarily on the defection of voters who in past years had cast their ballots for progressives in the Republican primary but who in 1932 voted in the Democratic primary. Some concluded that the progressive, in order to survive, must either bolt the GOP and form a new party or enter the Democratic party. In fact, the primary results did not completely support this analysis. Although the shift of voters to the Democratic side may have accounted for Blaine's narrow defeat, it did not account for La Follette's loss. Even if the shift had not occurred, he would still have fallen short of the number of votes necessary for victory.[79]

After the disastrous primary Bob La Follette deliberated over what his public stance in the presidential race should be. Although opposed to Hoover, he was reluctant to endorse the Democratic candidate, Franklin D. Roosevelt, as most of his progressive colleagues had already done. As he explained to his close friend Sen. Bronson Cutting of New Mexico, "There are two things that deter me from coming out

78. Letters, box 9-C, Family Papers.
79. PFL, *Memoirs*, pp. 177–83; *New York Times*, 21–24 September 1932.

for him flat-footedly. One is that I sense in his speeches confirmation of my estimate of the lack in depth and breadth of his fundamental progressivism." La Follette also feared that many people would interpret an endorsement of Roosevelt as an endorsement of Democratic candidates in Wisconsin: "The Democratic organization in the state is virtually an adjunct of the reactionary Republican organization. Besides that, the nominee for the United States Senate is an out and out reactionary, and the nominee for Governor a nice, but weak, man."[80]

Roosevelt, through his close aid Louis Howe, actively sought La Follette's support. Finally, three weeks before the election, La Follette issued a qualified endorsement of the Democratic contender. He later explained that two of Roosevelt's campaign speeches, one in Atlanta and the other before the Commonwealth Club in San Francisco, convinced him that Roosevelt "saw the crux of this problem, . . . and had the courage to announce his position upon it." In both speeches, Roosevelt declared that the way out of the depression was to restore mass purchasing power. At the same time, La Follette publicly endorsed the Democratic candidates for senator and governor in Wisconsin. Obviously he had decided that the "out and out reactionary" F. Ryan Duffy was preferable to Republican Red-baiter John Chapple, and that the "nice, but weak" Albert G. Schmedeman was preferable to Kohler.[81]

When the Democrats swept Wisconsin and the nation in November, La Follette sent Roosevelt a cordial note of congratulations.[82] Yet he still harbored doubts about Roosevelt's "fundamental progressivism." He decided that if Roosevelt wanted the progressives to support his administration, he would have to earn that support. And if in the months before the inauguration the president-elect wanted advice from the progressives, Roosevelt would have to make the first move.

In January 1933, Roosevelt appeared to do just that. Through his advisers Henry Morgenthau, Sr., and John F. Sinclair, Roosevelt sent word to La Follette that he would like to meet with him. Before accepting this indirect invitation, La Follette made it clear that Roosevelt, not he, was taking the initiative. To Sinclair he wrote: "I think I should reiterate the statement made to you and to Mr. Morgenthau, Sr. over the telephone. I said then, and I wish to repeat now,

80. RML to Bronson Cutting, 1 October 1932, box 9-C, Family Papers.
81. *CR* 73:1, 1933, vol. 73, pt. 3, p. 2521; *New York Times*, 20 October 1932.
82. Roosevelt to RML, 19 November 1932, box 10-C, Family Papers.

that I am not seeking an interview with the Governor." He went on to say that although he had endorsed Roosevelt during the campaign, "I did not anticipate then, nor do I feel now, that this places me in any position to urge upon him any course concerning the policies of his administration." However, he concluded, if Roosevelt, "of his own volition," "really desires me to meet with him . . . I shall be glad to do so."[83]

When La Follette visited Roosevelt at the Mayflower Hotel in Washington on 19 January, Roosevelt confirmed a rumor that had been circulating through the capital since the election. "I want Phil in my official family," he told La Follette. "I do not know just where yet, but he must come in." Curiously, before La Follette could respond, Roosevelt changed the subject.[84]

Several days later La Follette learned from Bronson Cutting why Roosevelt had seemed reluctant to discuss in detail the matter of Phil entering the administration. According to Cutting, Roosevelt had offered the post of attorney general to Sen. Thomas J. Walsh, a Democrat from Montana. However, the president-elect expected Walsh to decline, in which case he planned to offer the position either to Felix Frankfurter, of the Harvard Law School, or to Phil La Follette. Roosevelt had also asked Cutting to become secretary of the interior. Cutting asked for time to consider the offer and suggested to Roosevelt that he would be more inclined to accept were Phil also to be in the cabinet.[85]

Meanwhile, Roosevelt invited Cutting and Bob La Follette to his winter home in Warm Springs, Georgia. The two senators went there on 22 January and spent three hours with him. This was La Follette's first opportunity to talk at length with Roosevelt, and he came away impressed. "The Governor," he told reporters, "gave us a very attentive and sympathetic hearing. So far as his general attitude was concerned it was very gratifying." In a letter to his brother he elaborated on the meeting. Roosevelt's "attitude . . . on power, farm relief, unemployment relief, public works, was in substantial accord with the progressive position," he reported with satisfaction. Roosevelt also had agreed with La Follette that inflation must be a part of his program.

83. RML to John F. Sinclair, 17 January 1933, enclosed in Sinclair to Franklin D. Roosevelt, 18 January 1933, President's Personal File 1792, Franklin D. Roosevelt Papers, Franklin D. Roosevelt Library, Hyde Park, New York.

84. Roosevelt quoted in RML to PFL, 20 January 1933, box 43-A, Family Papers.

85. RML to PFL, 20 January 1933, box 43-A, Family Papers.

On the matter of cabinet appointments, the ostensible purpose of the meeting, Roosevelt told La Follette that if Walsh declined the attorney generalship, he would offer it to Phil. If Walsh accepted, he wanted to know "what position other than a cabinet office" Phil would accept. La Follette, however, was skeptical of Roosevelt's offer. "You will see, of course," he wrote to Phil, "that in so far as you are concerned, two and two do not make four in this situation." La Follette suspected that Roosevelt knew Walsh would probably accept the post but dangled the attorney generalship in front of Phil in order to secure "a more friendly personal attitude in so far as we are concerned toward his administration." [86]

Subsequent developments proved La Follette to have been correct. Walsh did accept; but before the inauguration he died of a heart attack. Then, rather than appointing Phil, Roosevelt selected party loyalist Homer Cummings of Connecticut. Roosevelt, however, did offer Phil the choice of two other positions, chairmanship of the Power Commission or a seat in the Federal Trade Commission, both of which Phil turned down. The La Follette brothers were probably more relieved than disappointed when Roosevelt failed to bring Phil into the cabinet. Even before the final turn of events, Phil had written to Bob: "I think it will be for the best if it works out that none of us are in his cabinet, and are left free to use this year to organize ourselves into a close and more definitely organized group." "There is real danger," he thought, "that by going into his cabinet we would become prisoners to his future." [87]

While Roosevelt selected his cabinet, the lame-duck session of the Seventy-second Congress was drawing to a close. During the session, La Follette and Costigan, now joined by Bronson Cutting, again pressed for direct relief to the unemployed. They argued that the Emergency Relief Act of 1932, which had empowered the Reconstruction Finance Corporation to make loans to the states, had failed to relieve distress. They pointed out that the RFC had been niggardly in its dispensation of relief funds; although some state governors begged for loans, the RFC, after eight months, had released little more than half of the $300 million authorized by the Relief Act. The only solution, the senators concluded, was to take control of relief

86. *New York Times*, 23 January 1923; RML to PFL, 24 January 1933, box 41-A, Family Papers.

87. RML to Fola and George Middleton, 24 February 1933, box 41-A, Family Papers; PFL, *Memoirs*, p. 205; PFL to RML, 5 February 1933, box 42-A, Family Papers.

funds away from the RFC, set up a federal relief board, and make outright grants, not loans, to the states.[88]

Even Robert F. Wagner, the principal author of the Emergency Relief Act, admitted its failure but he argued that the Senate was still too conservative to approve direct relief and that even if Congress passed the La Follette-Costigan-Cutting proposal, Hoover would surely veto it. Wagner countered with a bill that would retain the RFC's control of relief money and continue the use of loans but would liberalize the RFC's lending policies.[89]

During the debate, La Follette was uncharacteristically bitter and short tempered. Obviously the strain of the protracted relief battle was beginning to show. One day he became annoyed at colleagues for talking while he had the floor. "Senators who are not interested in the misery of millions in the United States," he said, should "retire to the cloakroom to carry on their conversations." When the talking continued, La Follette stopped in midsentence and, his voice rising in anger, expressed his hope that the *Congressional Record* would record the interruption "so that millions of persons now ground down to the level of paupers may understand that in the highest legislative body in this land there is no interest in their suffering or their degradation."[90] He also attacked Wagner, unfairly at times, with a vengeance he usually reserved for the most ardent foes of relief. Stung by the attack, Wagner struck back. "I do not want to indulge in pure futilities," he said of the direct-relief bill. Turning to La Follette he continued, "I do not see that it gets bread to the destitute to stand for some so-called principal of grants as against loans if, in the end, by pursuing that policy, we invite a veto and the hungry get nothing."[91] In the end, the Senate agreed with Wagner and adopted the compromise measure.

La Follette and Wagner then carried the fight to the House of Representatives. Both appealed to President-elect Roosevelt, Wagner urging him to persuade House Democrats to enact the bill, La Follette urging him to advise against passage. In making his case, La Follette assured Roosevelt that a "worthwhile bill, acceptable to you, social welfare experts, and the country can be passed early in the extra session" of Congress, which was only a few weeks away. Roosevelt followed La Follette's advice and withheld support from the

88. *CR* 72:2, 1932–1933, vol. 76, pt. 1, p. 162; *New York Times*, 22, 23 January 1933.
89. Huthmacher, *Wagner*, pp. 127–28.
90. *New York Times*, 23 February 1933.
91. Quoted in Schwarz, *Interregnum of Despair*, p. 211.

Wagner bill, and on 4 March, Inauguration Day, the House adjourned without having acted on it.[92]

For La Follette, the frustration of two years and the irritability of past weeks gave way to cautious optimism. He hoped that with a new Congress and especially with a new president the nation might yet find its way out of the depression.

92. Telegram, RML and Edward P. Costigan to Roosevelt, 23 February 1933, box 11-C, Family Papers; *New York Times*, 5, 6 March 1933.

CHAPTER 7

La Follette and the New Deal

During the first year and a half of the Roosevelt administration, La Follette played a key role in the formulation and passage of important New Deal legislation, especially in the areas of relief, public works, and taxation. During the same time, however, he emerged as one of the administration's most persistent critics. The administration, he charged, was not going far enough or fast enough to restore mass purchasing power. Above all, the glaring inconsistencies and contradictions within the New Deal appalled him. By 1934 La Follette had taken a position on the leftward periphery of the New Deal, a position he maintained for the duration of the depression.

The warm personal relationship La Follette and Roosevelt had formed during their Warm Springs meeting in January survived despite their frequent differences over domestic policy. Indeed, from the beginning Roosevelt went out of his way to cultivate La Follette's support and friendship. In contrast to Hoover, who had scrupulously avoided any personal contact with the Wisconsin senator, the new president frequently invited La Follette to the White House, often sent him cordial notes addressed "Dear Bob" and signed "from F.D.R.," and occasionally telephoned him at the office or at home to confer on some matter or another. During his first year in office Roosevelt also dismayed Wisconsin Democrats by appointing many La Follette progressives to important positions in the government. Clearly, Roosevelt wanted La Follette to feel that he was a part of the administration and that the administration was receptive to his views, even when it was not.

Political considerations in large part prompted these friendly overtures. Roosevelt was fully aware that La Follette's criticism had helped topple the Hoover administration, and he hoped to avoid the same fate. Then too, La Follette held a strategic position in the Senate. As a leader of the progressive Republicans and as a member of three of the most important Senate committees—Education and Labor, Finance, and Foreign Affairs—he could influence, for good or for ill, the course of New Deal legislation.

But aside from politics, Roosevelt also had a high personal regard for Young Bob. Unlike some visitors to the Oval Office, like Louisiana Democrat Huey Long who sometimes failed to remember that Roosevelt was the one who was president, La Follette was always polite and respectful. Yet he was no sycophant. When he disagreed with Roosevelt, he said so openly, though he showed enough discretion to suggest that the president was in error only because he had been misled by an adviser. La Follette also appeared to be genuinely unambitious for higher office and thus no threat to rival Roosevelt for the presidency, a fact that Roosevelt doubtless appreciated. Finally, Roosevelt seemed to identify with Young Bob's family background. Perhaps he viewed the La Follettes as the Roosevelts of the Middle West, a family with a strong sense of tradition and loyalty, a family whose members considered it their natural duty, almost their noblesse oblige, to lead and to do service to mankind. Rexford G. Tugwell, an intimate Roosevelt adviser, later expressed his belief that "if Franklin had not been a Roosevelt I am quite certain he would have liked to be a La Follette."[1]

Initially La Follette seemed to be a little self-conscious about his relationship with Roosevelt. After all, from Theodore Roosevelt to Herbert Hoover the La Follettes had traditionally battled with presidents, and he did not want people to think he was "going soft." As if to reassure himself, he pledged to his brother after the Warm Springs meeting that neither his friendship with Roosevelt nor any favors from the White House would interfere with his objectivity and independence. "I shall be governed by the position which he takes upon public questions," he declared. "And I shall support his policies when they are in conformity with progressive principles and shall do all in my power to make his administration a success so long as it is evident that he intends to advocate genuine progressive policies." "So far as I am concerned," he said another time, "I am going with [Roosevelt] when I think he is going in the right direction and I am going to be against him when I think he is not."[2]

La Follette wasted no time asserting his independence and attacked Roosevelt's initial legislative recommendations, the banking and the economy bills. On 5 March, his first full day in office, Roosevelt swiftly moved to avert the complete collapse of the banking system by closing the nation's banks. On 8 March, the day before the banks were to reopen, the president summoned La Follette and Edward P.

    1. Rexford G. Tugwell, *The Democratic Roosevelt: A Biography of Franklin D. Roosevelt* (Baltimore, 1969 [1957]), p. 298.
    2. RML to PFL, 24 January 1933, box 41-A, RML to Thomas M. Duncan, 17 March 1933, box 10-C, Family Papers (see list of appreviations p. x).

Costigan to an evening meeting at the White House. The two senators felt certain that Roosevelt wanted their advice on the banking crisis, so before leaving for the White House they hastily outlined their recommendations. The banking system, they believed, needed a complete overhaul. They felt that eastern banks, especially those in New York, had too much power. The government, therefore, should reorganize the system so that banks in no one section of the country dominated. More important, the government should tighten its regulation of the whole banking structure. They realized, however, that it would take months to work out the details of reorganization and reform, and they believed that, in the meantime, it was essential that Roosevelt maintain firm control over the banks. Apparently at no time did the two senators consider recommending outright nationalization of the banks.

For La Follette and Costigan the meeting with the president went badly. They quickly discovered that Roosevelt had already decided upon a course of action, and rather than ask for their advice, he proceeded to describe the bill that he intended to submit to Congress the next day. The most striking characteristic of the proposal was its conservatism. Indeed, in formulating the measure Roosevelt and his advisers had collaborated with prominent bankers and with Treasury Department officials who remained from the Hoover administration. The bill allowed banks with liquid assets to reopen immediately with only a minimum of government supervision. It also empowered the comptroller of the Treasury to appoint "conservators" to reorganize unsound banks. Although the bill contained many technical and complicated provisions, it was clear that there would be no fundamental reform of the banking system. The dejected senators left the White House that evening without even having had the chance to outline their own recommendations.[3]

The next day La Follette attacked the bill on the Senate floor but failed miserably in his attempt to rally opposition. After listening restlessly to him and to a few other dissenters, the Senate passed the bill, 73 to 7, and sent it on to the White House where the president signed it that night.[4] Roosevelt had acted shrewdly. The stunning swiftness with which he dealt with the banking crisis brought an out-

3. RML to Hiram W. Johnson, 8 March 1933, RML and Edward P. Costigan to Franklin D. Roosevelt, 8, 9 March 1933, box 11-C, Family Papers; Frank Freidel, *Franklin D. Roosevelt: Launching the New Deal* (Boston, 1973), p. 226; Arthur M. Schlesinger, Jr., *The Age of Roosevelt: The Coming of the New Deal* (Boston, 1958), p. 5.

4. *CR* 73:1, 1933, vol. 77, pt. 1, pp. 63–65.

pouring of public support and caught opponents off guard, leaving them no time to ready concrete alternatives.

During the campaign Roosevelt had scolded Hoover for excessive government spending and had vowed that if elected he would slash spending and balance the budget. At the time, La Follette doubtless hoped that such talk was merely idle rhetoric employed by Roosevelt to ward off attacks from the Right. But Roosevelt intended to keep his pledge, and on 10 March he asked Congress for the power to reduce, or even eliminate, veterans' pensions and to reduce by up to 15 percent the salaries of all federal employees.

The economy bill, as it was called, ran counter to La Follette's plan to end the depression. He argued that it would further diminish mass purchasing power and that it would set a bad example for state and local governments and private industry, which would probably also cut wages. Although he did not mention it, and understandably so, he doubtless did not relish the prospect of having his own salary of approximately ten thousand dollars reduced, since he had debts to pay off and would have had to find an outside source of income, probably the despised lecture tour. During the Senate debate La Follette decried the "hysteria of this hour." Still reeling from the furious reaction that had followed his vote against the bonus bill the year before, La Follette took up the veterans' cause. To reduce pensions, he said, would be a "cruel injustice" that Congress and the nation would regret once they returned to "sanity." When it became clear that the bill would pass, La Follette tried to soften its impact by offering two amendments, one to reduce veterans' pensions by 15 percent, but no more; the other to exempt from the salary reduction government employees who earned one thousand dollars or less a year. Both amendments failed, and the Senate, after only two days of debate, approved the measure, 62 to 13.[5]

La Follette learned from these initial bouts with the administration that it was much harder to play the insurgent role under a popular president than it had been under the unpopular Hoover. "I realize," he wrote a friend, "that something akin to a war psychology has been created and that people generally are critical of all those who do not 'stand back of the President.'" Several Wisconsin newspapers came

5. Ibid., pp. 442–43, 466–68; *Progressive*, 25 March 1933; RML to Fola and George Middleton, 3 April 1933, box 41-A, Family Papers; on La Follette's personal finances, see income records in box 640-C, Family Papers. In 1932 he earned $13,373 from the following sources: Senate salary—$9,500; government travel allowance—$278; and lecture fees—$3,595.

out with editorials castigating La Follette's "obstructionist tactics."
Even some of his progressive colleagues seemed to be casting disapproving glances in his direction. For example, Norris, who had never
before buckled under to presidential discipline, felt that "regardless
of party, and regardless of every other consideration it seems to me
that every patriotic citizen should help [Roosevelt] in every way."[6]
Despite the pressures to back the president, La Follette held firm.
It seemed to him that the administration and the Congress had been
taking action merely for the sake of action, without thorough deliberation over the consequences.

La Follette's spirits lifted a bit when, on 21 March, Roosevelt sent
to the Congress his first message on the subjects of unemployment and
relief. The president urged Congress to take two steps immediately,
to create a civilian conservation corps that would employ five hundred thousand young men on conservation projects and to provide
direct relief grants to the states. Roosevelt also said that a broad program of public works would be part of his approach to unemployment
but that he was not yet prepared to submit a specific plan.[7]

Since the inauguration, La Follette had been working out the details of a relief bill with Secretary of Labor Frances Perkins, who in
turn had been consulting with relief experts, other senators, and members of the administration. On 27 March, a week after Roosevelt's
message, La Follette joined Senators Costigan and Wagner to introduce a relief bill. Except for a larger appropriation it was virtually
identical to the La Follette–Costigan measures of 1932. It authorized
$500 million in outright grants to the states for relief and created a
federal emergency relief administration to supervise relief activities.
With the administration behind it, the bill encountered little serious
opposition. The Senate passed it on 30 March by a vote of 55 to 17,
and the House concurred three weeks later, 326 to 42. "At last your
labors on behalf of unemployment relief have been rewarded," Felix
Frankfurter, of the Harvard Law School, wrote to La Follette. "Of
course it has been delayed too long, but that has not been your fault,
and that we have achieved what we have . . . is largely your accomplishment."[8]

6. RML to Thomas M. Duncan, 17 March 1933, box 10-C, unidentified newspaper clippings, box 664-C, Family Papers; Norris to Ellery Sedgwick, 1 May
1933, quoted in Freidel, *Launching the New Deal*, p. 305.

7. J. Joseph Huthmacher, *Senator Robert F. Wagner and the Rise of Urban
Liberalism* (New York, 1971), p. 139.

8. Freidel, *Launching the New Deal*, pp. 258–59; Schlesinger, *Coming of the
New Deal*, pp. 264–65; Felix Frankfurter to RML, 31 March 1933, box 74, Felix
Frankfurter Papers, Library of Congress, Washington, D.C.

La Follette experienced something of a letdown after the successful culmination of his two-year fight for relief legislation. When his sister Fola and her husband, George Middleton, congratulated him, he replied, "I am afraid that I do not get the satisfaction from its passage which you feel I should. . . . I have felt from the beginning . . . that it was unfortunate that one's energies should be absorbed on relief rather than in making a drive for a fundamental and far-reaching attack on the causes of the depression."[9] La Follette was right, of course: federal relief did deal with the symptoms of the depression and not with its causes. Yet, by providing millions of citizens money with which they could buy the basic necessities of life, relief funds definitely eased the desperate condition of the unemployed.

Another reason for his bleak mood was the administration's delay in revealing its promised public works program. "Just now," he wrote to Fola and Mid in April, "I feel that a decision of the administration upon the question of a gigantic program to stimulate recovery through re-employment is hanging in the balance." He explained that the cabinet was "divided on the issue and what the ultimate outcome will be no one can say. Those in the cabinet who are opposed to such a program cling to the theory which motivated . . . the Hoover administration, namely, that the balancing of the budget and the restoring of confidence are ends in themselves and will pave the way for the 'normal' forces of recovery to intervene." And he predicted that unless the administration moved quickly to expand public works, there would be "a sharp recession within the next two or three months which will create another crisis and one . . . more severe than any we have yet experienced."[10]

Still Roosevelt continued to hedge on the issue of public works. In mid-April, La Follette, Costigan, Cutting, and Wagner spent an hour with Roosevelt discussing the subject. "We all got the distinct impression," La Follette reported to a friend, "that he was committed to a large program to put people back to work and wanted us to formulate such a program as soon as possible." But then, only a few days later, Roosevelt, "without consultation with any of us . . . told the newspaper men that he had decided that there was not much to be accomplished by such a program. We are going ahead, however, in drafting a bill in case he changes his mind and comes to our theory again." Roosevelt's vacillation puzzled La Follette. "I cannot yet make out what the President is driving at," he confessed. But he

9. RML to Fola and George Middleton, 3 April 1933, box 41-A, Family Papers.
10. Ibid.

added perceptively, "My own impression is that he has no concerted plan and is prone to meet each situation as it arises in the way which seems best at the moment. With lots of luck this technique may prove effective." "However," La Follette explained, "it is so contrary to my own way of thinking and training that I find it difficult to be patient. It also seems to me clear that in a crisis of this gravity . . . the policy of leaping and looking afterwards may very easily prove disastrous."[11]

La Follette found some consolation in the actions the administration did take during the spring. He approved of Roosevelt's attempt to raise domestic prices by abandoning the international gold standard; he gave qualified support to the administration-sponsored Agricultural Adjustment Act, which sought to raise farm prices by paying farmers to limit production; and he was gratified by Roosevelt's whole-hearted support of the Tennessee Valley Authority Act, which established public control over the facilities producing electric power at Muscle Shoals. Throughout, however, La Follette warned that the New Deal was doomed to failure unless the administration moved to restore purchasing power by expanding public works.[12]

Finally, La Follette decided to force the administration's hand. On 8 May, without Roosevelt's approval, he, Cutting, and Costigan introduced a $6 billion public works bill. This action was just one symptom of the growing feeling in Congress that the president was moving too slowly in the area of industrial recovery. For a time it appeared that the administration had lost the initiative and that Congress, under the leadership of the progressives, was prepared to seize it.[13]

The administration rebounded in mid-May when it came forth with its national-industrial-recovery bill. This complex and wide-ranging measure contained three key provisions. The most important and controversial provision sought to bring order and planning to industrial affairs. It suspended the antitrust laws and permitted business firms in each industry to formulate "codes of fair competition," which prescribed minimum price levels, production quotas, and wage and hour levels for workers. Before the codes went into effect, the president had to approve them. A second provision, section 7(a), recognized the right of labor to organize and engage in collective

11. RML to Alfred T. Rogers, 20 April 1933, box 11-C, Family Papers.
12. Congressional Intelligence, Inc., pamphlet, "Your Congressman's Vote on the New Deal" (Washington, D.C., 1934).
13. *CR* 73:1, 1933, vol. 77, pt. 3, p. 2966; William E. Leuchtenburg, *Franklin D. Roosevelt and the New Deal, 1932–1940* (New York, 1963), pp. 55–57.

bargaining without interference from employers. And the third provision, a concession to La Follette and other advocates of public employment, appropriated $3.3 billion for public works.

La Follette had mixed feelings about the bill. He liked section 7(a) with its guarantees to labor; and although he considered the public works provision inadequate, it was at least a start in the right direction. But the section suspending the antitrust laws and allowing business to write codes posed a profound dilemma. Like his father and like most Western progressives, he had always advocated strict enforcement of the antitrust laws. Yet since the beginning of the depression, he had also emphasized the need for economic planning, the achievement of which, he sensed, was impossible under a system of unfettered industrial competition. La Follette regarded the decision of whether or not to support the recovery bill as one of the most important of his career. Passage of the bill, he wrote in the *Progressive*, would mark the end of an epoch. "Once we have entered upon this field of attempted government regulation of industry, we have crossed the Rubicon, and we shall never recross it."[14]

Torn by conflicting feelings, La Follette never did make up his mind. As the bill made its way through the Senate, he swayed one way, then the other. During the Finance Committee's deliberations on the bill, he voted down the line for the measure in its original form. He reported to Fola that at one point he even "pulled the industrial recovery bill out of the fire for the President" by persuading a swing-vote senator on the committee to back the administration on a crucial vote. He quickly added that he would never get credit for it and perhaps he would never want to receive credit for it.[15] For the most part he kept quiet during the floor debate, although he did succeed in attaching to the revenue section of the bill an amendment that opened income tax returns to the public. At the conclusion of the debate, he voted with the majority to pass the bill. Apparently he had decided to cross the Rubicon to economic planning.

Yet, when the bill returned from the House-Senate conference committee, he reversed himself and voted against it in final form. The conference committee had watered down his amendment for public disclosure of income tax returns, and that, he said, was the reason he could no longer support the bill.[16] That La Follette would vote against the entire measure because of a minor amendment to a peripheral

14. *Progressive*, 3 June 1933.
15. RML to Fola and George Middleton, 6 June 1933, box 41-A, Family Papers.
16. CR 73:1, 1933, vol. 77, pt. 6, pp. 5284, 5380–83, 5398–5403, 5764–68.

section of the bill was highly doubtful. Perhaps he was playing politics. If the recovery act succeeded in its objectives, he could always point to his affirmative vote when it first passed the Senate; if it failed, he could cite his final, negative vote. But more likely, La Follette's inconsistency reflected genuinely conflicting feelings. And in the end, he was not committed enough to the concept of planning to give this experiment his endorsement.

Nor was La Follette alone in his confusion. Other senators had similar shifts of opinion. Even supporters of the National Industrial Recovery Act were of two minds. On the one hand they argued that the NIRA was a step toward economic planning and that it would lead to a greater concentration in industry; on the other hand they said that the NIRA would not alter the free enterprise system and that it would not reduce competition in industry, but rather enhance it. Apparently everyone wanted the benefits of planning without sacrificing one iota of the old, competitive system.[17]

By June, Roosevelt had had time to decide who were his enemies and who were his friends. Huey Long of Louisiana was an enemy. In June, Roosevelt took the first step in his attempt to destroy Long politically by stripping him of federal patronage favors in Louisiana. Although La Follette had been just as critical of the administration as Long, albeit without the same bombast, and although La Follette had a voting record very similar to Long's, Roosevelt apparently held no grudges against La Follette. To the contrary, he seemed to go out of his way to stay on good terms with the Wisconsin senator. Early that month, he again indicated that he was anxious to find a spot for Phil in the administration.[18] Roosevelt also invited Bob to become a member of the American delegation to the upcoming London Economic Conference, which was to consider international monetary and tariff policies. La Follette declined, writing a friend that Roosevelt "was very considerate of my point of view, and accepted my decision in good spirit." Other people were not so considerate of his point of view. Several Wisconsin newspapers criticized him for refusing the president's call to duty, thus reminding him again of the perils of opposing or even seeming to oppose Roosevelt.[19]

17. Ellis W. Hawley, *The New Deal and the Problem of Monopoly* (Princeton, N.J., 1966), pp. 474–78.

18. T. Harry Williams, *Huey Long* (New York, 1969), pp. 636–37; RML to PFL, 1 June 1933, box 41-A, Family Papers.

19. *New York Times*, 30 May 1933; RML to Thomas R. Amlie, 29 May 1933, box 10, Thomas R. Amlie Papers, State Historical Society of Wisconsin, Madison; "Silencing Critics," *Appleton Post-Crescent*, 3 June 1933, and other editorials, box 664-C, Family Papers.

After the passage of the NIRA in mid-June, Congress recessed for the rest of the year. Nearly everyone agreed that the first hundred days of the Roosevelt administration had been the most exciting and, at least in terms of the sheer volume of legislation enacted, the most productive in history. In his assessment of the session for readers of the *Progressive*, La Follette found much to criticize. Yet he conceded that a start had been made toward improving the economic condition of the country. But he also warned that since Congress would not meet again until January 1934, everything depended on the administration's implementation of the various programs that Congress had set up during the hundred days.[20]

La Follette spent the summer in Wisconsin, then in the fall, in order to pay off family debts, he went on an extended lecture tour through the Middle West and West. All the while he kept a close watch on Washington. In July he became alarmed when he read newspaper reports indicating that Roosevelt's advisers were urging him to delay implementation of the public works program that Congress had authorized. By July factory production had increased dramatically, and some people in the administration believed, falsely as it turned out, that the nation was finally coming out of the depression and that public works were no longer necessary. La Follette dispatched an urgent telegram to the president emphasizing that a public works program was still "the principal hope for economic recovery." As for those people who thought the depression nearly over, "My answer is that these same men have held these same views at about six month intervals ever since the stock market crash." La Follette warned that "unless the farmers and workers are given purchasing power through public works to meet increased costs of living this period of hope will turn to one of the deepest despair." "In the name of these men and their wives and children," he concluded, "I appeal to you to act with that boldness which has endeared you to the people of this country."[21]

Roosevelt responded immediately, assuring La Follette that he had no intention of scuttling the public works program. And, as if to further mollify the Wisconsin senator, Roosevelt told him in the same letter that he was considering George C. Mathews, a Wisconsin progressive, for a seat on the newly created Securities and Exchange Commission. Months later Roosevelt appointed not only Mathews but also two other La Follette progressives to key posts in the government, David E. Lilienthal to a directorship on the Tennessee Valley

20. *Progressive*, 24 June 1933.
21. Telegram, RML to Roosevelt, 8 July 1933, box 11-C, Family Papers.

Authority and John J. Blaine to a directorship on the Reconstruction Finance Corporation.[22]

In the fall, while on an extensive speaking tour of the West, La Follette had further cause for alarm. "It is the same story everywhere I have been thus far," he wrote to his wife. "No action on public works, farm refinancing nor home loans. People are losing faith in the NRA and unless Roosevelt cuts loose on this recovery program and pumps out purchasing power and relief in other agencies my judgment is that his administration is going to fail tragically." La Follette also thought that he detected a swing to the Left in the public mood. As further evidence of this, he cited the victory of progressive Republican Fiorello La Guardia in the November mayoral contest in New York City. In that race, Postmaster General James A. Farley had thrown the support of the administration and the Democratic party behind La Guardia's Democratic opponent. The outcome delighted La Follette. "It confirms my judgment held right along," he wrote, "that if there is a reaction against Roosevelt it will not be back to reactionary-ism but to more fundamental progressivism than he is providing." La Follette also exclaimed gleefully that La Guardia's victory "ought to shrink down Mr. Farley's head size and I hope it will open the eyes of Mr. Roosevelt."[23]

The Washington to which La Follette returned for the 1934 session of Congress seemed different somehow. The ebullient optimism and the "we can do anything" spirit of the first hundred days had dimmed. People were beginning to realize that, despite all the dramatic actions of 1933, economic conditions remained deplorable. The most noticeable change was in Roosevelt, who, more than anyone else, set the tone in the capital. In 1933 his theme had been "action, and action now." In 1934 it seemed more like "retrenchment, and retrenchment now."

The first major issue of the new year concerned public works. In November 1933 Harry L. Hopkins, head of the Federal Emergency Relief Administration, had gone to Roosevelt with a complaint. Hopkins charged that the Public Works Administration (PWA), under the direction of Secretary of the Interior Harold L. Ickes, had been much too slow to set up works projects. After five months in operation, Hopkins pointed out, the PWA had employed less than one million out of an estimated ten to twelve million jobless. Hopkins persuaded

22. Telegram, RML to Roosevelt, 13 July 1933, President's Personal File 1792, Franklin D. Roosevelt Papers, Franklin D. Roosevelt Library, Hyde Park, New York. In the telegram RML summarized Roosevelt's letter.

23. RML to Rachel, 7, 8 November 1933, box 41-A, Family Papers.

Roosevelt to divert part of the money that Congress had appropriated for the PWA to a new agency under Hopkins's direction, the Civil Works Administration (CWA). In contrast to Ickes, Hopkins moved with lightning speed. By the middle of January 1934, he had pumped nearly $1 billion into the CWA and had provided jobs for over four million men and women. Although some people called it a "Santa Claus" handout program, by and large, the CWA was a spectacular success. It built highways, schools, airports, and other public buildings. The imaginative Hopkins also utilized the special skills of many of the unemployed by hiring thousands of out-of-work teachers, writers, and artists. During the winter of 1933–1934, there was a slight increase in production, particularly in consumer industries, that was almost certainly the result of CWA activities.[24]

La Follette liked the CWA and thought that it should be expanded. Thus, he was dismayed to learn that Roosevelt, in one of his budget-balancing moods, had decided to phase out the CWA as soon as possible. In words that would have gratified Herbert Hoover, Roosevelt told advisers that if the CWA were to continue much longer, it would "become a habit with the country. . . . We must not take the position that we are going to have permanent depression in this country, and it is very important that we have somebody to say that quite forcefully to these people."[25] Roosevelt picked an unhappy and reluctant Harry Hopkins to break the news. In February, Hopkins announced that the CWA would wind up its activities by 1 May. At the same time he asked Congress for $950 million to tide the fated agency over until the terminal date.

Defenders of the CWA, however, did not go down without a fight. In the Senate, Bronson Cutting offered an amendment appropriating $2 billion for the agency and thus extending it far beyond 1 May. La Follette sensed that more was at stake than just one particular agency. The administration, he felt, was challenging the whole concept of massive public works as a solution to the depression.

In support of Cutting's amendment, he delivered one of the most impressive and thoughtful speeches of his career. During the address he rehashed a lot of old arguments but also sounded a significant new theme. The speech presented the economic and historical theories behind the concept of public works and, as a whole, was an impressive defense of that concept.

24. Schlesinger, *Coming of the New Deal*, pp. 269–73; Leuchtenburg, *Roosevelt and the New Deal*, pp. 121–24; CR 73:2, 1934, vol. 78, pt. 11, pp. 11661–63.
25. Roosevelt to National Emergency Council, quoted in Leuchtenburg, *Roosevelt and the New Deal*, p. 122.

He began with a long and detailed analysis of the origins and causes of the depression. Unlike the panacea vendors of the 1930s, such as Sen. Huey Long and radio priest Charles Coughlin, both of whom peddled oversimplified analyses of causation with equally oversimplified solutions, La Follette stressed that the causes were many and complex. Nonetheless, he singled out two developments during the 1920s that, more than any others, led to the depression. The first development was a large increase in agricultural and industrial production that was primarily due to technological advances. The second development was an acceleration in the concentration of wealth and a resulting decline in mass purchasing power. Finally, he explained, by 1929 production exceeded the ability of people to consume to such an extent that industries were forced to curtail production, cut wages, and lay off workers. This further decreased mass purchasing power and plunged the nation into depression.

As evidence of the maldistribution of wealth, La Follette cited a study of wealth distribution that the Taylor Society of New York, a private economic study organization, had compiled. Using the amount of $100 to represent the total wealth of the population and the number 100 to represent the total population, the study determined that in 1929, before the crash, one individual had $59; a second individual, $9; twenty-two persons, $1.22 each; and seventy-six persons, only $0.07 each. La Follette pointed out that the problem with such an uneven distribution of wealth was that the majority of people, those at the bottom end of the income scale, simply could not afford to purchase enough goods to keep agriculture and industry functioning at high levels. Nor could the few persons at the top of the income scale consume enough goods to sustain mass production. For example, he said, if a wealthy individual "has 12 or 13 suits of clothes, if he has 9 or 10 pairs of shoes, 35 or 40 suits of silk underwear, 100 pairs of socks, 200 shirts, 350 neckties, 8 or 9 . . . overcoats, and 7 hats, we do not expect that individual to buy any more clothing or haberdashery in the near future."

Having established that sapped purchasing power was the root cause of the depression and the chief barrier to recovery, La Follette moved to the crucial part of his speech. He argued that the federal government was the only agency, and massive public works the only instrument, that could restore mass purchasing power and thus end the depression. Those people who thought otherwise, he said, were blind to the economic changes that had taken place since the last serious depression. The most fundamental change and "the most significant economic factor that confronts us today" was "the closing of the frontier in this country, together with the closing of the frontiers in other countries, due to the rising tide of economic nationalism." In the past, he claimed, an expanding frontier had provided inducement for businessmen to reinvest surplus capital into new or expanded enterprises, and it was this "reinvestment of private capital for capital-expenditure purposes that pulled us out of the depressions of the past." But now, with the frontiers closed, he argued, this process could no longer take place. "If we had $10 billion on the table here this afternoon," he said, "I would challenge senators to say where it could be reinvested by private investors for capital expenditure purposes with a hope of getting a return upon the investment." Thus, industry had expanded to its outer limits; by itself it could not expand further. La Follette argued that the federal government, in conjunction with local and state governments, must now provide funds for use in capital expenditure. This it could do through massive spending on public works.[26]

In the end La Follette's long analysis had little impact on most of his colleagues. The Senate overwhelmingly defeated Cutting's amendment to extend the CWA by a vote of 58 to 10. Harry Hopkins then dismantled the CWA as fast as he had set it up, and by the end of April the four million men and women who had worked in CWA projects were out of jobs and back on relief.[27] To La Follette, Roosevelt's attitude toward the CWA was a prime example of the inconsistency of the New Deal.

Aside from public works, no issue aroused La Follette's interest more than taxation. Since 1925 he had played an active role in every revenue debate, all the while learning more and more of the intricacies of tax law. By 1934 observers and colleagues, however much they might disagree with his views, generally regarded him as one of the handful of senators who had mastered the subject.[28] It therefore came as no surprise when in April, La Follette eagerly plunged into the Senate debate on taxation and, in the process, scored his major success of the session.

Two principles guided his thinking on taxation. "I contend," he said repeatedly, "that all history demonstrates that concentration of wealth such as has taken place in the United States is inimical to the perpetuity of democratic institutions." He believed that a genuinely

26. *CR* 73:2, 1934, vol. 78, pt. 2, pp. 2164–73.
27. Leuchtenburg, *Roosevelt and the New Deal*, pp. 123–24; Huthmacher, *Wagner*, pp. 156–57.
28. Frank Kent, "The Tail Wags the Dog," *Baltimore Sunday Sun*, 15 April 1934, clipping, box 664-C, Family Papers.

progressive tax structure, based on the ability to pay, was the most effective instrument for achieving an equitable distribution of wealth and thus preserving democracy. In 1934 La Follette stressed the second principle even more. The federal government, he believed, must always maintain its fiscal integrity and its credit rating. This did not mean that the government had to balance the budget, he was quick to add. It could no more balance the budget during a depression than it could during wartime: "In 1917 what Senator would have dared to rise on the floor of the Senate and suggest that we could not fight the war against Germany . . . because it would unbalance the Budget? The first thing we did during the war . . . was to unbalance the Budget $7 billion in the first few weeks." But the government, in order to maintain its credit, did have to display a willingness to pay off its debts. This, he explained, it could do in one of two ways: either by cutting spending or by raising taxes. Since massive spending was the only way to restore purchasing power and thus lift the country out of the depression, La Follette argued that the only alternative was to increase income, inheritance, and gift taxes along progressive or graduated lines. But La Follette also added that once the depression ended, the government could and should return to a balanced budget.[29]

La Follette believed that the administration-backed revenue bill that the House passed and sent to the Senate in April neither raised sufficient revenue nor placed enough of the tax burden on the wealthy. Having failed to amend the bill in the Finance Committee, he carried the fight to the Senate floor. First he tried to revise the income tax section of the bill. The House bill imposed a normal tax of 4 percent on the first four thousand dollars of individual net income; it imposed surtaxes ranging from a minimum of 4 percent on income in excess of four thousand dollars to a maximum of 59 percent on income over $1 million. La Follette proposed raising the normal tax to 6 percent. And he called for a surtax schedule that went from a minimum of 6 percent on incomes of four thousand dollars to a maximum of 71 percent on incomes over $1 million. If adopted, La Follette's amendment probably would have made the tax structure the most sharply graduated one in the nation's history, even exceeding the rates that had been in effect during World War I.[30] But its main purpose, he emphasized, was to raise revenue, $185 million in contrast to the $27 million of the House bill.

29. *CR* 73:2, 1934, vol. 78, pt. 6, pp. 5973–74.
30. Ibid., pp. 6086–87; Sidney Ratner, *American Taxation: Its History as a Social Force in Democracy* (New York, 1942), p. 465, table 3 in app.

In proposing the amendment, La Follette called the administration's bluff on the spending issue. He felt that if the administration was so concerned about excessive spending, as it had seemed to be in the CWA fight, then logically it should want the increased revenue that his amendment would bring in. But large tax increases, such as the one La Follette proposed, were sure to be unpopular; and since 1934 was an election year, administration Democrats answered to the logic of politics, not to the logic of economics. In the end, the Senate turned back the La Follette amendment, 47 to 36.[31]

After this initial setback, however, La Follette scored three impressive victories in rapid succession. First he won Senate acceptance of his sharply graduated estate tax schedule.[32] Then he managed to persuade the Senate to revise upward the rates on gift taxes. The resulting estate and gift tax schedules were the most sharply graduated in American history.[33]

La Follette's most surprising victory came when the Senate approved his amendment opening income tax returns to the public. In June 1933 he had gotten a similar amendment through the Senate, only to have the House-Senate conference committee revise it in such a way as to make it ineffective. The committee had raised the very valid objection that open returns infringed upon personal privacy. But in 1934 the Congress was more receptive when La Follette argued, first of all, that open returns would deter tax evasion and fraud and, secondly, concerning the privacy issue, that if a person had nothing to hide, he had nothing to fear from public disclosure. Congress and the public generally had come to suspect that wealthy individuals were escaping their fair share of the tax burden. Fueling these suspicions were the sensational disclosures of a recently concluded Senate probe into alleged misdeeds and machinations by Wall Street bankers. Among other things the investigation had revealed that twenty partners in the House of Morgan had failed to pay any income taxes for several years. In final form, the La Follette amendment required taxpayers to submit with their returns a pink slip listing their total gross income, total deductions, net income, total

31. *New York Times*, 6 April 1934.
32. The estate tax was the tax that the government levied on an estate upon the death of the owner. It differed from an inheritance tax in that it was levied on the estate before the estate was divided and passed on to the heirs. The La Follette amendement raised the maximum rate from 45 percent to 60 percent on portions of estates over $10 million.
33. *New York Times*, 6, 13 April 1934; Ratner, *American Taxation*, pp. 466–67, table 3 in app.; Roy G. Blakey and Gladys C. Blakey, *The Federal Income Tax* (London, 1940), pp. 364–65.

credits, and taxes paid. Failure to comply resulted in a five-dollar fine. Anyone could have access to another individual's pink slip simply by paying a small fee.[34]

La Follette's performance during the tax fight impressed many observers. They pointed out that he had rewritten key sections of the bill, a remarkable achievement for anyone, but especially for a member of a minority party. Columnist Frank Kent, who disagreed with La Follette's views on taxation, concluded that no matter how people felt about his philosophy, they had to admit that "there is no more effective man in the Senate."[35]

Encouraged by his success in the tax fight, La Follette again challenged the administration in June, this time over its failure to do anything about the increasingly urgent labor problem. Section 7(a) of the National Industrial Recovery Act had given new life to the labor movement. During the year following passage of the NIRA, labor organizers had made impressive gains; they even had managed to gain a foothold in such bastions of antiunionism as the automobile and steel industries. Yet, employer opposition to unions increased proportionately, and by 1934 many industries had launched all-out efforts to block any further labor gains. Some industries established employer-dominated company unions—"kiss me clubs" workers scornfully called them. Other industries were less discrete. They resorted to brute force, employing such techniques as espionage, stockpiling of munitions, and strikebreaking in order to block the growth of organized labor. As industrial conflict mounted, one thing became abundantly clear: section 7(a) was wholly inadequate as a guarantee of labor's right to organize. For one thing, it was too vague; it did not explicitly prohibit company unions or other antilabor devices. For another thing, it had failed to establish any effective machinery to protect labor rights.[36]

Early in 1934 La Follette began work on legislation to clarify and strengthen the labor guarantees of section 7(a).[37] Sen. Robert F. Wagner had the same idea, and La Follette, recognizing Wagner's

34. *CR* 73:2, 1934, vol. 78, pt. 6, pp. 6543–54; Blakey and Blakey, *Federal Income Tax*, p. 360.

35. Frank Kent, "The Tail Wags the Dog," *Baltimore Sunday Sun*, 15 April 1934, Frank Kent, "Little Bob's Battle," *Baltimore Sun*, 17 April 1934, clippings, box 664-C, Family Papers.

36. Irving Bernstein, *Turbulent Years: A History of the American Worker, 1933–1941* (Boston, 1969), chaps. 2–6 passim.

37. Edwin E. Witte to Professor Francis D. Tyson, 2 February 1934, box 1, Edwin E. Witte Papers, State Historical Society of Wisconsin, Madison.

expertise on the subject, left to the New York senator the actual task of drafting the legislation. On 1 March Wagner introduced into the Senate a labor-disputes bill designed to guarantee workers the right to organize and to choose their own representatives for collective bargaining.

Roosevelt and other administration spokesmen believed that the Wagner bill was too prolabor. They wanted a measure that would appease labor, but that at the same time would not alienate large segments of the business community, an impossibility given labor's demand for the guaranteed freedom to organize on the one hand, and business's almost complete opposition to unionization on the other. Under administration pressure, the Education and Labor Committee, to which the Wagner bill was referred, hacked away at key sections of the bill. The final product, although labor considered it inferior to the original, was still an improvement over section 7(a). Predictably, business leaders still adamantly opposed the bill. Roosevelt, fearing that business would retaliate by opposing the Democrats in the November elections, decided that Congress should postpone the whole issue until the following year. He then persuaded Wagner not to press for Senate consideration of his bill. In a last minute attempt to soothe the ruffled feelings of labor, Roosevelt submitted to Congress an innocuous resolution that would authorize him to set up a board to investigate controversies that arose between employers and employees as a result of section 7(a).[38]

In all his maneuvering Roosevelt had failed to take La Follette into account, and in the end the Wisconsin senator threatened to upset the administration's plan. On 16 June, when the Roosevelt resolution came up for debate in the Senate, La Follette proposed as a substitute the Wagner bill along with amendments that would restore it to its original form. Congress was scheduled to adjourn in two days, but La Follette, perhaps hinting at a filibuster, insisted that it should remain in session until it took action on the Wagner bill. Unless the bill passed, he warned, "we shall have the most serious labor conditions with which the United States has ever been confronted." Neither Wagner nor anyone else, he said, had presented "one sound reason why the Congress should not legislate upon one of the most important questions . . . that has confronted the Congress in recent years."

La Follette's bold move especially embarrassed Wagner, who had

38. The fate of the Wagner bill is discussed in Huthmacher, *Wagner*, pp. 160–71.

promised Roosevelt that he would delay action on his bill. Doubtless dreading the prospect of voting against his own bill, Wagner pleaded with La Follette to withdraw the substitute and promised him that action on that bill, or on an even better one, was certain in the next Congress. La Follette very reluctantly agreed. With the bill's author in opposition, there was no chance of passage. And anyway, La Follette had made his point. But before withdrawing his substitute, he could not resist taking a parting shot at the New York senator and through him at the administration. Turning to Wagner, he said, "I was not brought up 'to march up the hill and march down again.' So far as I know, I have never started a fight in this body and quit." La Follette then moved to amend the Roosevelt resolution to include a reaffirmation of the right of workers to "strike or engage in other concerted activities." The Senate, relieved at not having to confront the labor issue, unanimously accepted the amendment and the resolution.[39]

The heated debate over labor policy revealed La Follette's uncompromising combativeness. But it also served to point up another characteristic. Since the beginning of the depression, he had spoken out much more forcefully about the problems of urban workers than about the problems of farmers. Although he had authored numerous bills dealing with industrial unemployment, he had not offered any significant legislation that directly affected farmers. And, although he had voted for the Agricultural Adjustment Act and for other farm measures, he had done so with a notable lack of enthusiasm. La Follette deliberately subordinated the farm problem to the problem of urban unemployment. It would do no good, he said repeatedly, to artificially raise farm prices through inflation or production controls if urban workers, the chief consumers of farm products, could not afford to buy them. Thus, the only real solution to the agrarians' plight was to restore purchasing power to the urban masses.[40]

Economically, La Follette's reasoning was sound. Politically, it was perilous. He had to face reelection in the fall, and if enough farmers felt that he was neglecting their problems he might well go down to defeat. Warning signs had appeared already. In 1933 hundreds of Wisconsin dairy farmers had staged scattered strikes—withholding milk from market, blocking highways, and dumping milk by the roadside—all in an attempt to call the attention of politicians, includ-

39. *CR* 73:2, 1934, vol. 78, pt. 11, pp. 12044–45, 12027–29; *New York Times*, 17 June 1934; Huthmacher, *Wagner*, pp. 163–71.

40. *CR* 73:1, 1933, vol. 77, pt. 3, pp. 2520–22; *Progressive*, 29 April 1933.

ing La Follette, to their desperate plight. In 1933 Orland Loomis, a member of the Wisconsin legislature, reported to La Follette that many farmers were saying, "Yes, it is allright for Bob to support unemployment relief, but he isn't putting up the fight he ought to for inflation. . . . They insist that you are not radical enough." In 1934 Joseph D. Beck, a commissioner of the Wisconsin Department of Agriculture and Markets, also warned La Follette about agrarian discontent: "While I believe your efforts for legislation to get people back to work offers the only way to permanent relief, yet farmers, not acquainted with all the ins and outs of our economic situation . . . have been saying, 'Well, Bob is all right, but why doesn't he give us a little attention. We need it as well as the wage earners.'" Although no one predicted a full-scale revolt against La Follette's leadership, there was cause for concern.[41]

Understandably then, La Follette devoted more attention to farm problems during the 1934 session than he had for years. He did not abandon his position that farm recovery ultimately depended on recovery of the urban-industrial sector, but he did look for ways to reassure his agrarian constituents that he was concerned. In March he succeeded in tacking onto a minor farm bill an amendment appropriating $150 million in aid for cattlemen and dairy farmers. The largest part of the appropriation went toward the eradication of diseased cattle, particularly those infected with Bang's disease. The amendment also authorized the government to purchase dairy and beef products and to distribute them to people on relief. Toward the end of the session, La Follette had another opportunity to perform a service for farmers. During the spring and early summer, a devastating drought hit three-fourths of the country, including Wisconsin. One observer painted a graphic portrait of conditions: "Vegetation refuses to grow. Streams have stopped running. . . . Trees, with leaves blighted, shriveling and falling with every gust of furnace hot air, produce little or no shade. Cattle, starved for proper nourishment, refuse to put on flesh." La Follette spent weeks traveling through the state, observing conditions, talking with farmers, and assuring them that he would do everything possible to bring them government aid. True to his word, in June he pushed through the Senate a bill that made $500 million available to drought victims. By the time

41. A. William Hoglund, "Wisconsin Dairy Farmers on Strike," *Agricultural History* 35 (1961): 24–34; Loomis to RML, 24 April 1933, box 5, Orland S. Loomis Papers, State Historical Society of Wisconsin, Madison; Beck to RML, [spring 1934], box 11-C, Family Papers.

Congress adjourned in mid-June, La Follette had repaired the political fences in the agrarian districts of his home state.[42]

Also by that time he had firmed up his position on the leftward periphery of the New Deal. La Follette still supported Roosevelt's leadership, and he said that if he had it to do over again, he would still have endorsed Roosevelt in 1932. Nor did he have any basic objection to many of the actions that Roosevelt had taken during the past fifteen months. He just thought that even the best of those actions had not gone far enough. Thus, he criticized the administration for its timidity on spending for public works, on labor policy, on tax reform, and on many other specific issues. Above all La Follette attacked the administration for its inconsistent approach to the depression. He had identified declining purchasing power as the root cause of the crisis, and he had formulated a coherent plan for combating it. The administration, he thought, should do likewise. He was fond of comparing Roosevelt to a general in war who had decided upon the impossible course of fighting both a defensive war and an offensive war at the same time.[43]

In one important respect, however, La Follette closely resembled Roosevelt and most other New Dealers. Like them, he offered no fundamental challenge to the basic structure of capitalism, even though at times he appeared to be on the brink of repudiating its ability to remain viable. "Our economic system has failed," he said often. But then he quickly pulled back. It was not so much the economic system that had failed but the politicians in charge. "The disaster of 1929 and the acute distress and suffering of the American people that followed," he declared in May 1934, "were made possible by the betrayal of the people's trust by men in both parties, controlled through their party organizations by privileged interests. This catastrophe could have been avoided. It could not have occurred if the people of this country had been provided with party machinery responsive to their needs." Thus, while Marxists and other radicals saw the depression as an inevitable product of capitalism, La Follette viewed it as the avoidable result of political mischief. At other times La Follette did indeed argue that some fundamental changes were needed in the economic structure. But he was always vague about the nature of these changes, and he argued that in any event they should not take place until the nation had recovered from the depression. One time, while he was giving a speech in Boston, several so-

42. CR 73:2, 1934, vol. 78, pt. 4, p. 4073; Doan, *Wisconsin Idea*, pp. 175–76; *Progressive*, 9 June 1934.
43. CR 73:2, 1934, vol. 78, pt. 11, pp. 11661–63, 11668.

cialists in the audience kept interrupting. Finally, La Follette stopped and addressed himself to the socialists. "I admit that the house is on fire," he said in reference to capitalism, "but not until the fire is put out will I argue what is to be done, and then I shall argue."[44] His emphasis on recovery rather than on fundamental reform set him even further apart from the radicals of the time, who believed that the depression afforded an opportunity to erect a new economic system from the bottom up.

Although La Follette was vague about what long-term changes were needed in the economy, he dropped abundant hints about what changes he did not desire. Socialism, for example, was clearly out. When he talked of socialism he tended to equate it with "disorganization" and "mob rule." In that same Boston speech, he also said that "socialization of any country disregards the people who are living now, and he for one was not willing to disregard the living for an unknown future." La Follette's attitude toward collectivism was more complex. The chief proponent of collectivism in Washington was Rexford G. Tugwell, a Roosevelt adviser, an undersecretary of agriculture, and a close personal friend of La Follette. Tugwell wanted to do away with a highly competitive, individualistic society in favor of a cooperative commonwealth in which everyone worked together for common goals. He viewed the centralizing trends in industry as a positive good. He advocated national economic planning whereby the government, with the public good as its foremost consideration, would make the major economic decisions. Tugwell believed that La Follette agreed with him. "Bob La Follette," he later wrote, "of all the progressives of that time, had made the most complete transition to modernism. He had become a collectivist by hard thinking and in the course of political experience in a tough school."[45] La Follette may have approached collectivism at times but he never embraced it. Even though he talked of the need for planning, his only concrete proposal had been the national economic council, a far cry from the type of planning mechanism Tugwell desired. Moreover, the way in which he agonized over the NIRA and his final vote against it revealed his hesitancy to endorse the planning concept. Perhaps in private conversations with Tugwell he indicated that he shared Tugwell's views. If so, he declined to state those views to others, either publicly or privately.

Basically, La Follette was skeptical of any theories of compre-

44. *Progressive*, 26 May 1934; account of Boston speech in *Boston Post*, reprinted in *Progressive*, 22 December 1934.
45. Tugwell, *Democratic Roosevelt*, p. 220.

hensive change. Americans, he said, wanted results, not theories. "During the present economic crisis there has been a tendency to oversimplify problems and to assume that our economic ills will be solved automatically if we . . . only adopt some new 'system.' "[46] In part La Follette meant this as a warning against any simple panaceas or cure-all formulas, whether they be socialism, collectivism, or Huey Long's "share our wealth" scheme. In part, too, it was a view that meshed with his intellectual temperament. One reason La Follette chose to delay discussion of the necessary permanent restructuring of the economy was that he was intellectually unsuited to the type of disciplined, painstaking thought that such a process would entail. Although he was more of an intellectual than many of his colleagues, he still found little pleasure in speculative thinking over extended periods. And even if he had been so inclined, the press of events left him little time. By mid-1934 he was already in the process of founding a new party.[47]

46. *Progressive*, 25 April 1936, cited by Theodore Rosenof, "'Young Bob' La Follette on American Capitalism," *Wisconsin Magazine of History* 55 (Winter 1971–1972): 135.

47. Rosenof, "'Young Bob' La Follette on American Capitalism," pp. 130–39, is a good critical analysis of La Follette as an economic thinker.

CHAPTER 8

Founding the Progressive Party

Nineteen thirty-four was a year of political turbulence. Huey Long founded the "share our wealth" movement, then he alarmed liberals and conservatives alike by attracting millions of supporters; a sixty-seven-year-old California doctor, Francis Townsend, organized millions of elderly citizens in a crusade for old-age pensions; forty million listeners tuned in weekly to hear radio priest Charles Coughlin offer his latest cure-all for the depression; novelist Upton Sinclair excited thousands of Californians with his End Poverty in California movement and his "production for use" platform; and Minnesota's Farmer-Labor governor, Floyd Olson, on his way to a smashing reelection victory in November, boasted, "You bet your life I'm a radical. You might say I'm radical as hell." It was the fifth year of depression with no end in sight. In increasing numbers, people reached out, desperately it seemed at times, to anyone who could promise relief. They also began to ask disturbing questions, chief among them being whether the traditional two-party system offered any hope for the future.[1]

Nowhere was the ferment more evident than in Wisconsin. There, in May 1934, progressives condemned the two major parties, bolted the GOP, and set up a party of their own. In November, just six months after its birth, the new party triumphed at the polls. Bob La Follette won reelection to the Senate; his brother Phil recaptured the governorship; and scores of progressives emerged victorious from state and local races.

In terms of things personal, the political turmoil markedly tormented Young Bob's sensitive, peace-loving, self-doubting soul. All this was apparent in the Hamlet-like vacillation he exhibited on the question of whether there should be or should not be a third party. Initially La Follette opposed the idea. Then, as the movement picked up momentum, he retreated to a position of indecision. Only when the establishment of a third party seemed almost certain, with or without

1. William E. Leuchtenburg, *Franklin D. Roosevelt and the New Deal, 1932–1940* (New York, 1963), pp. 95–117; Olson quoted in William Manchester, *The Glory and the Dream: A Narrative History of America, 1932–1971* (Boston, 1973), pp. 101–2.

him, did he lend his support, and then with noticeable reluctance. For all his marked superiority as a United States senator, Young Bob La Follette definitely was not a leader of movements.

Although before 1934 there had been recurrent rumors about a third party in Wisconsin, there had been no action. Following his defeat in the 1924 presidential contest, the elder La Follette committed himself to building a national party on a state-by-state basis, starting with Wisconsin.[2] His death in 1925, however, halted the momentum. For several years thereafter, Young Bob was too busy making his way in the Senate to give much thought to the matter. Moreover, he and Phil had enough trouble holding the old progressive coalition together without taking on the additional problems of leading a third-party movement. Nor was there any appreciable sentiment for a new party among state progressives. Old Bob's disastrous campaign in 1924 had probably convinced most of them that it would be suicidal to venture outside the familiar confines of the GOP.

The 1932 elections, however, forced progressives to reconsider. Phil La Follette and Sen. John J. Blaine lost in the Republican primary, and most observers blamed their defeats on the resurgence of the state's Democratic party and the defection of progressive voters to Democratic primary races. Many progressive office seekers feared for the future. With the liberal vote divided between the Republican and Democratic primaries, Republican progressives would have a difficult, if not impossible, task gaining nomination. Even if they did succeed, they would then have to face another grueling, money-consuming campaign against the Democrats in the general election. For these reasons, many progressives concluded that it would be suicidal not to leave the GOP.[3]

Phil was one of the first to reach that conclusion. In a July 1933 letter to his sister Mary and her husband, Ralph Sucher, he expressed his opinion that if Bob ran for reelection as a Republican in 1934, he would probably be defeated. Phil saw two alternatives, joining the Democrats or forming a third party. "I think Bob could be nominated and elected in the Democratic party," he said, but "the great question would be the ultimate result in going to bed with that organization." Like most progressives, he considered Wisconsin Democrats to be as reactionary as the regular Republicans. He might have added that

2. Belle Case La Follette and Fola La Follette, *Robert M. La Follette* (New York, 1953), 2:1156–58.
3. Roger T. Johnson, *Robert M. La Follette, Jr. and the Decline of the Progressive Party in Wisconsin* (Madison, 1964), pp. 27–29.

the Democrats, who had waited so long for their moment in the sun, would hardly welcome an influx of opportunistic progressives. Phil conceded that a third party would be a "gamble" but left no doubt that that was the course he favored. Although he saw a third party as a means for political survival, he also dreamed of making it the nucleus of a national organization. In this and subsequent comments about the third party, Phil conspicuously left himself out of the picture. He doubtless realized that a third party would provide a vehicle for his own ambitions, but he wanted to give the appearance of having only the future of his brother and of other progressives at heart. Having decided on the desirability of a third party, Phil now had to sell his brother on the idea.[4]

Bob did not buy it. Unlike Phil, he feared that a third party would jeopardize his reelection chances, since he thought that voters were too entrenched in the two-party habit to accept a change as soon as 1934. He also feared that bolting the Republican party would adversely affect his position in the Senate, especially his committee assignments. After nine years in office, he had climbed high on the seniority ladder and held seats on several key committees; and he dreaded the prospect of starting all over again, as his father had had to do after the 1924 campaign. In addition, his cautious nature held him back. "I sense your desire for action," he wrote Phil in October 1933, "and yet all my training leads me to want to know where we are going before we leap." Bob was not alone. Many older progressive leaders felt a deep commitment to the Republican party and were reluctant to abandon it. Then too, the few progressive officeholders who had survived the disaster of 1932, chief among them being Secretary of State Theodore Dammann, felt no practical need to leave the GOP.[5]

Bob's opposition placed his brother in an awkward position. Phil did not want to break openly with Bob, nor did he want to fuel the frequently circulated rumor that he was trying to push Bob in new directions for his own political gain. Phil therefore decided to assume

4. PFL to Ralph and Mary Sucher, 9 July 1933, box 135–2, PFL Papers (see list of abbreviations p. x); Bronson Cutting to H. Phelps Putnam, 3 October 1933, PFL to Bronson Cutting, 19 October 1933, box 10, Bronson Cutting Papers, Library of Congress, Washington, D.C.

5. Johnson, *La Follette, Jr.*, pp. 30–32; Mrs. PFL, "Isen's Political Diary," 21 June 1934, p. 6, box 161-3, PFL Papers; RML to PFL, 18 October 1933, quoted in Johnson, *La Follette, Jr.*, p. 32; Thomas R. Amlie to Alfred Bingham, 7 November 1933, box 10, Thomas R. Amlie Papers, State Historical Society of Wisconsin, Madison; Edward N. Doan, *The La Follettes and the Wisconsin Idea* (New York, 1947), p. 180.

a neutral stance in public. However, he decided that in private he would continue to pressure Bob and to encourage the third-party movement.[6]

During the winter of 1933–1934 the third-party movement gathered momentum and also took on an ideological hue. Most of the politicians who clamored for a new party did so out of expediency; quite simply, they did not think they could win elections as Republicans. But when the Farm Holiday Association and the Wisconsin Milk Pool, which had led the milk strikes of 1933, endorsed the movement, a new dimension was added. Members of these militant farm organizations wanted a genuine alternative to the two existing parties. "The Republican party," said one farm leader, "has done nothing for the farmer and hasn't a ghost of a chance in the next election."[7] Farmers expressed similar sentiments about the state's Democratic party, since the Democratic legislature and the Democratic governor, Albert G. Schmedeman, had done little if anything to ease the agrarian plight. Moreover, during the milk strikes Schmedeman had incensed farmers by calling out the National Guard to restore order. Support from organized labor further altered the complexion of the movement. Henry Ohl, Jr., president of the Wisconsin Federation of Labor, and Joseph Padway, federation attorney, called for creation of a Farmer-Labor party.[8]

With Phil La Follette temporarily confined to the sidelines, leadership of the third-party effort in the early stages fell into the eager hands of ex-congressman Thomas R. Amlie. Thirty-six years old, the son of a North Dakota farmer, and a graduate of the University of Wisconsin Law School, he had served one term in the House of Representatives before going down to defeat in 1932. Amlie had hopes of regaining his old House seat or possibly even running for governor. Like other progressives, he pinned his hopes on a third party. More significant, however, Amlie wanted nothing less than to lead the third party down the path to revolution.

Of all the Wisconsin progressives Amlie was probably the only genuine radical. His intellectual heroes were Thorstein Veblen and Karl Marx, and by 1933 he had concluded that capitalism was "no longer worth saving." "In my opinion," he said in July of that year, "when the Roosevelt plan fails we will have no alternative but to demand a complete socialization of all productive machinery." Amlie

6. Amlie to John R. Retzer, 9 November 1934, box 12, Amlie Papers.
7. Quoted in Doan, *Wisconsin Idea*, p. 179.
8. Ibid., pp. 178–79; Johnson, *La Follette, Jr.*, p. 30.

believed that a revolution, probably a violent one, would be necessary to overthrow capitalism.[9]

Beginning in the fall of 1933, Amlie set about paving the way for "the revolution." In October, along with a group that included Selden Rodman, editor of the radical journal *Common Sense*, Amlie founded the Young America movement. According to Rodman, this organization was to be a "militant radical youth movement" that would organize young people for political action. Amlie, however, had broader objectives in mind. "In a figurative sense, (if not in an actual sense) this group must be the storm troopers," he said. His use of the phrase *storm troopers* was deliberate. "We have more to learn from the methods of organization used by fascists than we have to learn from any other group," Amlie explained and added, "First, because these methods are highly efficacious; and secondly, if we are realistic, we will not let those methods lie around unused, for sure as shooting the capitalists will organize and finance a fascist movement that will immediately pick up all of these weapons and use them to our great sorrow."[10]

Amlie thought that the youth movement would provide leaders for the revolution, but he also believed that something had to be done to organize the rank and file. And this was where the third party came in. "It seems to me," he wrote in November 1933, "that conditions are ripe at the present time for a third party movement, having for its objective: the bringing together of the farmers and the laborers on common ground." Third parties, he thought, should organize on a state-by-state basis, then eventually merge into a national organization. Amlie realized that the average man was most concerned with immediate problems. "The farmer is interested in securing cost of production so that he may preserve his status as an individual capitalist. The laborer is interested in jobs and economic security. Obviously, these demands cannot be met by a contracting capitalism. But the great mass of the farmers and the laborers do not understand this." Moreover, "the average American carries the tradition of the frontier with him. He does not think of himself as a member of the proletariat. While the slogan, 'Workers Unite' may have real meaning on the Continent, it leaves the American working

9. Amlie to Parley P. Christenson, 18 October 1933, Amlie to Professor Charles Dietz, 18 July 1933, Amlie to L. G. Scherer, 9 October 1933, box 10, Amlie Papers.

10. Selden Rodman to Amlie, October 1933, Amlie to Goodwin Watson, 17 November 1933, Amlie to Selden Rodman, 30 October 1933, box 10, Amlie Papers.

man and farmer singularly unmoved. He does not think of himself as a worker. He thinks of himself as a doer of things." Therefore, Amlie thought, in order to gather support, third parties must offer "rather anomalous" programs with emphasis on immediate problems and short-term goals. "The appeal . . . must be middle class, rather than proletarian."[11]

Amlie was convinced, however, that once farmers and workers were organized into a third party, they would see the light and act accordingly. "In this respect we are proceeding on the theory of the U. S. Government during the war. The government did not try to put the fighting spirit into the drafted boys. They knew that if they put them in the front line trenches with a gun, with the enemy shooting at them from the other side, that there would be no necessity of telling them what to do." Amlie thought that organizing a Farmer-Labor party would bring the same result. He saw yet another advantage to the third-party movement. The "vested interests," he predicted, would fight to resist any revolutionary movement. They "could hire any number of young men to do their fighting for them at the rate of $1.00 a day." But if Farmer-Labor parties managed to gain control of state governments, "you have the national guard and the machine guns on your side. It is only a matter of detail to have the whole organization function 100% for your plan."[12]

Most people probably remained unaware of Amlie's revolutionary motives for establishing a third party, since he wisely confined talk of storm troopers and machine guns to private correspondence with like-minded comrades. Still, in public pronouncements he left no doubt that he favored radical economic and social changes and that he considered a third party a vehicle for achieving those changes. Many people thought that Amlie was an intelligent, eminently rational spokesman of radicalism. This belief was evident in an assessment of Amlie by Sylvester W. Muldowney, a close personal friend of Bob La Follette: "I must admit that I am inclined to agree with [Amlie's] thesis that the capitalistic system is not worth saving because the bozos running it seem to be so impervious to the changing events taking place all about them." Muldowney was chairman of the board of the National Union Radio Corporation.[13]

The third-party movement under Amlie's leadership threatened

11. Amlie to Goodwin Watson, 17 November 1933, box 10, Amlie Papers.
12. Amlie to Goodwin Watson, 17 November 1933, Amlie to L. G. Scherer, 9 October 1933, box 10, Amlie Papers.
13. Sylvester W. Muldowney to RML and Rachel, 8 November 1933, box 41-A, Family Papers.

the La Follette brothers' continued dominance of the state's progressive organization. By early 1934 it appeared likely that a third party would form, with or without the brothers' support. It also appeared possible that Amlie would lead the movement in a direction entirely unsatisfactory to them.

Time was running out for the La Follettes, and no one realized it more than Bob. But he found himself helpless to act. At times he appeared on the verge of changing his mind and backing the movement; at other times he was as opposed as ever. On 15 February 1934 he wrote to his father's old law partner and trusted adviser, Alfred T. Rogers, "I confess that I find the decision a difficult one to make, although it seems to me that the logic of the situation tends strongly in favor of a new party movement." The very next day, however, he wrote his brother that he had considered all of the arguments in favor of a third party but still had doubts about "the practical aspects of the situation."[14]

Part of his problem stemmed from the fact that he continued to receive conflicting advice from those whose advice he trusted. Republican colleagues in the Senate, like Charles L. McNary of Oregon and Arthur H. Vandenberg of Michigan, urged him to stay in the GOP. His closest friends in Wisconsin were older men who had been active in the progressive movement since the days of his father, and they too advised against a third party. For example, Alf Rogers warned Bob of "menacing obstacles and grief galore in attempting to bring a new party into being in Wisconsin next campaign." Unfortunately for La Follette, by this time old-timers like Rogers were out of touch with the younger progressives who had emerged since the days of progressive glory. On the other hand, Phil continued to press for a third party. And late in February, La Follette received another opinion in favor of it, this time from a most unexpected source, President Roosevelt. The president told him that, although he wanted La Follette to win reelection, he hesitated to say so publicly for fear of offending Wisconsin Democrats. Roosevelt added, however, that if La Follette ran as a third-party candidate rather than as a Republican, Roosevelt would be in a better position to extend a public endorsement.[15] With all the conflicting advice, La Follette found it impossible to make up his mind. In the end he decided to leave the decision to others.

14. RML to Alfred T. Rogers, 15 February 1934, box 12-C, Family Papers; RML to PFL, 16 February 1934, quoted in Johnson, *La Follette, Jr.*, p. 32.
15. RML to Rogers, 15 February 1934, box 12-C, RML to PFL, 27 February 1934, box 41-A, Family Papers.

Late in February, Bob La Follette, Theodore Dammann, and Herman L. Ekern invited county leaders from throughout the state to meet in Madison to discuss the third-party issue. On Saturday morning, 3 March, over four hundred progressives answered the summons, crowding into the ballroom of the Park Hotel. La Follette delivered the major address. The decision as to a third party, he told the delegates, was up to them. He would abide by it either way. Third-party enthusiasts, who were in the vast majority, breathed a sigh of relief. "While Bob was not so obviously pro third party, he nevertheless put no obstacles in the path of such movement," a relieved Thomas Amlie wrote a friend. The assembly probably would have voted then and there to establish a new party had it not been for an uncertain legal situation. Some doubt remained as to whether Wisconsin law would permit third-party candidates to appear on the ballot in the 1934 election. The conference adjourned to await a ruling from the state supreme court.[16]

The court gave the go-ahead on 1 May, and progressive leaders immediately made plans for a convention to meet later that month. As convention day approached, Bob La Follette seemed as nervous as a bridegroom on the eve of his wedding. Troubling questions were probably racing through his mind: Should he have followed his own instincts and spoken out against the idea at the March convention? Could he go through with the third party? A few friends who were opposed to the idea, like Theodore Dammann, only added to his doubts. They kept telling him there was little support among Wisconsin voters for a third party.[17] But the time for turning back had long since passed.

On Saturday, 19 May, progressives held a daylong convention in Fond du Lac. After sitting through a dull welcoming speech by William Mothe, a casket manufacturer in the hosting city, the delegates, as expected, voted to establish a new party by a lopsided tally of 252 to 44. Later in the day Young Bob addressed the convention. If the delegates hoped for a rousing call to action they were disappointed. Instead he proceeded to outline the causes of the depression, review the policies of the Roosevelt administration, and then, with some hedging, state the rationale for the third party. At one point he said that he was "in complete accord with" the convention's decision. He added, "I believe the necessity for a new party exists."

16. Johnson, *La Follette, Jr.*, pp. 33–34; Amlie to Howard Y. Williams, 5 March 1934, box 11, Amlie Papers.
17. RML to PFL, 11 May 1934, box 41-A, Family Papers.

It was clear to at least some of the delegates that La Follette did not fully believe his own words.[18]

The only flurry of excitement during the proceedings came when delegates wrangled over the party name. Labor and farm leaders, socialists, and Tom Amlie and his followers favored *Farmer-Labor* as a name. They chose that label to emphasize the class, or group, basis of the party and, more importantly, to stress that the party was a radical departure not only from the policies of the Republicans and Democrats but also from the worn-out progressivism of the past.[19] The La Follette brothers wanted to stick with the traditional designation of *Progressive*. The acrimonious debate that ensued revealed that more was at stake than a name. As Phil La Follette's wife, Isen, noted, "Any aware observer could see that certain elements were trying to undermine the La Follette leadership and run away with the new party." Labor leaders Henry Ohl, Jr., and Jack Handley argued that adoption of the *Farmer-Labor* name was the best way to attract the support of organized labor. If workers got the impression that the party was "merely to be the old Progressive office-seekers under a new name," Ohl and Handley warned, they would not back it. Phil La Follette, who had remained in the background for most of the proceedings, arose to deliver an impassioned defense of the name *Progressive*. "We have had 25 years' education under the Progressive name," he pointed out. "I am convinced that the great bulk of our people are not farmers first or laborers first—we must appeal to them as Americans, and not . . . on the basis of their occupation." "For whatever my judgment is worth," he concluded, "I think it is a fatal error, an irretrievable blunder, to launch this as a class party." The La Follettes had their way. By a vote of 236 to 41, the convention adopted the Progressive label.[20]

By the end of the day, progressives had their new party, and they had the La Follette brothers' promise to lead it. But some of the delegates left bitterly disappointed. "The convention," grumbled Tom Amlie, "was entirely in the hands of the old Progressive office-holding and office-seeking group, who are really not in favor of doing much of anything, except that which is necessary in order to get elected

18. *Progressive*, 26 May 1934; Johnson, *La Follette, Jr.*, pp. 34–35.

19. Amlie to Alfred M. Bingham, 2 May 1934, box 11, Amlie Papers; Philip F. La Follette, *Adventure in Politics: The Memoirs of Philip La Follette* (New York, 1970), pp. 210–11.

20. Mrs. PFL quoted in PFL, *Memoirs*, p. 211; Ohl and Handley paraphrased in Amlie to Alfred Bingham, 21 May 1934, box 11, Amlie Papers; *Progressive*, 26 May 1934.

to office." Fred S. Gram, editor of a Racine labor newspaper, reported widespread dissatisfaction. "The general feeling is, so far as I can find out, that the organized farmers and organized workers were betrayed by the conference. They went expecting a radical party to be organized. They got, instead, some more old-time La Follette progressivism." Gram quoted one militant farm leader as saying that "farmers would never leave their plows to vote for the progressives."[21]

In the weeks following the convention, disgruntled progressives, under Amlie's leadership, formed the Farmer Labor Progressive League. According to Amlie, the purpose of the league was to "further our ideas within the Progressive party." At the end of June the league held a convention in Fond du Lac. The La Follettes feared that the convention would adopt a radical platform and send candidates into the primary to challenge the other progressives. Phil spoke to the gathering and pleaded for unity. His appeal was effective, and the delegates announced their support of the Progressive party and endorsed Young Bob's candidacy.[22]

The La Follettes further subdued the left wing when they unveiled their long-awaited platform. Although the document, especially the statement of principles, fell short of what Amlie and his followers wanted, it was far-reaching enough to ensure support from even the most militant farm and labor groups. "Our economic system has failed," it stated boldly at the outset. "In the midst of an abundance of everything we suffer from widespread and continued poverty and insecurity." But then, in typical La Follette fashion, the platform suggested that the depression was not so much the fault of the system as the fault of the "reactionaries" in charge. The solution to the depression, it implied, was not structural reform of the economy but political reform. "We must have a political realignment that will place the exploiting reactionary on the one side and the producer, consumer, independent business and professional interests on the other."

Most of the planks dealt with national issues. The first plank echoed the demands of the Milk Pool and the Farm Holiday Association. It declared that the government should guarantee the farmer a profit on his investment, but it did not explain how this was to be accomplished. For industrial workers, the platform declared that if private employment failed, the government should provide jobs for everyone willing and able to work. Furthermore, the government should out-

21. Amlie to Howard Y. Williams, 28 May 1934, Fred S. Gram to Howard Y. Williams, 20 May 1934, box 11, Amlie Papers.
22. Amlie to John Girman, 4 June 1934, Howard Y. Williams to Amlie, 23 May 1934, box 11, Amlie Papers; PFL, *Memoirs*, p. 212.

law company unions and guarantee labor's right to organize without employer interference. One plank called upon the federal and state governments to launch a variety of welfare programs: unemployment insurance, old-age pensions, accident insurance, and financial aid to homeowners. Another plank supported a "government-owned central bank which will make the monopoly of credit in private hands impossible." The platform also included traditional progressive demands: tax reform; public ownership of utilities, especially electricity; government ownership of munitions industries "so that none will prosper from slaughter"; and public approval through a referendum before the United States could enter another war.[23]

Before opening the campaign, a final task remained: finding a candidate for governor. This would have posed no problem had it not been for Bob. Most progressive leaders thought Phil the obvious choice. He had served one term as governor, was an experienced vote getter, bore the magic name, and had supported the third party from the beginning. Despite his frequent denials, everyone knew that he was more than eager to run. Bob, however, opposed his brother's candidacy because he thought that voters might rebel at "too much La Follette" and send both of them down to defeat. He probably also felt that people might come to think of the Progressive party as the La Follette party, a vehicle for the brothers' selfish ambitions.[24]

Phil appeared to accept Bob's decision in good spirits. He told his wife that he agreed with his brother's reasoning and that "under *no* circumstances" would he "encourage, directly or indirectly, any 'boom'" for himself. Those close to Phil La Follette knew better; he wanted the governorship and he wanted it badly. They knew also that the relationship between the brothers could never again be quite as close as it had been.[25] First there had been Bob's nearly disastrous delay in supporting the third party. And now this. Phil's burning ambition must have compelled him to ask himself why it was he rather than Bob who always had to sacrifice his ambition and his future.

This time, as it turned out, Phil did get what he wanted. For over a month, Bob conducted an exhaustive search for an acceptable candidate. He could find none. Finally, reluctantly, he turned to Phil.

By midsummer the La Follette brothers held firm control over the Progressive party. But privately Bob still doubted the wisdom of the whole venture. For one thing, the task of launching a new party

23. Progressive Platform of 1934, *Progressive*, 6 October 1934.
24. PFL, *Memoirs*, pp. 211–12; Johnson, *La Follette, Jr.*, p. 36.
25. PFL to Mrs. PFL, 5 July 1934, box 135-2, PFL Papers; interview, Gordon Sinykin, August 1972.

turned out to be every bit as hard as he had feared. He had to plan his campaign, help plan Phil's, and coordinate campaign strategy for all Progressive candidates. These things required endless rounds of meetings with local leaders and intensive attention to detail. As Phil's wife, Isen, told it, one day Bob quarreled with a group of leaders because they would not follow his advice concerning campaign strategy. Bob threw up his hands in disgust and threatened to "get out of politics." Observed Isen, "It was obvious to me that Bob shuns the rough and tumble scrap for leadership which is certainly going to be unavoidable in the situation in the state this year." Isen, who understood Bob's temperament as well as anyone, added, "He feels that if he works hard in Washington in the interest of the state, that they 'owe' him (he does not put it that way of course) support. The burden of political life bears very heavily on him—he feels that it is a big sacrifice and I don't think he gets real joy out of it, as Phil or Blaine do for instance."[26]

Although most political experts predicted easy victory for him, Bob continued to worry that the third party had endangered his chances for reelection. To help things along he arranged for the usual contingent of outside speakers to canvass the state on his behalf. American Federation of Labor chief William Green; New York's mayor, Fiorello La Guardia; and Senate colleagues Burton K. Wheeler, Gerald P. Nye, and Edward P. Costigan all made appearances during the campaign.[27]

Most of all, La Follette wanted President Roosevelt's endorsement. If the election proved to be as close as he feared, the popular president's support might tip the balance in his favor. La Follette had discussed the matter with Roosevelt late in February but had come away discouraged, telling Phil, "My view is that we can pretty well count on Roosevelt's not doing anything in Wisconsin which will be at all effective so far as we are concerned." Early in June, however, La Follette reported to his brother that George Norris had conferred with the president and that Roosevelt "was much interested in my re-election to the Senate and that he was having Mr. Farley take the matter up with the Democratic leaders in Wisconsin in an effort to have something done that would be helpful to my candidacy." If Farley failed, Roosevelt "intended . . . at the proper time to make a statement that if he were a citizen of Wisconsin he would be doing

26. Mrs. PFL, "Isen's Political Diary," 21 June 1934, p. 5, box 161-3, PFL Papers.

27. *Progressive*, 28 June 1934; Johnson, *La Follette, Jr.*, p. 37.

all in his power in this campaign to bring about my re-election to the Senate." Later that month a White House reporter asked Roosevelt if he would pressure Wisconsin Democrats to support La Follette. Cautiously keeping his remarks off the record, the president replied, "My own personal hope is that they will find some way of sending Bob La Follette back here. But I cannot compel the Democracy of Wisconsin to go ahead and nominate him." Postmaster General and party boss James A. Farley exemplified Roosevelt's dilemma. "I hate to think of anything happening to Bob La Follette," he said but added, "It would be a wonderful thing if the Democrats could carry Wisconsin."[28]

Roosevelt probably gave Young Bob more support in 1934 than he gave any other non-Democrat. On 9 August, the president visited Wisconsin, almost certainly for the sole purpose of aiding La Follette. Intense speculation preceded the trip. Although everyone expected an endorsement of some sort, all were curious as to how Roosevelt would handle it. And what about Phil? "To bless Robert without inferring blessing Philip would not be easy," commented the *New York Times*. At Green Bay, Roosevelt invited La Follette and Wisconsin's other senator, Democrat F. Ryan Duffy, aboard his train. From the back platform Roosevelt told the crowd, "Your two senators, Bob La Follette and Ryan Duffy, both old friends of mine, they and many others have worked with me in maintaining excellent co-operation between the executive and legislative branches of the government. I take this opportunity of expressing my gratitude to them." Roosevelt said nothing about Phil but did thank his opponent, Schmedeman. The president's remarks fell short of an outright endorsement of Young Bob, but they were enough to gratify La Follette and to anger state Democrats, some of whom wished that Roosevelt had stayed away. Later in the campaign, Roosevelt invited La Follette to visit the White House after the elections and gave his consent for La Follette to make the invitation public. One key progressive campaign worker, Glenn Roberts, later claimed that the Democratic National Committee secretly funneled money into La Follette's campaign chest.[29]

28. RML to PFL, 27 February, 4 June 1934, box 41-A, Family Papers; Roosevelt quoted in James MacGregor Burns, *Roosevelt: The Lion and the Fox* (New York, 1956), p. 206; Karl M. Kahn, "The House that Farley Built," *Progressive*, 11 August 1934.

29. *New York Times*, 5 August 1934, sec. 4; *Milwaukee Sentinel*, 10 August 1934; RML to Roosevelt, 21 October 1934, box 2-C, Family Papers; interview, Glenn D. Roberts, 3 July 1973.

Once the campaign got underway, aides observed a remarkable, almost miraculous, transformation in La Follette. All of the doubts, all of the second-guessing of the past months, seemed to disappear. The old crusading spirit returned. Again the coming election was to be the battle between good and evil, or as La Follette put it, "between the Progressives who stand for more equal distribution of wealth and the reactionaries of both Republican and Democratic parties who have banded together to exploit the people who have produced the wealth." The audiences that heard him speak five, sometimes six, times a day would not have believed anyone who told them that only months before Young Bob had opposed a third party. The change in La Follette was characteristic. One close friend and aide later recalled that "it was like pulling teeth" to get La Follette involved in a campaign. He had to be carried into it kicking and screaming; but once involved, this aide noted, he became an enormously effective and tireless campaigner.[30] Few if any people outside the circle of family and close friends realized that La Follette, despite outward appearances, regarded the campaign, any campaign, as a duty, and a loathsome one at that.

Because the La Follette brothers ran unopposed in the September Progressive primary, they focused their efforts on the November contest. Young Bob had the good fortune of facing two rather weak and ineffectual opponents. His Republican foe was John B. Chapple, the young Ashland newspaper editor who had upset John J. Blaine in the 1932 primary but then had lost to F. Ryan Duffy in the general election. A longtime La Follette hater, Chapple conducted a contradictory and inflammatory campaign. He borrowed freely from the Progressive platform, advocating a referendum before the United States could enter war and supporting numerous progressive domestic proposals. Chapple also dredged up the Red-baiting tactics that had worked so well against Blaine. He denounced Senator La Follette for supporting diplomatic recognition of the Soviet Union, claimed that the pro-La Follette faculty at the University of Wisconsin had fostered free love and communism, and declared that Young Bob was under the influence of communists.[31] Clearly, Chapple was desperate.

John M. Callahan, La Follette's Democratic opponent, was only slightly more effective. He represented the conservative Al Smith faction of the Democratic party. In the campaign, Callahan urged

30. *Progressive*, 6 October 1934; interview, Gordon Sinykin.
31. Alan Edmond Kent, "Portrait in Isolationism: The La Follettes and Foreign Policy" (Ph.D. diss., University of Wisconsin, 1956), p. 239.

that the United States stay out of foreign entanglements, supported old-age pensions, but stressed budget balancing as the best way to end the depression.[32] President Roosevelt's early endorsement of La Follette had placed an insurmountable barrier in Callahan's path before he ever got started.

As the campaign drew to a close, La Follette displayed cautious optimism. Responding to Roosevelt's inquiry on 21 October, he said it was especially difficult to predict the outcome of the election in this "the fifth year of the depression." "Unless I am mistaken, people are becoming mentally and emotionally fatigued. The pressure and anxiety of the past few years is becoming almost unbearable." "Nevertheless," he concluded, "if the signs on the surface mean anything, I think I am likely to be re-elected." In the final weeks La Follette was confident enough to devote most of his time to helping Phil, who was involved in a much closer race.[33]

On election night the La Follettes gathered with family and friends in the library of the Maple Bluff Farm. The scene was familiar: Phil crouched down next to the radio; Bob seated at the desk, on the phone to the newsroom of the *Capital Times*. The final results pleasantly surprised even the most hopeful among them. Bob won with 48 percent of the vote, compared to 24 percent for the Democrat, Callahan, 23 percent for the Republican, Chapple, with the remaining 5 percent divided among minor candidates. Phil narrowly defeated incumbent Governor Schmedeman by less than a seventeen-thousand-vote margin. Progressive Theodore Dammann was reelected secretary of state, but Democrats took the other top state offices. Progressives captured 58 of 133 seats in the legislature and 7 of 10 seats in the House of Representatives. For the first time out, almost everyone agreed, it was an impressive showing.[34]

Jubilant supporters hailed the Progressive party as the new force in American politics, destined to sweep the nation and replace one of the two major parties. In light of the strides the party had made during its first months of existence, Progressives could hardly be blamed for overlooking the barriers that blocked the road to national prominence. The most formidable obstacle was Franklin D. Roosevelt. In November 1934, with the obvious exception of Wisconsin, the Democratic party had scored one of the most spectacular off-year

32. Ibid.
33. RML to Roosevelt, 21 October 1934, President's Personal File 1792, Franklin D. Roosevelt Papers, Franklin D. Roosevelt Library, Hyde Park, New York; PFL, *Memoirs*, p. 215.
34. Interview, Gordon Sinykin; Johnson, *La Follette, Jr.*, pp. 38–39.

election victories in history. Most experts interpreted the results as an endorsement of Roosevelt's leadership.[35] Perhaps no president had ever had such full command of the public trust. Although continuing depression could quickly alter things, it appeared in November 1934 as though the president and his party were secure from third-party attack.

A second barrier was factionalism within the Progressive organization. During the campaign the party had been relatively free of internal discord. But as soon as the elections were over, dissension reappeared. By the winter of 1934 Tom Amlie was again grumbling about the basic conservatism of the La Follette party. Now he was talking about the need for a fourth party.[36] Before progressives could realize their national ambitions, they would have to deal with dissension within their own ranks. Finally, to extend its influence beyond Wisconsin, the party needed bold and aggressive leadership from its best-known member, Bob La Follette. But his performance during 1934 had raised serious doubts about his willingness or ability to fill that need.

35. *Progressive*, 17 November 1934; Leuchtenburg, *Roosevelt and the New Deal*, pp. 116–17.
36. *Progressive*, 15 December 1934.

CHAPTER 9

The Pressures of Political Life

His reelection in 1934 gave Bob La Follette a pleasant, though temporary, respite from the turmoil of Wisconsin politics. Phil, he decided, would manage state affairs while he devoted himself to more important things. But victory at the polls brought no relief from the pressures of national politics. Again during 1935 La Follette had to force a hesitant Senate and an oftentimes sluggish administration into wrestling with the issues of public works, relief, and tax reform. Again he had to bear the innumerable pressures and annoyances of public life that weighed so heavily on him. Nevertheless he was doing what he did best. While in the process of founding a new party he had appeared indecisive and weak; now he performed as the bold leader of old.

In February 1935 La Follette turned forty. The passage of years had changed him little. He was a bit stockier and his oval face was slightly fuller; but everyone called him Young Bob and it still seemed appropriate. He also looked healthier than ever. His last serious bout with illness had been in 1929, and by 1935 he had been free of health problems longer than for any other period in his life. Still, old habits died slowly: his medicine cabinet looked like a pharmacy, and he continued to down an assortment of pills and potions daily.[1]

Nor had his personality and temperament changed much over the years. Friends still found him warm and friendly and ever considerate of others. Those who met him for the first time were apt to discover that this person they so often had heard thundering in the Senate chamber was by nature rather quiet and shy. Almost everyone agreed that he was "a good listener," especially when they compared him to Phil. No matter how hectic his day, he would never turn away anyone who had come to plead some cause. Civil rights activist Oswald Garrison Villard remarked, "You cannot go to him for sympathy for starved miners or frantic share croppers or half-famished unemployed . . . and come away empty handed." It was in these personal contacts

1. RML medical history, "Summary in the Case of Robert M. La Follette," June 1949, box 26-C, Family Papers (see list of abbreviations p. x); interview, Mary La Follette, 22 February 1973.

or in small groups that La Follette showed his best qualities. Unlike Phil, who would automatically plunge into a crowd to shake hands, whether at a political rally or in a railroad station, Bob was uncomfortable in large gatherings and he sometimes gave a false impression of being cold and aloof.[2]

Another aspect of his personality, his sense of humor, was a source of lively dispute. Some said he had one, others said he did not. "Humorless," recalled his sister-in-law Isen without qualification. Two veteran reporters wrote, "Grimness rather than gaiety is a La Follette characteristic, as it is their weakness." Others, however, detected in him, if not thigh-slapping humor, at least a dry wit. When Philadelphia lawyer Francis Biddle came to Washington to sit on a government labor board, he had frequent contact with La Follette. After a while Biddle asked the senator if he could call him "Bob." "Sure can," La Follette shot back. "Everyone in Wisconsin calls me Bob, or that son of a bitch."[3]

La Follette himself seemed sensitive about the prevailing "gloomy Gus" image, but when he tried to counteract it he usually ended up confirming it. Years later, *Current Biography* was preparing a biographical sketch of La Follette, and it sent him a rough draft. La Follette objected to one sentence: "He lacks a sense of humor; he cannot appreciate a joke or a wisecrack, unless they be of the ironic variety." La Follette retorted in a letter, "Of course this is a matter of opinion upon which my testimony may seem prejudiced but I have always considered that I had a very keen sense of humor, and I think any of my colleagues and associates would testify to this effect. I therefore suggest the elimination of this statement." The publisher obligingly complied.[4]

If anything about La Follette had changed over the years it was his attitude toward public life. The change was not sudden or drastic, and only a few close friends and relatives were aware of it. From the very beginning of his career he had regarded political life as something he had to endure rather than enjoy. But he had endured remarkably well and with little complaint. During the middle 1930s and after, however, he seemed a little less able to withstand the pres-

2. Oswald Garrison Villard, "Pillars of Government: Robert M. La Follette, Jr.," *Forum* 96 (August 1936):90. Interviews, Mrs. PFL, 5 July 1973; Mary La Follette; Gordon Sinykin, August 1972; Morris H. Rubin, 1, 8 August 1972.

3. Interview, Mrs. PFL; Ray Tucker and Frederick R. Barkley, *Sons of the Wild Jackass* (Boston, 1932), p. 155; Francis Biddle, *In Brief Authority* (New York, 1962), pp. 132–33.

4. RML to Miss Maxine Block (of *Current History*), 18 May 1944, box 46-C, Family Papers.

sures and demands of public life; the annoyances increased, his complaints became more frequent.

One aspect of public life that increasingly disturbed him was the frequency of intrusions on his privacy. Certainly he enjoyed some of the perquisites of prominence, like the recognition and the respect people accorded a well-known senator. But he enjoyed these things much less than did most public figures. When traveling by train he wanted to be able to sit by himself and nap or leaf through a newspaper. What usually happened was that someone would spot him, plop down in the seat beside him, and want to talk politics. Phil, by contrast, would pace the aisle until he found someone who recognized him. One time while in New York, Bob and his close friend Ruth Muldowney went to Harlem's Cotton Club to see dancer Bill Robinson. Afterward Bob described to Rachel what had happened: "My evening was ruined by a photographer who snapped my picture from a distance." His first impulse was to get up and chase after the photographer, but he held back for fear of making a scene. "It makes me pretty tired not to be able to ever have one evening of relaxation," he grumbled. "Next I expect to find a camera . . . behind the shower curtain to snap a picture of me on the 'Johnny.' "[5]

A more serious invasion of privacy involved a mentally disturbed woman from Taylor, Wisconsin, named Nettie Matson. To his knowledge La Follette had never met her. Yet between 1929 and 1936 she sent him hundreds of passionate "Darling Bobbie" letters, each one ten pages or longer. Nettie fantasized an entire relationship between herself and La Follette. Among other things she believed that "Bobbie" had promised to marry her. When he married Rachel instead, she accused him of having "led her on" and then betrayed her. In one letter Nettie threatened to commit suicide if Bob did not call her. For years La Follette and his staff passed the letters off as the harmless ravings of a disturbed mind. Some of her letters were so outrageous that they could not help but have a laugh at the unfortunate woman's expense. After 1934, however, the letters took a more serious turn. Nettie began to threaten La Follette and his family. Equally disturbing, she wrote many letters on the stationery of hotels located in cities where La Follette had recently appeared, indicating that she was following him around. One letter even bore the name of a Washington hotel. La Follette was at a loss to know what to do. Apparently it never occurred to him to contact the authorities; or perhaps he wanted to protect both himself and Nettie from the effects of nasty publicity. In 1934 he did take the letters to a Washington psychiatrist

5. RML to Rachel, 2 December 1936, box 42-A, Family Papers.

for analysis and advice. He also asked Phil to try to locate any relatives Nettie might have. But nothing worked and for two more years the letters kept coming. Finally about 1936, for some unexplained reason, Nettie stopped writing. La Follette probably regarded Nettie Matson more as an annoyance than as a threat. Nevertheless the whole affair increased his distaste for public life.[6]

A tragic event in the spring of 1935, the death of his closest friend in the Senate, Bronson Cutting of New Mexico, had a similar effect on him. In his forty-six years of life Cutting had had the best of everything: a prominent family name, great wealth, education at Groton, a Phi Beta Kappa key at Harvard, and a distinguished war record. Cutting was urbane, witty, brilliant, fluent in several languages, and best of all in La Follette's opinion, he believed in a progressive political philosophy. Early in life, poor health had forced him to forsake his native New York for the dryer climate of New Mexico, where he entered politics and soon built up "one of the tightest little political machines in the country," called by some the "Tammany of the Southwest." Upon entering the Senate in 1927 he struck up a close and lasting friendship with La Follette. The two youthful senators had much in common. Both had experienced the strains of having to live up to a distinguished family name. Their similar health problems meant that they could sit for hours swapping medical histories. They also saw eye to eye on most public issues, and over the years they had joined forces in many a lonely battle for relief and public works. Too, Cutting had contributed money to the La Follette brothers' campaigns and on occasion had helped save the *Progressive* from financial ruin.[7]

In 1934 Cutting experienced some misfortunes that finally ended in tragedy for him. After he narrowly won reelection in 1934, his Democratic challenger, Dennis Chavez, charged fraud and contested the election. That in turn led to White House interference. Although a progressive Republican who had supported much of the New Deal, Cutting had had an earlier falling-out with Roosevelt over a relatively minor issue. To the dismay of La Follette and other progressives, a vindictive Roosevelt backed Cutting's opponent, both in the election and in the subsequent dispute over the outcome. In May 1935, Cutting flew to New Mexico to gather evidence to support his case before the Senate committee investigating the election. On the way back to

6. Nettie Matson letters, box 33-C, Family Papers.
7. [Drew Pearson and Robert S. Allen], *Washington Merry-Go-Round* (New York, 1931), pp. 204–6; Tucker and Barkley, *Sons of the Wild Jackass*, pp. 196–220; "Financial Statement," September 1930, box 1-1, PFL Papers.

Washington, his plane went down over Missouri, and he was killed. Upon hearing the news La Follette burst into tears. Weeks later when New Mexico's Democratic governor selected Dennis Chavez to fill Cutting's vacant seat, La Follette and several other progressives stomped out of the swearing-in ceremony in angry protest. They blamed Chavez and Roosevelt for Cutting's death. They reasoned that Cutting might still be alive if only Roosevelt had supported him in the first place; if only Chavez had not contested the outcome; if only Roosevelt had not egged Chavez on. Their reaction was childish, and La Follette probably realized it once he recovered from the initial shock. Months later La Follette learned that Cutting had bequeathed fifty thousand dollars to him and twenty-five thousand dollars to Phil.[8]

The Cutting tragedy made La Follette all the more aware of what a bitter game politics could sometimes become. Of course all politicians had to confront the tensions of public life. But for many, if not most, of them, driving ambition helped smooth the rough edges. Unfortunately for his state of mind, La Follette was an oddity among public figures in that he seemed to genuinely lack that ambition.

If he so disliked public life, a few of his friends wondered, why did he continue to administer this self-inflicted punishment? His father's mentor Alf Rogers once put it to Bob bluntly. "Get out of politics as a means of earning a living," he advised. Yet, La Follette persisted for several reasons. One reason was that he disliked only certain aspects of public life. He detested the loss of privacy, the speaking tours that separated him from family, and especially the campaigns. But he enjoyed his Senate role. Many a time he must have thought how pleasant it would be to be able to remain in the Senate without having to go through the annoyance of a campaign. For another thing, La Follette at age forty was too young to retire and too old to enter another profession. After all, politics was the only life he had ever known. But most important, he continued because of his father. He knew that this was the life Old Bob had wanted for him. It seemed almost as though father and son had struck a sacred pact, and now Young Bob was driven to carry out his part of it. Consequently, La Follette persisted and coped as best he could.

During the mid-1930s a growing family provided some relief from public tensions. After the death of their first baby, Rachel bore them a son, Joseph Oden, in 1933. Three years and a miscarriage later, the

8. Arthur M. Schlesinger, Jr., *The Age of Roosevelt: The Politics of Upheaval* (New York, 1960), pp. 139–41; Philip F. La Follette, *Adventure in Politics: The Memoirs of Philip La Follette* (New York, 1970), p. 257.

birth of Bronson Cutting, named after the late senator, completed the family. Rachel, who resented the intrusion of politics even more than Bob, tried to insulate their children and home life from public affairs, a task she found almost impossible. As Bob put it, "It is tough that we have to be separated so much and even when we are together life is so hectic that we really have very little uninterrupted time."[9]

La Follette's social life evidenced his desire to escape the pressures of public life. Although much sought after by Washington hostesses, Bob and Rachel avoided the party circuit whenever possible, since the conversation at such affairs invariably centered on politics. The La Follettes much preferred a quiet evening at home by themselves or in the company of a few close nonpolitical friends. Guests in the La Follettes' simply furnished, rented house on Cathedral Avenue could expect an informal and relaxed evening. Bob would grill steaks over the backyard barbecue. Then after dinner and a few drinks he would roll back the carpet and turn on the phonograph for dancing, always his favorite entertainment. In the course of an evening the La Follettes and their guests would exchange political gossip, but no decisions had to be made, no strategy plotted. These were the times La Follette liked best.

La Follette was on good personal terms with almost all of his Senate colleagues. He also had many close friends in the administration and in various government posts. Harry Hopkins, Rexford Tugwell, Thomas Corcoran, William O. Douglas, and Aubrey Williams were just a few of them. Yet he rarely saw these people socially. The friends he saw most frequently and the ones with whom he seemed most comfortable were nonpoliticians, like John Clifford Folger, a Nashville businessman who later moved to Washington; Sylvester Muldowney, chairman of the board of the National Union Radio Corporation; and Wellwood Nesbit, a Madison doctor.

Occasionally on a Friday or Saturday evening Bob and Rachel went to their favorite nightspot, the ballroom of the Shoreham Hotel. But even that was sometimes hard to enjoy, because the orchestra, under the direction of Wisconsin native Barney Breeskin, would blare out "On Wisconsin" to announce La Follette's presence. When time permitted, which was not often, he took in a ball game at Griffith Park stadium or played a "rotten" game of golf. When the pressure of Washington became too much he went on vacation, sometimes leaving Rachel and the children behind. Every year he managed to squeeze in several short trips, to New York for a weekend with Fola and Mid or to Atlantic City. And he found time for at least one longer

9. RML to Rachel, 18 October 1933, box 41-A, Family Papers.

holiday of from ten days to two weeks. He often went to Florida; and in the fall of 1935 he and Phil took a cruise to Bermuda. Rarely did he vacation in Wisconsin, for that meant politics.[10] As Isen accurately observed, "Most of Bob's personal friendships, his vacations, etc. are an attempt to escape from the strain of politics."[11]

But escape was hard, since the work seemed endless. On a normal day La Follette left home between eight and nine o'clock in the morning, arriving at his office fifteen minutes later. He spent the next hour sitting behind his desk making phone calls and leafing through the mounds of letters he was always late in answering. The huge volume of mail he received attested not only to his prominence but also to the mushrooming of the federal bureaucracy during the New Deal. Each week hundreds of constituents requested the senator's help in dealing with various government agencies. For example, a farmer would want La Follette to put in a good word for him with the Farm Security Agency; another person would ask him to find out what was delaying his loan from the Home Owners Loan Corporation. Since 1933 La Follette, like all his colleagues, had assumed a new role. He had become the contact point between nameless government agencies and the people they served. Constituent problems required endless paperwork, countless phone calls, and occasionally a personal visit to the agency involved, thus placing a heavy burden on La Follette and his small staff of about seven persons. La Follette once estimated that constituent problems consumed from one-half to three-fourths of the average senator's time.[12]

By ten o'clock La Follette had left his office for committee meetings. He sat on six standing committees, of which Finance, Education and Labor, and Foreign Relations demanded the most time. The rest of the morning and most of the afternoon he spent shuffling back and forth between committee sessions and the Senate floor. "Young Bob is one of the most conscientious members of the Senate," observed Drew Pearson and Robert S. Allen. "He works hard on the floor and in committee. He attends all sessions."[13] His attendance

10. The foregoing is based primarily on the following sources: Interviews, Bronson C. La Follette, 5 July 1973; Mrs. PFL; Mary La Follette; Morris H. Rubin; Wilbur and Rosemary Voigt, 9 July 1973; and Gordon Sinykin. RML letter files, boxes 41–50-A, and miscellaneous articles and clippings, boxes 661–664-C, Family Papers.

11. Mrs. PFL, "Isen's Political Diary," 26 July 1934, p. 8, box 161-3, PFL Papers.

12. Interviews, Bronson C. La Follette; Mary La Follette; and Roderick H. Riley, 11 June 1973. Robert M. La Follette, Jr., "Congress Wins a Victory Over Congress," New York Times, 4 August 1946, sec. 4.

13. [Pearson and Allen], Washington Merry-Go-Round, p. 193.

record was not that good, but it probably was one of the best in the Senate.

By late afternoon he was back in his office receiving visitors and dictating letters. If he planned a Senate speech within the next two weeks he would also be beginning the long drafting process. During his first years in the Senate he had written most of his speeches almost entirely alone, but as the work load became heavier he relied more on his staff. The process began when he called in a secretary and dictated a general outline. An aide would then take the outline, assemble the mass of facts and statistics that always went into a La Follette address, and write a rough draft. Next, La Follette went through the copy line by line, rearranging paragraphs, crossing out words, and scribbling abundant comments in the margin. The whole process repeated itself several times before a final product emerged. La Follette considered speechmaking a serious business, and he would have been appalled at the later practice of legislators submitting unseen and undelivered speeches for publication in the *Congressional Record*. He acted as though a well-reasoned, well-documented address could convert colleagues to his side. "Making the *Record*," also helped salve the wounds of defeat, for he seemed to believe that if only he could get his arguments down on the permanent record, whatever the immediate outcome, some future historian would justify his stands.[14] Thorough preparation, however, paid off even in the short run. "When he rises to speak in the Senate Chamber," one newsman commented, "he does not want for an audience, because what he has to say makes up in meatiness whatever it lacks in rhetorical brilliance."[15]

Barring a night session or a late appointment, La Follette usually made it home by 7:00 P.M. There followed a cocktail, dinner, an hour or so with Rachel and the boys, then more work—often stretching past midnight. It was a grueling schedule. "The weeks are just a blur, the days merging into one another," he once complained. "At the end of each week I wonder where the time has gone and seem to have accomplished so little."[16]

Aside from his family and a few close friends, almost no one realized the extent to which La Follette regarded public life as a heavy burden. He kept his worries and doubts to himself. Thus Senate col-

14. Interviews, Norman M. Clapp, 3 August 1972; Maurice B. Pasch, 25 July 1972; Roderick H. Riley; Morris H. Rubin.

15. *New York Times*, 18 August 1935, sec. 4. See also Francis Brown, "La Follette: Ten Years a Senator," *Current History* 42 (August 1935):475–80.

16. Interview, Mary La Follette; RML to Fola, 4 March 1932, box 42-A, Family Papers.

leagues, the press, and the public could envision him as a self-assured, intense, aggressive statesman, a person comfortable in, and eminently suited to, his job. The initial success of the Progressive party and La Follette's victory in 1934 strengthened that impression. Bob La Follette's next move in politics, people were saying, would be not out but up.

Indeed, never had his political stock been higher. *Time* magazine placed him on the cover of its November 1934 election issue. Some observers forecast a Bob La Follette third-party presidential candidacy in 1936 or 1940. Others predicted that Roosevelt, in order to ward off the progressive threat, would pick La Follette as his running mate in 1936. According to newspaper accounts, in March 1935 a "group of Administration Democrats" had met to discuss the possibility of a Roosevelt–La Follette ticket. They reasoned that if Huey Long ran for the presidency on a third-party ticket, which seemed likely at the time, La Follette might be able to hold the Middle West and West for Roosevelt. Columnist John Franklin Carter, the self-designated "Unofficial Observer," saw another advantage to a La Follette candidacy. "It might offend some of the old-line Southern Democrats," he wrote, "but Bob would not alarm the Eastern conservatives more than Roosevelt has already alarmed them." "In fact," Carter thought, "he might alarm them less, for he is slower, steadier, and stays put, whereas they are never sure what Roosevelt will do next."[17] La Follette doubtless realized that the chances of Roosevelt selecting a non-Democrat for the vice-presidency were slim. He probably was even relieved that such was the case. Yet, the talk was flattering.

If being thrust even farther into the national spotlight made La Follette uneasy, he gave no sign of it as he took his seat for the 1935 session of Congress. The first problem he and his colleagues had to confront was the fifth consecutive year of massive unemployment. Conservative estimates put the jobless rate at 9 percent, but the true percentage was probably much higher. And these figures did not take into account the millions of Americans who could find only part-time work nor the millions more who earned subsistence wages. Depression, it seemed, was becoming a permanent way of life.

Roosevelt's answer was a $4.8 billion public works program. Although this unprecedented figure stunned conservatives, it was, when measured against the problem, modest indeed. At most, the pres-

17. *Time*, 19 November 1934; "A Third Party," *Vanity Fair* 42 (August 1934):24; *New York Times*, 23 March 1935; John Franklin Carter [The Unofficial Observer], *American Messiahs*, (New York, 1935), p. 104.

ident's proposal would directly employ only 3.5 million persons, fewer than half of those who needed jobs. Moreover, Roosevelt omitted from his plan any provision for direct relief. With an approach reminiscent of Hoover's, he told Congress that "continued dependence upon relief induces a spiritual and moral disintegration fundamentally disruptive to the national fibre." He compared relief to "a narcotic, a subtle destroyer of character." "The Federal Government," he concluded, "must and shall quit this business of relief." [18]

During the battle over relief, La Follette maintained his perfect record for staying several steps ahead of the administration. In 1933 when Roosevelt had asked for $3.3 billion in public works, La Follette had called for $6 billion. Now when Roosevelt requested $4.8 billion, the Wisconsin senator raised his demand to $9.8 billion. When the Senate took up the issue in March 1935, La Follette delivered a two-hour speech in behalf of his amendment to the president's proposal. He sounded like a teacher lecturing a class of unusually slow learners. As he had done so many times in the past, he patiently reviewed the purchasing power theory of the depression. The president's proposal, he argued, would not raise purchasing power to the level needed for recovery. As for Roosevelt's intention to end direct federal relief, La Follette thought it was folly. He asserted that without federal aid, state treasuries would crack under the strain. He cited California as an example. As of December 1934, 790,000 Californians were on relief. Of that number, the Federal Emergency Relief Administration estimated that 458,000, or 52 percent, were unemployable: children under sixteen years of age, elderly persons, housewives, persons mentally and physically disabled, and students. Even if all the rest of the jobless found work of some sort, which was unlikely, California would still have to provide for the unemployables, and this it could not do adequately without federal assistance. La Follette concluded his lecture with his father's favorite prediction. If legislators did not heed his advice, he warned, they would be demoted to private life. [19]

The tide running against any further relief was particularly strong in the Senate. A few weeks before, Thomas P. Gore, the blind senator from Oklahoma, had told his colleagues a story. Gore had asked a young man on his staff to put on some overalls and a workshirt, to let his whiskers grow, and to go down to the District of Columbia relief distribution center and mingle with the recipients. The young staff member came back shocked. Most of the reliefers he had en-

18. Quoted in Schlesinger, *Politics of Upheaval*, pp. 267–68.
19. *CR* 74:1, 1935, vol. 79, pt. 4, pp. 4147–52.

countered were ex-convicts. "To what extent, if at all, that is typical I do not know," Gore generously conceded.[20] Although most senators probably did not think it typical, the feeling that many of those on the dole were of questionable character was widespread. Hearing their leaders suggest that a lot of them were slackers and cheats getting a free ride at public expense, perhaps many people on relief came to believe it themselves.

In any event the Senate was anxious to comply with Roosevelt's request to end relief. It let La Follette have his say, then it turned down his amendment for public works and relief by a thumping vote of 77 to 8. Yet, La Follette's effort had advanced the public works cause, and perhaps that had been part of his strategy. After confronting a proposal for $9.8 billion, most senators now considered the president's request for a paltry $4.8 billion a bargain. The final measure, known as the Emergency Relief Appropriation Act, cleared the Senate in March and became law in April.[21]

At the end of March the Senate dealt La Follette another blow by repealing the statute he had maneuvered through Congress the year before requiring public disclosure of income tax returns. This action followed the most emotional and bitter debate of the session. According to the provisions of the publicity statute taxpayers had to fill out and submit with their returns a pink slip on which they listed gross income, deductions taken, and taxes paid. Then, by paying a small fee, any citizen could obtain a copy of any other citizen's pink slip. In February 1934, Sen. Royal S. Copeland and Rep. Robert L. Bacon simultaneously introduced repeal measures in both houses of Congress. During the ensuing debate, the National Chamber of Commerce and other business groups lobbied intensively for repeal.[22]

The repeal forces argued that the "pink slip provision" already had led to abuses and had the potential for even greater abuses. They claimed that business firms were snooping into the financial affairs of competitors and that credit organizations and mail-order concerns were using pink slips to compile customer lists. One opponent of publicity quoted a tax official as saying that most requests for pink slips had come from "widows seeking to find an eligible widower with a good income" and vice versa. The repeal forces also warned that open returns encouraged kidnappers to scour pink slips in search of families who could afford to meet ransom demands. The kidnapping and murder of the Lindbergh baby in 1932 remained fresh in the

20. Ibid., pp. 3458–59.
21. Ibid., p. 4152.
22. *New York Times*, 11, 25 February 1935.

public mind, and foes of income tax publicity played up this theme.[23]

Support for repeal came unexpectedly from La Follette's home state. From 1923 to 1934 Wisconsin was the only state to open state income tax returns to the public. And it was largely the supposed success of that experiment that had prompted La Follette to press for open federal returns in the first place. But in 1934 the Wisconsin Tax Commission, after investigating the effects of the practice, uncovered many abuses and concluded that open returns caused more harm than good. The commission's report undercut one of La Follette's basic arguments for retaining the publicity statute: he had claimed that what worked so well in Wisconsin should also be employed on the national level. The disclosure of the damaging study prompted the *New York Times* to editorialize, "If in the most sacred enclave of progressive virtue it works so ill, what is to be expected from its effects in a Commonwealth less inured to lofty purpose and the art of meddling?"[24] But the most persuasive argument in favor of repeal concerned the simple matter of personal privacy. During the Senate debate Millard Tydings of Maryland put it best: "I believe . . . that there are some things that a man is entitled to call his own business, and one of them is how much money he makes."[25]

La Follette, along with George Norris and Huey Long, struggled to hold back the rising tide for repeal. As in the past, La Follette contended that publicity deterred outright fraud; that it deterred "legal evasion" (a person claiming deductions or exemptions that, while not unlawful, would prove embarrassing if exposed to public scrutiny); that it increased revenue collection; and that ultimately it would restore people's confidence in the tax system. La Follette downplayed the Wisconsin Tax Commission study, even though he had the reputation for relying on the advice of experts. However, he did concede that some abuses had taken place. To prevent them in the future, he offered an amendment imposing a fine or imprisonment on anyone, except newspapers and public speakers, who obtained pink slips or disseminated information from them for financial compensation—presumably he wanted to prevent mail-order firms and the like from harassing consumers.

Thus far La Follette had presented a strong case; even opponents conceded to him the practical arguments. Open returns probably did deter fraud and evasion, and they probably did increase revenue. But these were not the central issues. Neither was kidnapping, although

23. Ibid.; *CR* 74:1, 1935, vol. 79, pt. 4, pp. 4444–46, 4501.
24. *New York Times*, 11 February 1935.
25. *CR* 74:1, 1935, vol. 79, pt. 4, p. 4450.

at times some of the most zealous proponents of repeal tried to make it so. The real issue was personal privacy, and it was this issue that defeated La Follette and his supporters. They might have been wise to argue that the prevention of tax fraud outweighed minor infringements on personal privacy; but they did not. Instead they ignored the whole issue, implying that the only reason a person could have for opposing something so sensible as open returns was a desire to cheat on his taxes. Huey Long, for example, pointed to the presence of businessmen in the ranks of the repeal forces and claimed that this was "proof in and of itself that they mean to rob the United States Government in the future as they have been robbing the . . . Government in the past." La Follette, although not quite as graphically, implied much the same. It apparently never occurred to La Follette and his supporters that a middle- or lower-income person might be just as eager to keep his personal finances out of the reach of inquisitive neighbors or relatives.[26]

On 11 March the House voted to repeal the publicity amendment, 302 to 98. Three weeks later the Senate concurred by a margin of better than two to one. Congressional action did not completely foreclose publicity, however, since the president still had the power to make income tax returns public, and congressional committees retained the power to subpoena any returns.[27]

As if the two setbacks of March were not enough, La Follette also had to worry about the administration. Thus far its performance had been disappointing: first an inadequate public works program; then Roosevelt's inaction in connection with several key measures that had bogged down in Congress, including the social-security bill, a Wagner sponsored labor proposal, and a measure revamping the banking system. By the end of April, La Follette was complaining that Roosevelt "hates a fight and would rather bust his program than face a row."[28]

On 15 May La Follette had a chance to express his concern to the president in person. That evening Roosevelt entertained a small group of progressives at the White House. Attending were Senators La Follette, Norris, Costigan, Wheeler, and Hiram Johnson; cabinet members Henry A. Wallace and Harold Ickes; and frequent presidential advisers Felix Frankfurter and David K. Niles. Apparently all of them had the same idea: they must tell the president discreetly but firmly to get moving and show some leadership. La Follette assumed

26. Ibid., pp. 4442–56.
27. *New York Times*, 13, 28, 29 March 1935.
28. RML to PFL, 22 April 1935, box 135-2, PFL Papers.

the initiative in this unpleasant task, prompting Frankfurter to say later of the others, "It was funny, wasn't it, how some who roar outside can become doves, indeed almost silent ones within."[29]

The main topic of conversation was how Roosevelt should handle the growing threats from both the Right and the Left. Two weeks before, the annual convention of the U.S. Chamber of Commerce had denounced Roosevelt and the New Deal. This action, climaxing a year of growing criticism from business and conservative quarters, had disturbed Roosevelt deeply. He had done much for business, he rightly felt, and now they were turning on him. La Follette reassured the president. The Chamber of Commerce attack, he said, was a "most fortunate happening." By this he undoubtedly meant that business had broken with the administration on its own initiative and that now Roosevelt was free of always having to appease business. La Follette had broken the ice. After he had his say, everyone agreed with him, Ickes adding that Roosevelt should capitalize on business opposition.[30]

The conversation then shifted to the threat from the Left, particularly the increasing support for Huey Long and Father Charles Coughlin. Roosevelt worried that Long, if he ran on a third-party ticket in 1936, might pick up enough votes to give the Republicans the election. Again La Follette took the lead, telling Roosevelt, according to Ickes's account, that Roosevelt had "a fine legislative program pending before Congress and that the best answers to Huey Long and Father Coughlin would be the enactment . . . of the Administration bills now pending there." At this point Burton K. Wheeler interrupted to say that two key Democratic leaders in the Senate, Joseph T. Robinson and Pat Harrison, opposed much of the administration's program and therefore posed an obstacle to its enactment. La Follette countered by reminding the president that Theodore Roosevelt had not shied away from taking issue with members of his own party; the president, La Follette suggested, might have to do the same thing. In making this analogy, La Follette must have smiled inwardly, knowing as he did that when Theodore Roosevelt had taken issue with fellow Republicans, it had usually not been with the conservatives but with the elder La Follette and the progressives.[31]

Several days later, Felix Frankfurter wrote La Follette praising him

29. Felix Frankfurter to RML, 22 May 1935, box 74, Felix Frankfurter Papers, Library of Congress, Washington, D.C.
30. Harold L. Ickes, *The Secret Diary of Harold L. Ickes* (New York, 1953–1954), 1:363.
31. Ibid.

for "the extraordinary combination of forthrightness, practical wisdom and tact with which you led the discussion into the right channels, kept it there, and said the things that needed to be said and that nobody else would have come within forty percent of saying." "I verily believe," Frankfurter continued, "there are not half a dozen men who leave the same impact on [Roosevelt] that you do, and fundamentally because he knows that your downrightness and simple honesty are used for wholly disinterested ends." Most important, said Frankfurter, Roosevelt had gotten the message. He concluded by praising La Follette in the best way he could: "Your statesmanship would be no surprise to your father . . . but how proud he would have been over such a performance as yours was the other night."[32]

The meeting with the progressives, along with the earlier Chamber of Commerce attack and a later Supreme Court decision overturning the National Industrial Recovery Act, gave Roosevelt the courage he had lacked. During the summer of 1935 the president asserted leadership as he had not done since the first hundred days of his administration in 1933. On 13 June, just as legislators were putting the finishing touches on their vacation plans, Roosevelt insisted that they postpone adjournment and remain in Washington until they passed four key measures: a bill curbing the spread of holding companies, a banking-reform measure, the Wagner labor proposal, and the social-security bill. A week later he added tax reform to the list.[33]

La Follette, obviously delighted with the president's change of mood, sprang into action. During that hectic summer, as Congress simultaneously deliberated over a half dozen or more major pieces of legislation, La Follette seemed to have his hands in everything. In June, when the social-security bill came before the Senate, defense of the measure fell to La Follette and a handful of Democrats who supported the administration. Not only did the Wisconsin senator help steer the bill through the Senate and later through the conference committee, but he also managed to attach a crucial amendment to the unemployment compensation section.[34]

Even though many of La Follette's activities escaped public notice, his role in the long, drawn-out tax fight did not. La Follette had been

32. Frankfurter to RML, 22 May 1935, box 74, Frankfurter Papers.
33. William E. Leuchtenburg, *Franklin D. Roosevelt and the New Deal* (New York, 1963), pp. 143–50; Schlesinger, *Politics of Upheaval*, pp. 291–92.
34. For La Follette's role in the social-security fight, see Edwin E. Witte, *The Development of the Social Security Act* (Madison, 1962), pp. 105, 107, 141, 160, Arthur J. Altmeyer, *The Formative Years of Social Security* (Madison, 1962), p. 40, Edwin E. Witte to RML, 5 July 1935, box 2, Edmond E. Witte Papers, State Historical Society of Wisconsin, Madison.

pressing for tax reform since the beginning of the year. In March he had tried unsuccessfully to turn the debate over open returns into a full-fledged debate over tax policy. At the end of April, during an address over the CBS radio network, he announced that it was the intention of Senate progressives to fight for "drastic increases in the taxes levied upon wealth and income" before Congress adjourned. The attitude of the administration, however, made any extended tax debate seem unlikely. In January, Roosevelt told Congress that he did not "consider it advisable at this time to propose any new or additional taxes." A month later, he rejected a sweeping tax-reform proposal that Treasury officials had submitted to him for consideration. Then in May, not long after La Follette's radio address, he reiterated his stand against tax legislation.[35]

Consequently, it came as a shock when, on 19 June, Roosevelt dramatically reversed himself and sent a blistering tax-reform message to Congress. In words that La Follette had used many times, the president told stunned legislators that the time had come to strike at the concentration of wealth and power. Specifically, he urged Congress to impose a sharply graduated inheritance tax, to raise gift and estate taxes, and to increase tax rates on incomes and dividends. Roosevelt left the reasons for his change of direction unexplained, but the knowledge that La Follette and the progressives intended to wage a tax fight, with or without his support, may have influenced the timing of his message. Also, the recent anti-Roosevelt attacks of big business may have provoked the president into retaliation. Or he may have been trying to "steal [Huey] Long's thunder."[36]

Oddly enough, although Roosevelt handed down a complete set of tax proposals, he failed to specify any timetable for congressional consideration. Thus, it was unclear whether he wanted action before Congress adjourned or at some future time, the following year perhaps. When reporters and administration floor leaders sought out the president for clarification, they discovered that he had left town for the Harvard-Yale boat races. In the absence of any direction from the White House, Democratic leaders, most of whom were unenthusiastic about the president's message anyway, announced that Congress would delay action until 1936.[37]

They reckoned without La Follette, who had waited too long for

35. *New York Times*, 28 March, 28 April 1935; Roosevelt quoted in Raymond Moley, *After Seven Years* (Lincoln, Nebr., 1971 [1939]), n. 13, p. 308; Schlesinger, *Politics of Upheaval*, p. 326.

36. Schlesinger, *Politics of Upheaval*, pp. 326–29; Leuchtenburg, *Roosevelt and the New Deal*, p. 152; Moley, *After Seven Years*, p. 308.

37. *New York Times*, 21 June 1935.

tax reform to allow this opportunity to slip away. In a series of clever maneuvers he forced action before adjournment. There was at that time a joint resolution pending before the Senate to extend excise, or "nuisance," taxes that were due to expire on 30 June. The Senate had to act on the resolution before the terminal date or face the loss of millions of dollars of revenue. On 19 June, just a few hours after Roosevelt sent down his tax message, La Follette announced that he would force immediate consideration of the president's proposals by attaching them and a few proposals of his own to the already pending excise tax resolution. The next morning La Follette made his move in the Finance Committee. But the Finance Committee's conservative chairman, Pat Harrison, blocked the move by pressuring a committee majority to vote down the La Follette amendments. Emerging from the session to face reporters, Harrison confidently predicted that Congress would not take up tax reform until the following year. La Follette disagreed and pledged to wage a floor fight. But with Roosevelt still unavailable for comment, most observers concluded that tax reform was dead at that session.[38]

Again they underestimated La Follette's resourcefulness. Along with Senators Norris, Borah, and Hiram Johnson, he began to circulate a round-robin statement among colleagues. By the night of 21 June, twenty-one senators had signed a statement pledging "to stay in session until action is taken" on the president's tax program. The round robin forced Roosevelt out of hiding. A few days later he summoned congressional leaders to the White House and directed them to take up the tax issue before adjournment. Yet one danger remained: Congress might begin consideration of tax reform but then, tiring of it, adjourn without final action. Taking no chances, La Follette, presumably on behalf of the round-robin signers, threatened to obstruct passage of the excise tax resolution unless the Democratic leadership pledged not to adjourn until a tax bill had passed. Outmaneuvered, Pat Harrison, on behalf of the leadership, reluctantly complied. La Follette's precaution later proved wise, for in mid-July, while the House was still holding hearings on the tax bill, a drive for adjournment got underway. But true to their word, Democratic floor leaders kept Congress in session until final action.[39]

Thus far everyone had assumed that La Follette's skillful maneuverings were intended solely to advance the Roosevelt tax program. All along he had been saying something about having proposals of

38. Ibid., 20, 21 June 1935.
39. Press release, 22 June 1935, file 1935, State Historical Society of Wisconsin, Madison; *New York Times*, 22 June, 16 July 1935.

his own, but nobody had paid much attention. Once the tax debate got underway, however, it became clear that, although La Follette supported and would work for the Roosevelt reforms, he was even more anxious to secure adoption of his own proposals.

La Follette had laid the theoretical groundwork for his proposals earlier in the session, in his March speech on public works and in his April radio address. Both times he had reiterated his belief that massive spending for relief and public works was the only way to restore purchasing power and thereby end the depression. "But," he was quick to add, "it is clear from the experience of other countries, that we cannot carry on these extraordinary expenditures . . . without taxing to the limit." He feared that massive spending without drastic tax increases would damage the government's credit rating and lead to "uncontrolled inflation." For La Follette, "taxing to the limit" meant not only increasing rates on business and upper-income groups, as the Roosevelt plan proposed, but raising rates on middle- and lower-income groups as well. It also meant widening the base of the tax structure. The success of the British tax system, with its broad base and sharply progressive rates, profoundly influenced La Follette's thinking. In his April speech he noted that even though the British government had spent heavily in fiscal 1934, it had managed to balance its budget. "It is obvious," he concluded, "that if we had had the courage to tax as heavily . . . as they have done in Great Britain, we would have had a balanced budget both in 1933 and 1934."[40]

La Folette endorsed Roosevelt's plan to increase tax rates on corporations and great wealth, but he thought that it was inadequate because it would not raise enough revenue to safeguard government credit, ward off inflation, and finance needed spending programs. Thus, in addition to the president's proposals, La Follette recommended a variety of changes in the income tax schedules. One of them would start a sharply graduated surtax schedule at three thousand dollars net income rather than the four thousand dollars of the current law. Another would raise surtax rates on net incomes over eight thousand dollars. Roosevelt had proposed increasing surtax rates only on net incomes over $1 million. La Follette's most important and most controversial proposal would widen the tax base by reducing personal exemptions from twenty-five hundred dollars to two thousand dollars for married persons and from one thousand dollars to eight hundred dollars for single persons. This last provision would

40. *CR* 74:1, 1935, vol. 79, pt. 4, pp. 4147–52; transcript, RML radio address, 28 April 1935, President's Special File—La Follette, Franklin D. Roosevelt Papers, Franklin D. Roosevelt Library, Hyde Park, New York.

bring almost a million and a half new taxpayers into the system and would raise approximately $40 million in additional revenue.[41]

La Follette's proposals and the ideas behind them revealed an aspect of his economic philosophy that conservative opponents often overlooked. He still remained in basic disagreement with those who wanted to slash government spending in order to bring the budget into balance. But what conservatives ignored was that he also kept his distance from the followers of British economist John Maynard Keynes, who advocated deficit spending and lower taxes during depressions and decreased spending and higher taxes during prosperous times. Not only did La Follette think that such a policy stimulated "uncontrolled inflation" and endangered government credit, he also thought that the policy of spending now and taxing later was naive. Recalling the prosperous 1920s, he reminded the Keynsians that both major parties had been trying to outdo one another in cutting taxes. La Follette said that he had been around Washington long enough to know that Congress would never take the unpopular step of raising taxes when good times returned.[42] La Follette clearly was far from being the wild and irresponsible spender some of his critics tried to make him out to be. In fact, he often seemed more consistent and more responsible than many of his conservative detractors. He always matched his spending proposals with demands for increased taxes. On the other hand, the conservatives who cried loudest for a balanced budget rigidly rejected tax increases, probably because they feared incurring the wrath of outraged taxpayers.

La Follette's taxation philosophy did contain several flaws. Certainly he exaggerated when he said that the alternative to higher taxes was uncontrolled inflation. In 1935 the problem was deflation, not inflation. The nation could not only have survived but desperately needed a healthy inflationary surge to lift sagging wages and prices. By proposing higher taxes and lower exemptions, La Follette also contradicted his theories about purchasing power. Tax hikes, especially in the middle- and lower-income brackets, would further sap mass purchasing power. Of course La Follette hoped that Congress would funnel much of the revenue derived from tax increases back into the economy through public works. But in light of the past performance of the Congress and the administration, La Follette was taking a risk.

Early in August the House passed and sent to the Senate a tax bill that conformed closely to the president's recommendations. As the

41. Sidney Ratner, *American Taxation: Its History as a Social Force in Democracy* (New York, 1942), p. 469; *Progressive*, 24 August 1935.

42. *CR* 74:1, 1935, vol. 79, pt. 4, pp. 4073-76, 4147-52.

Finance Committee began deliberations, La Follette planned his strategy. He would attempt to preserve the major features of the House bill, except for the income tax section. For that he would try to substitute his own revenue-producing amendments.

The committee closeted itself for five days. On Saturday, 10 August, it disclosed the details of the tax bill it intended to present to the Senate early the following week. To almost everyone's surprise, the committee had adopted the La Follette amendments. But it had also gone on to slash key sections out of the House bill, the most important being the inheritance tax. These changes it made over La Follette's opposition. The bill as it stood would raise a lot of revenue—some $450 million as compared to the $250 million of the House bill—but otherwise it had been so watered down that it bore almost no resemblance to Roosevelt's "soak the rich" plan.[43]

The Finance Committee had completed its work on a Saturday morning. Within hours its bill was under attack from all sides. Business leaders, who had been lobbying against tax increases from the start, denounced the bill, saying it was still too hard on business. But the sharpest criticism came from liberal quarters. George Norris and William Borah singled out the La Follette amendments for attack. Borah thought that to lower exemptions and increase surtaxes in the lower-income brackets would cause hardship and lower the standard of living for families who were already paying more than their fair share of taxes. Both Norris and Borah pledged to fight the La Follette amendments on the Senate floor. Other liberals dubbed the La Follette amendments a "soak the poor" plan.[44] Roosevelt was also unhappy with the committee bill, and when he invited Alben W. Barkley, a leading Democrat on the Finance Committee, for a weekend cruise down the Potomac, the rumor circulated that Roosevelt was pressuring the committee to reconsider.

When the committee reconvened Monday morning it did just that. By one vote it struck out the La Follette amendments and also replaced some of the features of the House bill. When the bill reached the floor, La Follette tried to reinstate his amendments but without success.[45]

The Wealth Tax Act of 1935, which Congress finally passed late in August, hardly seemed worth all the effort. True, it was a significant improvement over the existing law. It increased gift and estate taxes and imposed the highest and most progressive income surtax rates in

43. *New York Times*, 11 August 1935.
44. Ibid., 12 August 1935.
45. Ibid., 13, 16 August 1935.

history. But it contained no inheritance tax. Although it imposed a variety of corporation taxes, it did little to diffuse corporate wealth and power. Nor did the act do much to distribute wealth. Other New Deal programs, like Social Security with its regressive payroll tax, offset any leveling affect the Wealth Tax Act might have had.[46] For La Follette the final results were doubly disappointing. He had lost his fight to strike at the concentration of wealth and to raise revenue. Moreover, he had exposed himself to criticism from both the Right and the Left: conservatives criticized him for having supported Roosevelt's proposals, and liberals criticized him for trying to increase rates in the lower-income brackets. Yet he could at least take consolation in the knowledge that had it not been for his initiative, there would never have been a bill at all.

46. Leuchtenburg, *Roosevelt and the New Deal*, p. 154.

CHAPTER 10

"Digging Out the Rats"

La Follette reached the height of his national prominence between 1936 and 1940 when, as chairman of the Senate Civil Liberties Committee, he conducted an investigation into violations of labor's right to organize. The investigation, one of the most extensive, productive, and controversial congressional probes in history, exposed the heavy-handed, often brutal, manner in which many employers tried to prevent workers from organizing. La Follette approached the investigation as he approached his other Senate duties, with diligence, with determination to make it succeed, and with a certain reluctance. Inwardly he seemed to regard the investigation as an unpleasant, though necessary, chore that it was his duty to perform.

Many persons and organizations were responsible for the creation of the Civil Liberties Committee. For years the American Civil Liberties Union had pleaded for a government investigation not only of oppressive labor practices, but of civil liberties infractions in general. Several religious organizations had also called for an investigation. In 1935 the American Federation of Labor sought a congressional inquiry. Initially, however, these demands were rebuffed by Congress. No one on Capitol Hill seemed willing to invest the time or risk the political consequences of initiating an investigation.[1]

The person who first tried to interest La Follette in the idea was Heber Blankenhorn, a staff member of the National Labor Relations Board. Blankenhorn, a staunch defender of organized labor, believed that a congressional investigation into antiunion practices was essential to the success of the Wagner Act, which had become law in July 1935. The Wagner Act affirmed in uncompromising language labor's right to organize and bargain collectively through representatives of its own choosing. The act also provided for a National Labor Relations Board (NLRB) to enforce its provisions. By the end of 1935, however, both the Wagner Act and the board were in serious trouble. Convinced that the Supreme Court would overturn the Wagner Act, many corporations simply refused to comply with it and

1. Jerold S. Auerbach, *Labor and Liberty: The La Follette Committee and the New Deal* (Indianapolis, 1966), pp. 30–32, 50–51.

continued their antiunion practices. When the NLRB tried to force compliance, corporation lawyers appealed its decisions in the courts, thereby tying up the board in litigation. Blankenhorn realized that the board needed help; and nothing, he thought, would help as much as a thorough investigation into antiunion practices. He believed that such an investigation would raise a public outcry so loud that big business would be forced to abandon its last-ditch efforts to scuttle the Wagner Act.[2]

In December 1935 Blankenhorn sought out his friend from Wisconsin. "It's again a case of going first to Bob La Follette for advice," he wrote the senator. Blankenhorn explained the problem and then asked La Follette for advice on how to go about initiating a Senate investigation, whom to see, and "how to set it up with as little noise as possible and get it through, the objective being a complete tear-up of labor espionage, strike breakers and strike munitions companies, and their hook-up with high-placed legal defenders." Blackenhorn did not come right out and say so, but he probably hoped that Young Bob would volunteer to take it from there. If he had that in mind, he was temporarily disappointed, for La Follette apparently did little more than put Blankenhorn in touch with a few other senators. Several years earlier someone had come to La Follette and asked him to launch an investigation into the munitions industry and its effects on American foreign policy. La Follette had begged off, saying that he was just too busy to undertake it. Since that time his work load and responsibilities had increased. Although he undoubtedly sympathized with Blankenhorn's problem, he probably hoped to avoid direct involvement. Blankenhorn, meanwhile, tried unsuccessfully to interest other senators in the project.[3]

The problem did not go away. Two months later, on the evening of 21 February 1936, La Follette, several of his liberal colleagues, farm and labor leaders, and a few social-minded clergymen attended a private dinner meeting at the exclusive Cosmos Club in Washington. The topic of discussion was the dire state of civil liberties, especially among sharecroppers in the South, who for years had been trying to organize but had encountered violent opposition from planters in collusion with law enforcement authorities. Just recently, in Tampa, Florida, a gang of thugs, apparently with the help of police officers,

2. Ibid., pp. 53–61.

3. Heber Blankenhorn to RML, 5 December 1935, box 1-8, Heber Blankenhorn Papers, Archives of Labor History and Urban Affairs, Wayne State University, Detroit; Wayne S. Cole, *Senator Gerald P. Nye and American Foreign Relations* (Minneapolis, 1962), p. 67; Auerbach, *Labor and Liberty*, p. 62.

had beaten and killed Joseph Shoemaker, a farm-labor leader. During the course of the evening everyone agreed that something should be done, not only about sharecroppers but about the labor situation in general. Gardner "Pat" Jackson, a longtime social activist and one of the sponsors of the dinner, raised the possibility of a congressional investigation. The response was discouraging. Labor leader John L. Lewis thought Jackson well intentioned but naive. Lewis said scornfully that Congress would never authorize an investigation until blood flowed in the streets. Jackson went around the room asking the legislators present if Lewis was right. One by one they sadly agreed. A disheartened Jackson finally turned to the only guest who had yet to be heard from. "What do you think?" he asked Bob La Follette. La Follette probably wished that he had escaped the question. Although no one seemed willing to initiate an investigation, La Follette thought one was needed; and even though he had turned down Blankenhorn, he could not refuse again. "Pat," he said to Jackson, "if you'll set up a committee of [the] people here . . . and we get a resolution, I will try to get it passed."[4]

Shortly after the Cosmos Club dinner, Gardner Jackson got in touch with Heber Blankenhorn, and together they and a few other people drafted a resolution. On 23 March La Follette introduced Senate Resolution 266 directing the Committee on Education and Labor, of which he was a member, "to make an investigation of violations of the right of free speech and assembly and undue interference with the right of labor to organize and bargain collectively." After preliminary hearings, the Senate, on 6 June, approved the resolution and appropriated fifteen thousand dollars for the probe. The Education and Labor Committee's chairman, Hugo Black, appointed La Follette and Democrats Elbert D. Thomas of Utah and Louis Murphy of Iowa to the investigating subcommittee. Since La Follette had sponsored the enabling resolution, he became chairman. Before the hearings ever got underway, Murphy was killed in an automobile accident; his seat remained empty until 1939 when Democrat David I. Walsh of Massachusetts filled it.[5]

For many reasons La Follette seemed like the ideal person to head the inquiry. Civil libertarians acknowledged him as one of their most faithful champions. Organized labor could cite no one in the Senate, save perhaps Robert F. Wagner, who had so consistently supported prolabor legislation. La Folette even went so far as to say that workers

4. RML quoted by Gardner Jackson, cited by Auerbach, *Labor and Liberty*, p. 47.
   5. Ibid., pp. 63–75.

not only had the right but also the duty to organize.[6] His knack for attracting publicity also qualified him for the job. The ostensible purpose of the inquiry was to determine the nature and extent of infractions on the rights of labor with a view to remedial legislation. But another, equally important, purpose was public education, and that necessitated widespread publicity. With his flair for drama and his modest talent for showmanship, La Follette ensured maximum press coverage for his committee. A final asset La Follette brought to the investigation was his third-party affiliation. With a Progressive in charge rather than a Republican or a Democrat, it appeared less likely that the inquiry would degenerate into a purely partisan controversy.

Initially, however, not everyone was convinced that La Follette was the right person to conduct the probe. In the fall of 1936 Blankenhorn attended the annual convention of the American Federation of Labor to secure the convention's endorsement of La Follette's committee. At the time, the AFL was engaged in a bitter conflict with the Congress of Industrial Organizations (CIO), an insurgent labor organization that had broken away from the AFL. Even though the AFL had demanded an investigation the year before, Blankenhorn encountered "covered opposition" not only to La Follette but also to the committee itself. "This La Follette thing is a CIO business, started by them, wasn't it?" one AFL leader asked Blankenhorn. The convention, however, did pass a resolution backing the committee. At first John L. Lewis, head of the CIO, also expressed reservations about La Follette. Apparently he suspected that La Follette would not be aggressive enough. Even Blankenhorn had some initial doubts along the same line.[7] Before the investigation ended, however, they would have reason to change their minds.

During the summer of 1936 La Follette faced the task of assembling a staff. As in any congressional investigation, the quality and character of staff members were vitally important. Although La Follette, and to a lesser extent Senator Thomas, would determine the general outlines of the investigation and would conduct the public hearings, the actual investigation—collecting evidence, selecting witnesses, and the like—would fall to the staff. For the top position of committee secretary, La Follette, at Blankenhorn's request, selected Robert Wohlforth, a liberal Republican from Connecticut who had just

6. Ibid., p. 77; "Progressive State Party Platform of 1934," *Wisconsin Blue Book, 1935* (Madison, 1935), p. 478.
7. Blankenhorn to National Labor Relations Board, 30 November 1936, box 1-4, Blankenhorn to J. Warren Madden, 7 December 1936, box 1-2, Blankenhorn Papers.

finished serving on the staff of the Senate Special Committee Investigating the Munitions Industry. The second most important position, that of committee counsel, went to John J. Abt, a brilliant Chicago lawyer who had held posts in a variety of New Deal agencies. To fill other positions, La Follette borrowed freely from several federal agencies. Blankenhorn, who was probably La Follette's closest adviser during the investigation, led a large delegation of persons on loan from the National Labor Relations Board. The committee also attracted many idealistic, reform-minded young men and women who were just out of college and anxious to put their ideals into practice. During the first hundred days of the Roosevelt administration, they might have gone to Washington to work in any number of New Deal agencies; after 1936 they went to the La Follette committee.[8] As La Follette later suspected, the committee may even have attracted a few Communist party members or sympathizers.

The composition of the committee, from the chairman on down, gave a clue as to the nature of the impending investigation. As a whole the committee was young, liberal, prolabor, and anti–big business. Clearly this was not to be a detached, scholarly inquiry into the nature of labor-management relations. Before the hearings ever got underway the committee assumed that great evils existed and that big business was the chief villain. Its tasks were to document the evils and to force the villains to account for their sins before the court of public opinion. Blankenhorn put it bluntly. The purpose of the investigation, he said, was "to really dig out the rats and those responsible for them."[9]

In August the committee began to locate witnesses and collect evidence for the first round of public hearings. It immediately encountered resistance. Witnesses tried to elude subpoena-bearing investigators. One witness, Blankenhorn reported, "was chased by airplane from city to city in North and South Carolina before we got him." After testifying, he was "excused by mistake." La Follette signed a new subpoena and committee investigators resumed the chase. They finally found the elusive witness hiding out in the bathroom of a southbound train. The committee's efforts to subpoena the office files of corporations and of private detective agencies that engaged in antiunion activities proved equally difficult. One investigator arrived at the Detroit office of the Pinkerton Detective Agency just in time to find an agency official "sneaking out with a bundle of

8. Auerbach, *Labor and Liberty*, pp. 82–86.
9. Blankenhorn to J. Warren Madden, 19 December 1936, box 1-8, Blankenhorn Papers.

files." Other businesses stripped their files and tossed incriminating documents into trash bins. Ingenious committee investigators countered attempts to destroy evidence by befriending janitors and getting their permission to sift through wastepaper baskets for shredded documents. "In various business quarters," La Follette wryly observed, "record-keeping has gone out of fashion and systems of book-keeping seem to have given way to systemized 'book cooking.' "[10]

The scene of the committee's public hearings, which opened on 22 September 1936, was room 357 of the Senate Office Building. La Follette, his partner Senator Thomas, and staff members sat at a large, carved wood, crescent-shaped desk located at the front and center of the room and raised a few steps from the floor. Directly in front of and below them was a long table where witnesses testified. Behind the witness table were ten rows of seats for visitors. The room could comfortably hold two hundred spectators, but many days as many as seven hundred persons managed to cram in. Spectators came in droves because of the widespread publicity the hearings received and because they expected a good show. They rarely left disappointed. For four years the committee treated them and the millions more who followed the hearings in their newspapers to the unfolding of a drama that one observer described as "stranger than fiction."[11]

From the outset La Follette took command of the hearings. Thoroughly versed in the subject matter and working from elaborate lists of questions that the staff had prepared beforehand, he led the examination of witnesses. He proved to be a superb inquisitor. His questions—short, incisive, and coming in rapid-fire order—sought to elicit facts, not opinions. He pursued witnesses relentlessly. A witness pretended not to hear the question. La Follette repeated it. The witness gave an evasive response. La Follette rephrased the question. The witness mumbled his answer. Speak louder, the chairman commanded. "You won't get anywhere if you fence with me, so please be frank," he told one witness. Only rarely did La Follette lose his composure and allow himself to become angry, to characterize testimony, or to argue with witnesses. "The brisk little Senator, dapper in a different suit each day, was too smart to indulge in any personal his-

10. Blankenhorn memorandum, "La Follette Hearings, September," box 1-7, Blankenhorn to J. Warren Madden and Edwin S. Smith, 12 September 1936, box 1-4, Blankenhorn to Madden, 10 September 1936, box 1-2, Blankenhorn Papers; RML quoted in Edward N. Doan, *The La Follettes and the Wisconsin Idea* (New York, 1947), p. 205.

11. "Strike Terrors," *Literary Digest* 122(3 October 1936):8–9. See also *Literary Digest* 122(5 September 1936):9–10, clipping, box 664–C, Family Papers (see list of abbreviations p. x).

trionics," a reporter noted. "He simply directed his actors, the witnesses."[12] Indeed, throughout the hearings, the most damaging facts and admissions came from the wrongdoers themselves.

La Follette also displayed a reasonable sense of fair play. He permitted witnesses to bring attorneys and to confer with them whenever they wished. Although neither witnesses nor attorneys could cross-examine other witnesses, they did have ample opportunity to comment upon or refute previous testimony. La Follette also encouraged witnesses to submit written statements and to bring to the committee's attention potential witnesses or evidence it might have overlooked. La Follette was less successful in maintaining decorum in the hearing room. Partisan spectators delighted in seeing businessmen on the "hot seat," and they occasionally laughed when they thought an employer was lying. One time La Follette had to remind the visitors that they were "guests of the Committee" after they had hissed at a witness's response. Laughing spectators and reporters so rankled one company executive that, when he finished testifying, he turned to reporters and snarled, "You're nothing but a bunch of goddamned Communists."[13]

The other senator on the committee, Elbert D. Thomas of Utah, played Doctor Watson to La Follette's Sherlock Holmes. Fifty-eight years old, balding, and bespectacled, this former college professor "devoted himself to the more philosophical side of the inquiry."[14] While La Follette probed for the factual details of wrongdoing, Thomas searched for the attitudes and motives of the wrongdoer. Frequently he engaged antiunion employers in long discussions about their moral obligations to society and about the nature of communism, which many of them blamed for labor unrest. The Utah senator's quiet, unassuming, genial manner nicely complemented La Follette's tough, cold, prosecutorial style.

The initial phase of the committee's investigation, from the fall of 1936 to the spring of 1937, focused on the four principal weapons of antiunionism: industrial espionage, strikebreaking, private police systems, and the stockpiling of munitions. The first of these, industrial

12. U.S. Congress, Senate, Committee on Education and Labor, *Private Police Systems*, S. Rept. 6, pt. 2, 76th Cong., 1st sess., 1939, p. 161; *Time*, 12 July 1937, pp. 17–18.

13. Auerbach, *Labor and Liberty*, p. 81; U.S. Congress, Senate, Subcommittee of the Committee on Education and Labor, *Hearings Pursuant to S. Res. 266, Violations of Free Speech and Rights of Labor*, 74th–76th Congs., 1936–1940, pt. 14, p. 4769 (hereafter cited as *Hearings*); *Washington Post*, 25 September 1936. Expletives in this and other newspaper accounts are only partially spelled out.

14. *Washington Post*, 25 September 1936.

espionage, was the employers' hiring of private detectives to infiltrate employee ranks. Masquerading as a worker, the detective reported to the company the names of union organizers and sympathizers. The company then harassed, or if necessary fired, these "agitators." Detectives also recruited, or "hooked," employees to inform on fellow workers, thereby enlarging the spy network. If an employer could not prevent his workers from organizing, he planted spies in the union; some spies even became union officials. Through espionage many corporations managed to stop unions from forming and to weaken those that existed.

Industrial espionage dated back at least to the 1870s, and its existence was common knowledge long before La Follette's committee began its probe. But the extent to which businesses engaged in the practice came as a shock. After combing the files of five detective agencies, the committee compiled a list of twenty-five hundred firms that between 1933 and 1936 had hired spies. The list, the committee noted, "reads like a bluebook of American industry."[15]

Many labor spies confessed their sins before the committee. Some of them looked and sounded the part, like the unregenerate Pinkerton agent who said he would spy on the White House if a client wanted him to. But most of them were ordinary workers whom detective agency officials had tricked into becoming spies. When one young, clean-cut worker admitted "ratting" on close friends and fellow workers, La Follette asked him, "Why did you do it? You don't look like that kind of fellow to me. Why?" The man lowered his head in shame, then went on to describe how he had been "hooked."[16]

The hearings produced several dramatic scenes. One day Charles Rigby, a worker at the Electric Auto-Lite Company in Toledo, was explaining how a Pinkerton detective had tried to induce him into becoming a "stool pigeon." During a break in the testimony, Rigby glanced over his shoulder only to spot the detective sitting in the back of the hearing room. Jumping to his feet and shaking his fist at the agent, Rigby screamed, "I said I'd get you for this; you dirty son of a bitch, and I will! There he is, the yellow rat who tried to frame me and my family, and I exposed him. He ought to be tarred and feathered." But there were some lighter moments, too. Arthur "Frenchy" Dubuc, who, though president of a union local at General Motors, spied on fellow workers, had spectators roaring with laughter as he told about meeting his company contact in a cemetery in the dead of night. Later, Frenchy even forced the usually deadpan La Follette

15. *Time*, 3 January 1938, pp. 9–10; Auerbach, *Labor and Liberty*, pp. 97–98.
16. *Washington Post*, 22 February 1937, 23 September 1936.

to crack a smile. To whom did he submit his intelligence reports, La Follette asked him. "Well," Dubuc replied, "to start with it was Pugmire and then a man by the name of Mathews, but since then I know is Mason. Of course, that might be a different alias, but I know him as Mason now. Then Parker, but now I know he is Peterson." Dubuc caught his breath and then continued: "Then Sullivan came in the picture and then after Sullivan there was a man by the name of —no Roberts came in the picture and then Sullivan came and finally a man by the name Riley, but Pugmire told me that it was Riley and to call him Ed, that his real name was John."[17]

Detective agency and corporation executives followed the labor spies to the witness table. Confronted with documents from their own files and with previous testimony, they reluctantly admitted that they engaged in espionage. But, they corrected La Follette, they hired "operatives," not spies. And in the words of one detective agency official, the purpose of espionage was not spying but rather "promoting efficiency and happiness among employees, looking for leaks and violations, and improving employee morale." They also claimed that operatives helped ferret out radicals and communists who tried to stir up the workers. "Frankly," La Follette asked officials of the Pinkerton Detective Agency, "don't you regard any attempt by men to organize in labor unions as Communistic?" "It's Communistic until we find out different," one of them replied.[18]

In its final report the committee rejected the justifications of corporations and detective agencies. It concluded that the real purpose of espionage was to hamper workers from exercising their rights to organize, and it recommended federal legislation to abolish the practice.[19]

The committee next turned its attention to strikebreaking, which like espionage had a long and sordid history. When a strike began, many employers automatically rejected collective bargaining and thought instead of how best to crush the strike. Again they utilized the services of the ever faithful detective agencies, which supplied not only spies but strikebreakers as well. Corporations could choose one of the reliable big names in the field, like the W. J. Burns International Detective Agency, or they could choose from among the more than fifty other agencies specializing in strikebreaking.[20]

17. Ibid., 29 January 1937; *Hearings*, pt. 6, pp. 2139, 2147.
18. *Time*, 8 February 1937, p. 16; *Washington Post*, 26 September 1936.
19. Auerbach, *Labor and Liberty*, p. 99.
20. U.S. Congress, Senate, Committee on Education and Labor, *Strikebreaking Services*, S. Rept. 6, 76th Cong., 1st sess., 1939, pp. 214–15.

On the stand, corporation executives openly admitted that they hired "strike personnel" during walkouts. But they denied the charge of strikebreaking. Rather, they explained with straight faces, they hired workers to continue plant operations, and they hired "watchmen" and "guards" to protect plant property and insure the safety of loyal employees who remained on the job.

The evidence, however, suggested otherwise. In most of the strikes that the committee examined, the men who supposedly ran the factory in the absence of striking employees were not qualified workmen. They only "made a show of working," so that strikers, getting the impression that the company was operating without them, would fear for their jobs, end the strike, and return to work. Most of the so-called watchmen or guards were in reality professional strikebreakers, many of whom had long criminal records. And rather than protect property and loyal employees, they fomented violence. Sometimes they tried to break strikes with brute force. Organizing themselves into "slugging crews," they attacked pickets and beat up strike leaders. Frequently they vandalized plant property and then blamed strikers for the damage. Paradoxically, although hired to end strikes, strikebreakers often tried to prolong them in order to remain on the job. Thus, when a settlement appeared near, they would, as one strikebreaker admitted to the committee, "slug a picket or two . . . or go in and throw a rock through a business representative's window, or something like that."[21]

Of all the witnesses who appeared before La Follette's committee, none made as deep an impression as the strikebreakers themselves, who seemed to epitomize the sordid nature of their occupation. They were, commented Heber Blankenhorn, "probably the strangest collection of witnesses that had ever appeared before a Senate committee: thugs and plug-uglies, one of them of such enormous bulk, with tremendous chops and no forehead, such that his photograph went all over the United States as a specimen of his craft." Blankenhorn was referring to 266-pound Sam "Chowderhead" Cohen, a twenty-year veteran of industrial warfare. In between his strikebreaking activities, Cohen had served time in the Elmira Reformatory for receiving stolen goods, in the Atlanta Penitentiary for conspiracy, and in Sing Sing for burglary. Shortly after his much publicized appearance before the committee, a New York jury convicted him for yet another crime. Despite Cohen's questionable background, many companies, including Remington Rand and Borden Dairy Products, had

21. Ibid., pp. 2, 71, 136; *Hearings*, pt. 22, p. 9383, quoted in Auerbach, *Labor and Liberty*, p. 104.

had no second thoughts about putting him on the payroll "to protect property" during strikes. The same day Cohen testified, Jack "Eat Em Up" Fisher put in an appearance. Among his credentials for strike-breaking were previous arrests for grand larceny, rape, and car theft. Such was the character of the strikebreaker. The practice, the committee observed, approached a "gangland racket."[22]

Strikebreakers, the La Follette committee concluded, "not only . . . tend to provoke violence and disorder, but their purpose is to discredit and destroy instruments of collective bargaining and make amiable settlement of disputes an impossibility." Furthermore, "through their acts of intimidation, coercion, and provocation such persons violate the rights of free speech and free assembly and the freedom of association of employees." The committee promised to recommend legislation abolishing the practice.[23]

From March to May of 1937, the committee turned the spotlight on yet another antilabor practice, the use of private police forces. Ostensibly a corporation hired its own policemen to guard plant property and employees and to supplement often inadequate public law enforcement agencies. In practice, however, company police served functions little different than those of professional strikebreakers. They intimidated and harassed workers, perpetrated acts of violence, and crushed strikes. This phase of the investigation focused on the coal-mining company towns of Harlan County, Kentucky. Later in 1937 the committee added another case study, the private police systems of the Republic Steel Corporation.

By 1937 Harlan County had already become a national scandal. A year before the La Follette probe, a Kentucky governor's commission reported finding "a monster-like reign of oppression" in the county. Tales of terror emanating from Harlan so frightened one La Follette committee investigator that he "wanted either the troops out or permission to carry a gun" before he would enter the county. According to Blankenhorn, "La Follette nearly went through the ceiling when the request for guns fell into his hands." La Follette refused the request, but he was concerned enough about the safety of his investigators that he directed them to enter Harlan only during daylight hours. At night they were to take refuge in neighboring Bell County.[24]

22. Blankenhorn memorandum, "La Follette Hearings, September," box 1-7, Blankenhorn Papers; *Strikebreaking Services*, pp. 83, 85, 189.

23. *Strikebreaking Services*, pp. 136–38.

24. Kentucky report quoted in *Private Police Systems*, p. 13; Blankenhorn to J. Warren Madden, 6, 16 March 1937, box 1-3, Blankenhorn Papers.

Harlan County more than lived up to its reputation. The committee found that the miners, who lived in company-owned houses located in company-owned towns, endured wretched economic and social conditions. The coal companies paid meager wages, then managed to retrieve part of the wages through a variety of devious practices. One company forced miners to do all their shopping at the company store, which charged exorbitant prices; overcharged miners for medical services; and twice a month compelled them to buy chances in a phony used-car raffle. Even more appalling was the near total absence of freedom. In company towns, the employers administered town government and strictly regulated the social life of residents. In some towns the company controlled the right of inhabitants to come and go as they pleased. A locked gate barred the only road into the town of Louellen. Residents had to request permission from the company office to come or go or to receive visitors. In the appropriately named town of Lynch, company police carefully scrutinized all visitors. If visitors did not meet their approval, the police whisked them out of town.

Mine operators, organized into the Harlan County Coal Operators' Association, successfully resisted attempts by miners to form unions. The agents of resistance were the private police that each company employed, the chief law enforcement officer in the county, High Sheriff Theodore Middleton; and Middleton's deputy sheriffs, many of whom were convicted criminals and most of whom were on company payrolls. Occasionally coal operators beefed up these forces by hiring "thug gangs." Company agents harassed miners who showed even the slightest interest in organizing; they broke up union meetings; and they arrested organizers on trumped-up charges. Should union organizers persist, deputy sheriffs and "thug gangs" got rough. They shot union organizers and threw sticks of dynamite through the front windows of their homes. One month before La Follette's committee took up the Harlan investigation, the seventeen-year-old son of Marshall Musick, a field representative of the United Mine Workers, was shot and killed. Musick's wife and another son were wounded. The evidence indicated that the shooting was done by coal company henchmen.[25]

Day after day during the Harlan hearings, spectators sat in stunned silence, as though they could not believe all that they were seeing and hearing. Indeed, many of the witnesses and much of the testimony seemed almost to defy belief. The deputy sheriffs who testified, wear-

25. *Private Police Systems*, pp. 1–114 passim, 207–10.

ing broad-brimmed black hats and with pistols strapped to their sides, looked like bad guys straight out of a western movie. Some of the testimony contained elements of black humor. For instance, when La Follette asked a coal company executive why none of his employees belonged to a union, he responded, "Our people have never seemed to want the union."[26] Another company official assured La Follette that miners had every opportunity to join unions, but they simply had not wanted to. He said that on one occasion his employees "with a secret ballot voted 267 to 5 that they did not want any union there." When La Follette inquired as to the nature of the "secret ballot," the official admitted that he had required the miners to sign their names to the ballots.[27]

The La Follette committee's shocking exposé of the practices of mine employers produced salutary results. Simultaneous with the hearings, the United Mine Workers sent organizers into Harlan County. With the national spotlight fixed upon them, coal operators and their agents dared not disturb the union organizers. The hearings also prompted a federal grand jury to hand down sixty-nine indictments, naming as defendents company officials and law enforcement officers. Under these pressures, Harlan coal operators signed contracts with the United Mine Workers.[28] Due in large part to the efforts of La Follette's committee, the reign of terror ended, at least temporarily.

In addition to espionage, strikebreaking, and private police systems, the committee exposed a fourth antilabor device, the stockpiling of munitions by corporations. When labor trouble threatened, many companies bought huge supplies of weapons, including tear-gas and nauseating-gas grenades, guns with which to shoot the grenades, revolvers, rifles, billy clubs, handcuffs, and in some cases machine guns. Corporation officials claimed that they needed armaments for the protection of payrolls and of plant property during strikes. Such reasons, however, did not explain the clearly offensive nature of some weapons contained in corporation arsenals, like sawed-off shotguns, machine guns, long-range rifles, and guns that could project gas grenades long distances. Nor, as the committee pointed out, did they explain why corporations frequently resorted "to all manner of subterfuge to conceal their purchase and possession of arms and gas." Presumably, if employers bought armaments to protect property, they would be

26. Quoted in Auerbach, *Labor and Liberty*, p. 118.
27. *Private Police Systems*, p. 68.
28. Auerbach, *Labor and Liberty*, p. 120.

anxious to publicize their purchases and thereby deter potential thieves and trespassers.[29]

The committee concluded that the real purpose for stockpiling munitions, at least in such vast quantities, was to enable the employers to engage in "aggression" against striking workers. Further, it found a "marked correlation" between employers' purchases of weapons and their policies toward labor. "Almost invariably those employers who have assumed an attitude of hostility to bargaining with so-called outside unions, have been discovered to be the largest purchasers of industrial munitions." The committee documented numerous strikes during which companies distributed munitions to private police and strikebreakers, who in turn used them to combat strikers. In May 1935, during a strike at the Berger Manufacturing Company of Canton, Ohio, a subsidiary of Republic Steel, heavily armed company police attacked picket lines and roamed through the city indiscriminately tossing tear-gas grenades at strikers and innocent bystanders alike. What had started as a peaceful strike turned into a bloody confrontation between police and workers.[30]

The committee also investigated the three major suppliers of industrial munitions: Federal Laboratories, Lake Erie Chemical Company, and the Manville Manufacturing Corporation. These vulturelike companies preyed on labor unrest for their livelihood. Munitions vendors testified that, in selling their wares, they were only doing their patriotic duty: working to combat radicalism and defend the American way. The documents that the committee subpoenaed from the vendors' files told a different story. One Federal Laboratories salesman in California once wrote to his boss, "I will let you know as soon as possible the outcome of the milk strike. Here's hoping it is a good one." "We are surrounded with strikes," wrote a Lake Erie salesman, "but they are all too peaceful to suit me." Another munitions seller wrote his lawyer that he was "waiting for a nice juicy strike up here. The darn things don't happen enough to suit me."[31]

"The possession and use of industrial munitions by employers," the committee concluded, "is the logical end of a labor relations policy based on nonrecognition of unions—in opposition to the spirit of national labor laws." It found that the deployment of munitions during strikes resulted in violence, embittered labor-management re-

29. U.S. Congress, Senate, Committee on Education and Labor, *Industrial Munitions*, S. Rept. 6, pt. 3, 76th Cong., 1st sess., 1939, pp. 69–70, 72–80.
30. Ibid., pp. 3, 107–15.
31. Ibid., p. 90.

lations, provoked strikers to violent retaliation, and hampered the peaceful settlement of disputes. Moreover, because strikebreakers and company police often turned their weapons on persons not involved in strikes, munitions menaced the public peace. Finally the committee recommended stiff federal regulation of the sale and possession of munitions.[32]

When, in mid-May 1937, the committee concluded its hearings on the four weapons of antiunionism, it faced an uncertain future. La Follette favored ending the investigation as soon as possible.[33] Although his reasons were not entirely clear, he may have felt that the committee should quit while it was still ahead. For eight months it had battered the nation with sensational and shocking disclosures. Perhaps he sensed that the public had reached the saturation point and that further disclosures might numb rather than outrage people. Moreover, by May the committee had more than enough evidence with which to frame remedial legislation, and perhaps he thought it should seize upon the widespread revulsion at employer practices to push that legislation through Congress. Then too, the labor situation no longer seemed as urgent as it had a year earlier. In March the Supreme Court had upheld the constitutionality of the Wagner Act and thereby freed the National Labor Relations Board from debilitating challenges to its legality. Organized labor, especially the CIO under the leadership of John L. Lewis, also appeared to be on firmer ground. Since the beginning of 1937, the CIO had experienced phenomenal growth in membership and had managed to topple such bastions of antiunionism as United States Steel, General Motors, and Chrysler. La Follette's committee had contributed mightily to the CIO's success, and La Follette may have believed that organized labor had reached the point where it could stand on its own feet. Finally, La Follette had wearied of the investigation. It cut into the time he felt he should devote to his other responsibilities. "I am working so hard," he complained to Rachel in June, "and spread out so thin between so many committees that I do not feel at all satisfied with any of my work."[34]

La Follette also came under pressure to continue the investigation. Gardner Jackson slipped word of the senator's mood to Roger Baldwin of the American Civil Liberties Union, and he in turn lavishly praised La Follette for what he had accomplished and appealed to him to press forward. The committee's staff also urged its chairman to con-

32. Ibid., pp. 188–90.
33. Auerbach, *Labor and Liberty*, p. 121.
34. RML to Rachel, 18 June 1937, box 45-A, Family Papers.

tinue. But it was an incident in Chicago on Memorial Day 1937 that finally impelled La Follette to extend the life of his committee.[35]

On 26 May the Steel Workers Organizing Committee, an arm of the CIO, called workers out on strike against Republic Steel, Inland Steel, and the Youngstown Sheet and Tube Company. This was the start of the so-called Little Steel strike. On 30 May, Memorial Day, there occurred a tragic incident at Republic Steel's South Chicago plant. At midafternoon that day, several thousand strikers, their families, and a few spectators gathered at Sam's Place, a former tavern that was serving as strike headquarters. After listening to a few speeches, the crowd decided to march en masse to the plant, some five blocks away. The Chicago police, expecting trouble, had three hundred men stationed outside the factory gates. According to the official police account, the "mob," armed with clubs, bricks, and chunks of concrete, tried to storm police lines and enter the plant. During the ensuing melee, strikers stoned, clubbed, and knocked down policemen, injuring at least thirty-five of them. The police finally dispersed the rioters by firing tear gas at them. Several policemen had to shoot attackers in self-defense. When it was over, ten strikers had been killed, more than one hundred wounded. The next day newspapers throughout the country spread the police version of the incident across page one. Editorials roundly condemned the brutal tactics of the strikers and by implication condemned the CIO. It seemed to be a clear-cut case of mob violence.

Perhaps it was too clear-cut; or so thought the secretary of the La Follette committee, Robert Wohlforth. Soon after the incident he learned that Paramount Newsreel had filmed the incident but was refusing to distribute the film to movie theaters because it might incite riots. His suspicions aroused, Wohlforth persuaded a friend at Paramount to slip him a copy of the film for private showing to the committee. The newsreel, running just under eight minutes, convinced committee members that the account they had read in the newspapers was patently false. After viewing the film they were privately referring to the incident as the "Chicago massacre."[36]

During a meeting with La Follette and Thomas, staff members strongly recommended an investigation. Although the senators considered the incident "unfortunate," they were reluctant to involve the committee. "If there was an objection to investigating that was not raised," Blankenhorn complained, "I did not hear it. There were even

35. Auerbach, *Labor and Liberty*, pp. 120–22.
36. Ibid., pp. 121–23; Blankenhorn to J. Warren Madden, 14 June 1937, box 1-3, Blankenhorn Papers.

some invented." The senators and staff argued back and forth for three hours. Finally, La Follette consented to a preliminary investigation. Several days later, after continued prodding from Blankenhorn, he agreed to public hearings.[37]

The hearings on the Memorial Day incident lasted from 30 June to 2 July and were easily the most dramatic that the committee held over the four years of its existence. "Tingling," said one reporter. Thirty witnesses testified, including ten police officers and eighteen persons who had either taken part in the march or had witnessed it. In addition, the Chicago police department provided the committee with twenty-three sworn affidavits from patrolmen who had been present. Adding to the suspense was the knowledge that when the committee finished with the witnesses, it planned the first public showing of the Paramount newsreel.[38]

The policemen, in order of rank from the commissioner down to the patrolmen, led off the testimony. Basically they stuck to their original story, although they embellished it here and there. In short they claimed that several thousand heavily armed strikers, "marching as if under commands" and "executing their maneuvers with military precision," marched from Sam's Place toward the plant. When they approached the police line they stopped momentarily. Captain Mooney told them that he wanted no trouble and that they should turn back. With cries of "Kill the lousy coppers" and "Forward, we will take the plant," the mob surged forward. The police used only such force as was necessary to repel the attack.[39]

Several officers claimed that communists had instigated and led the assault. Fourteen of the marchers, they said, were "known Communists." Two patrolmen swore that they heard the mob singing the communist anthem, the "Internationale." Sergeant Lyons testified that many, if not most, of the marchers were "probably [of] foreign extraction," an additional proof of their radicalism.[40]

The bluecoats had a difficult time squaring their testimony with the physical evidence the committee had gathered. On the first day of hearings, La Follette made public for the first time the coroner's report indicating that of the ten strikers killed, seven had been shot in the back, three in the side. Even more damaging were the more than twenty-five photographs the committee had subpoenaed from news-

---

37. Blankenhorn to J. Warren Madden, 14, 18 June 1937, box 1-3, Blankenhorn to RML, 17 June 1937, box 1-1, Blankenhorn Papers.
38. *Time*, 12 July 1937, pp. 17–18; *Hearings*, pt. 14.
39. *Hearings*, pt. 14 passim.
40. Ibid., pp. 4692, 4767, 4832, 5039.

men on the scene. Except for one photograph, which showed a few marchers carrying rocks, clubs, and ax handles, the pictures raised serious questions about the police account. One photograph showed a long, winding, rather disorganized column of people approaching the police line—hardly an army "executing their maneuvers with military precision." Another picture, taken just after the shooting began, showed the crowd in full retreat, their backs to the police. On the far left of the photograph was a policeman, his right arm outstretched toward the fleeing marchers. La Follette told Sergeant Lyons to hold a magnifying glass over the picture of the officer. "You see that hand," La Follette asked. "Yes sir," said Lyons. "What is in it?" asked La Follette. Although the officer appeared to be aiming a pistol, Lyons said it looked like a rock. Perhaps realizing the improbability of a policeman pointing a rock at a crowd, Lyons changed his answer. It was neither a rock nor a pistol, he concluded, but a smudge in the picture. Although police witnesses consistently claimed that they had drawn their pistols only in self-defense, in one photograph an officer was reaching for his holster, even though no striker was anywhere near him. Senator Thomas asked Lyons, "What is he doing with his right hand?" Responded Lyons, "He may be drawing a handkerchief." "Out of his holster?" asked Thomas. One photograph showed an unarmed marcher down on the ground, covering his head to fend off police clubs; another showed policemen dragging an injured striker along the ground by his feet.[41] Although the subject matter was "grim and gruesome," spectators occasionally could not help but laugh. Patrolman George Higgins, for example, trying to explain how he had "defended" himself from a woman attacker, said: "I didn't strike her. Like a gentleman I shoved her."[42]

The next set of witnesses, the marchers and observers, told a story completely contradicting the police version. The strikers, they said, had no intention of breaking into the factory. They only wanted to set up a mass picket line out in front of the gates. According to Ralph Beck, a reporter for the *Chicago Daily News*, when the crowd arrived at the police line, marchers informed the officials of their plan. The police told them they could go no farther. After five minutes of discussion between the marchers and the police, someone in the back of the crowd tossed a tree branch toward police. "Watch out," a policeman shouted. Another bluecoat fired his gun in the air. Two more shots followed. Then came a barrage of rocks and clubs from the strikers. With this, some policemen threw tear-gas grenades into the

41. Ibid., pp. 4650, 4758–81, photographs.
42. *Time*, 12 July 1937, pp. 17–18.

crowd, while others fired their revolvers point-blank at the backs of already fleeing marchers. Then police chased after the strikers, clubbing and kicking the fallen and wounded. A string of witnesses followed Beck to the stand, confirming various parts of his account and adding details of police brutality.[43]

On the final day of the hearings the moment came that everyone, except the police, had been waiting for. Shortly before noon La Follette ordered the room darkened and the projector turned on. Seven hundred spectators sat on the edges of their seats, watching the Paramount newsreel and then a repeat showing of it in slow motion. Actually the film was somewhat anticlimactic. Between the jiggling camera and the clouds of tear gas, it was difficult to follow the action. Moreover, because the photographer had changed lenses just when hostilities began, those crucial seconds went unfilmed. But even with those limitations, the newsreel proved beyond doubt that the police version of the incident was sheer fabrication. Here were policmen chasing unarmed men and women, pushing them to the ground, then wildly beating the unmoving bodies with nightsticks. One graphic scene showed policemen shoving a man, semiconscious and with a blood-soaked shirt, into the back of a patrol wagon. They acted as though they were handling a sack of potatoes. When the film ended, the hearings broke for lunch; it was doubtful that anyone had the stomach for it that day.[44]

In its report on the Memorial Day incident the committee concluded that the strikers were fully within their rights to march to the plant and set up a picket line. If the Chicago police had not interfered, "the day would have passed without violence or disorder." Although conceding that strikers had provoked the police by using abusive language and by hurling objects, the report concluded that, "from all the evidence we think it plain that the force employed by police was far in excess of that which the occasion required. Its use must be ascribed either to gross inefficiency in the performance of police duty or a deliberate effort to intimidate the strikers."[45]

43. *Hearings*, pt. 14, pp. 4853–86, 4893–4974.
44. Ibid., p. 4891; *Time*, 12 July 1937, pp. 17–18; Auerbach, *Labor and Liberty*, p. 127.
45. U.S. Congress, Senate, Committee on Education and Labor, S. Rept. 46, pt. 2, 75th Cong., 1st sess., 1937, pp. 33–39, quoted in Auerbach, *Labor and Liberty*, pp. 127–28.

CHAPTER 11

Temporary Alliance

Even though the civil liberties investigation demanded much of his time, La Follette was determined not to slight his other political and legislative responsibilities. Hence, during the first two years of the investigation he managed to play a prominent role in the 1936 presidential election, to help lead the fight for Roosevelt's controversial "court packing" plan in 1937, and to continue his battles for public works and tax reform. In 1938 he became an unenthusiastic partner in his brother's ill-fated attempt to launch a new third party, the National Progressives of America. The 1936 election and the ten months following it marked the peak of La Follette's active cooperation with Roosevelt. Indeed, so close was their personal and political relationship that for a time, in the fall of 1937, the talk in Washington was that Roosevelt intended to support the Wisconsin senator for the Democratic presidential nomination in 1940. Yet their alliance was short lived. Due to disagreements about how to handle the recession of 1937–1938 and about foreign policy and especially due to the formation of the National Progressives of America, La Follette began to drift away from the president.

Immediately following La Follette's reelection as a Progressive in 1934, political observers, believing him to be a reliable gauge of liberal sentiment in the country, began to speculate about his stance in the 1936 presidential contest. No one of course expected him to support the standard-bearer of the GOP, the party he had so recently repudiated. But they did wonder whether he would support Roosevelt, help organize a third party, or simply remain neutral.

Early in 1935 Roosevelt feared that La Follette was leaning toward a third party. To Woodrow Wilson's old mentor, Colonel House, Roosevelt wrote, "Progressive Republicans like La Follette, Cutting, Nye, etc., . . . are flirting with the idea of a third ticket . . . with the knowledge that such a third ticket would be beaten but that it would defeat us, elect a conservative Republican and cause a complete swing far to the left before 1940."[1]

1. Roosevelt to House, 16 February 1935, in Elliott Roosevelt, ed., *F. D. R.: His Personal Letters, 1928–1945* (New York, 1950), 1:452–53.

La Follette figured prominently in Roosevelt's reelection strategy, and the president seemed to work hard to secure his support. For one thing, he continued to grant patronage and other favors to Phil's administration in Wisconsin. In July 1935, for example, he appointed a La Follette man, Ralph Immel, as administrator of federal public works projects in the state. Wisconsin Democrats were outraged, since in most other states that choice position went to loyal Democrats. Roosevelt undoubtedly realized that from Young Bob's reformist point of view, his performance in office left much to be desired. He therefore compensated for what he lacked in performance with promises for the future. According to Rexford Tugwell's later account, Roosevelt indicated to Tugwell, Bob La Follette, and Harry Hopkins that he intended to work for the realignment of the political parties along liberal and conservative lines. Tugwell, La Follette, and Hopkins were unsure of how Roosevelt would bring about realignment, whether he would transform the Democratic party into a vehicle for liberal ideas by purging the conservatives within, or whether he would at some time form a progressive third party. But, according to Tugwell, they were convinced of the president's sincerity.[2]

Roosevelt's strategy paid off. In August 1935, La Follette scotched rumors of a third party. "We could preach a crusade and probably roll up an impressive vote, but we could do little more," he told a reporter. At the same time Roosevelt invited the La Follette brothers to Hyde Park to help him plan campaign strategy.[3]

As the election drew near, La Follette stepped up his activities on Roosevelt's behalf. In September 1936 he helped organize, then became chairman of, the Progressive National Committee, a bipartisan organization pledged to insure Roosevelt's reelection. Funded largely by contributions from organized labor, the committee succeeded in attracting large numbers of independent liberals to the Roosevelt camp. Under the committee's auspices La Follette stumped throughout the Middle West and West, calling upon "Progressive-minded citizens" to "close ranks" against "the forces of reaction which are solidly behind" Gov. Alfred Landon, the Republican challenger.[4] Not

2. Philip F. La Follette, *Adventure in Politics: The Memoirs of Philip La Follette* (New York, 1970), pp. 220–25; *New York Times*, 28 July 1935, sec. 4; Rexford G. Tugwell, *The Democratic Roosevelt: A Biography of Franklin Roosevelt* (Baltimore, 1969[1957]), pp. 410–14.

3. *New York Times*, 18 August 1935, sec. 7; PFL, *Memoirs*, pp. 226–27.

4. Arthur M. Schlesinger, Jr., *The Age of Roosevelt: Politics of Upheaval* (Boston, 1960), pp. 595–96; *New York Times*, 12 September 1936; *Washington Post*, 29 September 1936.

since his father's campaign in 1924 had Young Bob displayed so much enthusiasm for a presidential campaign.

The outcome of the 1936 election delighted him. Roosevelt carried all but two states. In Wisconsin, Phil easily won a third term, and the Progressive party reached the zenith of its electoral strength. It swept seven of the House seats and secured a near majority in the state legislature. La Follette viewed the election as a significant step toward realignment. "The last election," he told a reporter, "did not seem to me between Democrats and Republicans as much as between two sets of ideas." Pointing to the victories of George Norris, who ran as an independent in Nebraska, of William Borah, who ran as a Republican in Idaho, of the Progressives in Wisconsin, and of Roosevelt in each of those states, La Follette concluded that the voters were "not voting for parties but for ideas—choosing between liberalism on the one hand and conservatism or reaction on the other." La Follette also viewed the election, not as an expression of appreciation for what Roosevelt had done during the first term, but as a "mandate to go ahead and do more."[5]

Roosevelt's first legislative recommendation of 1937, the Court-reform proposal, drew La Follette's enthusiastic support and convinced him that the president took his "mandate" seriously. Since 1935 the Supreme Court had been waging war on the New Deal. It had invalidated the National Industrial Recovery Act, the Agricultural Adjustment Act, and numerous other federal, as well as state, laws. By 1937 it appeared likely that the Court would overturn such key measures as the Social Security and Wagner Labor Relations acts. On 5 February of that year, Roosevelt struck back. In a message to Congress he requested the power to expand membership on the High Court from nine to possibly fifteen justices.

It was no surprise that Roosevelt chose to confront the Court crisis, which threatened to cripple government attempts to fight the depression. But the manner in which he acted and the nature of his proposal shocked and outraged much of the nation. He sprang the plan on Congress without warning. Even his congressional leaders, who would have to muster enough votes to insure passage of the plan, received but one hour of advance notice. Worse still, Roosevelt seemed devious, for in his message to Congress he disguised his real purpose under the cloak of efficiency. The justices, he said with feigned sympathy, were overburdened with work. To help them out

5. *Milwaukee Journal*, 24 January 1937, clipping, box 665–C, Family Papers (see list of abbreviations p. x).

he would appoint additional members. This silly pretense fooled no one, and Roosevelt quickly dropped it.

He probably expected opposition from Republicans and conservative Democrats, who regarded the Court as the only remaining barrier to New Dealism run wild; but he did not anticipate the storm of protest that issued from liberal quarters. In the Senate, liberal Democrats Burton K. Wheeler and Joseph C. O'Mahoney and progressive Republicans Borah, Nye, and Hiram Johnson sharply attacked the plan. Some opponents accurately pointed out that the proposal did not go to the heart of the problem. Packing the Court might get Roosevelt out of trouble, but what, they asked, would happen if some future, conservative president tried to stack the Court with reactionaries? Other critics maintained that, if the Court's powers were to be trimmed, Congress, rather than the chief executive, should be the beneficiary.[6]

In contrast to many of his liberal colleagues, La Follette greeted the president's message with enthusiastic approval. Like his father, Young Bob was a longtime critic of the Court. As far back as 1930, when the Senate debated the nomination of Charles Evans Hughes for chief justice, La Follette had denounced the Court for usurping legislative functions. "The Supreme Court . . . has now placed itself in the position where it defeats the popular will as expressed in legislation enacted by Congress," he had declared. Prior to the president's message La Follette had advocated a variety of Court reforms, including a constitutional amendment granting to Congress the regulatory powers the Court denied it and a drastic proposal permitting the Court to rule on the constitutionality of a statute coming from a lower court only after the attorney general had ruled that such a review was in the national interest. Initially, opponents of Court packing, like Wheeler, hoped to have La Follette on their side. Wheeler later recalled that he had appealed to La Follette by saying that if the elder La Follette were alive, he would have opposed the president's scheme. The Montana senator also reminded La Follette that he, Wheeler, had lifted his alternative to Court packing—a constitutional amendment allowing Congress to override Court vetoes—from Fighting Bob's 1924 platform.[7] La Follette was unmoved.

La Follette became one of the president's most vocal supporters.

6. William E. Leuchtenburg, *Franklin D. Roosevelt and the New Deal, 1932–1940* (New York, 1963), pp. 232–95; James MacGregor Burns, *Roosevelt: The Lion and the Fox* (New York, 1956), pp. 293–99.

7. *CR* 71:2, 1930, vol. 72, pt. 4, pp. 3561–64; Schlesinger, *Politics of Upheaval*, p. 228; *New York Times*, 14 February 1936; interview, Burton K. Wheeler, 4 December 1973.

Six days after Roosevelt's message to Congress, the Wisconsin senator delivered a widely publicized address over the NBC radio network. During the protracted debate over Court packing, few if any persons on the Court-reform side lashed out at the Court in language as harsh as what La Follette used that night. "When the Court substitutes for the will of the people . . . its own will; when it supplants the prevailing economic theory with its own smug theory of days gone by; when it decrees that it is beyond the power of the people to meet the national needs—then," said La Follette, "it has become a dictator and we have succumbed to a fascist system of control which is inconsistent with fundamental principles upon which our government is founded."[8]

On 4 March, before a gathering of party faithful at the Mayflower Hotel, Roosevelt made his first public appeal for Court reform. The next day La Follette congratulated Roosevelt for "an inspiring, fighting speech . . . delivered in your most masterful style" and assured him that "the overwhelming majority of people will answer by coming to your support with renewed determination to win the battle you are waging to save our fundamental institutions of democracy." "It is a great privilege," he concluded, "to fight in the ranks under your courageous leadership in this historic struggle." These were rare words indeed from one who had so often criticized the president's leadership. "It is a grand battle and you know how happy I am to have you with me," Roosevelt responded.[9]

In addition to his many public speeches, La Follette helped lead the Court fight in the Senate. Roosevelt had placed Joseph T. Robinson, Democratic majority leader, in charge of the effort. Although Robinson was upset over the president's failure to consult with him prior to springing the plan on Congress and although he probably had strong reservations about Court packing, the loyal majority leader promised his best effort. But he was slow to move. A month after the message, Robinson had yet to organize the Senate supporters of Court reform; so La Follette moved in to fill the leadership vacuum. On 16 March he reported to Roosevelt, "I am sure you will be glad to know that I got Senator Robinson to call an informal conference of Senators supporting the Supreme Court proposal on last Saturday." La Follette, who had never thought highly of Robinson, perhaps was subtly pointing out to the president that Robinson had been remiss in his duties. Nine senators attended the strategy session. "We went

8. *New York Times*, 14 February 1937.

9. RML to Roosevelt, 5 March 1937, President's Personal File 1792, Franklin D. Roosevelt Papers, Franklin D. Roosevelt Library, Hyde Park, New York; Roosevelt to RML, 11 March 1937, box 15-C, Family Papers.

over the list of senators very carefully and made arrangements to do all that we properly can with regard to those who are in doubt," La Follette wrote. He also reported that all of the senators attending expressed "supreme confidence in the ultimate outcome. They regarded the suggestions of compromise coming from opponents as an indication of . . . weakness."[10] La Follette was usually a keen judge of sentiment in the Senate. This time, however, he badly misjudged his colleagues.

By the spring of 1937 the Court-packing bill was all but dead. Many circumstances had contributed to that state of affairs. Roosevelt's inept handling of the matter at the outset had gotten his "grand battle" off to a bad start, and the opposition was stronger and better organized than anyone had expected. With such prominent liberals as Burton Wheeler in opposition and with other New Dealers, like Wagner, sitting on the sidelines, the Republicans needed only to sit back and watch gleefully as the Democratic party ripped itself apart. But it was the Court itself, through a series of decisions in the spring, that administered the death blow. On 29 March, in a 5 to 4 decision, it upheld a Washington minimum-wage law almost identical to a New York statute it had previously invalidated. Two weeks later it ruled the Wagner Act constitutional. On 18 May anti-New Deal Justice Willis Van Devanter, an opponent of the New Deal, announced his retirement from the High Court. Finally, on 24 May, the Court upheld the Social Security Act. The Court's actions thus eliminated the sense of urgency that had been Roosevelt's trump card.[11]

But these developments did nothing to change La Follette's opinion of the Court. Speaking in Philadelphia shortly after the decisions for the Washington minimum wage and the Wagner Act, he declared that the Court-reform struggle was between "the reactionaries of business, finance, and politics" on the one hand and "the representatives of the people" on the other. Referring to Justice Owen J. Roberts, who had voted against New Deal legislation in the past but who had voted to uphold the minimum-wage law and the Wagner Act, La Follette declared, "Just because a Justice has changed his mind, shall we abandon the effort to release our Government from the thralls of judicial usurpation of power? No! A thousand times no!"[12]

In addition to his stated reasons for supporting the Court-packing proposal, La Follette possibly hoped that, if the proposal passed,

10. RML to Roosevelt, 16 March 1937, box 15-C, Family Papers.
11. Leuchtenburg, *Roosevelt and the New Deal*, pp. 234–38.
12. *Philadelphia Evening Bulletin*, 20 April 1937, clipping, box 665-C, Family Papers.

Roosevelt would reward him with an appointment to the Court. According to his sister-in-law Isen, when Justice Van Devanter resigned, Bob asked Phil if he was interested in serving on the Court. "Phil said No. Then Bob said he would like it himself." Isen wrote in her diary: "Phil and I . . . think it would be a great stroke for Roosevelt to appoint Bob; . . . Bob really hates the wear and tear of every day political life. . . . We agreed that he wants to serve in the Progressive cause, but badly wants security, and the Court would be an ideal place for him and he would do a superb job."[13]

The Court controversy dragged on into the summer. Finally, in late July the Senate voted to recommit a compromise plan to the Judiciary Committee, where it was killed. Loyal to the end, La Follette joined nineteen senators in opposition to sending the bill to committee.[14]

There was a second controversy during the summer, about the future of relief and public works, in which La Follette again staunchly backed the administration. Roosevelt's budget message of April sparked the controversy. In it he announced his intention to slash federal expenditures for public works and for work relief and thereby balance the budget within a year. The chief victim of this cutback was the Works Progress Administration, the work relief agency under the direction of Harry Hopkins. In 1935 Roosevelt had created the WPA and turned over to it most of the $4.5 billion that Congress had appropriated for public employment that year. In his budget message the president requested only $1.5 billion to continue WPA activities. With this reduced sum the WPA would have to cut its payroll drastically, perhaps laying off a million or more employees.

Roosevelt's budget message reflected his belief that the nation was well on the way to recovery, and there was some justification for his optimistic assessment. By the spring of 1937 industrial production had at long last surpassed 1929 predepression levels. The unemployment rate, although still high, had dropped by about one-half since 1933. Prices were rising, and the stock exchange was experiencing a modest boom.[15]

The president's message, however, deeply disturbed La Follette, who felt that the depression was far from over. He also feared that spending cuts would wipe out previous gains. Moreover, by this time he had come to believe that, even when prosperity returned, the

13. Mrs. PFL, "Isen's Political Diary," 15 May 1937, p. 44, box 161-3, PFL Papers.

14. New York Times, 23 July 1937.

15. Leuchtenburg, Roosevelt and the New Deal, pp. 243–44; New York Times, 23–25 April 1937.

government would have to continue public works in order to maintain full employment. He envisaged a system of "modified capitalism" wherein the government, through taxation and spending policies, played a permanent role in regulating the economy.[16]

When the WPA appropriation bill reached the Senate in June, La Follette carefully refrained from criticizing the president for offering the meager appropriation. And, for the first time during a public works debate, he did not offer an amendment to increase the appropriation. Doubtless the reason for this uncharacteristic restraint was his realization that the Senate would not only defeat a higher appropriation but that it might also insist on cutting the president's modest $1.5 billion request. As usual, conservative Republicans and Democrats favored slicing the appropriation. But they received unexpected support from two powerful Democratic moderates in the Senate, James F. Byrnes of South Carolina and majority leader Robinson. In the past Byrnes and especially Robinson had generally supported administration measures. Both, however, believed that the depression was over and that public works should be phased out as soon as possible. "Joe Robinson has thrown in his lot with the reactionary Democrats and Republicans who are out to wreck Roosevelt," La Follette remarked to Rachel.[17]

Confronted with this small-scale rebellion on the part of his usually reliable Senate leaders, Roosevelt refused to back off. By so doing he enhanced his reputation with La Follette, who had been upset with the president's decision to curtail spending. "Roosevelt is certainly driving the wedge deep into his party," La Follette wrote approvingly. "If he keeps on he may bring about the party realignment so essential if democracy is to work in the future." With the defection of Robinson, Byrnes, and several others, Roosevelt turned to La Follette and to a handful of liberal Democrats to lead the WPA fight. This group finally managed to salvage the president's request for $1.5 billion. "The irony of the relief fight," La Follette wrote to Rachel, "is that I regard the sum of $1.5 billion as woefully inadequate as do many of us who are carrying the brunt. Time will prove we are right on that score."[18]

16. RML to Rachel, 19 June 1937, box 45-A, Family Papers; Fred C. Kelly, "Senator La Follette Chats," *Milwaukee Journal*, 24 January 1937, clipping, box 665-C, Family Papers.

17. James T. Patterson, *Congressional Conservatism and the New Deal: The Growth of the Conservative Coalition in Congress, 1933–1939* (Lexington, Ky., 1967), pp. 140–43; RML to Rachel, 19 June 1937, box 45-A, Family Papers.

18. RML to Rachel, 19 June 1937, box 45-A, Family Papers; Patterson, *Con-*

Although La Follette and Roosevelt worked closely on the Court-packing and relief-bill efforts, the tax issue continued to divide them. In June, La Follette tried to capitalize on the budget-balancing craze then sweeping Congress by proposing income tax increases. His proposals, in the form of amendments to an excise tax bill then before the Senate, called for increasing surtaxes along graduated lines on taxable income over six thousand dollars and for broadening the tax base by lowering personal exemptions. By offering his amendments without advance warning, La Follette caught administration forces off guard. On 24 June the Senate adopted the first of his amendments, 35 to 31. But administration supporters quickly regrouped, called for another vote, and defeated the amendment, 42 to 29. Had the administration not intervened, the Senate probably would have accepted La Follette's proposals.[19]

The tax fight was filled with ironies. As conservative columnist Frank Kent pointed out, "It is interesting that from Senator La Follette, whose name is linked with so much that is radical, should come this essentially conservative, courageous and eminently sound proposal" to reduce the federal deficit. Kent thought it "strange" that businessmen who "have been howling their heads off about the unbalanced budget" should oppose tax increases. "But stranger still is to find Mr. Roosevelt, who has not hesitated to adopt and make his own various La Follette ideas, the soundness of which were at least open to question, wholly indifferent to this one, so unquestionably sound and so clearly the way to avert the dangers of which [Roosevelt] has warned."[20] The administration probably opposed La Follette's plan not because it considered tax increases unsound fiscal policy, but because it knew that such increases were sure to be unpopular with the voters.

The tax fight revealed the two approaches to economics that were current during the 1930s. Both La Follette and Roosevelt wanted to find a way to balance the budget; but they differed over the means by which to achieve that goal. Roosevelt sought to reduce the deficit by curtailing spending, La Follette by increasing taxes.

Aside from their brief skirmish over tax policy, La Follette and Roosevelt had displayed unusual harmony during the first eight months of 1937. During the Court-packing controversy, the most

gressional Conservatism, pp. 143–44; RML to Rachel, 19 June 1937, box 45-A, Family Papers.

19. Arthur Krock, "In Washington," *New York Times*, 25 June 1937.

20. Frank R. Kent, "The La Follette Plan," *Baltimore Sun*, 10 August 1937.

serious political crisis yet to beset the administration, Roosevelt had found Young Bob standing with him to the end. In the WPA fight of June, the Wisconsin senator had helped save the president from another embarrassing defeat. La Follette, for his part, had reason enough to be satisfied with Roosevelt's performance. True, Roosevelt's spending cuts deeply disturbed him. On the political front, however, the president had, or so it seemed to La Follette, made efforts to stand up to the conservatives within his party.

During the late summer and fall a rumor circulated through Washington that Roosevelt might select the Wisconsin senator as his successor in 1940. In August, Roscoe Fertich, an aide to Harold Ickes, related to Ickes the substance of a conversation he had had with Leo T. Crowley, a Wisconsin Democrat who was head of the Federal Deposit Insurance Corporation and a Roosevelt adviser. Crowley claimed to have it " 'straight' from the White House that the President's first choice for 1940 is Bob La Follette." According to Crowley, Roosevelt's second and third choices were Secretary of Agriculture Henry A. Wallace and Assistant Attorney General Robert H. Jackson, respectively. Ickes, who quite possibly had presidential aspirations of his own, regarded the report with skepticism. "So many people have things 'straight' from the White House!" he grumbled in his diary. "I have always believed, and I still do, that the President hasn't made up his mind whom he will favor in 1940." Moreover, Ickes thought, even if Roosevelt had made up his mind, "he wouldn't be telling anyone. That isn't the way the President works." Besides, he added, the Democratic convention would never nominate the Wisconsin Progressive.[21]

Variations of the rumor cropped up in other places as well. In September, *News-Week* reported that Roosevelt favored La Follette in 1940. But, like Ickes, it considered the nomination of a non-Democrat exceedingly unlikely. At the same time, Stanley High, a Republican who had signed on with the Roosevelt campaign in 1936 as a presidential aide and speechwriter and who presumably possessed some inside knowledge, came out with his book, *Roosevelt— And Then?*. "If Mr. Roosevelt were free to choose his own successor without regard for party-political considerations," High wrote, "he would probably select" La Follette. High also believed that "more nearly than any other American of political importance, Senator La Follette is what Mr. Roosevelt would be if Mr. Roosevelt did not have a national political party to think about." At least one of Roosevelt's

21. Harold L. Ickes, *The Secret Diary of Harold L. Ickes* (New York, 1953–1954), 2:201.

opponents seized upon the La Follette rumor in an apparent attempt to stir up opposition to the president. In September, Sen. Royal S. Copeland of New York, a Democrat who had broken with Roosevelt over Court packing, told reporters that Roosevelt would run for a third term. But if unsuccessful, Copeland predicted, the president would back La Follette for the nomination; if that failed, Roosevelt would support labor leader John L. Lewis.[22]

That Roosevelt ever seriously considered La Follette as a successor was highly doubtful. Young Bob was too far to the Left on most issues to satisfy the president's basically conservative instincts. Moreover Roosevelt was too devout a Democrat to support someone who was not a party member, and he was too realistic to think that he could force what would surely be an unwilling convention to accept La Follette as its candidate. Yet, given his state of mind during and after the Court fight, it was possible, perhaps even likely, that he started or at least encouraged talk of La Follette in 1940. The decision of many Democrats to oppose Court reorganization disturbed and angered Roosevelt. He may have intended the La Follette rumor as a warning to party rebels that they had best return to the fold before it was too late. La Follette, for his part, must have been flattered by the rumors; but he doubtless knew Roosevelt well enough not to put much faith in them. Moreover, everyone who knew the La Follette clan knew that it was Phil, not Bob, who aspired to the presidency. However improbable the talk of Roosevelt backing La Follette for the presidency, it was at least indicative of the close political and personal relationship between the two that had existed since the 1936 elections.

Late in 1937 and early in 1938, a series of developments combined to drive a wedge between the president and the Wisconsin senator. The first of these was the recession of 1937–1938. During the later months of 1937, industrial production fell off sharply; farm prices and farm income plummeted; and the unemployment rate, which had been slowly declining since 1933, soared upward once again. By 1938 the country was experiencing an economic nightmare: a recession in the midst of a depression. The psychological impact of the setback was devastating because it came at the very time when many people believed that the economy had finally turned that elusive corner toward prosperity.

There ensued within the administration a lively debate about the causes of the recession and about the possible solutions. Secretary of the Treasury Henry Morgenthau, Jr., counseled Roosevelt to follow

22. *News-Week* 10 (13 September 1937):9; Stanley High, *Roosevelt—And Then?* (New York, 1937), pp. 310–15; *New York Times*, 22 September 1937.

traditional practices. The recession, he argued, stemmed from low morale in business quarters. Businessmen, fearing that continued deficit spending by the government would stimulate inflation and necessitate higher taxes, were reluctant to reinvest their profits and to expand production. Balance the budget, Morgenthau advised, and businessmen, their confidence restored, would put the nation on the road to recovery. Other Roosevelt advisers, like Hopkins, Ickes, and Marriner S. Eccles, governor of the Federal Reserve Board, scoffed at Morgenthau's analysis. Pointing out that the recession had immediately followed Roosevelt's spending cuts, they insisted that, for the time being at least, the president should forget about balancing the budget and resume heavy spending. A third group of advisers placed primary blame for current ills on monopolistic control of industry and prescribed a heavy dose of trust busting. Thoroughly confused, Roosevelt did nothing for months.[23]

As economic conditions worsened, La Follette resumed his normal role as a critic of the administration. In January 1938, during two nationally broadcast radio addresses, he blamed the recession on Roosevelt's decision to curtail spending. He said, "Unfortunately for everyone . . . the government made a tragic mistake when it yielded to the clamor to balance the budget by drastic reductions in expenditures." That action, he charged, had "made inevitable the present crisis within a crisis, and the crisis was intensified by the unjustifiable increase in prices in the segment of our economy which is subject to monopolistic control." La Follette went on to completely reject the notion that "balancing the Federal budget by reducing expenditures" would induce business to undertake new investment and to expand production. "Certain fundamental changes in our economic environment," he argued, "have drastically curtailed the opportunity for private capital investment." "Among the more important of these changes" were the closing of the frontier, the decline in population growth, "reduced foreign markets due to economic nationalism," and "the financial control over business which makes profits for the insiders by making scarcity for outsiders." But La Follette maintained that the most important change was the low level of mass purchasing power. Because people could not afford to buy products, business had no incentive to expand production and thereby create jobs. Indeed, people could not even afford to buy goods that had already been produced; hence, business had to curtail production and lay off work-

23. Leuchtenburg, *Roosevelt and the New Deal*, pp. 244–47; Burns, *Lion and the Fox*, pp. 319–36.

ers. To bolster his arguments, La Follette cited the testimony of several industrialists who had recently appeared before a Senate committee. According to La Follette, William F. Knudsen, vice-president of General Motors, had "put his finger on the major difficulty. He said he had to lay men off, although he had ample factory space and over two hundred million dollars of cash surplus in the bank, simply because the customers are not buying cars." La Follette concluded by calling upon the administration to restore buying power by resuming spending for public works and work relief.[24]

As economic conditions worsened, Roosevelt finally yielded to La Follette and the other advocates of increased spending. In April he announced his intention of allowing the PWA and the WPA to resume their pump-priming activities. But to La Follette the president's request for some $3.75 billion was too little too late.[25]

Critical of Roosevelt's response to the recession, La Follette was also growing suspicious of the administration's foreign policy. Between 1935 and 1937 a series of dramatic developments abroad threatened to ignite another world war. In 1935 Italian forces, under the direction of fascist dictator Benito Mussolini, invaded the North African kingdom of Ethiopia. That same year, German dictator Adolph Hitler announced his nation's plans for massive rearmament. In the summer of 1936 a bloody civil war broke out in Spain, and within a few months Italy and Germany were supplying men and munitions to right-wing Gen. Francisco Franco and the rebels who were trying to topple the ruling republican government. Events on the other side of the world were equally alarming. In July 1937 an expansionist-minded Japan attacked China, setting off a full-scale, though undeclared, war.

On 5 October, three months after the Japanese attack, Roosevelt delivered his so-called quarantine speech in Chicago. Decrying the "present reign of terror and international lawlessness" that "has now reached a stage where the very foundations of civilization are seriously threatened," Roosevelt declared that "the peace-loving nations must make a concerted effort in opposition to those violations of treaties and those ignorings of human instincts which today are creating a state of international anarchy and instability from which there is no escape through mere isolation or neutrality." Then, in the words that made the headlines, Roosevelt said, "It seems to be unfortunately true that the epidemic of world lawlessness is spreading. When an

24. Transcript of radio address, 13 January 1938, box 556-C, Family Papers.
25. Leuchtenburg, *Roosevelt and the New Deal*, p. 257.

epidemic of physical disease starts to spread, the community approves and joins in a quarantine of the patients in order to protect the health of the community against the spread of the disease."[26]

Although Roosevelt quickly denied that his quarantine address signified a departure from the policy of American neutrality, La Follette and other so-called isolationists suspected that the president was leading the country in a dangerous new direction that might eventually involve the United States in war. On 16 November, in response to Roosevelt's address, La Follette introduced into the Senate a constitutional amendment providing "that authority of Congress to declare war or conscript men for military service overseas shall not become effective until confirmed by a majority of all votes cast in the nationwide referendum thereon." The only exception to this would be a direct attack upon the United States, its territorial possessions, or "any other North American or Caribbean nation." La Follette did not originate the idea of a war referendum. Immediately before American entry into World War I, his father had proposed a resolution requiring a nonbinding, advisory referendum before the United States could enter any war. In February 1937, Lewis Ludlow, a congressman from Indiana, introduced a similar amendment in the House of Representatives. With the administration vehemently opposed to the referendum idea, which it believed would cripple the president's conduct of foreign policy, La Follette was unable to muster enough support even to bring it to a vote in the Senate.[27]

In the meantime, the debate over foreign policy shifted from the war referendum to defense spending. In January 1938 Roosevelt proposed a $1 billion defense budget, with the bulk of the money allotted for naval expansion. As Roosevelt explained it, the United States needed a navy that could protect both the Atlantic and the Pacific coasts at the same time. La Follette opposed the two-ocean-navy bill for several reasons. He believed that the current size of the navy was more than adequate for national defense, and he felt that the United States was invulnerable to attack, either in 1938 or in the foreseeable future. Too, he feared that by expanding naval forces beyond defense needs, Roosevelt might be initiating a new foreign policy. La Follette implied that Roosevelt might be planning to involve the nation in Asian or European conflicts. Also, he believed that the money could

26. "Quarantine" address, in Samuel I. Rosenman, ed., *The Public Papers and Addresses of Franklin D. Roosevelt* (New York, 1938–1950), 6:406–11.

27. *CR* 75:2, 1937, vol. 82, pt. 1, p. 24; Belle Case La Follette and Fola La Follette, *Robert M. La Follette* (New York, 1953), 1:565; Leuchtenburg, *Roosevelt and the New Deal*, p. 229.

be better spent on domestic needs. During an address in Chicago, he declared that rather than build new ships, the government should expand public works projects. He pointed out to his Chicago audience that building one battleship would give work to only eight thousand persons, whereas a public housing project in Chicago could provide work for all of that city's unemployed. La Follette also believed that if the economy geared itself to an expanding armament program, then when the expansion stopped, the United States would experience the worst depression ever and "probably revolution." Finally, he suspected that another of Roosevelt's reasons for requesting naval expansion was to help pull the nation out of the recession by following the course of military spending that European nations had taken to help relieve their economic problems. To his brother, La Follette wrote, "Many people rather close in to the administration are fearful if the slump continues his remedy will be a large armament program."[28]

Suspicious of the president's motives and convinced that the naval-expansion bill would move the nation closer to involvement in foreign turmoil, La Follette led the opposition in the Senate. But he did not reckon with developments in Europe and Asia. In March, Germany overran Austria and set its sights on Czechoslovakia; and Japan swept farther into China. In May, by large majorities in both houses, Congress passed the navy bill.[29]

In the long run, disagreements about foreign policy would bring relations between La Follette and the administration to the breaking point. In the short run, however, the launching of the National Progressives of America party was proving more divisive.

Ever since the founding of the Wisconsin Progressive party in 1934, Phil La Follette had been awaiting the opportunity to organize the third party on a national level. He planned to encourage the formation of third parties in many states with the hope that eventually these state parties would coalesce into a new national party. The 1936 elections, in which Wisconsin Progressives swept the state, probably convinced him that, with his own state secure, the time had come to make his move. In May 1937, on the occasion of the third anniversary of the Progressive party, Phil declared that "The Progressive party looks forward to a national existence and to a national political realignment. The time is close at hand for the formation of a new national alignment which will defeat the reactionary forces of America, just as the Progressive party had defeated the reactionary forces in

28. *New York Times*, 6 February 1938; RML to PFL, 6 January 1938, box 135-2, PFL Papers.
29. *New York Times*, 14–18 May 1938.

Wisconsin."[30] Early in August, when the La Follette brothers spent a weekend with Roosevelt aboard the presidential yacht, Phil suggested to the president that "we should try to get a movement started in other states as had been done in Wisconsin and Minnesota." " 'Go Ahead,'" Phil remembered Roosevelt saying enthusiastically. "I got the impression," Phil later recalled, "that Roosevelt had given up hope of liberalizing the Democratic party and was ready to go along with realignment."[31]

That Phil should confide his plans to Roosevelt, perhaps in an attempt to secure the president's approval, indicated that he did not envisage the third-party movement as an anti-Roosevelt, anti–New Deal movement. Moreover, at this stage Phil apparently had no definite timetable for establishing a national third party. "Any sound political realignment must be built state by state," he wrote to a friend in the fall of 1937, adding that "we learned in my father's campaign in 1924 that it can't be done overnight in the nation, but must be developed in the states after a great deal of organization work." As late as January 1938 Phil apparently was thinking "in terms of . . . six or ten years rather than in terms of next election."[32]

The recession, however, altered his strategy. Doubtless realizing that the recession had badly eroded Roosevelt's prestige and power and sensing that liberals might welcome a new leader and a new party, he decided to launch the third-party movement ahead of schedule, in the spring of 1938. He also decided to give the new party a decidedly anti-Roosevelt thrust. In April he delivered a series of four radio addresses during which he sharply attacked the president for causing the recession. He also pronounced the New Deal a failure. In his final speech he summoned progressives to a mass meeting on 28 April at the University of Wisconsin Livestock Pavilion.[33]

As long as the third party had remained in the planning stage, Young Bob had supported it enthusiastically. Since 1934 he had repeatedly called for political realignment along liberal and conservative lines. Throughout 1937 he had corresponded regularly with Phil about a third-party movement and displayed lively interest in Phil's progress.[34] But in March of 1938, when Phil began to make definite

30. Ibid., 20 May 1937.
31. PFL, *Memoirs*, p. 252.
32. PFL to Edwin Hadfield, Jr., 7 October 1937, quoted in Donald R. McCoy, *Angry Voices: Left-of-Center Politics in the New Deal Era* (Lawrence, Kans., 1958), p. 162; Mrs. PFL, "Isen's Political Diary," 31 January 1938, p. 48, box 161-3, PFL Papers.
33. McCoy, *Angry Voices*, pp. 166–67; PFL, *Memoirs*, p. 253.
34. For example, see RML to PFL, 3 August 1937, box 135-2, PFL Papers;

plans, Bob backed away. In her diary Isen La Follette described Bob's reaction to the venture. "This morning," she wrote on 29 March, "I have re-read my notes on the year we formed the Wisconsin Third Party, and I could almost write ditto marks about Bob's reaction to the present venture. Bob is for it theoretically and evenutally, but can't bear to face the difficulties of immediate action." A few weeks later Isen described what had happened when Phil went to Washington to outline to Bob his plans for the new party, which Phil had decided to name the National Progressives of America. "Bob," wrote Isen, "is tired; he sees all the risks; he's discouraged . . . he kept repeating, 'Well, all right if what you want is to retire from politics!' " However, she continued, "By the end of the talk . . . when Phil had developed his speech and the symbol, he says Bob's eyes began to sparkle and he had the craftman's appreciation of the possibilities of the thing." Isen concluded, "The upshot is, however, that Phil will have to go it alone, as he did in 1934."[35]

Feeling as he did, Young Bob played almost no role in planning the NPA. During March and April, Phil pleaded with Bob to return to Wisconsin to discuss the matter with him and with other Progressive leaders. Bob always declined. At one time, according to Isen, Wellwood Nesbit, a Madison doctor and Bob's best friend in Wisconsin, "telephoned Bob in Washington . . . and urged him to come out, saying that Bob should know what was going on and it would help Bob to get his feet on the ground." When Bob refused, "Wellwood had the feeling that Bob did not want to come, that he dreaded facing the various issues which would confront him."[36]

Although La Follette almost certainly believed that the NPA would probably damage his own and his brother's political careers, he could not bring himself to stand in Phil's way. On 25 April, three days before the stock-pavilion meeting, he told reporters, "A national third party is inevitable and now is the time to form one." Two days later he declared that he was "in" the third-party movement "all the way."[37]

On the evening of 28 April some four thousand persons, including newsmen from all over the country, packed the livestock pavilion at the University of Wisconsin. Several thousand more, many of them curious university students, stood outside the building and listened to

PFL to RML, 27 November, 5 December 1937, RML to PFL, 7 December 1937, box 45-A, Family Papers.

35. Mrs. PFL, "Isen's Political Diary," 29 March, 18 April 1938, pp. 51–55, box 161-3, PFL Papers.

36. Ibid., 18 April 1938, p. 55, box 161-3, PFL Papers.

37. *New York Times*, 26, 28 April 1938.

the proceedings over loudspeakers. Senator La Follette did not attend, prompting speculation that he was not in sympathy with the movement. But he did send a telegram, saying that although he regretted his absence, the naval-expansion bill then pending in the Senate made it necessary for him to remain in Washington.[38]

After introductory remarks by Judge Alvin C. Reis, Phil La Follette delivered the major address of the evening. A new party was needed, he declared, because the two major parties had failed to stop the depression. Although Phil praised Roosevelt's "brilliant leadership," his speech, as journalist Elmer Davis correctly noted, "was all based on the postulate that Roosevelt is through, that somebody else must carry the torch hereafter." In a thinly veiled attack on New Deal welfare measures, La Follette called for an end to "coddling or spoon-feeding of the American people." Announcing the formation of the National Progressives of America, the governor proclaimed, "Make no mistake, this is NOT a *third* party. As certain as the sun rises, we are launching THE party of our time."[39]

Although, as Elmer Davis observed, Phil's speech "offered little detail as to how NPA was going to save the country," La Follette tried to compensate for the lack of substance with abundant theatrical effects. Floodlights ringed the stage from which he spoke. Behind the stage hung a huge flag containing the NPA emblem: a blue X against a white background and surrounded by a red circle. As Phil later explained it, "the X stood for multiplication of wealth instead of less; placed in a circle, it represented American equality in the ballot box— abundance in economic life, equality and freedom at the polls."[40]

Aside from the crowd at the stock pavilion, the NPA stirred little enthusiasm. Many liberal leaders, like Senator Norris, feared that the La Follette party would divide liberal forces. To some observers, the NPA smacked of fascism. One critic dubbed the cross-in-a-circle emblem a "circumscribed swastika." To others, the stock-pavilion meeting, with the flags, spotlights, and Phil's talk of "The party" resembled a typical Hitler rally. Press accounts, especially photographs of the meeting, reinforced this image. *Life* magazine ran a full-page picture of Phil standing alone on the platform, his right hand outstretched in a manner that resembled the "heil Hitler" salute of the Nazis. In its account, *Time* magazine ran two devastating photographs. In one picture Phil had both arms outstretched over the crowd

38. Telegram, RML to Alvin C. Reis, 28 April 1938, box 16-C, Family Papers.
39. Elmer Davis, "The Wisconsin Brothers," *Harper's Magazine* 178(February 1939):275.
40. Ibid.; PFL, *Memoirs*, pp. 252–53.

with his hands hanging down as though he were a magician casting a spell. In the other picture, Phil's hair hung down over his forehead, his eyes bugged out, and his lips were curled in a fiendish expression.[41]

Oddly enough, Phil had expected some people to compare the NPA emblem, which he designed personally, to a swastika. One month before the rally, Isen wrote in her diary: "We have shown [the emblem] to our 'inner circle' and while it has shocked some of them, they are all for [it] eventually. Of course if we use it there will be a howl of 'Nazi,' comparison to the Swastica, etc." But, she added, "Phil declares that he wants that; that *if* we are right in our program, or solution economically, we must get publicity, get people aroused and arguing, so long as we have given our people the answers to the argument." Besides attracting publicity, Phil apparently believed that the emblem would give people a sense of belonging. Isen wrote, "People are looking for security, they want to 'belong' even to march; we are living in that era; I hear even good Progressives say apologetically 'I certainly hate Hitler, but you have to hand it to that guy; he gets things done.' "[42]

The public reaction to the NPA confirmed Young Bob's worst fears. Nevertheless he gamely defended his brother and the NPA and repeatedly denied rumors that he privately opposed the party movement. On 10 May writer John Chamberlain wrote to La Follette, saying that one of the things that had frightened Chamberlain's New York friends concerning the NPA was the flag, "which they think smacks of Fascism." La Follette replied that he did "not understand the reaction of some people concerning the insignia of the new party. It was our idea that rather than to permit some cartoonist to give us a meaningless and perhaps ridiculous designation in the form of some animal, crippled or otherwise, that it would be wise to work out an insignia that had some meaning."[43] That La Follette should shoulder the blame for something he opposed, evidenced his loyalty to his brother.

In the meantime, observers anxiously awaited some indication of Roosevelt's reaction to the NPA. Publicly he said nothing, but privately he was closely watching NPA developments. On 12 May, Max Lerner of the *Nation* gave Roosevelt and Secretary of the Interior Ickes a firsthand account of the stock-pavilion meeting. According to

41. McCoy, *Angry Voices*, pp. 172–75; PFL, *Memoirs*, p. 254; *Life*, 9 May 1938, p. 9; *Time*, 9 May 1938, pp. 11–13.
42. Mrs. PFL, "Isen's Political Diary," 29 March 1928, p. 50, box 161-3, PFL Papers.
43. John Chamberlain to RML, 10 May [1938], RML to Chamberlain, 13 May 1938, box 665–C, Family Papers.

Ickes, Lerner, who "has been close to the La Follettes and has been a booster of them," was shocked at the Hitler-like trappings of the rally. Ickes wrote, "Lerner was not only disturbed but disgusted with the whole proceeding." One week later, in a letter to the American ambassador to Italy, William Phillips, Roosevelt poked fun at the NPA and its emblem: "All that remains is for some major party to adopt a new form of arm salute. I have suggested the raising of both arms above the head, followed by a bow from the waist. At least this will be good for people's figures!"[44]

Roosevelt, however, was much more worried about the threat that the NPA posed to his administration and to the Democratic party than he let on to Phillips. Two weeks after the Madison rally he was thinking of ways to deal with the pesky La Follette brothers. On 12 May he told Ickes that he had invited Senator La Follette for a weekend cruise down the Potomac. Ickes wrote, Roosevelt "has in mind to do a little confidential and, if possible, persuasive talking with Bob La Follette. He thinks Bob is much more substantial than Phil. What he indicated that he would say to La Follette was that their Progressive movement was all right if they didn't get out too far." Roosevelt also informed Ickes that sometime before the 1940 election he would try to make a deal with the La Follettes, presumably in an effort to make sure that they would support the Democratic presidential nominee rather than a third-party candidate. As part of the deal Roosevelt would offer to make Young Bob secretary of state after 1940. Roosevelt, said Ickes, "thinks Bob would make a good next Sec. of State . . . and then Phil could go into the Senate and this would take care of both of them. He thinks that Bob would have better qualities for the Cabinet than Phil would have." Ickes observed, "This talk about Bob La Follette rather negatives [sic] the idea that the President is thinking of supporting him for the Presidential nomination on the Democratic ticket in 1940. As a matter of fact, he is distinctly of the mind that it will be necessary, in order to hold the Democrats together, to nominate a party Democrat."[45]

As it turned out, Roosevelt did not have to conclude a deal with the La Follettes in order to ward off the threat of a new party. The November 1938 elections killed the NPA movement for him. In Iowa and California, candidates affiliated with the NPA suffered lopsided, embarrassing defeats. But the fatal blow came in Wisconsin, where Republican Julius Heil trounced Phil La Follette in the governor's

44. Roosevelt to William Phillips, 18 May 1938, in *F. D. R.: His Personal Letters*, 4:785.
45. Ickes, *Secret Diary*, 2:394–95.

race. Republicans also captured eight of the ten House seats and gained a majority of seats in the state legislature. The election marked the death of the NPA and the beginning of the end for the Wisconsin Progressive party. For Roosevelt, the outcome in Wisconsin was one of the few bright spots in an otherwise dismal off-year election. In a letter to Ambassador Josephus Daniels in Mexico City, he wrote, "Besides clearing out some bad local situations, we have on the positive side eliminated Phil La Follette and the Farmer-Labor people in the Northwest as a standing Third Party threat. They must and will come to us *if* we remain definitely the liberal party."[46]

46. McCoy, *Angry Voices*, pp. 178–82; Roger T. Johnson, *Robert M. La Follette, Jr. and the Decline of the Progressive Party in Wisconsin* (Madison, 1964), p. 46; Davis, "The Wisconsin Brothers," pp. 276–77; Roosevelt to Josephus Daniels, 14 November 1938, in *F. D. R.: His Personal Letters*, 4:785.

CHAPTER 12

Concluding the Investigation

From 1938 to its termination in mid-1940, La Follette's Senate Civil Liberties Committee continued to investigate infractions of civil liberties in the area of labor relations. Specifically, it examined the union-busting policies of employers' associations, the Little Steel strike of 1937, and the explosive farm-labor problem in California. The final two and a half years of the investigation proved difficult for La Follette. The press appeared to lose interest in the committee's hearings, which were less dramatic and more complex than the hearings of 1936–1937; consequently the committee's most important findings went largely unnoticed. Moreover, much of the publicity it did receive was unfavorable. Critics accused it of conducting a vendetta against business and of aiding a communist conspiracy. In this hostile atmosphere the Senate came close to prematurely terminating the investigation. And when the investigation did end, Congress failed to pass La Follette's bill to outlaw oppressive labor practices, which contained the committee's legislative recommendations.

The La Follette committee's investigation of employers' associations revealed a paradox. Although many employers prevented workers from organizing, they themselves found the lure of organization to be irresistible. As Senators La Follette and Thomas cleverly put it, employers "have frequent occasion to exercise their constitutional rights of free speech and assembly, and to form associations of their own choosing to advance their own interests." The committee properly noted that many business organizations were beyond reproach. But "in some cases . . . employers have formed associations the principal function of which has been to combat efforts by employees to exercise their rights of association," and it was to these that the committee devoted its attention.[1]

Out of hundreds of business organizations throughout the country, the committee chose three to subject to careful scrutiny: the National Metal Trades Association, which had a membership of 952 manufacturing plants, including subsidiaries of General Motors,

1. U.S. Congress, Senate, Committee on Education and Labor, *Labor Policies of Employer Associations*, S. Rept. 6, pt. 4, 76th Cong., 1st sess., 1939, pp. 1–2.

Chrysler Corporation, and Republic Steel; the Associated Industries of Cleveland, composed of some five hundred employers in the Cleveland area; and the most powerful association of them all, the National Association of Manufacturers. The committee discovered that both National Metal Trades and Associated Industries had destroyed incriminating files and doctored records in anticipation of the investigation. In addition, both ran espionage and strikebreaking services for their members, and when Congress passed the Wagner Act, both had encouraged members to disregard the law. National Metal Trades appeared to make violation of the Wagner Act a necessary qualification for membership. It even went so far as to blacklist any "wayward" businessman who had the temerity to allow his employees to organize.[2]

The primary target of the La Follette inquiry was the National Association of Manufacturers. Dominated by a "small but powerful minority of corporations," the committee charged, the NAM had "consistently fought . . . national labor policy." The association lobbied against section 7(a) of the national-industrial-recovery bill in 1933 and against the Wagner bill of 1935. When the Wagner bill became law, the NAM "deliberately organized and coordinated the efforts of employers and employers' associations in a planned nation-wide campaign to nullify the administration of the National Labor Relations Act, impairing the successful operation of the law." The association's legal department, convening itself into an unofficial supreme court, ruled the act unconstitutional and inapplicable to manufacturing industries. The NAM also initiated a movement to repeal the act, and leading members of the association tied up the National Labor Relations Board in court litigation. La Follette's committee also exposed the NAM's massive covert "propaganda" campaign to influence public opinion. The committee found that "through newspapers, radio, motion pictures, slide films, stockholders' letters, payroll stuffers, billboard advertisements, civic progress meetings and local advertising" the NAM tried to turn the public "against 'labor agitators,' against governmental measures to alleviate industrial distress, against labor unions, and for the advantages of the status quo in industrial relations."[3]

The committee condemned the NAM for promoting "organized disregard for the National Labor Relations Act. Such action by a powerful and responsible organization encourages disrespect for the law and undermines the authority of government." It also deplored

2. Ibid., pp. 108, 112–13; pt. 5, pp. 178–85.
3. Ibid., pt. 6, pp. 154–79, 218–19, 221.

the NAM's failure "to adapt themselves to changing times and to laws which the majority of the people deem wise and necessary."[4]

The investigation of the employers' associations presented La Follette and his committee with a problem they had not yet faced. To abolish strikebreaking, espionage, and munitions stockpiling, the committee had simply recommended enactment of laws prohibiting such practices. The practices of employers' associations, however, did not lend themselves to so easy a solution. However much La Follette might condemn the activities of the NAM, his probe had turned up nothing illegal in its activities; nor could he properly recommend legislation outlawing those activities. Clearly, the NAM possessed the right to lobby for or against bills before Congress and to attempt to influence public opinion. Thus the La Follette committee was left with exposure and moral condemnation as the only weapons it could use to attempt to curb employers' associations like the NAM.

Following the probe of employers' associations, La Follette and his colleagues turned their attention to the Little Steel strike of 1937. One of the bloodiest conflicts in labor history, the strike began in May 1937 when steelworkers affiliated with the CIO walked out against Republic Steel, Bethlehem Steel, and Youngstown Sheet and Tube Company, collectively known as the Little Steel industry. For two months chaotic violence racked the many communities in which Little Steel operated plants. The Memorial Day incident, which La Follette's committee had already investigated, was the most dramatic single event during the strike. The strike was a near total disaster for labor. Under the leadership of Republic Steel chieftain "Terrible Tom" Girdler, whose hatred for unions was almost pathological, Little Steel routed the strikers. At the time, it seemed, much of the public could not have cared less. Fed up with labor tactics such as the sit-down strikes in the automobile and rubber industries earlier in the year, many people blamed labor as much as management for the strike against Little Steel and the ensuing violence. President Roosevelt seemed to catch the public's mood when, toward the end of the strike, he declared, "The majority of people are saying just one thing, 'A plague on both your houses.' "[5]

Nearly a year after the strike, from 18 July to 11 August 1938, La Follette's committee conducted public hearings. From the hearings and from many months of behind-the-scenes investigation, it compiled an account of the strike markedly different from the account

4. Ibid., pp. 221–22.
5. Quoted in Irving Bernstein, *Turbulent Years: A History of the American Worker, 1933–1941* (Boston, 1969), p. 496.

that the public had received at the time. The committee laid blame for the outbreak of the strike squarely on the shoulders of Little Steel: "The refusal of the steel companies, at the outset of negotiations, to enter into any kind of written agreement [with the union] was evidence . . . of bad faith, and tantamount to a refusal to bargain at all. The strike arose out of this one issue." The committee also held Little Steel primarily responsible for the "bloodshed, bitterness, and economic disorganization of communities" that occurred during the strike.[6]

The committee's most important finding was that, although the steel companies had resorted to traditional strong-arm practices during the strike, they had also developed a new and more effective technique of strikebreaking. The technique was to "incite a spirit of vigilantism in the citizens and to subvert the community to strikebreaking activities." When the strike broke out, Little Steel encouraged the formation of citizens' committees in the towns where it owned plants. On the surface a typical committee appeared to be the spontaneous creation of disinterested citizens. In reality the committee's organizers and leaders usually had close ties to the company. Once formed, the citizens' committee whipped up antistrike sentiment in its community to the point of hysteria by claiming that only a minority of workers supported the strike; that radical agitators were behind the walkout; and that if allowed to continue, the strike would threaten law and order. The citizens' committee urged the community to take action to put down the strike. In Massillon, Ohio, the site of a Republic Steel plant, the citizens' committee called itself the Law and Order League. This league falsely claimed that law and order had broken down in the community because of the strike, and it badgered the chief of police until he reluctantly expanded his force by swearing in local citizens as deputies. On the night of 11 July, the police force, which had become little more than a mob of vigilantes, attacked a group of strikers peaceably gathered outside the union hall. During the ensuing melee, three strikers and strike sympathizers were killed; many others were injured. Later that night police rounded up scores of strikers and threw them into jail without cause. The "riot" broke the morale of the workers and ended the strike. Events followed a similar pattern in other communities until the strike finally collapsed.[7]

6. U.S. Congress, Senate, Committee on Education and Labor, The "Little Steel" Strike and Citizens' Committees, S. Rept. 151, 77th Cong., 1st sess., 1941, pp. 321, 330.
    7. Ibid., pp. 229–52, 316–30.

Mobilizing communities through citizens' committees appeared to be the ultimate antiunion weapon. By comparison, the traditional methods of strikebreaking seemed hopelessly old fashioned. Employers could save themselves the expense of hiring strikebreakers, who were often unreliable anyway and, as La Follette's committee had already revealed, often tried to prolong strikes in order to remain on the job. Moreover, by importing the likes of a Chowderhead Cohen to crush strikes, employers ran the risk of inadvertently creating sympathy for the strikers.

The Civil Liberties Committee sadly discovered that the significance of the Little Steel strike was not lost on the business community. The National Association of Manufacturers "brought to the attention of its entire membership the importance of the citizens' committee technique in the breaking of the 'Little Steel' strike." The NAM did "nothing to stem the flow toward vigilantism or to condemn the dangerous effects of citizens' groups fomented by the employer in time of labor strife." Instead it suggested to its members that they might find it useful to employ similar techniques. "The cynical approval which the National Association of Manufacturers gave to citizens' committees and vigilante organizations in the summer of 1937," the committee declared, "is one of the most dangerous tendencies ever exhibited by any of the belligerent employer associations in their long struggle against labor organizations."[8]

Because citizens' committees and vigilantism posed a grave threat to the future of both labor-management relations and civil liberties, the Little Steel probe ranked in importance at or near the top of the committee's investigations. Unfortunately, the committee's hearings and final report, which it issued three years after the strike, attracted little attention. "With magnificent thoroughness," wrote partisan newsman Kenneth G. Crawford, the committee "stripped away the curtain of pretense and told the real story . . . but the newspapers were not interested. Truth was too slow to catch up with untruth."[9]

As public interest in its findings waned, the committee itself increasingly became the target of criticism. Over the years it had accumulated its share of critics. Right-wing extremist groups had accused it of aiding the communist conspiracy. Anti-Semitic organizations had tied it to a vague Jewish conspiracy. From time to time more responsible critics had taken La Follette to task for narrowly focusing on

8. Ibid., p. 328.
9. Kenneth G. Crawford, *The Pressure Boys: The Inside Story of Lobbying in America* (New York, 1939), p. 131.

employer misdeeds to the exclusion of labor excesses. Yet, before 1938 the committee's supporters easily outnumbered its detractors, and the committee never faced a serious threat to its continued existence.[10]

In the spring of 1938, however, it became evident that opposition to the investigation was increasing, particularly in the Senate. By April the committee had nearly exhausted its funds. La Follette therefore introduced a resolution appropriating sixty thousand dollars to continue the probe. Congress was scheduled to adjourn the second week in June, and unless the Senate approved the resolution before then, the committee would go out of existence. The resolution encountered stiff opposition. Early in May the Committee to Audit and Control the Contingent Expenses of the Senate, under the chairmanship of South Carolina Democrat James F. Byrnes, grudgingly reported out the La Follette resolution "without recommendation." According to Heber Blankenhorn, La Follette observed that "previously opposition Senators did not care to record themselves against the investigation; now several, . . . mostly southerners, are believed to be looking for a chance to oppose it on the floor."[11]

With adjournment fast approaching, the parliamentary situation in the Senate favored the opponents of La Follette's committee. The resolution was to come up under the "call of the calendar," and if even one senator objected to consideration of the resolution it would most likely be dead for the session. La Follette, apparently aware that at least one senator planned to raise an objection, offered a compromise; he pledged that if the Senate approved the resolution, he would request no more funds in the future and would complete the investigation within eight months. With this assurance, La Follette's foes dropped their opposition, and on 18 May the Senate passed the resolution extending the life of the committee.[12]

In August 1938 there arose an even greater threat to the La Follette committee: an investigation by the House Un-American Activities Committee. Under the chairmanship of Texas Democrat Martin Dies, this committee provided a platform for extreme critics of the La

10. For reactions, pro and con, to the committee, see Jerold S. Auerbach, *Labor and Liberty: The La Follette Committee and the New Deal* (Indianapolis, 1966), pp. 152–63.

11. Heber Blankenhorn to J. Warren Madden, 12 May 1938, box 1-3, Heber Blankenhorn Papers, Archives of Labor History and Urban Affairs, Wayne State University, Detroit.

12. RML to Hiram W. Johnson, 24 January 1939, RML to Culbert L. Olson, 15 February 1939, box 44-C, Family Papers (see list of abbreviations p. x).

Follette investigation. On the second day of hearings, John P. Frey, president of the American Federation of Labor's Metal Trades Department, testified and in the process caused a sensation. Frey charged that the Congress of Industrial Organizations, the AFL's bitter rival, was infested with communists. He went on to implicate the La Follette committee in a communist conspiracy. Committee investigators, Frey claimed, had worked with communists in planning the civil liberties investigation. During the ensuing months, a string of witnesses before the Un-American Activities Committee flung similar unsubstantiated accusations at La Follette's committee. For a short time Dies even considered investigating La Follette's committee. La Follette and his colleagues, in defending themselves against these charges, found themselves in good company. Witnesses before Dies's committee accused hundreds of organizations, groups, and individuals of being communists. One witness even implicated the Boy Scouts of America and the Camp Fire Girls. As columnist Kenneth G. Crawford, with only slight exaggeration, put it, "No patrioteer was too wacky to be taken seriously" by Dies's committee.[13]

Although witnesses before the Un-American Activities Committee presented no convincing evidence to support their charges, the claim that some staff members of La Follette's committee had communist leanings may have been true. Years later, after La Follette had left the Senate, he wrote an article in *Collier's* magazine saying, "I know from first-hand experience that Communist sympathizers have infiltrated into Committee staffs on Capitol Hill in Washington." "A few years ago," he recalled, "when I was Chairman of the Senate Civil Liberties Committee, I was forced to take measures in an effort to stamp out influence within my own committee staff." In addition to his own committee, La Follette implicated three other Senate committees. In the highly charged atmosphere of the late 1940s and early 1950s, several former Civil Liberties Committee staff members, including John Abt, the committee's secretary from 1936 to mid-1937, came under suspicion of having been Communist party members during the 1930s.[14]

Aside from the political ramifications, the possibility that com-

13. Auerbach, *Labor and Liberty*, pp. 164–66; William E. Leuchtenburg, *Franklin D. Roosevelt and the New Deal, 1932–1940* (New York, 1963), p. 280; Crawford, *Pressure Boys*, p. 112.

14. Robert M. La Follette, Jr., "Turn the Light on Communism," *Collier's* 119(8 February 1947):22; Auerbach, *Labor and Liberty*, p. 168; Earl Latham, *The Communist Controversy in Washington: From the New Deal to McCarthy* (Cambridge, Mass., 1966), pp. 107–10, 117–21, 161–62.

munists served on the committee mattered little unless they significantly influenced the course of the investigation. There was no evidence that they did so. Occasionally various staff members did abuse their powers, and it was to those abuses that La Follette apparently referred in the *Collier's* article. One time, for example, one of the committee's investigators, A. L. Wirin, without authorization released confidential committee files to a magazine, an action for which La Follette fired him.[15] La Follette once confided to an adviser that one or more staff members, whom he suspected of being communists, deliberately misused the committee's subpoena powers.[16] Yet, leaks to the press or abuses of subpoena power, which may or may not have been evidence of communist activity, did not significantly alter the course of the investigation.

Presumably, if communists had played a major role, they would have managed to incorporate their ideas in the committee reports, which contained summaries and analyses of evidence, conclusions, and recommendations. Senators La Follette and Thomas signed the reports, but staff members researched and wrote them and thus had ample opportunity to influence their contents. The thoroughly documented reports, approximately twenty in all, did contain blistering denunciations of antiunion employers. But they did not contain any Marxist thought, at least not any Marxist thought that was distinguishable from progressive or liberal thought. For example, the reports never claimed, as communists might have, that all, or even a majority of, employers resorted to oppressive labor practices; nor did they suggest that such practices were endemic to capitalism. One report stated that "the majority of American businessmen today have conformed to the National Labor policy and have not interfered with the right of labor to organize for the purpose of collective bargaining." It went on to say that "there have been outstanding examples of industrial statesmanship since 1937" and that "certain of the most powerful corporations in the country have in good faith entered into collective bargaining agreements with their employees in conformity with the law and have contributed to the success of the national labor policy." The report on strikebreaking expressed the committee's belief that "many employers . . . have already renounced the barbaric methods used in the past to fight strikes." The committee also felt that

15. RML to Gen. Hugh Johnson, 10 March 1937, transcript, "Long Distance Conversation Between Senator La Follette and Frank Palmer of the *People's Press*," 11 March 1937, box 15-C, Family Papers.
16. Interview, Wilbur and Rosemary Voigt, 9 July 1973.

"the majority of employers will welcome a prohibition of the utilization of persons to engage in the brutal or deceptive practices of strikebreaking."[17] Finally, the committee's reports ended by recommending remedial legislation, not fundamental alterations of capitalism, to ameliorate the abuse of employees by their employers.

By early 1939 it appeared that La Follette's committee would soon go out of existence. It had nearly exhausted its last appropriation on a preliminary investigation of the farm-labor problem in California, and La Follette had promised the Senate the previous May that he would request no additional funds. Even if he reneged on the pledge, Senate foes of the committee, armed with the testimony of the Un-American Activities Committee's witnesses, appeared to have enough strength to block any move to continue the investigation. Yet, committee supporters outside the Senate were unwilling to watch the committee die without putting up a fight. At the end of January, social activist and former editor of the *Nation* Oswald Garrison Villard, journalist Bruce Bliven, and others formed the National Committee to Save the La Follette Committee. Gov. Culbert L. Olson of California personally appealed to La Follette to continue the investigation in his state. But the most significant agitation came from the Roosevelt administration. "Strictly speaking," the president wrote to La Follette in March, "it is . . . none of my business to say anything out loud about the continuation of the Senate Civil Liberties Committee. I can, however, tell you personally of my real interest in it and my belief that . . . it should be continued."[18]

In March, Sen. Lewis B. Schwellenbach of Washington introduced a resolution granting additional funds to the committee. The administration threw its full weight behind the appropriation. When the resolution bogged down in the Committee to Audit and Control the Contingent Expenses of the Senate, Roosevelt publicly urged continuation of the civil liberties investigation. He also fired off a stern message to the chairman of the Audit Committee, James F. Byrnes of South Carolina, who was no friend of La Follette's committee. "I hope much you will go through with the . . . request for more money for the Civil Liberties Committee," Roosevelt said. "From the point

17. *Labor Policies of Employer Associations*, pt. 6, p. 221; U.S. Congress, Senate, Committee on Education and Labor, *Strikebreaking Services*, S. Rept. 6, 76th Cong., 1st sess., 1939, p. 138. For a different view on this issue, see Auerbach, *Labor and Liberty*, pp. 166–69, 174.

18. Auerbach, *Labor and Liberty*, pp. 64, 173; Culbert L. Olson to RML, 7 February 1939, box 44-C, Roosevelt to RML, 8 March 1939, box 17-C, Family Papers.

of view of the preservation of Civil liberties, I recommend it strongly
—and from the point of view of good politics, I recommend it equally
strongly. Can I make a stronger statement to you?"[19]

La Follette, meanwhile, gave no encouragement to the movement
to revive his committee. To Sen. Hiram Johnson of California, who
evidently opposed continuation of the investigation, La Follette
wrote, "There has been . . . considerable agitation for a continuation
of the Committee but I assure you this has not been prompted by me
nor anyone connected with the Committee's work." In answer to those
who urged him to fight for continuation of the inquiry, La Follette
cited his pledge to the Senate of the previous May. "Naturally," he
said, "I feel personally bound by this commitment." His explanation,
however, did not satisfy everyone. In an editorial appealing to "pro
gressives throughout the country . . . to muster every bit of influence
at their command in a fight to save the La Follette investigation," the
Nation noted that "an unfortunate element in the situation is the hesitation exhibited by Senator La Follette. A combination of politics
and punctilio has led him to pull his punches in the fight for his own
inquiry." Although the *Nation* conceded that the senator felt honor
bound to abide by his pledge to the Senate, it also claimed that "his
political advisors in Wisconsin fear that the powerful enemies the
investigation has made will spare no expense to defeat him for reelection."[20]

Even though La Follette seemed content to allow the investigation
to end, others were not. At least one committee staff member, Heber
Blankenhorn, quietly worked behind the scenes for continuation of
the probe, possibly without La Follette's knowledge. The most significant pressure, however, continued to come from Roosevelt, and
in the end it proved decisive. In August, after months of delay and
a rancorous debate, the Senate granted the committee a final appropriation of fifty thousand dollars.[21]

Intermittently between December 1939 and May 1940, the committee conducted its final investigation. The subject of inquiry was
the strife-torn farm-labor situation in California. In the spring of
1939 the publication of John Steinbeck's stirring novel *The Grapes*

19. Roosevelt to James F. Byrnes, 26 July 1939, in Elliot Roosevelt, ed.,
F. D. R.: His Personal Letters, 1928–1945 (New York, 1950), 2:907.
20. RML to Hiram W. Johnson, 24 January 1939, RML to Culbert L. Olson,
15 February 1939, box 44-C, Family Papers; "Funds for La Follette," *Nation*
149(15 July 1939):61.
21. Blankenhorn to Nathan Witt, 29 May 1939, box 1-7, Blankenhorn Papers;
Auerbach, *Labor and Liberty*, pp. 172–73.

of Wrath had momentarily drawn national attention to the bitter and too long neglected plight of migrant farm workers. "There is a crime here," Steinbeck wrote of California, "that goes beyond denunciation. There is a sorrow here that weeping cannot symbolize. There is a failure here that topples all our success."[22] In less eloquent but no less passionate words, La Follette and his colleagues were to agree.

The investigation, which included one month of hearings on the West Coast and testimony from over four hundred witnesses, exposed a problem so severe and so complex as to seem almost insoluble. The heart of the problem was the sad fate of the migrants. "These families," explained University of California professor Paul S. Taylor, "face low earnings, unemployment, instability and insecurity, meager housing, interrupted schooling of children, prejudice, and hostility of established residents." Culbert L. Olson, the governor of California, testified that migrant workers "for the most part . . . lack the means, individually and collectively, to defend themselves against illegal practices of the type that will be revealed during the course of your investigation." For example, said Olson, "it is inherently difficult . . . for a nondescript army of migratory workers to organize themselves into trade unions."[23]

The obstacle to unionization that most concerned La Follette was the organized opposition of the fruit and vegetable growers who owned the "farm-factories" that dominated the state's agriculture. Like their cousins in the manufacturing industries, California growers confronted labor militancy with espionage, strikebreaking, and the deployment of munitions. Like the coal company operators of Harlan County, they dominated local law-enforcement agencies. At their behest, county sheriffs spent most of their time running labor "agitators" out of the community. And like the Little Steel industries, when labor strife threatened, California growers whipped the citizenry into a state of frenzy and encouraged vigilantism. Through their powerful employers' association, Associated Farmers of California, they also played a conspicuous role in political affairs. Throughout the state, local chapters of Associated Farmers persuaded communities to enact vaguely worded antipicketing ordinances, which crippled the organizing activities of labor and curtailed freedom of speech and assembly.[24]

22. John Steinbeck, *The Grapes of Wrath* (New York, 1939), p. 385.
23. U.S. Congress, Senate, Subcommittee on Education and Labor, *Hearings Pursuant to S. Res. 266, Violations of Free Speech and Rights of Labor*, 74th–76th Congs., 1936–1940, pt. 47, pp. 17219, 17246 (hereafter referred to as *Hearings*).
24. Auerbach, *Labor and Liberty*, chap. 8 passim.

Testifying before the committee, the growers vigorously defended their actions. Unions, they said, were fine in the manufacturing industry; but in agriculture, where strikes would delay the harvesting of crops, unions would prove ruinous. They also viewed labor unrest as the product of a communist conspiracy. At the conclusion of his testimony, Philip Bancroft, past president of an Associated Farmers chapter, told La Follette that he was "a great admirer of your father, and I admired the stand you took in trying to keep us out of war, and the stand he took in trying to keep us out of the first war." But, Bancroft added, "I cannot understand why you are giving aid and comfort to the Communists now by trying to smear the farmers and the law-enforcement officers of the State."[25]

The committee's report urged the federal government to extend the protection of the Wagner Act and of other federal statutes to cover farm workers. But its plea fell on deaf ears. Like the Little Steel investigation, the probe of working conditions in California attracted little attention. Nor did it lead to any measurable improvement in the conditions of migrant farm laborers.[26]

The California hearings concluded the committee's four-year investigation. But La Follette still had to persuade skeptical colleagues in the Senate to enact the committee's recommendations. In March 1939 he and Thomas had introduced an oppressive-labor-practices bill that prohibited industrial espionage, strikebreaking, the sale and possession of industrial munitions, and the use of private armed guards by an employer in any place other than his own premises. At the same time Democrat Reuben T. Wood of Missouri introduced an identical measure in the House of Representatives.

Reaction to the bill split along predictable lines. The administration endorsed it, and so did organized labor, including the AFL and the CIO. On the other hand the National Association of Manufacturers and the United States Chamber of Commerce denounced it. Calling the bill "drastic and unfair," the NAM said that "only the blind and the prejudiced can view this legislation as designed to protect civil liberties or civil rights."[27]

The Senate took up the La Follette–Thomas bill in May 1940, five years after it had passed the Wagner Act and four years after it had overwhelmingly approved the Civil Liberties Committee's investiga-

25. *Hearings*, pt. 49, p. 18051.
26. Auerbach, *Labor and Liberty*, chap. 8 passim.
27. Auerbach, *Labor and Liberty*, pp. 198–201; statement of the National Association of Manufacturers, in U.S. Congress, Senate, Subcommittee of the Committee on Education and Labor, *Hearings on S. 1970*, 76th Cong., 1st sess., 1939, p. 87.

tion. The debate evidenced the extent to which sentiment in that body had shifted against organized labor since the middle 1930s. Without defending the practices the bill outlawed, opponents charged that it was one sided, saying that although it prohibited certain practices used by employers, it did nothing to curb the excesses of labor that sometimes made such practices necessary. Critics also seized upon the war scare then sweeping the Congress. Alarmed by Nazi Germany's recent advances in Europe, they argued that the bill would cripple the defense industry. Without espionage, employers could not detect the presence of foreign agents among their workers; without munitions, factories would be vulnerable to sabotage. On 27 May the Senate passed the bill, 47 to 20, but only after adding two amendments that completely altered its nature. Resistance was so strong in the House that Representative Wood could not even muster enough votes to bring the measure to a vote.[28]

Congress's refusal to enact the bill, however, did not give employers license to engage in oppressive labor practices. By 1940 the National Labor Relations Board, after five years of interpreting and enforcing the Wagner Act, had ruled the antiunion practices exposed by the investigation to be clear violations of the Wagner Act.[29] Thus, from a legal standpoint, the failure of Congress to enact the La Follette–Thomas bill was not as serious a setback for labor as it seemed to be at the time.

Despite the trying last years of the investigation, La Follette could justifiably take pride in the accomplishments of his committee. Clearly, the investigation did not by itself eliminate the tendency of employers to resort to force and violence in order to settle labor-management disputes. But the committee, working alongside the National Labor Relations Board, probably did force most employers to rely less on strong-arm practices. By 1940 even the committee's bitter foe, the National Association of Manufacturers, felt it necessary to publicly renounce "the use of espionage, strikebreaking agencies, professional strikebreakers, armed guards, or munitions for the purpose of interfering with or destroying the legitimate rights of labor to self-organization and collective bargaining."[30] Though it was impossible to precisely measure the investigation's impact on public opinion, it seemed probable that the committee, by exposing the obsta-

28. Auerbach, *Labor and Liberty*, pp. 202–3.
29. Bernstein, *Turbulent Years*, p. 648.
30. *Hearings on S. 1970*, p. 201.

cles workers faced when they tried to organize, increased the public's tolerance of organized labor. Certainly a fair reading of the committee's record suggested that orderly collective bargaining between union and management was preferable to bloody warfare. Finally, the committee bequeathed to future generations a vast documentary record on industrial relations during the turbulent 1930s. In seventy-five volumes of transcripts and documents and in twenty-odd reports, the committee provided later historians with essential source material for recounting the events of the decade. Significantly, although many historians added new information to the committee's findings, they did not significantly alter its conclusions on, for example, Harlan County, the Memorial Day incident, the Little Steel strike, and the migrant-labor problem.

La Follette could also take pride in having maintained a high standard of procedural fairness in his conduct of the hearings. In this regard, comparison of his committee with the House Un-American Activities Committee offered an illuminating contrast. The latter, especially in its early stages, permitted witnesses to make sweeping, unsubstantiated accusations without subjecting them to careful scrutiny. Furthermore, Dies's committee rarely gave an accused person the opportunity to reply to charges made against him. La Follette, on the other hand, subjected almost every witness to painstaking cross-examination and allowed ample opportunity for each person accused of misconduct to present his side of the story, usually at, or close to, the time that witnesses made the charges against him. To many observers, La Follette's committee, in terms of procedures, was a model of what a congressional investigation should be and Dies's committee a model of what it should not be.[31]

La Follette's fairness was reflected in the sharply conflicting assessments that his style of questioning sometimes prompted. For example, during the California hearings, a foe of the committee said to La Follette, "I have listened to you question some of the sheriffs, and I must say . . . that it is very unfair and not an impartial questioning as defined by any dictionary that I have seen." Yet when Republic Steel's Tom Girdler testified during the Little Steel hearings, journalist Paul Y. Anderson, an avid committee supporter, complained that "La Follette . . . treated Girdler with elaborate courtesy and consideration, and failed to confront him with a number of facts that were calculated to embarrass him." Anderson continued, "Bob has

31. For example, see Richard L. Strout, in *Washington Post*, 30 October 1938.

got into the habit of leaning over backward so far that he is constantly losing his balance."[32]

The investigation and La Follette's conduct of it, however, were not without defects. For one thing, the scope of La Follette's investigation was too narrow. The Senate resolution setting up the committee had authorized it to investigate "violations of the rights of free speech and assembly and undue interference with the rights of labor to organize and bargain collectively." Although various organizations and individuals frequently called the committee's attention to civil liberties infractions outside the field of labor relations—such as racial injustice, terrorism by the Ku Klux Klan, and infringements on academic freedom—La Follette failed to respond. Limitations of time and money and La Follette's belief that labor-management relations constituted the most pressing threat to civil liberties made the committee's limited scope understandable, but no less regrettable.[33]

The most frequent and ultimately the most valid criticism of the La Follette investigation was that it told only one side of the story.[34] Rep. Clare E. Hoffman of Michigan charged that La Follette and his colleagues "were more interested in disclosing the violation of civil liberties on the part of the employers than they were on the part of the strikers, labor organizers, and unions." The National Association of Manufacturers accused the committee of ignoring union violence and of operating on the asumption that "the employer alone is responsible for violence, and . . . that all labor organizations are law-abiding and above reproach."[35] In fact the committee did not ignore violence perpetrated by workers. But it did tend to rationalize it. In strikes during which both labor and management resorted to force, the committee almost invariably interpreted labor's actions as an understandable reaction to provocations by management.[36] Undoubtedly the committee told the most important side of the story; but by failing to condemn labor's excesses with the same force with which it condemned employers' excesses, it relinquished its claim to complete impartiality. A more balanced approach probably would have increased La Follette's chances of securing adoption of his remedial legislation.

32. *Hearings*, pt. 50, p. 18381; Paul Y. Anderson, "La Follette Pulls Punches," *Nation* 147(20 August 1938):170.

33. Auerbach, *Labor and Liberty*, n. 63, p. 121; Benjamin C. Marsh, *Lobbyist for the People: A Record of Fifty Years* (Washington, D.C., 1953), p. 212.

34. Auerbach, *Labor and Liberty*, pp. 129–30, 158–60.

35. *Hearings on S. 1970*, pp. 207–8.

36. For an example of the committee's handling of labor violence, see *The "Little Steel" Strike*, pp. 328–29.

The investigation greatly enhanced La Follette's reputation as a champion of civil liberties and as a defender of organized labor. Roger Baldwin, head of the American Civil Liberties Union, praised him for "a job without parallel in American history." Doubtless the praise that most pleased him came from Socialist Norman Thomas. "The country," said Thomas, "owes Bob La Follette a debt comparable to that owed his father."[37]

When the investigation ended, La Follette seemed satisfied with his own performance and with the work of his committee. Yet, one aspect of the investigation, the possibility that communists had served on the committee, would later come back to haunt him. In 1940, however, La Follette was relieved to have the investigation behind him, for by this time his thoughts had turned to the international crisis and to keeping the United States out of war.

37. Baldwin and Thomas quoted in Workers Defense League pamphlet entitled "Labor, Defense, and Democracy," 1941, box 668-C, Family Papers.

CHAPTER 13

Deadly Parallel

From the onset of the depression in 1929, until 1939, La Follette, like most of his countrymen, devoted relatively little attention to foreign affairs. He considered domestic issues such as unemployment, taxation, and labor relations far more important to the nation's welfare than any developments abroad. The outbreak of war in Europe in September 1939, however, forced him to rearrange his priorities. By 1940 he was calling foreign policy the "supreme issue" confronting the nation. La Follette perceived in the events from September 1939 to December 1941 and in the Roosevelt administration's response to them a "deadly parallel" with the events preceding America's entry into World War I.[1] And like his father twenty years earlier, he was convinced that the United States must at all costs avoid involvement in the European war. La Follette became so preoccupied with foreign policy during these years that he continued to neglect Wisconsin affairs. As a result he almost lost his Senate seat in the 1940 election.

La Follette's views on foreign policy, even more than his views on domestic matters, evidenced the continuing influence of his father. By way of contrast, because Old Bob had never faced a major depression while in office, his record had provided little guidance on the most pressing issues of the 1930s. For example, before dealing with the problems of unemployment and economic recovery, Young Bob had been forced to search out the facts and decide what his position would be; although these positions were probably consistent with his father's principles, they were his own. In the realm of foreign policy, La Follette accepted his father's view of the world and of America's proper role in it.

Many beliefs and attitudes, most of them inherited from his father, underpinned La Follette's views on foreign policy and conditioned his response to international developments between 1939 and 1941. First of all, he believed that America's entry into World War I had been a tragic mistake—a "mad adventure," he called it. Britain and France, he thought, had duped the United States into believing that

1. *CR* 76:3, 1940–1941, vol. 86, app., p. 5650; 77:1, 1941, vol. 87, pt. 8, p. 8316 (see list of abbreviations p. x).

democracy was at stake in their war against Germany. In reality all they had wanted was a partner in plunder. In luring the United States into war, those two Old World powers had received assistance from American financiers and munitions makers who stood to profit financially from the war. They had also received help from President Woodrow Wilson's administration, which between 1914 and 1917 skewed American policy in favor of the Allies. According to La Follette's version of history, when the war ended, Britain and France showed their true colors; with the connivance of President Wilson at Versailles, they fashioned a "peace of spoils and indemnities, of cruel, inhuman exercise of power of the conqueror over the conquered, such as had never been known to the civilized world."[2] La Follette repeatedly maintained that nothing good had come out of World War I and the cruel peace that followed it. For the United States the war caused needless bloodshed, accelerated the concentration of wealth, and contributed to the agricultural depression of the 1920s and the Great Depression of the 1930s. For Europe the war and the Versailles treaty brought economic and social chaos; sowed the seeds of resentment, especially among the German people; and made another war almost inevitable.[3]

La Follette's analysis of the causes and consequences of World War I clearly revealed another of his attitudes toward foreign policy: he had a deep distrust of Europe. He persisted in calling it the "Old World," and to him it was a place of despots and plutocrats, of purges, religious persecutions, and "isms." He once said that "intrigues and imperialism" dominated European diplomacy. La Follette seemed to consider Hitler's Germany, Stalin's Russia, and Mussolini's Italy the worst of the European lot; but Britain and France ranked a close second. In 1938 he declared, in reference to Britain and France, that "so long as other nations are governed by rancor, the lust for power, and financial and commercial interests, it is folly to consider joint action with them." When speaking of England, La Follette rarely passed up the opportunity to remind listeners that it was an imperial power and the seat of the British Empire; occasionally, to drive home

2. *CR* 69:1, 1926, vol. 67, pt. 3, p. 2578.

3. This summary of La Follette's views on the causes and consequences of World War I is based on bits and snatches of numerous letters, articles, and speeches. See especially the following speeches in *CR*: 69:1, 1926, vol. 67, pt. 3, pp. 2575–87, 3679–80; 73:2, 1934, vol. 78, pt. 2, pp. 2164–68; 76:1, 1939, vol. 84, app., pp. 3544, 3687; 76:2, 1939, vol. 85, pt. 1, pp. 144, 321–27; 77:1, 1941, vol. 87, pt. 8, pp. 8316–18. See also *La Follette's Magazine*, April, May 1926, March, September 1929; *Progressive*, 14 October 1933. RML letter files in boxes 21-A, 24-A, 27-A, Family Papers, also shed light on his views.

the point, he would list all of the empire's member nations. He was, however, not totally negative toward Europe. He felt sympathy and admiration for the European masses, whom he considered to be victims of oppressive regimes, greedy politicians, and the "special interests"; and for smaller nations, like Spain before it fell to the fascists, the Scandinavian countries, Finland, and later the nations that were overrun by the Nazis. La Follette even lauded some aspects of English government. Its tax structure, for example, served as a model for his own tax proposals. Yet, he repeatedly cautioned that sympathy with European problems was not enough reason for America to be drawn into the "maelstrom of European politics." That, he concluded, was the tragic lesson of World War I.[4]

A third key to La Follette's foreign policy was his suspicion of the role of the presidency in foreign affairs. Experience taught him that presidents, unless checked by Congress, tended to involve the country in international conflicts. Like his father, he was convinced that President Wilson had helped lead the United States into the World War. In 1926, he believed, President Coolidge had come perilously close to provoking war with Mexico. That same year Coolidge advocated American membership in the World Court, and La Follette helped lead the opposition, arguing that membership in the court might involve the United States in another war. In 1927 when Coolidge sent troops to Nicaragua, La Follette accused the president of usurping Congress's power to declare war. La Follette relaxed a bit during the Hoover administration and the early years of the New Deal. He praised Roosevelt's Good Neighbor policy in Latin America, and in 1934 he supported the reciprocal-trade agreements, which gave Roosevelt broad powers to adjust tariff rates and to negotiate trade agreements with other countries. But then in 1935 Roosevelt proposed that America join the World Court, and La Follette again became aware of the propensity of chief executives to create mischief in foreign affairs. A prime example involved a series of neutrality acts that Congress passed between 1935 and 1937. One of the provisions of these laws prohibited American citizens from selling munitions or making loans to nations at war. La Follette supported the measures; but he also vigorously fought attempts to give the president discretionary powers in administering the laws or in deciding when they should go into effect. La Follette also believed that not even Congress could be trusted to decide rationally the ultimate question of whether or not the nation should go to war. Hence, from 1937 on-

4. CR 69:1, 1926, vol. 67, pt. 3, p. 2587; 75:3, 1938, vol. 83, pt. 6, p. 5895; Progressive, 25 April 1936; New York Times, 5 April 1935.

ward he repeatedly sought adoption of a constitutional amendment making a congressional declaration of war, except in the case of direct attack, subject to a vote of approval by the people.[5]

Significantly, and in contrast to many of his colleagues, La Follette's distrust of presidential power did not spill over into the domestic arena. Even as he called for restraints upon the president's authority over foreign affairs, he supported measures to increase the president's power over domestic affairs. In 1937 he fought for Roosevelt's Court-packing plan, and in 1938 he was a prime proponent of a government-reorganization bill that would have extended Roosevelt's control over the federal bureaucracy. Similarly, the Wisconsin senator simultaneously criticized Roosevelt for being too aggressive abroad and too meek at home.[6]

The most important attitude underlying La Follette's views on foreign policy was a near total aversion to war. This attitude stemmed directly from his own and his father's experiences during the war. Young Bob had escaped service in 1917 through a medical deferment, but he had witnessed the ugly domestic consequences of war. Surely he never forgot those nightmarish years, when people called the elder La Follette a traitor, hung him in effigy, and spat upon him in the streetcar; when lifelong friends shunned the family; and when the Senate considered a motion to expel Old Bob for disloyalty. The war was also the time of Young Bob's critical illness, and perhaps he unconsciously associated that ordeal with war.

La Follette spoke more passionately and more emotionally about the domestic repercussions of war than he did about any other subject. "Modern war," he said, "poisons democracy, often fatally. Men cannot speak, think, or write freely. No longer do they participate as citizens of a free state." He predicted that if the United States ever again became involved in war, "tolerance will die. Hate will be mobilized by the Government itself. Neighbor will be set to spy on neighbor; bigotry will stalk the land; labor, industry, agriculture, and finance will be regimented, if not taken over, by the Central Government." In short, war would create a dictatorship and destroy democracy, perhaps permanently. La Follette sometimes sounded like a pacifist, but he was not. He believed that if a foreign power attacked the United States, its possessions, or other nations in the Western

5. *La Follette's Magazine*, January, May, June 1927, January 1928; *New York Times*, 12 March 1927; Alan Edmond Kent, "Portrait in Isolationism: The La Follettes and Foreign Policy" (Ph.D. diss., University of Wisconsin, 1956), pp. 226, 255–58, 262–63, 268–69. See also miscellaneous speeches and statements on neutrality legislation, box 407-C, Family Papers.
6. *New York Times*, 6 February, 6 March 1938.

Hemisphere, the United States would have to fight. But he considered such an attack most unlikely.[7]

On 1 September 1939, Germany invaded Poland. Two days later England and France declared war. La Follette was in Wisconsin when he heard the news, and he promptly declared that henceforth he would "test every international issue upon the question of whether or not it tends to keep the United States from becoming involved in another foreign war."[8]

The first test was not long in coming. Shortly after war broke out, La Follette hurried back to Washington, for Roosevelt had summoned Congress into special session. Congress, the president insisted, must revise the Neutrality Act of 1937. He wanted repeal of the arms embargo, and he also wanted Congress to put the sale of arms and other materials on a "cash and carry" basis, requiring belligerents to pay cash for goods, then carry them away from American ports on their own vessels. England controlled the Atlantic, so repeal of the arms embargo clearly would help the Allies in their fight against Germany. But Roosevelt de-emphasized this fact, claiming instead that revision of the Neutrality Act would lessen the chances of American involvement in the war. La Follette privately doubted the president's sincerity. "I found out today," he wrote Rachel, "that Donald Richberg," whom he presumed to be speaking on behalf of the administration, "has been meeting with businessmen and bankers in New York telling them they must get behind the President on repeal of the Arms Embargo because unless we give the Allies this support they may cave in and make peace soon. Compare this with Roosevelt's public appeal that it is to maintain our peace and neutrality!"[9]

Convinced that repeal would put the United States on the road to war, La Follette helped mobilize opposition in the Senate. On 21 September he met with twenty-three senators to plot strategy. "I made the group a pep talk," he told Rachel, "stating my firm conviction that the fight could be won despite the fact that the Administration *now* has the votes; providing that we organized the fight . . . and also organized the public opinion in the country so it could have some medium to function through." La Follette was "convinced that an overwhelming majority of the people are against the repeal of the arms embargo but unless that opposition is brought to bear on the Congress the President has all the advantage in the struggle." The

7. *CR* 77:1, 1941, vol. 87, pt. 2, pp. 1302, 1307.
8. *Progressive*, 9 September 1939, cited in Kent, "Portrait in Isolationism," pp. 294–95.
9. RML to Rachel, 25 September 1939, box 47-A, Family Papers.

next day, after consulting with Phil and with ardent noninterventionist Chester Bowles of the advertising firm of Benton and Bowles, La Follette pressed upon his colleagues the idea of forming a national organization to mobilize public opinion. The plan never materialized. According to La Follette, Sen. Arthur H. Vandenberg, a Republican from Michigan, called him "to say that two or three of the men who had been at the meeting . . . were fearful that the plan might bring criticism because it would be charged that the response was being manufactured." La Follette considered this objection "a lot of eye wash . . . but [Senators] Borah and Nye took the position that we could not go ahead if there was any dissent so we called it off." La Follette glumly concluded, "I think the fight was lost right there but what could Phil and I do?" [10]

On the eve of the embargo debate, La Follette seemed resigned to defeat. Organizing the opposition, he privately admitted, had proved difficult: "In the first place they are only agreed on that issue, in the second place . . . it is like driving two wild horses to try and keep Borah and [Hiram] Johnson pulling together. In any case I have done the best I could to pull the group together and one always has to be satisfied with one's best effort." [11]

On the Senate floor and in a radio address, La Follette pleaded for retention of the embargo. Repeal, he warned, would mark "a significant step toward participation in the European war." Once the United States started supplying munitions to the Allies, there might be no turning back. "That," he said, "was the lesson of the last war." La Follette displayed absolutely no sympathy for Britain and France, "these partners who will soon be asking us to join them in another waltz of death and destruction." He ridiculed the notion that the conflict was a war to preserve democracy and save civilization. Since 1914, he charged, Britain and France had pursued imperialistic policies and had shown wanton disregard for democracy. He further suggested that they had only themselves to blame for their current problems: "In the years after the war they helped to strangle every effort toward democracy in Germany. They thus became the illegitimate parents of nazi-ism and all the terrible things it has brought with it."

If the United States became involved in the war, he continued, it would have nothing to gain and everything to lose. War would destroy American democracy and wreck the economy. He did not believe that Allied victory was essential to American national security.

10. RML to Rachel, 23 September 1939, box 47-A, Family Papers.
11. RML to Rachel, 30 September 1939, box 47-A, Family Papers.

So destructive was modern warfare, he argued, "that a few months after this war is over, no one will be able to tell the victors from the vanquished." La Follette dismissed as "just so much eye-wash" the argument that Hitler, after conquering Europe, would mount an attack on the Western Hemisphere. "I do not believe any nation or group of nations can arise from the ashes of war's destruction to challenge the most powerful nation on the face of the globe." And even if, "by some miracle," Germany did launch an offensive, the United States could easily repel it. "Make no mistake about it," he declared, "we can have an invulnerable hemisphere. No nation or group of nations can successfully attack it if we but provide the necessary Army, Navy, and the bases needed for their efficient operation." La Follette considered unsolved domestic problems, like massive unemployment, a far greater threat to national security than Hitler. He similarly rejected the argument that either the war or possible German victory threatened America's economic development. He reeled off statistics indicating that the United States far surpassed other nations in productive capacity and wealth of natural resources. The Western Hemisphere, he seemed to say, could survive and prosper in a hostile world.[12]

As La Follette expected, on 27 October the Senate ended the embargo by a better than two-to-one margin. He then moved to soften the impact of repeal by offering two amendments. The first required a nonbinding national referendum "upon the question of war or peace prior to any declaration of war by Congress." The second amendment, which sought to "prevent the growth and subsequent collapse of a short-lived war boom, with its attended dangers to our peace, prosperity, and the cost of living," placed quotas on American exports. The Senate easily turned back both amendments. For La Follette and his noninterventionist colleagues, the repeal of the arms embargo marked the first in a long series of defeats.[13]

Following Hitler's conquest of Poland in September, an eerie calm fell over western Europe, since neither side wanted to launch an offensive during the winter months. World attention than shifted to the east, where on 30 November the Soviet Union invaded Finland. Like most Americans, La Follette sympathized with the Finns, and early in 1940 he voted for a modest loan to Finland. To a constituent who evidently wondered how La Follette could support aid to that country and not to Britain or France, he answered, somewhat lamely, that he had voted for the loan "only after the Senate Committee on

12. *CR* 76:2, 1939, vol. 85, pt. 1, pp. 321–33, app., pp. 144–45.
13. Ibid., pp. 841–57, 986–99.

Foreign Relations . . . received assurances that this would in no way jeopardize our neutrality." La Follette's position on the Russo-Finnish war emphasized the shift that had taken place over the years in his attitude toward the Soviet Union. He had always opposed communism, but before the late 1930s he had generally been tolerant of Russia. In 1928, after reading a sympathetic account of Russia by Dorothy Thompson, he told his sister Fola that Thompson's views were close to his own. He did add, however, that she was more "tolerant of [the Russians'] intolerance than I find it possible to be. Their cock-sureness that they alone were *right* was annoying to me as it always is with people who can so easily tell right from wrong."[14] La Follette was one of the earliest proponents of diplomatic recognition of Russia, and he wholeheartedly supported Roosevelt's action to establish ties in 1933. But then rumors of purges and the like began to leak out of the Soviet Union, and by the late 1930s La Follette had grown hostile. By 1940 he considered Stalin to be as evil as Hitler.[15]

The calm that fell over Europe during the winter proved to be the "calm before the storm." In the spring of 1940 Hitler launched a terrifying offensive. Between April and June, German armies overran Denmark, Norway, Holland, Belgium, Luxembourg, and finally France. By summer only England in the west and Russia in the east stood between Hitler and the conquest of Europe.

These alarming developments only intensified La Follette's determination to keep the United States out of war. "If we allow ourselves to be drawn into the European slaughter," he told a gathering of Wisconsin Progressives in May, "it will bleed us white and leave us as helpless as the rest." He also declared that "we must and shall provide adequate military defenses for this hemisphere to protect us against invasion or interference. I would vote the last man and the last dollar, if necessary to defend this hemisphere, but in the name of democracy I pledge to you that I shall never give my vote to send American boys to fight overseas in a foreign war." Two months later La Follette wrote an article for United Features Syndicate in which he said that "it would be a tragic mistake to go to war to defend the British Isles." He repeated the charge he had made during the embargo debate that Britain and France were responsible for the rise of Hitler. He wrote, "We cannot remedy the mistakes made by Great

14. RML to Ann Eckert, 18 April 1940, box 291-C, RML to Fola, 1 December 1928, box 36-A, Family Papers.

15. *CR* 76:2, 1939, vol. 85, pt. 1, p. 331. La Follette later discussed the evolution of his attitude toward the Soviet Union in *CR*, 79:1, 1945, vol. 91, pt. 4, pp. 5320, 5322.

Britain during the last twenty-two years in both foreign and domestic policy. What is happening now was decided long before Sept. 3, 1939." La Follette admitted that "it is tragic to see France defeated and brave Englishmen fighting against odds." "But," he concluded, "powerful as we are, we have not the strength to reverse the running of the European sands of time."[16]

Before 1940 La Follette could always take comfort in the knowledge that his heartfelt convictions on foreign policy closely reflected the views of his constituents. Even after the alarming events of the spring and early summer, most Wisconsinites doubtless hoped with La Follette that the United States would not again become involved in foreign war. Yet increasingly there were signs that at least some of them were unwilling to go as far as their senior senator to avoid involvement.

For evidence of discontent La Follette had to look no further than the pages of his own *Progressive* magazine. Since 1928 he, his brother, and his sisters had shared control of that weekly publication with William T. Evjue, the gruff, outspoken editor and publisher of the *Capital Times* of Madison. A Norwegian-American and one of the elder La Follette's staunchest backers, Evjue had 50 percent interest in the *Progressive* and also served as its editor. Since 1937 he and the La Follette brothers had frequently been at odds, but the real crisis came with the war in Europe. Although Evjue had supported Old Bob's antiwar stand in 1917, he militantly opposed Young Bob's noninterventionist position. After the embargo debate La Follette told Rachel that "Evjue would like to punish me for not supporting F.D.R. on the arms embargo and for unknown reasons which have made him so bitter against Phil and me in the past few years." La Follette even suspected that if Evjue "thought he could get away with it he would make a deal with F.D.R., Crowley, Farley et al. to give me the works." He concluded, "Well let them come on. I'll let them know they have been in a good fight before they get through next November."[17]

During and after Hitler's spring offensive, Evjue, in the *Progressive*, openly endorsed Roosevelt's policy of aiding Britain. In July the La Follettes finally severed their partnership with Evjue, once again

16. RML speech to Progressives, 19 May 1940, box 164-3, PFL Papers; Robert M. La Follette, Jr., "No! Says La Follette," *Washington Daily News*, 20 July 1940, clipping, box 667-C, Family Papers.

17. Kent, "Portrait in Isolationism," pp. 204–5; Herbert F. Margulies, *The Decline of the Progressive Movement in Wisconsin, 1890–1920* (Madison, 1968), p. 217; PFL to Joseph R. Farrington, 6 August 1940, box 136–1, PFL Papers; RML to Evjue, 28 April 1937, box 45-A, RML to Rachel, 16 December 1939, box 47-A, Family Papers.

assumed complete control of the magazine, and installed their own editor, Morris H. Rubin. A talented young man from New York City, Rubin had graduated from the University of Wisconsin, been a political reporter, and worked for Phil since 1937.[18]

Although Evjue was the most vocal critic of La Follette's foreign policy, one of the senator's closest political advisers in the state, Madison attorney and businessman Glenn D. Roberts, also expressed reservations. Roberts feared that La Follette was underestimating the extent of the menace that Hitler represented. Convinced that Germany would eventually attack the United States, Roberts pleaded with him to sponsor some national defense measures. Failure to do so, he warned, might destroy La Follette's career.[19]

La Follette dismissed all criticism, and during the summer and fall of 1940 he continued to battle the administration on practically every international issue. In August he tried unsuccessfully to defeat a bill establishing the first peacetime draft in the nation's history. "It seems a crime," he wrote, "to fasten such a system on a country where it is clear men can be gotten under the voluntary system." As an alternative to forced conscription, he recommended boosting voluntary enlistments by shortening the length of service, increasing pay, and barring volunteers from serving outside the Western Hemisphere or American possessions.[20]

On the evening of 11 September, La Follette went on the radio under the auspices of the newly formed America First Committee and delivered a scathing attack on administration policy. He singled out the recent "destroyer deal," in which Roosevelt had turned over to Britain fifty "overage" naval vessels while Britain signed over to America the control of its bases in the Western Hemisphere. The United States, La Follette charged, had come out on the short end. He said that the destroyers, far from being obsolete as Roosevelt had claimed, were "equipped with the latest protection devices and armaments." By the president's definition of obsolescence, "50 percent of the combat vessels in the . . . Navy could be declared overage and yet we know that our Navy is our first line of defense." La Follette warned that "unless we stop in our tracks there will be no end to the policy of taking everything that Britain wants and labeling it surplus or overage and obsolete. The next step after overage destroyers will

18. Kent, "Portrait in Isolationism," pp. 306–7; interview, Morris H. Rubin, 1, 8 August 1972.

19. Roberts to RML, 25 May 1940, box 18-C, Family Papers.

20. RML to family, 13 August 1940, constituent form letter, August 1940, box 47-A, Family Papers.

be middle-aged battleships. Then it will be youngish cruisers. In the end, they will be calling for our right-aged sons."

During the speech, he provided insight into the motives that impelled him to speak out. "One reason I feel so strongly about the course on which our country has embarked," he said, "is that I have seen this tragedy before. I feel as though I had walked into a movie only to discover that I have seen the picture years ago, under a somewhat different name and with a different cast." He reminded listeners that he had been at his father's side in 1917. "Fortunately for my education, I was close to the historic battle which raged in Washington. Its full, tragic meaning burned into me for life." "As I sit in the . . . Senate today," he continued, "the words that are spoken and the things that are done here in Washington have a tragic ring of familiarity. Some of the words and slogans are different. But in spite of new phrases cooked up by the best propagandists in the business we are going, step by step, down that same road we took in 1916–17."[21]

Throughout 1940 La Follette also carried the fight against intervention into the field of taxation. In the years immediately preceding America's entry into the First World War, American industrialists made huge profits from selling armaments and supplies to Britain and France. This lucrative trade, La Follette believed, had helped draw the United States closer to the Allies and eventually into war. At one time in his career, he had favored placing "the manufacture and sale of munitions and armaments . . . exclusively in the hands of the government, so that none shall profit from human slaughter."[22] But there was little congressional support for government ownership of the munitions industry, and by 1940 he had come to see a stringent exces-profits tax as the solution. In theory such a tax would fall heavily on corporate earnings derived from the war boom and thus would remove the profit incentive from war. La Follette also viewed the levy on profits as an important source of revenue for meeting federal expenditures.[23]

In June he nearly succeeded in attaching a profits tax to a pending revenue bill. The Senate adopted his amendment, but House-Senate conferees struck it out at the last moment. The fight was not over, however, for in July, Roosevelt insisted that Congress immediately enact a "steeply graduated excess profits tax, to be applied to all

21. RML speech, "Are We on the Road to War," 11 September 1940, *CR* 76:3, 1940, vol. 86, app., pp. 5649–50.
22. "Progressive State Platform, 1934," *The Wisconsin Blue Book, 1935* (Madison, 1935), p. 478.
23. RML constituent form letter, May 1939, box 47-A, Family Papers; RML speech to Progressives, 19 May 1940, box 164-3, PFL Papers.

individuals and all corporations without discrimination." The president's demand was largely a bluff. Although he abhorred the thought of corporations reaping huge profits from war, he was willing to settle for a token tax bill, which Congress could strengthen at some future time. With the November elections only four months away, he wanted to be able to point to an excess-profits tax, no matter how weak, in order to fend off Republican charges that the Democratic party was the "war party." Roosevelt also hesitated to press for a stiff tax of the La Follette type because he feared, with some justification, that corporations would then refuse to sign defense contracts. Secretary of the Treasury Henry Morgenthau, Jr., quoted Roosevelt as saying, "I want a tax bill; I want one damned quick; I don't care what is in it; I don't want to know."[24]

In this frame of mind, Roosevelt gave the conservative chairmen of the House Ways and Means Committee and the Senate Finance Committee complete freedom to write the tax bill as they saw fit. Not surprisingly the profits tax that took shape was extremely mild—a "sham," La Follette called it. "I cannot understand," he grumbled in August, "how the Administration can advocate conscription of men in peacetime and then draw a bill which lets the defense profiteers off with a slap on the wrist." A month later he complained that in all the years he had served on the Finance Committee, he had never seen members so unconcerned about what they were doing. Except for Chairman Pat Harrison of Mississippi, Walter George of Georgia, and himself, "no one on the committee . . . has made any effort to understand the bill or the issues at stake." Worse yet, Harrison and George were "both out to help the high profit, low capitalization companies and the committee follows them blindly." La Follette suspected that "they want to write such a lousy bill that it will discredit the whole idea of excess profits taxation and thus pave the way to slap the whole burden on the people by a sales tax in the end."[25]

In September the Finance Committee, with La Follette dissenting, reported out a seriously flawed bill. It contained numerous loopholes allowing corporations to escape all, or part of, the excess-profits tax. The bill also favored prosperous, well-established corporations at the expense of smaller, less well-to-do concerns. La Follette, with the

24. RML to Alfred W. Couch, 22 April 1942, box 298-C, Family Papers; Roosevelt quoted in Sidney Ratner, *American Taxation: Its History as a Social Force in Democracy* (New York, 1942), pp. 495–96; John Morton Blum, *From the Morgenthau Diaries: Years of Urgency, 1938–1941* (Boston, 1965), pp. 289–92.

25. Blum, *Years of Urgency*, p. 291; RML to family, 12 August, 7 September 1940, box 47-A, Family Papers.

help of Assistant Secretary of the Treasury John L. Sullivan, prepared an amendment to close the loopholes and pledged to "put up the best fight I know how to make on the floor."[26]

Meanwhile, Secretary of the Treasury Morgenthau pointed out to Roosevelt the defects in the tax bill and apparently urged him to support the La Follette revision. Morganthau informed La Follette that Roosevelt approved his amendment "a hundred percent" and that the president would privately direct Democratic leaders to support it. But Roosevelt was unwilling to go beyond this. He refused to endorse the amendment publicly, and during the Senate debate he left La Follette to fend for himself. The Senate defeated the amendment, 41 to 20, and went on to pass an excess-profits-tax bill that La Follette described as "a two-headed monstrosity that ought to be put in a Believe It or Not Odditorium rather than on the statute books."[27]

When the tax debate ended, La Follette returned to Wisconsin to campaign for reelection. Since 1938, when Phil and most other Progressives had gone down to defeat, almost everyone had been predicting a close race and possible defeat for the senator in 1940.[28] He seemed vulnerable for a number of reasons. The Progressive party was in a shambles, and neither of the La Follette brothers had done much to make the necessary repairs. The GOP, on the other hand, appeared stronger than ever. After going into eclipse during the middle 1930s, it had reappeared in 1938 to capture the governorship, the legislature, the other Senate seat, and a majority of House seats. Republicans were so confident of ousting La Follette in 1940 that seven of them scrambled for the nomination.[29] The Democratic party, which once again had fallen on hard times, posed no direct threat to La Follette except that possibly, in a close contest, its Senate nominee might attract enough liberal votes from La Follette to ensure a Republican victory.

La Follette's record in the Senate was his strongest asset, but even it contained potential weaknesses. To win he needed to attract both

26. Blum, *Years of Urgency*, pp. 294–96; RML to family, 12 August 1940, box 47-A, Family Papers.

27. Henry Morgenthau, Jr., Diaries, 304:171–79, 192–93, Franklin D. Roosevelt Library, Hyde Park, New York; Blum, *Years of Urgency*, p. 295; La Follette quoted in Edward N. Doan, *The La Follettes and the Wisconsin Idea* (New York, 1947), p. 223.

28. Daniel W. Hoan to RML, 6 January 1939, Glenn D. Roberts to RML, 3 August 1939, box 17-C, Family Papers; Harold L. Ickes, *The Secret Diary of Harold L. Ickes* (New York, 1953–1954), 2:654.

29. Roger T. Johnson, *Robert M. La Follette, Jr. and the Decline of the Progressive Party in Wisconsin* (Madison, 1964), pp. 46, 50–51, 54–55.

labor and farm votes. His efforts on behalf of the unemployed and his chairmanship of the Senate Civil Liberties Committee assured him of a good showing in the urban-industrial sections of the state. Organized labor, including the Wisconsin CIO, the railroad brotherhoods, and most labor leaders, endorsed him warmly.[30] But the farm vote posed a problem. Although he had consistently supported pro-farm legislation, the activities to which he had devoted the most time and for which he was best known affected urban workers far more than agrarians. Hence, farmers may have felt slighted. La Follette also had reason to worry about the voters' reaction to his unyielding stance on foreign policy, at least if William T. Evjue's criticism reflected widespread sentiment.

Above all, he was vulnerable to the charge that he was an absentee senator who returned home only at election time. Each year, it seemed, he was devoting less time to state affairs. His trips to Wisconsin were infrequent and of short duration, and they usually ended abruptly as some new crisis drew him back to Washington. At one point, between 1937 and 1938, an entire year went by without his making an extended visit. Until the late 1930s, his brother was able to compensate for the senator's neglect. Phil kept Young Bob's name before the public and handled the day-to-day affairs of the party organization, all of which Bob came to take for granted. As Isen once noted, "Bob absolutely overlooks or is unconscious of the Wisconsin set up, i.e. he assumes organization, men to do his bidding and work, without realizing that most senators not only have to do their jobs in Washington but have to take care of the home fires as well. " After his defeat in 1938, however, Phil became much less active in state politics, and Bob failed to adjust to the new situation. He shrugged off the repeated warnings of advisers that he must spend more time in the state. His response to one such warning from Daniel W. Hoan, the Socialist mayor of Milwaukee, was typical: "I realize," La Follette said, "that my enemies . . . criticize my not being in the state more. . . . I presume if I had spent more time in Wisconsin when the Senate was in session that they would criticize me for not being on the job in Washington."[31] La Follette seemed oblivious to the fact that friends as well as enemies criticized his neglect.

An annoying controversy over his Virginia "estate" symbolized the

30. Ibid., p. 70.
31. Mrs. PFL, "Isen's Political Diary," 8 November 1938, box 161-3, PFL Papers; Johnson, La Follette, Jr., p. 47; Philip F. La Follette, Adventure in Politics: The Memoirs of Philip La Follette (New York, 1970), p. 263; Hoan to RML, 6 January 1939, RML to Hoan, 13 January 1939, box 17-C, Family Papers.

problem. In 1931 he had purchased an old, ninety-one acre estate in the Virginia countryside. He paid seventeen thousand dollars for the property, which included a dilapidated but genuine colonial house. Originally he had planned to remodel the house and move in, but over the years he never had been able to afford the time or the expense of undertaking the project. Old Bob had always thought it politically unwise to own a home in Washington. His less shrewd son saw no danger in it. The property did not become an issue until 1940, when the senator's foes began urging voters to permanently return him to his "palatial" Virginia estate. La Follette responded by including a photograph of the run-down house in a campaign booklet. The house, the booklet explained, "has no heat, no plumbing, and the roof leaks. An aged Negro lives there, rent-free. Bob has never spent a night in the place."[32] This rebuttal missed the point. The controversy about the estate probably stemmed less from concern that La Follette was living in luxurious surroundings than from concern that his closest ties were to the Washington area rather than to Wisconsin.

The Democratic challenger who hoped to capitalize on La Follette's vulnerability was James E. Finnegan, a former state attorney general who represented the conservative faction of his party. At the Democratic national convention in July, he had opposed a third term for Roosevelt, supporting instead the conservative John Nance Garner. Once the campaign got under way, however, Finnegan, perhaps angling for an endorsement from Roosevelt, suddenly announced that he was in complete agreement with the president's domestic and foreign policies. Virtually no one gave him a chance of ousting La Follette.[33]

The man most likely to do that, everyone agreed, was Republican Fred H. Clausen, a wealthy farm-implement manufacturer from Horicon. Clausen concentrated on La Follette's liberal domestic record, attacking him for aiding and abetting the "insanity" that was the New Deal. He de-emphasized foreign policy, probably because, like most Wisconsin Republicans, he was a noninterventionist. But he did

32. RML to Fola and George Middleton, 15 May 1931, box 41-A, Belle to Fola and George Middleton, 7 May 1931, box 40-A, campaign brochure entitled "Bob's Record of Service," box 298-C, Family Papers. Since entering the Senate, La Follette had lived in several rented homes in the District of Columbia and Maryland. In the early 1940s, however, he bought a home in the District. For information on La Follette's financial status in 1940, see income tax records, box 641-C, Family Papers. His income for that year was $11,317, and it came from the following sources: Senate salary—$10,000; government travel allowance—$461; income from stocks and bonds—$856.

33. Johnson, La Follette, Jr., pp. 60, 68; Kent, "Portrait in Isolationism," pp. 318–19.

score against La Follette by criticizing him for publicly supporting the progovernment Loyalists in the Spanish Civil War. Many Catholics, and there were a sizable number of them in Wisconsin, considered the Loyalists procommunist and anti-Catholic.[34]

La Follette, for his part, conducted a curious campaign. Though worried advisers had been warning him for over a year that he faced a close race and possible defeat, he delayed a long time before organizing his supporters. According to Isen, he never did take the time to appoint an official campaign manager. In the end, Gordon Sinykin, Phil's former secretary and a Madison lawyer, and Glenn D. Roberts stepped in to share leadership responsibilities. Earlier in the year some advisers had urged La Follette to consider utilizing new campaign techniques such as drama, puppet shows, or newsreels. La Follette apparently was too busy to consider the suggestions and nothing came of them.[35]

On the stump he reiterated his stand against aid to Britain and defended his record on domestic issues. As usual he virtually ignored his opponents, except to imply that they were the tools of "organized wealth" and the "special interests." For some unexplained reason, he spent what some of his supporters considered an inordinate amount of time during the campaign attacking the incumbent Republican governor, Julius P. Heil, who was running against Progressive Orland "Spike" Loomis. This strategy did not stem from overconfidence, for he was pessimistic about his own chances of reelection. Isen noted in her diary that Phil attributed it to the fact "that Bob is innately modest and it was the hardest thing in the world for him to campaign for himself." "I believe that is true," she added, "but it was a real mistake, especially after being so little in Wisconsin, to spend most of his speech[es] on the Heil record rather than talk about what was going on in Washington."[36]

The most difficult decision La Follette faced during the campaign was whether or not to endorse Roosevelt for a third term. The recession of 1937–1938, the founding of the National Progressives of America, and especially the war issue had severely strained relations between him and the president. On the surface their relationship remained cordial enough, but La Follette no longer received frequent invitations to the White House, to Hyde Park, or to spend weekends

34. Johnson, *La Follette, Jr.*, pp. 55, 60–61.

35. Norman Clapp to Glenn D. Roberts, 3 May 1940, box 18-C, Mrs. PFL to RML, 13 August 1940, box 47-A, Family Papers; Mrs. PFL, "Isen's Political Diary," 9 February 1941, pp. 77–78, box 131-3, PFL Papers.

36. Johnson, *La Follette, Jr.*, pp. 63–64; Mrs. PFL, "Isen's Political Diary," 9 February 1941, pp. 77–78, box 161-3, PFL Papers.

aboard the presidential yacht. And apparently he no longer received patronage favors from the administration. As early as March 1939 he had explained to Glenn Roberts that "it is impossible for me to help people on these patronage appointments. I very much regret that such is the case, but we might as well face the facts." La Follette also knew that if he endorsed Roosevelt his opponents would surely remind voters that during the Coolidge administration he had sponsored that famous resolution declaring that "any departure" from the tradition of presidents retiring from office after two terms "would be unwise, unpatriotic, and frought with peril to our free institutions."[37]

But La Follette was also able to think of reasons for supporting Roosevelt, the most compelling of which was Wendell L. Willkie, the Republican presidential candidate. The senator could see no differences between Willkie's and Roosevelt's approaches to foreign policy. But on domestic policy, Willkie, with his Wall Street connections and his past defense of the utility conglomerates, was distinctly inferior to Roosevelt. La Follette probably also realized that if he supported the president he would attract much-needed votes from liberal Democrats who might otherwise cast their ballots for Finnegan. Finally, after much soul-searching, he decided to support the president.[38]

Roosevelt, meanwhile, was trying to decide what, if anything, he should do to help La Follette. He had been thinking about the Wisconsin situation for some time. In 1938, before the demise of the NPA, he had seemed anxious to appease the La Follette brothers; he may have even considered offering to make Young Bob secretary of state after 1940. But then, when the third party fizzled, he realized that the brothers, especially Bob, needed him far more than he needed them. In June 1939, according to Harold Ickes, the president predicted that "on the present lineup" La Follette would lose the election. Roosevelt went on to say that he was willing to help the senator, but only for a price. The president "said that Phil La Follette had not behaved himself any too well and that he would have to have a period of purification. He does not think he ought to run for governor next year." If the brothers came to him, Roosevelt said, he would offer them a deal: Phil must promise not to run for governor, and the La Follettes and their supporters must promise to support a progressive Democrat instead; in return Wisconsin Democrats would support

37. RML to Roberts, 9 March 1939, box 17-C, Family Papers; *New York Times*, 11 February 1928.
38. Johnson, *La Follette, Jr.*, pp. 66–67; Mrs. PFL, "Isen's Political Diary," 9 February 1941, pp. 77–78, box 161-3, PFL Papers.

Young Bob for the Senate.[39] Phil eventually decided not to run, although there was no indication that Roosevelt had in any way influenced his decision. In the meantime, however, foreign policy differences placed another barrier in the way of the president's aiding La Follette. Yet, as Roosevelt looked over the situation in the fall of 1940, he probably realized that he had nothing to gain and something to lose from a La Follette defeat. The Democrat, Finnegan, could not win. But the Republican, Clausen, might; and if he did he would provide no help to the administration on foreign policy issues and would only strengthen the conservative, anti–New Deal bloc in the Senate.

Roosevelt did not endorse La Follette directly, but he did provide substantial indirect aid. During the campaign four leading Democrats appeared in Wisconsin on La Follette's behalf: Senators Sheridan Downey of California and Robert F. Wagner of New York, Attorney General Robert H. Jackson, and Roosevelt's running mate, Henry A. Wallace. The latter two doubtless had Roosevelt's approval. Wallace's appearance caused a commotion. Shortly before his scheduled speech in Madison, Wisconsin's Democratic leaders urged him to endorse all of their party's nominees for state office, including Finnegan. When Wallace arrived, Finnegan and other Democrats joined him on the dais. Then Wallace dropped the bombshell. Ignoring Finnegan, he singled out La Follette for praise, without, however, directly endorsing him. But he came close enough, and the hapless Finnegan and two other Democrats promptly stood up and walked out.[40]

In addition to indirect endorsements, Roosevelt may have approved financial aid to La Follette. In fending off the well-organized, heavily financed Clausen challenge, the La Follette organization went into debt, and late in the campaign Phil was reaching into his own pocket to meet expenses. On 26 October, ten days before the election, La Follette's Washington secretary, Grace Lynch, wrote to one of the senator's campaign managers, Gordon Sinykin, and said that help was on the way. "Tom Corcoran," she wrote, "wanted me to wire you that another thousand dollars is on the way to you." She added, "I feel it unwise . . . in such an hour to be so plain in telegrams, so I send the word thus, thinking that one night will make little difference." Corcoran was a close personal friend of La Follette. But he was also one of Roosevelt's chief assistants, and it seemed unlikely that he would provide money to the La Follette campaign without the presi-

39. Ickes, *Secret Diary*, 2:654.
40. Johnson, *La Follette, Jr.*, pp. 67–69.

dent's authorization. Another of La Follette's 1940 campaign leaders, Glenn Roberts, later confirmed that the "Roosevelt administration" did help finance the senator's reelection effort.[41]

La Follette needed all the help he could get. As the 5 November election day approached, observers called the race a toss-up, with Clausen perhaps having a slight edge. La Follette himself believed that he would lose. During the final week of the campaign, Isen later recalled, "we talked . . . at length one evening, Bob insisting that he was ready for [defeat], would feel that he had done his duty to the people of Wisconsin, and that this would be a release." Isen tried to talk him out of it, but "Bob insisted . . . that he wouldn't care at all, so I finally desisted!"[42]

La Follette did win the election, but by a relatively small margin. He defeated Clausen by fifty thousand votes, out of 1.3 million votes cast. The final returns gave him 45 percent of the vote to 41 percent for Clausen and 13 percent for Finnegan. In 1934 La Follette had carried 66 of 71 counties; this time he won only 36. In other Wisconsin races, Roosevelt narrowly defeated Willkie, the Republicans retained the governorship and most other state offices, and the Progressive party continued its downward slide.

Analysis of the final returns indicated that two factors were decisive in the senatorial race. First, many Democrats had abandoned Finnegan and voted for La Follette. Without that crossover vote, La Follette would have lost. The second key was Milwaukee County, the most populous and one of the most industrialized counties in the state. Outside Milwaukee, La Follette narrowly trailed Clausen. But in the county he gathered nearly 50 percent of the vote and defeated Clausen by fifty-five thousand votes. And that was what gave him his margin of victory. His good showing in Milwaukee probably resulted in large part from the Socialist vote he received. In 1934 the senatorial candidate of the Socialist party polled 17 percent in Milwaukee. In 1940 the party decided not to challenge La Follette, and he apparently picked up votes from those who had voted for the Socialists six years earlier. Analysis of the final returns also indicated that La Follette's stands on foreign policy had little effect on the outcome. La Follette lost most of the German American counties which presumably were

41. William Benton to PFL, 13 November 1940, box 137-2, Mrs. PFL, "Isen's Political Diary," 9 February 1941, pp. 77–78, box 161–3, PFL Papers; Grace Lynch to Gordon Sinykin, 26 October 1940, box 18-C, Family Papers; interview, Glenn D. Roberts, 3 July 1973.

42. Johnson, *La Follette, Jr.*, p. 72; Mrs. PFL, "Isen's Political Diary," 9 February 1941, pp. 77–78, box 161–3, PFL Papers.

anti-interventionist, and he carried most of the Scandinavian counties where interventionist sentiment probably ran high.[43]

Having prepared himself for defeat, La Follette doubtless was pleasantly surprised at the outcome. Yet, the disturbing fact remained that although he was one of the best-known and most widely respected senators in Washington, a majority of Wisconsin voters—54 percent—had selected someone else to represent them in the Senate. To what extent voters were dissatisfied with him for neglecting Wisconsin affairs and to what extent they simply disagreed with his politics was impossible to determine. The closeness of the presidential race in the state and the impressive Republican showing in other contests suggested that conservatism was on the upswing and that even if La Follette had been more attentive to his constituents he still might have come close to defeat. The conservative upsurge was a force largely beyond his control. But he could control the amount of time and effort he invested in state and party matters. Whether La Follette would learn anything from the experience and act accordingly remained to be seen.

La Follette spent little time pouring over the election statistics or searching for the hidden meanings behind the results, because shortly after the election a new crisis in foreign affairs was commanding his attention. Late in 1940 a beleaguered Britain warned Roosevelt that it would soon be unable to pay cash for the munitions it needed to fight Hitler. Fresh from his electoral triumph and convinced more than ever that American security depended upon British victory, the president came up with the idea of "lend-lease." In January 1941 he asked Congress for the power to lend, lease, sell, transfer, or exchange war materials with any country whose defense he deemed vital to the defense of the United States.

In selling his plan to Congress and the public, Roosevelt displayed as perhaps never before the full range of his remarkable powers of persuasion. He appealed to common sense. All he wanted to do, he said, was "get rid of the silly, foolish old dollar sign" in supplying aid to Britain. Lend-lease, he argued, was as natural as one neighbor temporarily loaning his garden hose to another neighbor whose house was on fire.[44] Roosevelt appealed to the public's fear of Hitler. He

43. *Wisconsin Blue Book, 1935*, p. 618; *Wisconsin Blue Book, 1942* (Madison, 1942), p. 661; Kent, "Portrait in Isolationism," p. 322.

44. Quoted in James MacGregor Burns, *Roosevelt: The Soldier of Freedom* (New York, 1970), p. 26.

warned, "Never before . . . has our American civilization been in such danger as now," for Hitler was bent on world domination. Already, he claimed, enemy agents were at work in the Western Hemisphere, trying to soften it up for the kill. Roosevelt appealed to American idealism. The United States, he declared, should help build a world in which the four freedoms prevailed: the freedoms of speech and religion and the freedoms from want and fear. Throughout, he assured that lend-lease was not a step toward war. Rather, he argued that it would keep war away from American shores. The president's supporters in Congress were equal to the occasion. To lend-lease they affixed the patriotic number 1776 and the title, a bill "to Promote the Defense of the United States."[45]

La Follette considered the decision on lend-lease "the most momentous . . . America has ever been called upon to make." Addressing the Senate on 24 February, he charged that passage of the bill would give Roosevelt "the green light for war"; would invest him with dictatorial powers exceeded only by those of Hitler, Mussolini, and Stalin; and would permit Roosevelt "to strip the military and naval defenses of the United States to support a quixotic adventure overseas." The heart of La Follette's argument was that lend-lease and indeed the administration's entire foreign policy rested on the "false premise" that British victory was essential to American national security. "The victory of any nation," he asserted, "may be useful, but it is not vital, to the United States." He did not believe "that the fate of 130,000,000 Americans will either now or in the foreseeable future be dependent upon or determined by the outcome of war in Europe, Asia, or Africa." La Follette repeated his claim that even if Germany did win the European war, it could not launch a successful attack on the Western Hemisphere. He went on to criticize the administration for neglecting to strengthen military and economic ties with Latin America, "the one area in the world which is truly vital to our defense and prosperity."[46]

What alarmed La Follette as much as lend-lease itself was the nature of the debate, which at times degenerated into a verbal brawl, with persons on both sides throwing reckless, unsubstantiated charges that impugned the integrity and patriotism of their opponents. Roosevelt set the tone. He used phrases like "American appeasers" to describe the noninterventionist critics of his proposal and charged that

45. Roosevelt "Four Freedoms" speech, 6 January 1941, and Lend Lease Act, 11 March 1941, in Henry Steele Commager, ed., *Documents of American History* (New York, 1968), 2:446, 449.
46. *CR* 77:1, 1941, vol. 87, pt. 2, pp. 1299–1307.

some Americans in high places were unwittingly aiding the enemy. Some of the president's statements evoked memories of an embittered Woodrow Wilson on the eve of World War I. In March 1917, following the filibuster of the armed-ship bill in the Senate, Wilson had characterized the elder La Follette and other antiwar senators as "a little group of willful men, representing no opinion but their own" who had "rendered the great Government of the United States helpless and contemptible." At one point in his message to Congress on 6 January 1941, Roosevelt employed strikingly similar language. La Follette, vividly remembering the abuse to which his father had been subjected following Wilson's denunciation, must have cringed when he heard Roosevelt warn, "We must especially beware of that small group of selfish men who would clip the wings of the American eagle in order to feather their own nests."[47] Some of the noninterventionists responded in kind. Lend-lease, declared Sen. Burton K. Wheeler, was "the New Deal's triple A foreign policy; it will plow under every fourth American boy." Roosevelt promptly swung back, calling Wheeler's remark the most unpatriotic thing that had ever been said.[48]

As the debate turned ugly, La Follette expressed his concern to an old friend, Supreme Court Justice Felix Frankfurter. Frankfurter, although he disagreed with La Follette on foreign policy, had recently sent him a warm, sympathetic letter. La Follette replied, "Unless those in positions of responsible leadership on both sides of the issue make every effort to maintain a tolerant attitude towards their opposite numbers the future of democracy in this country will be dark indeed." But, he added, "several phrases used by the President in his last radio speech and in the message [to Congress] have given me great concern . . . for the ultimate survival of the democratic spirit here at home."[49]

La Follette himself was sometimes guilty of excess. Occasionally he portrayed the movement to aid Britain as a conspiracy to drag the United States into war—"a subtle, diabolically clever, and powerful effort to sneak up on our blind side," he once called it.[50] Certainly

47. Burns, *Soldier of Freedom*, pp. 26–28; Wilson quoted in *New York Times*, 5 March 1917, cited by Belle Case La Follette and Fola La Follette, *Robert M. La Follette* (New York, 1953), 1:626; Roosevelt, "Four Freedoms" speech, in Commager, *Documents of American History*, p. 447.

48. Wheeler-Roosevelt exchange cited by Burns, *Soldier of Freedom*, p. 44. On the nature and tone of this so-called Great Debate over foreign policy see Wayne S. Cole, *Charles A. Lindbergh and the Battle Against American Intervention in World War II* (New York, 1974), especially chaps. 16–18.

49. RML to Frankfurter, 30 January 1941, box 18-C, Family Papers.

50. RML speech, "Are We on the Road to War," 11 September 1940, *CR* 76:3, 1940, vol. 86, app., p. 5650.

he exaggerated when he said that lend-lease "means war" and that it gave Roosevelt dictatorial powers and allowed Roosevelt to strip America's defenses. For the most part, however, La Follette did not engage in the mudslinging and name-calling that too often marred the foreign policy debate in 1941. He acknowledged that his opponents, although misguided, were sincere; on one occasion he prefaced a Senate speech with the statement that "nothing in my remarks will be intended to impugn the motives, the character, or the high patriotism of those who disagree with me upon this issue."[51]

The senator's mail ran heavily against lend-lease. The public opinion polls, however, showed that a majority of citizens supported the measure. Despite a mighty effort by La Follette and his allies, lend-lease cleared the House in February, passed the Senate a month later, and became law on 11 March.[52]

During the next eight months Roosevelt moved the nation cautiously but steadily toward active participation in the war. La Follette fought the administration every step of the way, but to no avail. In the spring the president ordered the navy to expand its patrolling operations in the western Atlantic and to warn British ships laden with supplies from America of the location of German vessels. In July, when the United States occupied Iceland, La Follette accused Roosevelt of behaving more like dictators Hitler and Stalin than like a statesman. A month later the president symbolically affirmed America's commitment to England by meeting with Britain's prime minister, Winston Churchill, off the coast of Newfoundland. When the talks ended they issued a joint statement of principles, called the Atlantic Charter. "Just more words," La Follette grumbled, "but God alone knows what F.D.R. promised C."[53] As La Follette feared, the naval patrols eventually provoked retaliatory attacks from German submarines. After one such attack in September, the president ordered the navy to "shoot" German and Italian vessels "on sight." Later that month Roosevelt requested additional funds for lend-lease. And in October he sought and received from Congress a revision in the Neutrality Act. This revision gave him the power to arm American merchant ships and authorized American ships to transport cargo to Allied ports. La Follette attacked Roosevelt's "shoot on sight" order and voted with the minority against lend-lease and against revision of the

51. *CR* 77:1, 1943, vol. 87, pt. 8, p. 8316.
52. RML's office to Gordon Sinykin, 17 February 1941, box 19-C, Family Papers.
53. Kent, "Portrait in Isolationism," pp. 332–33; RML to family, 14 August 1941, box 48-A, Family Papers.

Neutrality Act. During the Neutrality Act debate, the senator, perhaps sensitive to criticisms that he was living in the past, said, "I have never advanced the claim, and I do not now, that this present war in the Old World is like World War No. 1." "But," he went on to say, "I do venture the prophecy that future unbiased historians, if such there may be, . . . will recite the deadly parallel between the steps whereby we entered World War No. 1 and those by which apparently we are entering the present conflict."[54]

La Follette did not confine his activities solely to attacks on the administration. Throughout the year he again pressed for a stringent excess-profits tax; but as in 1940 he failed. Perhaps in an effort to cast off the opprobrious label of *isolationist*, he also proposed sending shipments of surplus farm products to the civilian victims of the European war.[55]

During 1941 La Follette was as outspoken on the war issue as any of his noninterventionist colleagues. But he did not play as conspicuous a role as some of them in the public debate that raged outside the Senate. Senators Nye and Wheeler, for example, barnstormed the country, addressing rallies and delivering radio speeches under the sponsorship of the most prominent anti-interventionist organization, the America First Committee. La Follette's brother also traveled widely under the auspices of the committee. Persons affiliated with the organization urged La Follette, usually through Phil, to become more active in the national debate.[56] In January 1941 America First member Chester A. Bowles asked Phil, "Isn't it time Bob made a really important speech on the Radio?" In July, R. Douglas Stuart, Jr., America First's founder and national director, told Phil that he was "anxious to talk with you in the near future about the possibility of getting your brother . . . out on the road." The senator, Stuart thought, "is one of our most respected spokesmen. He is revered by labor. He is admired by everyone for his defense of civil liberties." In September 1940 La Follette did deliver a radio address for America First, but thereafter he kept his distance. Perhaps he felt uncomfortable with the committee because many of its leaders and backers were conservatives on domestic issues.[57] Perhaps he did not want to slight his Senate duties. Then too, he may have recoiled instinctively

54. *Progressive*, 27 September, 25 October 1941; CR 77:1, 1941, vol. 87, pt. 8, p. 8316.

55. Doan, *Wisconsin Idea*, pp. 224–27; CR 77:1, 1941, vol. 87, pt. 4, p. 4589.

56. Wayne S. Cole, *Senator Gerald P. Nye and American Foreign Relations* (Minneapolis, 1962), pp. 178–79; R. Douglas Stuart, Jr., to PFL, 14 July 1941, box 138-2, PFL Papers.

57. Telegram, Chester A. Bowles to PFL, 7 January 1941, R. Douglas Stuart,

from a more active national role for fear of exposing himself to the type of hysterical denunciation that his father had encountered in 1917. Consequently, La Follette never became as identified with the noninterventionist movement as did Nye, Wheeler, his brother, and many others.

Nevertheless he did come in for harsh criticism. As far as his political future was concerned, it was ominous that organized labor in Wisconsin was one source of the criticism. In November the Wisconsin State Industrial Union Council, an arm of the CIO, passed a resolution condemning La Follette and the rest of the state's congressional delegation for their "appeasement" policies. The council acted "in spite of the fact that some of them, notably Senator La Follette, have good labor records on other issues."[58] This marked the start of a long and bitter feud between the senator and Wisconsin CIO leaders.

Long before December 1941 La Follette seemed to sense that full American participation in the war was only a matter of time. Nevertheless the Japanese attack on Pearl Harbor on 7 December must have come as a shock. Preoccupied with Europe, he had paid little attention to the Asian war. Yet he had also repeatedly maintained that if any foreign power ever attacked the United States or its possessions, Congress would have no alternative but to declare war. When La Follette arrived at his office Monday morning, 8 December, he told an aide in effect, "We have no choice." Later that day he voted for war against Japan and two days later for war against Germany.[59]

La Follette never retracted any of his prewar statements. Nor did he make a point of insisting that he had been right and the administration wrong. And, unlike some bitter foes of Roosevelt, he never suggested that the president had bungled Japanese relations or perhaps even deliberately provoked Japan into attacking the United States. The time for debate was over, he felt. He wrote a constituent, "All of us must now unite wholeheartedly in support of the war effort until a just peace can be obtained."[60]

Jr., to PFL, 19 July 1941, box 138-2, PFL Papers; Wayne S. Cole, *America First: The Battle Against Interventionism, 1940–1941* (Madison, 1953), pp. 70–74.

58. Resolution enclosed in Walter J. Burke to RML, 13 November 1941, box 320-C, Family Papers.

59. Interview, Norman M. Clapp, 3 August 1972.

60. RML to Rev. Daniel Woodward, 19 December 1941, box 320-C, Family Papers.

CHAPTER 14

The Difficult War Years

World War II was the most frustrating period of La Follette's career. As the depression lifted at home and as American soldiers pressed toward victory abroad, he had to grapple with new and perplexing issues, like inflation, wage and price controls, consumer subsidies, and in foreign affairs the issue of American participation in a postwar international organization. His stands on those and other issues involved him in bitter and costly feuds with powerful segments of his constituency, especially organized labor. In Wisconsin, during the war years the Progressive party verged on collapse, and La Follette's popularity continued to decline. These years were also frustrating from a personal standpoint. Health and family problems unsettled him. As the war came to a close in 1945, La Follette, then fifty-one years of age, was physically and emotionally exhausted, and he seriously considered retiring from the Senate when his current term expired. The pressures of public life, he confided to friends, had finally become too much to bear.

Soon after Pearl Harbor, La Follette experienced the first of many wartime disappointments: Phil, at age forty-four, reenlisted in the army. He volunteered for overseas duty and was assigned to the Pacific theater as a public relations officer on the staff of Gen. Douglas MacArthur. Bob deeply resented his brother's decision. He doubtless worried about Phil's safety, but he was also concerned about the political situation in Wisconsin. Because of Phil's departure, the senator would have to assume leadership of the Progressive party and in general play a greater role in Wisconsin politics. According to his sister-in-law Isen, Bob complained that Phil had gone off and left him " 'holding the bag' politically."[1]

Shortly before Phil left, Bob indicated that he would assume his new responsibilities reluctantly, if he assumed them at all. Early in 1942 there was talk that many Progressives planned to bolt to the Republican or Democratic parties. "I am simply going to tell [Pro-

---

1. Philip F. La Follette, *Adventure in Politics: The Memoirs of Philip La Follette* (New York, 1970), pp. 266–68; Mrs. PFL to PFL, 12 May 1943, box 140-2, PFL Papers (see list of abbreviations p. x).

gressive leaders] what is in my mind and then they can do what they please and God Bless them whatever they decide to do," Bob wrote to Phil and added, "Life is too short and the future too obscure to put me in any frame of mind where I want to tell others what to do. I shall take whatever satisfaction can be extracted from hell on earth by trying to do what seems right for myself."[2]

During the war the brothers' relationship deteriorated steadily. Phil studied the news dispatches from Washington and read the letters from family and friends, and he became convinced that Bob was "wasting opportunities—and shirking responsibilities—that I would have welcomed."[3] In his letters to Bob, Phil criticized him for not speaking out more forcefully on the issues and for failing to spend more time in Wisconsin. Bob, upset by his brother's criticisms, tried to defend himself, but in vain.[4]

In his letters to Isen, Phil was more blunt. Bob, he said, was unsuited for public life and should have chosen the law or medicine as a profession. "Instead, he had the fortune—I was about to say misfortune—to plump into the Senate, at an early age and without the hardening foundation that [in] general is a prelude to such a position. His natural ability, keen intelligence, and knowledge of public affairs enabled him to do an outstanding job." "But," Phil added, "he never liked, and never will like the cost that staying in such a position exacts." Phil also brooded over the past. Bob, he believed, had received golden opportunities in life without having to fight for them and without even wanting them. He, Phil, on the other hand, had always had to scrap for what he wanted. Phil complained that the family, with the exception of Isen, had given more encouragement and support to Bob than to himself.[5] Bob probably never realized the extent of his brother's bitterness toward him. Nevertheless, his increasingly strained relationship with Phil doubtless contributed to his depressed state of mind during the war.

During the 1942 session of Congress, La Follette suffered more than his usual share of political disappointments. With unemployment no longer a serious problem, he tried to revive the monopoly issue, an issue that he had de-emphasized, though not abandoned, during the 1930s. He charged that the government, through its dis-

2. RML to PFL, 9 March 1942, box 139-2, PFL Papers.
3. PFL to Mrs. PFL, 18 March 1944, box 142-2, PFL Papers.
4. PFL to RML, 22 January, 12, 25 February, 14 June 1943, box 48-A, PFL to RML, 21 November 1944, box 49-A, RML to PFL, 9, 11 March, 24 June 1943, box 49-A, Family Papers.
5. PFL to Mrs. PFL, 15 May 1944, box 142-2, PFL to Mrs. PFL, 7 June 1943, box 190-2, PFL Papers.

tribution of war contracts, was fostering the growth of monopolies. He complained that "dollar-a-year monopolists," who placed self-interest above the national interest, had become entrenched in the War Production Board and other federal agencies that regulated the wartime economy. Convinced that the survival of small businesses was essential to winning the war and to preserving economic and political democracy, La Follette called for enforcement of the anti-trust laws. He sadly discovered, however, that the monopoly issue was not as potent as it had been in his father's day or even in his own first years in the Senate. Although Congress expressed its concern for small businesses by creating the Smaller War Plants Corporation in 1942, big business continued to receive the most lucrative defense contracts, and the concentration of industries proceeded apace during the war years.[6] Similarly, La Follette's major legislative proposals stirred little enthusiasm. Believing that war offered no excuse to curtail labor rights, he joined Senator Thomas in 1942 to introduce a revised oppressive-labor-practices bill. Secretary of War Henry L. Stimson, presumably with the president's approval, opposed the measure as it stood and recommended drastic changes. Stimson urged the sponsors to exclude striking workers from the protection of the bill, to eliminate the ban on industrial munitions, and to include a provision allowing the government to blacklist labor agitators. La Follette refused and the bill died in committee.[7]

Even more disappointing for La Follette was the outcome of the tax debate of 1942. As soon as the Finance Committee began deliberations on the revenue bill, La Follette sensed defeat. "We got started on the tax bill today," he wrote his family. "The majority is going to soak the little fellow something fierce and in the process everybody will get a terrific wallop." Nevertheless he waged an all-out effort. One of La Follette's assistants, Wilbur R. Voigt, later described the extensive preparations that preceded sessions of the Finance Committee and of other committees. In addition to gathering the statistics and facts with which to support his case, La Follette would prepare a whole series of amendments to each major section of the bill under discussion. Trying to anticipate every possible objection, he would design each amendment in the series so that it was

6. Edward N. Doan, *The La Follettes and the Wisconsin Idea* (New York, 1947), p. 234; *Progressive*, 29 August 1942; RML interview, enclosed in Charles G. Ross to RML, 17 September 1942, box 20-C, Family Papers.

7. Henry L. Stimson to Elbert D. Thomas, 20 July 1942, enclosed in Thomas to RML, 21 July 1942, box 355-C, Family Papers; Jerold S. Auerbach, *Labor and Liberty: The La Follette Committee and the New Deal* (Indianapolis, 1966), n. 23, p. 203.

slightly more moderate than the one preceding it. Then, if the committee voted down one of his amendments, he would immediately offer a "compromise" proposal. If it failed he would propose yet another amendment, and so on through the series. Occasionally La Follette would disguise his true intentions by leading off with amendments that he knew would be rejected. After each defeat he appeared to yield a bit more. Finally, feigning great disappointment, he would propose the amendment that he had actually wanted passed from the start.[8]

This time, however, his elaborate strategy failed to produce results. In committee he fought for a bill that would raise sufficient revenue to finance the war without placing an excessive burden on low-income groups. La Follette, in a reversal from past years, opposed efforts to broaden the tax base by reducing personal exemptions. A fairer way of raising revenue, he argued, was to increase tax rates for persons in the middle- and upper-income brackets, for corporations, and for gifts and inheritances. He also advocated compelling married couples to file joint, rather than individual, returns, eliminating the tax-exempt status of income derived from state and municipal securities, and eliminating the percentage depletion allowance for oil and gas companies. The committee rejected La Follette's proposals and over his objections reported out a tax bill in September. He then tried to amend the bill on the floor, but without success.[9]

The tax debate helped explain La Follette's growing sense of frustration. Over the years he had probably devoted more time to taxation than to any other issue. Nearly every year he played an active role in each stage of the revenue debate: from the Finance Committee, to the floor, to the conference committee. His thorough preparation, his dogged persistence, and his obvious mastery of the subject earned him the admiration of colleagues and reporters. When La Follette speaks on taxation, said one observer, "it is taken for granted that what will be said will be something approximating a last word on the subject."[10] Yet admiration did not always translate into votes. And, as the 1942 revenue debate demonstrated, the Wisconsin senator, for all his efforts, had very little impact on national tax policy.

In 1942 and for the duration of the war the most troublesome do-

8. RML to family, 24 August 1942, box 48-A, Family Papers; interview, Wilbur Voigt, 9 July 1973.

9. New York Times, 11 October 1942; CR 77:2, 1942, vol. 88, pt. 6, pp. 8060–61; Randolph E. Paul, Taxation for Prosperity (Indianapolis, 1947), pp. 96–114.

10. Stanley High, Roosevelt—And Then? (New York, 1937), p. 314.

mestic issue La Follette faced was inflation. Because wage earners and farmers clashed over the causes of, and remedies for, inflation, La Follette found himself in a crossfire between the two largest and most powerful segments of his constituency. It was clear from the outset that whatever stand he took on inflation-related issues, he was certain to alienate one group or the other.

By 1942 inflation had replaced unemployment as the most serious domestic problem confronting the nation. Between early 1941 and early 1942 the cost of living increased 15 percent, but what disturbed consumers most was food prices, which rose 20 percent. In 1942 Congress empowered Roosevelt to establish wage and price controls within certain limits. The administration, on its own initiative, also launched the so-called consumer-subsidy program. Using funds that Congress had appropriated for other purposes, the administration purchased farm products and other commodities and then sold them to consumers at reduced prices.

Although the government's anti-inflation program held down the cost of living, it pleased practically no one. Farmers and businessmen bitterly complained that price controls denied them a reasonable profit over the costs of production. In addition farmers denounced the consumer-subsidy program. Consumers, they reasoned, would become accustomed to substandard food prices; then, when the subsidy program ended, consumers would rebel at having to pay higher prices. Many farmers felt that government economic policy discriminated against them in favor of urban workers and consumers. On the other hand, wage earners and consumers supported price controls and consumer subsidies but grumbled about wage restrictions.[11]

The conflict between farmers and workers profoundly disturbed La Follette. It not only divided his constituency but also assaulted a fundamental principle of his political philosophy. Throughout his career he had maintained that, in the words of his 1934 platform, "the interests of farmers and labor are fundamentally in harmony. Neither can prosper long while the other is depressed."[12] But farmers and wage earners did not see it that way. Both groups were well organized in Wisconsin, and both groups pressured La Follette to support their conflicting demands.

11. Roland Young, *Congressional Politics in the Second World War* (New York, 1956), pp. 90–93; J. Joseph Huthmacher, *Senator Robert F. Wagner and the Rise of Urban Liberalism* (New York, 1971), pp. 285–87; James T. Patterson, *Mr. Republican: A Biography of Robert A. Taft* (Boston, 1972), pp. 260–61.
12. "Progressive State Platform," 1934, *The Wisconsin Blue Book, 1935* (Madison, 1935), p. 478.

On several key issues La Follette sided with farmers and thereby antagonized elements of organized labor. He fought to raise the ceiling on farm prices and to abolish the food-subsidy program.[13] Realizing that the abandonment of subsidies would impose a hardship on families with low or fixed incomes, La Follette joined Sen. George Aiken of Vermont in proposing an alternative: a food-stamp bill that would give low-income families food-purchase stamps "in whatever amount . . . necessary to provide enough additional food to meet minimum nutritional requirements." La Follette argued that whereas the subsidy program benefited rich and poor consumers alike, food stamps would only help those most in need. But organized labor wanted subsidies, not food stamps. A Milwaukee local of the United Auto Workers denounced food stamps as a form of "charity," degrading to the recipients. "You mean well," a union official wrote La Follette, "but you are either misled or mistaken, this time—Honest laborers are proud people." In 1944 the Senate defeated the La Follette–Aiken food-stamp bill, and the subsidy program was continued.[14]

La Follette further aggravated his relationship with labor and with urban consumers in general by aligning himself with Wisconsin dairy farmers in the oleomargarine controversy. Manufacturers of oleomargarine could produce and sell their product for only a fraction of the cost of butter. To protect the dairy industry, the federal government and many states had for decades placed a tax on margarine. Because of the high cost of food during the war, there were repeated efforts in Congress to reduce or repeal the federal tax. Each time, La Follette successfully led the opposition. He portrayed the controversy as a struggle between the oleomargarine monopoly and the small independent dairy farmers. "This is an issue of economic democracy, a way of life," he declared. But consumers took a different view. To them the federal tax on oleomargarine was a blatant example of special-interest legislation. One angry consumer wrote La Follette, "Suppose it does dislocate the agricultural economic situation in Wisconsin—Good God! the buggy-makers were 'dislocated' when

13. CR 77:2, 1942, vol. 88, pt. 6, pp. 7586–87; RML to M. E. Slattery, 17 March 1943, box 43-C, RML to R. T. Glassco, 22 February 1943, box 303-C, RML to Roscoe Smith, president of Wisconsin Farm Bureau Federation, box 310-C, Family Papers.

14. RML statement on food stamps, 17 March 1944, CR 78:2, 1944, vol. 90, app., pp. 1682–84; RML to Milo K. Swanton, 21 December 1943, box 318-C, Family Papers; Karl Bennewitz, chairman, Legislative Committee, UAW-CIO, Local 324, to RML, 2, 24 January 1944, box 304-C, 48-C, Family Papers.

the automobile was developed." This person went on to express his disappointment in the senator: "I have felt that Wisconsin had a Senator who could be depended upon to exercise a guiding leadership —Not to merely represent an interest."[15]

One other issue during the war also damaged La Follette's standing with labor. In 1943 and 1944 he tried to block attempts by the administration and its Senate supporters to commit the United States to participation in a postwar international organization.[16] Suspicious of the motives of Britain and Russia, he declared that "before this nation commits itself to any definite course in international collaboration, I for one want to be sure that the physical strength and moral force of this nation will be serving the forces of good rather than of evil in this world."[17] Organized labor and especially the CIO supported the creation of a new league of nations, and the Wisconsin CIO assailed La Follette's stand.[18]

Except for his stands on price controls and foreign affairs, La Follette compiled a nearly perfect labor record. In addition to sponsoring the bill to abolish oppressive labor practices, he called for resumption of the civil-liberties investigation. In 1943 he helped lead the unsuccessful fight against the antilabor provisions of the Smith-Connally Act. A year later he denounced the president's extraordinary request for "national service" legislation, which in the president's words would "prevent strikes" and "make available for war production or for any other essential services every able-bodied adult in the nation." La Follette declared that this so-called work-or-fight proposal was "either a diabolical scheme to bring fascistic controls into this country under the false guise of wartime necessity or a political hoax to curry favor among the labor-hating elements in the nation."[19]

15. RML press release, 24 March 1944, miscellaneous letters and speeches, box 312-C, Family Papers.
16. RML to PFL, 12 April 1943, box 49-A, RML to Frank C. Eustis, 13 May 1943, box 310-C, telegram, RML to Arthur K. Vandenberg, 6 October 1943, box 43-C, RML to Mrs. H. Kent Tenney, Jr., 16 February 1944, box 321-C, Family Papers; RML to PFL, 21 April 1943, box 140-2, PFL Papers.
17. RML to Ken Traiger, 26 June 1944, box 51-C, Family Papers. On RML's views of Britain and Soviet Union, see RML to PFL, 16 February 1943, box 140-21, PFL Papers; RML to PFL, 23 March 1943, box 49-A, Family Papers.
18. Philip Murray to RML, 12 December 1944, box 45-C, Family Papers; Roger T. Johnson, *Robert M. La Follette, Jr. and the Decline of the Progressive Party in Wisconsin* (Madison, 1964), pp. 139–40.
19. Franklin D. Roosevelt, "An Economic Bill of Rights," 11 January 1944, in Henry Steele Commager, ed., *Documents of American History* (New York, 1968), 2:484; RML, draft article for *Northern Lights*, enclosed in RML to Ray Gersheski, 29 February 1944, box 47-C, Family Papers.

Finally, just as he supported price increases for farmers, he supported wage increases and adjustments for workers. Yet for all his efforts La Follette received scant praise from organized labor and much criticism from labor's enemies.[20]

Two incidents illustrated La Follette's increasingly tense relationship with labor. In 1943, during one of his infrequent trips to Wisconsin, he stopped off in Milwaukee and conferred with many city and state labor leaders. Several months later, however, William R. McCabe, a Progressive party leader, reported to La Follette that Melvyn Heinritz, an official of the Wisconsin CIO, had "made a statement that [the] Milwaukee Federation of Labor and the CIO were rather opposed to you this year." "It seems," McCabe explained, "that when you were back in . . . Milwaukee you did not have any conference with any of the above named organization's leaders." McCabe added that Heinritz and other labor leaders "were much disturbed that you were against subsidies to help keep down the cost of living." McCabe's report angered La Follette. "I am getting a little bit tired of the way in which some individuals in the labor movement in Milwaukee are constantly endeavoring to prejudice their fellows against me," he replied. "There is absolutely no truth in the statement that I failed to see labor leaders when I was in Milwaukee last summer."[21]

On another occasion a delegation of Wisconsin labor leaders visited Washington to lobby for legislation they wanted passed. When they arrived at La Follette's office, they presented him with a long list of demands. After each demand there was a small space for him to write *yes* or *no*. La Follette refused to fill out the form, explaining that many of the demands were too complex for simple yes-or-no answers; he wanted the opportunity to explain his reasons for opposing certain of their demands. The labor leaders, however, insisted that he complete the form. As one of La Follette's aides remembered it, they became rude and "abusive." La Follette again refused and ordered the leaders to leave.[22] La Follette was unaccustomed to such treatment. And he doubtless was perplexed at the reasons behind this and other manifestations of labor's dissatisfaction with him.

Apparently La Follette believed that his troubles with labor were at least partly caused by communist infiltration of the labor move-

20. RML to Jack F. Whitton, 5 November 1943, box 44-C, RML to Luella Christianson, 27 May 1943, box 310-C, Family Papers.
21. W. R. McCabe to RML, n.d., RML to W. R. McCabe, 18 December 1943, box 41-C, Family Papers.
22. Interviews, Wilbur Voigt; Norman M. Clapp, 3 August 1972.

ment in Wisconsin. In the late summer of 1943, Isen La Follette reported to Phil the substance of a conversation she had had with the senator, who had just completed a tour of the state. Bob, she wrote, "is impressed as I am at the progress the Commies are making; [he] says that Ken Greenquist [a progressive leader] gives a very gloomy report as to their effectiveness in the labor movement in Racine and Kenosha." Bob also "says that their tactics are to divide and split every group they can penetrate and that they have been very successful in getting into high position in practically every field." La Follette's closest friends and advisers in Wisconsin shared his concern. They were convinced that communists had penetrated the labor movement, particularly the state CIO, and that one of their aims was to turn the unions against La Follette, particularly because of his frequent and outspoken criticism of the Soviet Union.[23] But such an analysis, even if true, underestimated organized labor's sincere opposition to La Follette's stands on domestic issues such as price controls and subsidies.

The wartime political situation in Wisconsin caused La Follette great anguish. The Progressive party was failing rapidly, and even though La Follette was managing to keep it alive, he could not restore it to health. Nor could he halt the steady erosion of his personal popularity.

In the spring of 1942, amidst rumors of the party's imminent collapse, La Follette summoned Progressive leaders from across the state to a meeting in Madison. The party should continue, he told them. Then, promising more than he would deliver, he pledged to devote as much time to state and party affairs as his Senate duties allowed. The leaders voted unanimously to field a slate of candidates for the fall campaign.[24]

The outcome of the 1942 elections demoralized the party faithful. The Progressives lost ten of their twenty-nine seats in the legislature and one of their three seats in the House of Representatives, and they were defeated in all but one of the contests for statewide office. But there remained at least a glimmer of hope. Their lackluster candidate for governor, Orland "Spike" Loomis, defeated the unpopular incumbent, Julius Heil. But then tragedy struck. Before Loomis could take office he died of a heart attack; and Lt. Gov. Walter S. Goodland, a

23. Mrs. PFL to PFL, 29 August 1943, box 141-2, PFL Papers. Interviews, Morris H. Rubin, 1, 8 August 1972; Glenn D. Roberts, 3 July 1973.
24. Johnson, *La Follette, Jr.*, pp. 88–89.

Republican, was sworn in as governor. "It was a cruel blow to lose Spike," La Follette wrote his sister-in-law. "He had expressed a fine attitude to Glenn [Roberts] and I had hopes of building up the Party. Now we will have to start all over again."[25]

The developments of late 1942 increased the pressures on La Follette. With Phil in the service and Loomis dead, he was the sole remaining hope of the party he had never wanted in the first place. During the first half of 1943 Progressive diehards pleaded with him to return to Wisconsin, for his own sake and his party's sake. Lloyd Larson, a Progressive leader in Mauston, wrote him: "Why don't you leave that nice house in Washington and come home and talk to some of the people you will want to vote for you next election and find out what the real sentiment is." A lot of the "old line boys" were beginning to ask questions, Larson added, and he could not answer them. From the South Pacific, Phil, as usual, led the chorus. "I am disturbed about your not getting out to Wisconsin," Phil wrote Bob. "Nothing that is happening or can happen in Washington is anywhere near as important as your relations with your state. Year after year has gone by and you have gotten further and further away from your constituents." The subject was on his mind, Phil said, "because this is the Old Man's birthday, [and] the one thing he never did was to let ANYTHING in Washington interfere with his relations with the folks back home."[26]

But La Follette always had an excuse. Naturally, he would like to spend more time in Wisconsin, he told Larson, but he felt "a certain obligation to discharge the responsibilities of my office by being present when legislation is under consideration in the Senate." In late winter he promised Phil that he would go home "as soon as the weather moderates," no later than spring or early summer. June came, and he was still in Washington. Now he offered a new excuse: "Perhaps never as much as now people are looking to Congress to help straighten out the mess created by the war and made worse by maladministration. Also, I have participated in a number of important fights on appropriation bills, which cannot be finished until the end of the fiscal year, June 30."[27]

Some of his Wisconsin friends threw up their hands in despair. No one, it seemed, could get through to him. "Phil, the La Follette leader-

25. Ibid., p. 93; RML to Mrs. PFL, 8 December 1942, box 140-2, PFL Papers.
26. Lloyd Larson to RML, 7 May 1943, box 41-C, PFL to RML, 14 June 1943, box 48-A, Family Papers.
27. RML to Lloyd Larson, 11 May 1943, box 41-C, Family Papers; RML to PFL, 24 February 1943, box 140-2, PFL Papers; RML to PFL, 24 June 1943, box 49-A, Family Papers.

ship in this state is dying of dry rot," wrote Old Bob's chief lieutenant, Alf Rogers, "and Bob is going to take it on the chin unless he changes his tactics. Bob, himself, sees, but has become so saturated with the atmosphere at Washington that he is sucked in as a moth to a flame." Rogers pointed out that "Bob is very much loved and respected in Washington by friend and foe, and how he and Rachel do enjoy basking in the luxury of the Senatorial sun. They glory in the 'great record' he has and is making for himself, and rely upon this to get the voters back home." But Rogers knew, as La Follette seemed not to, that the reverse was often true: "A rotten record in Washington, and personal contacts with the home folks will keep a man in the Senate a lifetime." Worst of all, "Bob doesn't really enjoy mixing with Tom, Dick, and Harry at home. It's a bore to him." The real question, Rogers concluded, is " 'How are we going to blast Bob into action?' So far as personal persuasion counts, I have done my best, and shall continue to do so. You also will persist. I am stumped at present."[28]

Finally, in July 1943, La Follette yielded to pressure and returned home after an eight-month absence. He then launched his most extensive tour of the state since the 1940 campaign. In each community that he visited he conferred with party supporters. He also set up a desk in the local courthouse and invited the townspeople to come and talk over with him any problems they might have concerning the federal government. He attracted some much needed publicity, but the turnouts were often small, prompting Phil to remark, "One cannot be out of contact with Viroqua, for instance, for ten years, and expect to blow in and have a hundred people standing in line to meet you at the court house." After several weeks on the road, La Follette decided that he had done all he could for the party. The next step, he explained to Phil, was up to the party's state leadership. "Without leadership within the state, there is nothing I can do from Washington or even by frequent trips to Wisconsin to keep the movement together." Despite its limitations, La Follette's tour came at a crucial time. Party members met twice during the summer to discuss whether to stay with the party or disband and move into other parties. They decided to stay, and their decision was probably determined by their leader's presence in the state.[29]

Toward the end of his stay in Wisconsin, La Follette contracted bronchopneumonia, his first serious illness in fourteen years. He was

28. Rogers to PFL, 4 June 1943, box 140-2, PFL Papers.
29. Mrs. PFL to PFL, 19 August 1943, PFL to Mrs. PFL, 12 August 1943, box 141-2, PFL Papers; RML to PFL, 1 September 1943, box 49-A, Family Papers; Walter A. Craunke to PFL, 9 September 1943, box 141-2, PFL Papers.

confined to Madison General Hospital for six weeks. Perhaps it was more than a coincidence that his illness occurred at the time when he was undertaking the task he hated above all others, tending to state affairs.[30]

The following year, 1944, was critical for the Progressive cause. Unless the party picked up strength, or at least held its own, in the fall elections, it seemed doubtful that it could survive. Early in the year La Follette found reason for optimism. In the spring he delivered the keynote address at the party's convention, and except for a few delegates affiliated with the CIO, who grumbled about his criticism of Roosevelt's foreign policy, the assembly gave him a warm reception. La Follette and other leaders came away encouraged about the party's prospects in November.[31] But the reaction of the convention was not an accurate gauge of sentiment across the state. For one thing the seven hundred delegates composed a most unrepresentative sample of Wisconsin voters. They were the true believers, the "old-time died-in-the-wool Progressives" La Follette once called them. They had probably been with the party since its founding; some of them had even taken part in Fighting Bob's crusades. The fact was that the party had failed to attract new generations of supporters. Alf Rogers, himself an old-timer, once told Phil that Old Bob's friends, who composed the core of Young Bob's and the Progressive party's supporters, "are dying off by the thousands each year, and if not dead, they are becoming so old that they do not carry weight politically in the communities in which they live." "The young people," Rogers observed, "think them back numbers, which they are, living in the past politically with nothing to interest the young people for the future."[32] What little time La Follette had devoted to party matters in the past few years was spent not in trying to attract new supporters but in trying to prevent old supporters from defecting.

The August primaries dramatically demonstrated the weakness of the party. Many Progressive candidates failed to receive the minimum number of votes needed to earn a place on the November ballot. Others just barely qualified. "Unbelievably bad" was the way

30. RML medical history, "Summary in the Case of Robert M. La Follette," June 1949, box 26-C, Rosemary McCormick to Samuel Robock, 11 November 1943, box 304-C, RML to Gordon Sinykin, 23 October 1943, box 21-C, Family Papers.

31. Johnson, La Follette, Jr., pp. 96–98; Mrs. PFL to PFL, 8, 12, 13 May 1944, box 142-2, PFL Papers; RML to Gordon Sinykin, 19 May 1944, box 22-C, Family Papers.

32. RML to PFL, 1 September 1943, box 49-A, Family Papers; Alfred T. Rogers to PFL, 4 June 1943, box 140-2, PFL Papers.

La Follette described the situation. Labor, he said, had deserted to the Democratic party, farmers to the Republican party. Panic set in among Progressive ranks. In a desperate effort to prevent a "debacle" in November, La Follette sent out a form letter to thousands of Progressive loyalists. He asked them to help in the upcoming campaign and promised to do all he could. Only a hundred persons bothered to reply. The party's chairman, Glenn Roberts, appealed to a thousand supporters for contributions. He received two replies.[33]

La Follette spent less than a week actively campaigning for Progressive candidates. He explained to his sister Fola that the gas rationing caused by the war had forced him to restrict his travel around the state. Moreover, he said, "meetings like we used to hold are out of the question because people will not attend." One decision La Follette made during the campaign actually harmed his own and the party's cause. For the first time since 1928 he refused to endorse either of the presidential candidates. Labor, he reported to Fola, is "very bitter toward me personally because of my failure to come out for a 4th term for F.D.R. Many of the leaders say they will get me for this in 1946."[34]

The outcome of the general election shocked even the most pessimistic Progressives. The party slate as a whole garnered only 6 percent of the vote and finished a distant third behind the front-running Republicans and the closely trailing Democrats. The party lost eight of its nineteen seats in the legislature and one of its two seats in the House of Representatives.[35]

When the initial shock wore off, Progressives began asking themselves what had gone wrong. Who or what was responsible for the demise of a party that had once been the talk of the nation? For some, perhaps many, of them the answer was simple: Bob La Follette. A party leader from Eau Claire wrote the senator that Progressives in his area "feel that you, personally, laid down in this campaign and that you could have done more. Maybe they are mistaken—I do not know." Naturally, La Follette denied the charge, replying that he had done everything possible.[36]

La Follette deserved some, but by no means all, the blame for what had happened. Clearly he had failed to provide the party with the firm, constant direction that it needed. Instead his leadership had

33. RML to Fola, 19 August, 28 September 1944, box 49-A, Family Papers.
34. Johnson, *La Follette, Jr.*, p. 99; RML to Fola, 28 September 1944, box 49-A, Family Papers.
35. Johnson, *La Follette, Jr.*, p. 100.
36. G. Earle Ingram to RML, 27 November 1944, RML to G. Earle Ingram, 30 November 1944, box 48-C, Family Papers.

come in irregular bursts. He would ignore the party for long periods of time, and then, as in the summer of 1943, frantically try to make up for lost time. But then, just as he started to gain control, he would return to Washington. La Follette had repeated this cycle again and again.

Yet, two other factors were of equal or greater importance in causing the downfall of the party. Except for the La Follette brothers, the party produced no leaders of exceptional talent. Over the years Progressive supporters had fallen into the habit of "letting the La Follettes do it," a habit that the brothers, particularly Phil, had encouraged. Consequently, when Phil withdrew from politics following his defeat in 1938 and when Bob faltered, no one emerged to take control. The closest exception to this was the uninspiring Spike Loomis. The most important cause of the party's decline, however, was factionalism. There had been divisions within the party from the beginning, and these divisions deepened through the years. The two most visible factions were farmers and wage earners. Initially both groups had submerged their long-standing differences and joined to fight mutual enemies: economic insecurity and a two-party system that ignored their common plight. But by the 1940s, as La Follette realized only too well, farmers and workers were drifting apart. The 1944 election marked the culmination of that trend. Labor moved into the party of Roosevelt and farmers returned to their traditional home base, the GOP. Another source of factionalism within the Progressive party was foreign policy. In the years immediately preceding Pearl Harbor the noninterventionists, led by the La Follettes, had clashed with the interventionists, who were led by William T. Evjue. They continued to clash during the war, only now the issue in dispute was whether or not there should be a new league of nations.[37] Thus, weak leadership, internal divisions, and repudiation at the polls had brought down the once powerful Progressive party. The only question that remained to be answered was not if the party would formally disband, but when.

As if La Follette's political difficulties were not enough, he also had to contend with problems of a personal nature. There was talk among some family members and close friends that he and Rachel were experiencing serious marital problems. Phil, after receiving one such report from Isen, who faithfully passed on to him every detail she

37. On labor defection, see RML to Fola, 28 September 1944, box 49-A, Family Papers; Johnson, *La Follette, Jr.*, pp. 77–101, discusses divisions among progressives, especially over foreign policy.

could glean about Young Bob's personal life, said that although he might be wrong, he had "sensed for a long time that there was rough weather there—and I think they are held together by circumstances rather than desire."[38]

If there was tension in the La Follette home, it was at least partly caused by the demands made on Bob and Rachel by politics. Rachel, like her husband, enjoyed the Washington side of political life but detested the Wisconsin side of it. She dreaded having to accompany Bob to the state. Born and raised in Virginia, she had few close friends in Wisconsin. She apparently disliked Phil and Isen, and the feeling was mutual. Worst of all, once there, she resented the demands that people made upon her. Having become used to the political style of Belle, Fola, and Isen, Wisconsinites had come to expect that the La Follette women would participate in campaigns and write articles in the *Progressive*. Bob's political strategists would therefore schedule Rachel for speaking engagements and luncheon appearances. But she disliked such activities, even though she carried them out well. Feeling as she did, Rachel would sometimes become annoyed with Bob when he decided that they had to return to Wisconsin. Thus he found himself caught between friends and advisers who pleaded with him to return home and a wife who thought that, if anything, he spent too much time in the state.[39]

La Follette's personal and political troubles affected him emotionally and physically. During the war he seemed more depressed than usual. At one point Isen wrote Phil that "from what people who have seen him over the past months say, he is in a depth of depression that is dangerous." A few days later she added, "It is obvious . . . that he cannot stand any more strain and that it is up to us all to do what we can to ease the situation." Other people also noticed that he was in low spirits. "He doesn't have the equanimity of his brother Phil and takes things pretty seriously," Sen. George Aiken wrote Phil. Fola, who was as close to Bob as anyone, sensed it too, and she tried to encourage him. One time she assured him that when historians wrote the history of the period, they would conclude that he was "as able, as courageous, and as outstanding" as his father.[40]

At the same time, La Follette's health began to deteriorate. First

38. Mrs. PFL to PFL, 7, 9, 14 July 1943, PFL to Mrs. PFL, 17 July 1944, box 142-2, PFL Papers.
39. Interviews, Mrs. PFL, 5 July 1973; Bronson C. La Follette, 5 July 1973.
40. Mrs. PFL to PFL, 9, 14 July 1943, box 140-2, George Aiken to PFL, 5 August 1943, box 141-2, PFL Papers; Fola to RML, 4 May 1944, box 49-A, Family Papers. See also Mary Rubin to PFL, 9 July 1943, box 141-2, Mrs. PFL to PFL, 29 November 1944, box 142-2, PFL Papers.

came the bout with pneumonia in the fall of 1943. Then in 1944 he entered the Naval Medical Center for tests, complaining of muscular pains in the neck, shoulders, and limbs and of slight swelling in his hands and feet. The doctors found evidence of a recent streptococcal infection. But they expressed the opinion that his symptoms "were secondary to such an infection and were most likely of the nature of rheumatic fever," a serious disease that is usually contracted in childhood but often goes undetected until adulthood.[41] Apparently this was the first time that he had been diagnosed as possibly having rheumatic fever. If the diagnosis was correct, it was probable that he had contracted the disease as a child and that many of the subsequent illnesses that had so baffled doctors, including his near fatal one in 1918, had in reality been attacks of rheumatic fever.

Declining health did not impair La Follette's performance in the Senate, but it did give him an excuse for not devoting more time to Wisconsin matters. In December 1944, for example, Phil sent him a letter outlining the steps he should take to rebuild his political support in the state. Bob now had an answer that even his brother would have to accept. Phil's program was a good one, La Follette replied, and he would "endeavor to carry out as much of it as my energy output will permit. This, as you probably know, is not as great as it was prior to my pneumonia of a year ago last fall and I have to cut my suit according to the cloth that is available."[42]

After awhile Isen, for one, began speculating that her brother-in-law's health problems might be a "psychological reaction to protect one's self from having added responsibilities or demands thrust on one."[43] The question of whether or not La Follette's illnesses were psychosomatic was of course impossible to answer. Often he had fallen ill during times of obvious emotional stress: in 1915 when he was in college and under intense pressure from his parents to improve his grades; in 1918 at the height of the family's wartime crisis; and now during the 1940s when he was experiencing numerous political and personal problems. In varying degrees each period of illness had allowed him to withdraw from a stressful situation. Yet, on the other hand, many of his specific ailments—streptococcal infections, pneumonia, and possibly rheumatic fever—were ones not usually considered by medical experts to be psychosomatic. The strong possibility remained, however, that his mental anxiety adversely affected such

41. RML medical history, "Summary in the Case of Robert M. La Follette," June 1949, box 26-C, Family Papers.
42. RML to PFL, 4 January 1945, box 143-2, PFL Papers.
43. Mrs. PFL to PFL, 18 February 1945, box 143-2, PFL Papers.

things as sleeping and eating habits and thereby weakened his body's ability to resist illness.

In early 1945, with the end of the war finally in sight, La Follette turned his full attention to the plans being made for the creation of a new league of nations. He had serious reservations about the proposed United Nations and about postwar policy in general, and he decided that the time had come for him to deliver his first major foreign policy address in the Senate since the bombing of Pearl Harbor. As two of La Follette's staff members later told it, Roosevelt, upon learning of the senator's intention, personally asked him to postpone the speech. Negotiations had reached a crucial stage, the president explained, and it would be unwise to provoke a national debate at this time. La Follette heeded the president's request.[44]

In April, Roosevelt died, Harry S Truman became president, and representatives from fifty nations assembled in San Francisco to begin writing the United Nations charter. La Follette, with the help of *Progressive* editor Morris Rubin and others, carefully put together a speech. Finally, on 31 May, after a month's preparation, he took the floor to deliver the most controversial speech of his career. "He was just fed up, and he let fly with everything he had," said journalist Allen Drury.[45]

The central theme of his three-hour address was that too much attention was being focused on the United Nations and not enough on the terms of the peace settlement ending the war. Unless the settlement was just, he argued, any international organization, no matter how skillfully constructed, was doomed to failure. In order to prove his point, he recalled in detail the problems that had faced the League of Nations. La Follette believed that the league had failed to keep peace not, as many people argued, because the Unitd States refused to join, but because the Versailles treaty, which the league was set up to enforce, was corrupt. The treaty, he said, was "shot through with injustice and war-breeding settlements," and no world organization could have enforced it. La Follette argued that the United States was largely to blame for the tragedy of Versailles, because during and immediately after World War I it failed to use its enormous power and prestige to exact commitments to a just and democratic settlement from its allies. Instead President Wilson, in the grossly mistaken belief that the League of Nations could right the in-

44. Interview, Wilbur and Rosemary Voigt, 9 July 1973.
45. Interview, Morris H. Rubin; Allen Drury, *A Senate Journal: 1943–1945* (New York, 1963), pp. 438–39.

justices of the treaty, needlessly yielded to the Allies' imperialistic demands.

As La Follette continued, the reason for the history lesson became apparent. "There is overwhelming evidence that up to the present we have not mastered these lessons of the past," he declared. "Thus far we have been traveling a road which, almost step by step, parallels the tragic road we took after the First World War." Once again the United States had failed to use its bargaining power to commit its allies, this time the Soviet Union and Britain, to a just peace settlement. Instead, American leaders had pursued a policy of "compromise and surrender" in dealing with its allies. La Follette went so far as to imply that the United States, in order to wrest concessions from Russia and Britain, should have threatened to withhold money and supplies during the war.

Thus far La Follette had talked in generalities. Now he became specific. But before doing so he ventured a prediction: He had no doubt, he said, that some of the remarks he was about to make would be "misinterpreted and distorted by the smear bund. It has become virtually impossible to criticize the activities of at least one of our allies—Soviet Russia—however constructively, without bringing down upon one's head a storm of smearing vilification and misrepresentation by a tightly organized minority in the United States." This minority was the "Russia-can-do-no-wrong chorus" and it employed Hitler-like tactics—"the big lie, the big smear, and the wholesale impugning of motives and character"—in order to intimidate and silence critics of the Soviet Union.

La Follette then launched a point-by-point attack upon Soviet actions in the field of world affairs. During the war Russian troops had moved into Poland, Rumania, Hungary, Austria, and other countries. But having liberated these nations from Nazi oppression, the Soviet Union was now trying to take them over and impose upon them governments "made in Moscow." Russia's actions, La Follette claimed, violated the Atlantic Charter to which it had subscribed and the solemn pledges that it had made to Britain and the United States at the Yalta Conference of 1945. Even worse, Soviet imperialism threatened the future peace of the world, since a permanent peace could only come when all peoples were free to decide their own destinies. That, he suggested, was the lesson of World War I and its aftermath.

Although he focused his attack on Russia, La Follette reserved some of his fire for Great Britain. He condemned "Mr. Churchill's dogmatic, and at times arrogant, refusal to discuss any definite plans for freedom for the subject peoples of the British Empire" and said that he was "no more prepared to commit the United States to enforcing British rule over India, Burma, or Malta" than he was "to commit my country to enforcing Russian domination over Poland, Rumania, Austria, the Balkans, or any nations in the Baltic States."

La Follette also condemned the United States for acquiescing to Soviet and British actions. The time had come, he said, "to stand firmly against any steps which may wreck the peace." However, he did not spell out the steps he thought the United States should take to reverse Soviet and British actions.

In the subsequent furor over La Follette's speech, one key aspect of it went almost unnoticed. He expressed a willingness to commit the United States to a high degree of international cooperation. For example, in discussing the proposed structure of the United Nations, he opposed the veto provision whereby any one of the five permanent members of the Security Council—the United States, Britain, France, Russia, or China—could prevent the United Nations from imposing military or economic sanctions on an aggressor nation. Rather, he argued, majority rule should prevail. Thus he was willing to subject the United States to the democratic rule of nations.[46]

On the surface, La Follette seemed to be repudiating his isolationist, noninterventionist past. La Follette, who had so often denounced the League of Nations and the World Court and who had urged the United States to remain "aloof" from "Old World" affairs, was now talking about international cooperation and supporting, despite deep reservations, a new league of nations. La Follette, who in the years before the attack on Pearl Harbor, had argued that the United States should not intervene in Europe to contain German aggression, now sounded willing to have the United States intervene in eastern Europe to block Soviet expansion.

Clearly, just as La Follette had viewed the events leading up to Pearl Harbor from the perspective of 1914–1917, so in 1945 he was viewing events from the perspective of the years immediately following World War I. He had always maintained that in 1919 President Wilson should have used the power and influence of the United States to block the imperialist demands of France and Britain. Now he was saying that the United States should use its power and influence to block the imperialist ambitions of the Soviet Union and Britain.

La Follette's address plus the condensed version he delivered over the CBS radio network a few days later attracted more attention than

46. *CR* 79:1, 1945, vol. 91, pt. 4, pp. 5315–30.

had any other speech in his career. When he finished speaking, Senate colleagues, even those who disagreed with what he had said, gathered around his desk to congratulate him. The next day other senators sent him letters of praise. "La Follette doesn't go in for needling," noted an admiring Allen Drury, "and when he makes a major speech people listen."[47]

The address also stirred controversy. Hundreds of favorable letters poured into the senator's office, most of them singling out for praise his criticism of the Soviet Union. Among them was a letter from Socialist party leader Norman Thomas, who urged La Follette to deliver a similar speech on the Japanese situation.[48] La Follette also came under sharp attack. The *Milwaukee Journal*, in an editorial entitled "La Follette Is Destructive," accused him of trying to "sabotage" the proposed United Nations. The conservative Republican *Wisconsin State Journal* criticized him for heaping "vituperation and abuse" on Russia and Britain. Yet the equally conservative *Appleton Post-Crescent* found the speech "of particular value because of the candor, restraint and honesty that pervaded its fiber from start to finish."[49]

The harshest criticism came from the Wisconsin CIO. Its spokesman, Melvyn Heinritz, said that the speech evidenced La Follette's intention "to spearhead the fight against a world security organization and blast the people's hopes for peace and security." According to a news summary, Heinritz also declared that La Follette's call for a " 'peace of tolerance not vengeance' disclosed his hope for leniency for war criminals and vestiges of European Fascism." In fact, La Follette had clearly stated his belief that war criminals should be brought to trial. La Follette received approximately three hundred identical postcards from persons in the Milwaukee area saying, "You are to be . . . condemned for grinding your personal axe of isolationism as a representative of a State which does not support your views. It is high time you begin to speak for the people whom you represent." Although the writers did not identify themselves, they were probably union members.[50]

Despite the intense reaction that La Follette's speech provoked, it

47. RML, CBS radio speech, 5 June 1945, box 565-C, Wallace H. White to RML, 1 June 1945, Arthur Capper to RML, 2 June 1945, Styles Bridges to RML, 1 June 1945, box 563-C, Family Papers; Drury, *Senate Journal*, pp. 438–39.
48. Letters, box 563-C, Norman Thomas to RML, 12 June 1945, box 56-C, Family Papers.
49. *Milwaukee Journal*, 3 June 1945, *Wisconsin State Journal*, 4 June 1945, *Appleton Post-Crescent*, 4 June 1945, clippings, box 666-C, Family Papers.
50. *Superior Telegram*, 4 June 1945, clippings, box 563-C, Family Papers; *CR* 79:1, 1945, vol. 91, pt. 4, p. 5330; postcards, box 666-C, Family Papers.

had no immediate impact on United States policy toward the United Nations. In late June the San Francisco Conference completed drafting the United Nations Charter without adopting the changes La Follette had recommended. In July, after an uneventful debate, the Senate ratified the charter, 89 to 2. La Follette voted with the majority. "I am disappointed in what seem to me the inherent weaknesses of the San Francisco Charter," he wrote a constituent, "but I intend to support it nonetheless."[51]

One day in the spring of 1945 La Follette met in Washington with his closest friends and advisers. From Madison came Morris Rubin, Glenn Roberts, and Dr. Wellwood Nesbit. Fola and her husband, George Middleton, were also present. La Follette told them that he was seriously considering retiring from the Senate when his current term expired. Roberts later recalled La Follette having said that he was under too much pressure. When he first came to the Senate, he explained, he had been free to exercise his own judgment on political matters, to follow an independent course. But over the years things had changed. Now he was under constant pressure from individuals and groups to pursue particular courses of action. And no matter what he did, someone was always criticizing him. Recalled Rubin, "Bob said that he had really had it and that he just didn't want to run."[52]

Roberts wrote La Follette a few weeks later and tried to change his mind. La Follette, Roberts said, was highly respected in Washington and the nation. If he retired he would disappoint, and possibly lose the respect of, his many admirers. "I am sure that will make you very unhappy—more unhappy than you are now—and far more unhappy than were you to be re-elected, or even defeated." Roberts added that if he did lose, "at least, you will have the satisfaction of having gone down fighting, and your name will live on with honor, where if you withdrew, I am afraid ... [you] will lose all of the respect you have built for yourself on your own merits."[53]

La Follette eventually did decide to stand for reelection. But at the same time he apparently decided that he would not put up a fight. If the people wanted him back in the Senate, he would serve. If they did not want him, that was all right too.

51. RML to Father Bloodgood, 12 July 1945, box 52-C, Family Papers.
52. Interviews, Glenn D. Roberts, Morris H. Rubin.
53. Roberts to RML, 12, 24 May 1945, box 49-A, Family Papers.

CHAPTER 15

Congressional Reorganization

La Follette sensed that the 1946 session of Congress would be his last, and he was determined to make the most of it. Above all he wanted Congress to adopt a series of comprehensive internal reforms, which he believed would restore to it some of the power and prestige that had shifted to the presidency during the war. During the session, he bent his every effort toward that end. And he succeeded. With the assistance of Rep. Mike Monroney and others, he sponsored and steered through Congress the Legislative Reorganization Act of 1946, a measure that streamlined the cumbersome committee system and in other ways modernized the structure and procedures of Congress. Observers, incredulous that Congress had actually voted to reform itself, hailed La Follette's performance as a "legislative miracle." Although the Reorganization Act never lived up to the expectations of its sponsors, it was a significant achievement and a fitting end to La Follette's twenty-one-year career in the Senate.

Passage of the act marked the end of a three-year struggle for the Wisconsin senator. Two related developments during the war had convinced him of the need for congressional modernization. They were the erosion of the power and prestige of Congress and the concurrent increase in the power of the presidency. Power had already begun to shift from the legislative branch to the executive branch during the 1930s, but the war greatly accelerated the trend. After Pearl Harbor, Roosevelt requested and received from Congress sweeping authority to mobilize the nation for war. Moreover, the president assumed additional powers that he claimed were inherent to his role as commander in chief during war. Roosevelt, through his agents in the executive bureaucracy, regulated nearly every aspect of American economic life. Various agencies rationed scarce commodities, set production priorities and quotas for industry, regulated wages and prices, and arbitrated labor disputes. The result of all this was that the executive branch during the war clearly emerged as the dominant branch of government.

In addition to relinquishing power to the presidency, Congress suffered a serious loss in prestige. Congress, of course, had never enjoyed very high esteem; from the first days of the Republic it had been a target of ridicule and scorn and a favorite subject for American humorists. Thus Mark Twain had written, "It could probably be shown by facts and figures that there is no distinctly native American criminal class except Congress." And some forty years later Will Rogers quipped that Americans had "come to feel the same when Congress is in session as we do when the baby gets hold of a hammer. It's just a question of how much damage he can do with it before we can take it away from him." During the 1930s foes of the New Deal criticized Congress for being a rubber stamp, while friends of the New Deal accused it of blocking needed reform.

During the war, however, criticism of Congress became unusually bitter. More was involved, as La Follette observed, "than the ancient and honorable pastime of 'running down Congressmen.'" There was, for example, a strangely intense outburst of public indignation early in 1942 when Congress passed a routine measure bringing legislators into the government's retirement system. Congressmen, people complained, were demanding sacrifices from everyone while lining their own pockets. Similarly, there was an uproar a few months later when the press disclosed that "those greedy legislators" had become eligible for X-cards, which permitted the holders to purchase unlimited quantities of gasoline. In both instances, no mention was made of the fact that members of the executive branch enjoyed the same privileges.[1]

The criticisms of Congress as an institution were of a more serious nature. It seemed to some people that Congress, with its petty partisan bickerings, its cumbersome procedures, and its long delays in considering legislation, was incapable of meeting the demands of war. Distinguished columnist Raymond Clapper broadened the indictment to include domestic affairs. "The ignorance and provincialism of Congress," he flatly stated, "render it incapable of meeting the needs of modern government."[2]

A dramatic incident in the fall of 1942, involving price controls, evidenced the precarious state of Congress. Early in 1942 Congress passed the Emergency Price Control Act, which gave Roosevelt the power to stabilize prices. One key provision of the act, however, prohibited the president from freezing farm prices until they reached

1. Robert M. La Follette, Jr., "A Senator Looks at Congress," *Atlantic Monthly* 172 (July 1943):91–92; Roland Young, *Congressional Politics in the Second World War* (New York, 1956), pp. 20–21.

2. Quoted in Charles A. Beard, "In Defense of Congress: Citadel of Our Freedom," *American Mercury* 55 (November 1942):529–35. In the same article noted historian Henry Steele Commager was quoted as saying, "Democracy apparently flourishes when the Executive is strong, languishes when it is weak."

110 percent of parity. This provision carried the endorsement of Roosevelt's own secretary of agriculture. During the spring and summer farm prices rose and so, naturally, did the cost of food for consumers. In response Roosevelt asked Congress to revise the Price Control Act so that he could freeze farm prices at 100 percent of parity rather than at 110 percent. When Congress stalled, Roosevelt, on Labor Day, issued a dramatic ultimatum. He charged that Congress, by its inaction, had endangered the whole economy and by implication the war effort. Congress, he declared, had three weeks in which to revise the parity provision of the Price Control Act. If at the end of that time it had failed to act, he, as commander in chief, would do it himself. It was a sweeping and probably unprecedented claim of presidential authority. As La Follette correctly pointed out, Roosevelt had "claimed for himself the power to override a law enacted by Congress with or without its consent."[3] Roosevelt never had to carry out his threat, since a humbled Congress promptly revised the price-control law in accordance with his wishes.

More astonishing than the president's bold assertion of power was the feebleness of the response to it. In 1938 his Court-packing proposal, a much less serious threat to the constitutional process, had caused a flood of protest. In contrast, Roosevelt's Labor Day ultimatum stirred hardly a ripple of dissent. True, many congressmen, most of them Republicans, expressed outrage. But it was also true that public opinion in general, which five years earlier had been unwilling to sanction a challenge to the independence of the judiciary, now seemed willing to sustain a more serious challenge to the independence of the legislative branch. But such was the state of Congress.

La Follette emerged during the war as perhaps the most outspoken defender of Congress. The controversies over pensions for congressmen and X-cards, he charged, were the latest manifestations of a "sinister campaign" that had long been underway "to undermine the prestige of Congress and build up the power of the executive branch." He accused Roosevelt of lending the prestige of the presidency to the campaign to undermine Congress and said that Roosevelt, in his Labor Day address, had "used the tone of a dictator" and had enunciated a false and dangerous doctrine of executive supremacy. The Wisconsin senator warned Americans "not to be betrayed into a repudiation of Congress as a representative institution . . . because if that ever happens, you are at the end of the road to fascism and dictatorship." La Follette vigorously defended the wartime record of the Congress, saying that most criticisms of it were simply unfounded. Rather, they

3. Young, *Congressional Politics*, pp. 94–98; *Progressive*, 19 September 1942.

stemmed from "personal prejudice, political bias, and above all from an utter lack of knowledge of the workaday problems with which a great legislative body must deal."[4]

Nonetheless, La Follette realized that talk alone would not restore power and prestige to Congress. He further realized that many of its problems were of its own making. "Its internal structure is antiquated and overlapping," he wrote. "Its contact with the Executive is irregular and spasmodic. Its supervision of executive performance is superficial. Much of its time is consumed by petty local and private matters." In short, it needed modernization.[5]

He drew together his thoughts on the subject in an important article for the July 1943 issue of *Atlantic Monthly*. He conceded that a strong presidency was vital to the nation's welfare, in war and in peace. But a strong, independent Congress, he argued, was also vital. As he saw it, the best way for Congress to reassert itself as a coequal branch of government was not to weaken the presidency but to strengthen itself through a series of internal reforms.

First he recommended "drastic" reorganization of the "outmoded" committee system. At the time there were thirty-three standing committees in the Senate and forty-five in the House. Many of these committees, he pointed out, had overlapping and poorly defined jurisdictions, which was "not conducive to the formulation of coherent and continuous legislative policy." In the Senate, for example, responsibility for military matters was spread out over at least four committees. Military Affairs and Naval Affairs were the principal ones; but the Pensions Committee handled soldier pensions, and the Finance Committee had jurisdiction over veterans' affairs. La Follette recommended merging Military Affairs and Naval Affairs and then letting this new committee assume the duties of the Pensions Committee and relieve the Finance Committee of veterans' affairs. In the field of business and commerce, La Follette proposed combining four committees with closely related functions: Interstate Commerce, Commerce, Manufactures, and Patents. And he continued to make such recommendations for the rest of the committees as well. He also recommended the complete elimination of some committees, like the one on the District of Columbia. Congress, he said, should grant home rule to the District "and quit doing a poor and time-consuming job as its common council." Through a process of combination and

4. *Progressive*, 19 September 1942; RML, "A Senator Looks at Congress," p. 92.
5. RML, "Modernizing Congress," enclosed in RML to James Shourt, 5 April 1945, box 56-C, Family Papers (see list of abbreviations p. x).

elimination La Follette thought it possible to reduce the number of standing committees in the Senate from thirty-three to ten or twelve, and he suggested that a similar process be undertaken in the House. One of the many advantages to simplifying the committee structure, he argued, would be that it would facilitate cooperation between companion committees in the House and Senate.

Secondly, La Follette recommended increasing the research and technical assistance available to the legislative branch. He noted that in recent years Congress, in framing legislation, had increasingly come to rely on the help of experts from executive agencies. The reason was that Congress had been "generous in providing expert and technical personnel for the executive agencies but niggardly in providing such personnel for itself." If Congress was to be independent, he concluded, it must have an adequate professional staff of its own.

La Follette also saw the need for redistributing the work load of legislators. For one thing, he thought, there should be a limit to the number of committees on which each congressman could serve. At the time more than half the senators served on six or more committees. One member held down ten committee posts. If congressmen were only allowed to serve on one, or at most two, committees each, he argued, they could specialize and become expert in a particular area. He also proposed relieving them of some of the petty chores that distracted them from more important matters. In those days Congress devoted an incredibly large part of its time to private legislation, which usually affected only one person. For example, if the crew building a federal highway happened to damage a person's property, that person would ask his senator or representative to introduce a bill compensating him for the damage. Ex-servicemen who wanted their military records corrected went through the same procedure. For each claim, the conscientious legislator had to investigate its merits, draft a private bill, and steer the bill through Congress. La Follette suggested creating a special court to settle claims against the government. But private legislation was just one aspect of the broader and even more time-consuming problem of constituent affairs. To meet this problem the senator urged increased appropriations for congressmen's office staffs.

Finally and according to La Follette most importantly, Congress needed to assume greater responsibility for overseeing the executive branch. He noted that one of the most important developments of recent years was the tendency of Congress to delegate to the president or his agents broad discretionary powers to implement legislation.

Congress did this, he explained, because when it framed a bill it obviously could not plan in advance for all contingencies. Yet, delegating such authority to the executive branch had its drawbacks. It weakened the policymaking capacity of Congress. And broad discretionary power in the hands of a "relatively irresponsible bureaucracy" was also subject to abuse. To regain its policymaking function and to prevent abuses in the implementation of laws, Congress should continually supervise, in a positive and constructive way, the executive branch. But so far, La Follette concluded, Congress had failed to do this.

Committee reorganization, he believed, would help considerably. Fewer in number, with their jurisdictions clearly defined, and with a staff of experts at hand, the committees would be better able to supervise the executive branch. La Follette also proposed the creation of a legislative-executive council, composed of a small number of senators and representatives, the president, and heads of executive departments and agencies. This council would meet regularly and discuss "broad questions of policy." It would permit Congress "to make certain that the delegation of its powers in various fields of government action was being exercised as Congress intended." Moreover, the council "would save the executive branch . . . from many a mistake and relieve it from the justifiable charge of usurpation and abuse of power." La Follette suggested that a final method by which Congress could oversee the executive branch was by requiring cabinet members and agency heads to appear at regular intervals before Congress for questioning.[6]

Shortly after the appearance of the *Atlantic* article La Follette introduced into the Senate a resolution containing many of his recommendations. The article and the resolution prompted much discussion about congressional reorganization, both within and without Congress. Congress, however, was preoccupied with the war, and it took no immediate action.[7]

But a year and a half later, in December 1944, it took the first tentative step toward reform. Acting on a joint resolution cosponsored

6. RML, "A Senator Looks at Congress," pp. 91–96.

7. *CR* 78:1, 1943, vol. 89, pt. 5, pp. 7182–84. In addition to La Follette's, other early calls for reform of Congress included, Charles A. Beard, "In Defense of Congress: Citadel of Our Freedom"; Albert Gore, "Congress Can Save Itself," *Collier's* 3(16 January 1943):13, 32–33; William Hard, "Congress's Biggest Job: A Better Congress," *The Reader's Digest* 41 (October 1942):16–20; and C. H. Woodring, "Modernization of Congress," *Editorial Research Reports*, 24 May 1943.

by Sen. Francis T. Maloney of Connecticut and Rep. A. S. Mike Monroney of Oklahoma, both of whom were Democrats, Congress set up
a joint committee to investigate reorganization. Maloney became
chairman and Monroney vice-chairman. Before the committee began
hearings, however, Maloney died and La Follette replaced him as
chairman. Historian Charles A. Beard, a longtime family friend, congratulated La Follette on his appointment and added, "The task in
hand is in many ways as important for our country as that tackled by
the Fathers in 1787, for, as you know, representative government is
at stake here and everywhere."[8]

As had been the case with the civil liberties investigation, La Follette was in many respects the ideal person to conduct this latest
probe. His third-party affiliation would help insulate the committee
from partisan politics. More important, he was as knowledgeable as
anyone in either house about the internal workings of Congress. By
1945, although La Follette was only fifty years old, only six of the
ninety-six senators had served more years in the Senate than he had.
And including the years he served under his father, La Follette had
more experience in Washington than any senator save two, eighty-
seven-year-old Carter Glass of Virginia and seventy-six-year-old Kenneth D. McKellar of Tennessee.[9]

Another asset La Follette brought to the task was his lofty stature
in the Senate. His popularity may have been on the decline in Wisconsin, but he had never been more popular among his colleagues.
In the gentleman's-club-like atmosphere of the Senate there existed
a certain formal camaraderie among members: the ritual handshaking, the perfunctory congratulations after a speech, the refusal to
personally criticize a colleague. But it went much farther than this in
La Follette's case. *Progressive* editor Morris Rubin, recalling the
many times he had visited La Follette at the Capitol, said: "You just
couldn't help but feel that everybody there, no matter what their
position was, thought he was one of the great men of the Senate."
Rubin remembered La Follette introducing him to people like Richard
Russell, Harry Truman, "and some of the other big names in the
Senate. And they all just seemed to have an enormous regard for
him."[10]

8. Edward N. Doan, *The La Follettes and the Wisconsin Idea* (New York,
1947), p. 270; Charles A. Beard to RML, 7 March 1945, box 52-C, Family
Papers.

9. *Congressional Directory* (Washington, D.C., 1945), p. 162.

10. Interview, Morris H. Rubin, 1, 8 August 1972. Interviews with Gordon
Sinykin, August 1972; Glenn D. Roberts, 3 July 1973; Norman M. Clapp, 3

Political writer Stanley High had once tried to account for what he termed "Bob La Follette's Class A status" among his colleagues. It was not, High thought, because the senator was a "hail-fellow-well-met"—one of the boys in loose translation. La Follette "knows the social game and, on occasion, he loves to play it," but he was also something of a loner, often dining alone in the Senate restaurant and generally preferring the company of personal friends to that of his colleagues. Nor did his status derive from any overwhelming support for his political or economic viewpoints. Indeed his positions were "poison" to many senators. Rather, High suggested, "most of the members of the Senate—being men of ordinary but not exceptional minds—admire men whose minds are extraordinary. Bob La Follette's mind is that kind." "Moreover," he said, "most of the members of the Senate—not being of a particularly studious turn of mind—have a good deal of respect for men who know their stuff. Bob La Follette knows his stuff." Certainly that was part of it. Journalist Allen Drury, himself an admirer of the senator, identified another trait that endeared La Follette to his colleagues: "the dogged persistence with which he has gone on fighting for 20 years for things he has only rarely succeeded in attaining." "It would have broken a less determined man long ago," Drury wrote in his diary, "and even he sometimes shows a certain humorless tiredness. But he sticks with it regardless, and by that fact alone contributes much to his country."[11]

However, keen intelligence, mastery of the issues, and persistence were not the only reasons for La Follette's high stature in the Senate. The elder La Follette, after all, had possessed these qualities in abundance, and yet the Senate had treated him like a pariah. What Young Bob had that his father did not was simply the willingness to play by the club's rules. Through the years the Senate had tolerated, even embraced, the occasional insurgent, as long as the insurgent adhered to the body's customs, both written and unwritten. But Fighting Bob had deliberately assaulted many customs. He had portrayed the Senate as a veritable den of iniquity, a haven for big business and the special interests. He had flouted senatorial courtesy by going into the home states of colleagues and campaigning for their defeat —"calling the roll" he termed it. Occasionally he had called the roll even as the offending senator sat next to him on the platform. The elder La Follette had also gloried in the fact that the Senate treated

---

August 1972; Wilbur and Rosemary Voigt, 9 July 1973; and John Clifford Folger, 5 June 1973, brought out similar recollections.

11. Stanley High, *Roosevelt—And Then?* (New York, 1937), pp. 312–14; Allen Drury, *Senate Journal: 1943–1945* (New York, 1963), p. 131.

him as an outcast, since that proved that he was not a part of the wicked establishment. "Alone in the Senate" was his proud, autobiographical description of his first years in the upper house.[12]

Young Bob, by contrast, had scrupulously adhered to Senate traditions. He could be cutting and sarcastic in debate, but he had never attacked a colleague personally. Nor had he ever campaigned against an incumbent, except, of course, in Wisconsin. And rather than criticizing Congress, he had become its most vocal defender. The senators had rewarded him for this and his other qualities by according him their admiration and respect.

From March through June of 1945 the twelve-member Joint Committee on the Organization of Congress held public hearings. It heard testimony from over one hundred witnesses, nearly half of whom were congressmen. At the conclusion of the hearings, the committee disappeared from public sight for nearly a year as it tried to shape concrete proposals from the literally hundreds of suggested reforms.

Finally, in March 1946, it issued its final report. Its thirty-seven recommendations ranged from the important to the trivial, from suggestions for reorganizing the committee structure to ideas for improving restaurant facilities in the Capitol. The committee's major proposals fell into seven categories. First it recommended streamlining the committee system by reducing the number of committees from thirty-three to sixteen in the Senate and from forty-five to eighteen in the House. The organization committee also carefully defined committee jurisdictions. A second set of proposals sought to improve the staffing of Congress by assigning expert researchers and clerical employees to each committee, expanding the Legislative Reference Service, and allowing each congressman to hire an administrative assistant at an annual salary of eight thousand dollars. The La Follette–Monroney committee next recommended relieving legislators of such time-consuming tasks as handling private claims against the government and running the District of Columbia. Fourth, the committee advised increasing the salaries of congressmen and bringing congressmen into the government's retirement system.

The most innovative and potentially most important proposal was aimed at strengthening congressional control over government spending. According to the detailed proposal, at the beginning of each session the four revenue and appropriations committees of Congress would meet and formulate a legislative budget detailing the expected

12. Robert M. La Follette, *Autobiography: A Personal Narrative of Political Experiences* (Madison, 1960[1911, 1913]), pp. 159, 178–79.

expenditures and expected receipts for the coming fiscal year. Once Congress approved the budget, it became binding. Then, if total expenditures during the fiscal year exceeded the budget ceiling, the president would be required to make uniform, across-the-board cuts (with a few exceptions) in appropriations.

Next the La Follette–Monroney committee urged Congress to make a greater effort to oversee the executive branch. Standing committees, it suggested, should be the primary agents of oversight. They should "conduct a continuous review of the agencies administering laws originally reported by the committees." Thus, for example, if the Senate Banking and Currency Committee reported out a price-control bill that evenutally became law, that same committee should constantly monitor the implementation of the law by the Office of Price Administration. This procedure would ensure that federal agencies were applying laws as Congress had intended. The organization committee also endorsed La Follette's idea for a legislative-executive council. Finally the committee recommended regulation of lobbying. Lobbyists, it advised, should register with Congress and periodically report to Congress on their activities. The committee's recommendations represented a triumph for La Follette. He had persuaded its members to adopt all of the reforms that he had originally proposed in 1943 and much more.[13]

On 13 May, two months after the committee made its report, La Follette introduced into the Senate an omnibus bill containing the committee's recommendations.[14] Representative Monroney offered a companion bill in the House. La Follette then made arrangements with the Democratic majority leader, Alben Barkley, to set aside four days in early June for Senate debate on the measure.

In spite of La Follette's legislative acumen, it seemed to others that he could not have chosen a worse time to press for adoption of the bill. Then pending before Congress were a host of controversial measures involving such key issues as the power of organized labor, continuation of price controls, and extension of the military draft. This being the case it appeared unlikely that the La Follette–Monroney bill, with all its provisions, any one of which was equivalent to a major bill in itself, could clear Congress before it adjourned in the first week of August. Moreover, 1946 was an election year, and con-

13. La Follette-Monroney Committee, preliminary report, box 331-C, Family Papers; *New York Times*, 5 March 1946; George B. Galloway, *The Legislative Process in Congress* (New York, 1953), pp. 591–623. Galloway was staff director of the La Follette-Monroney Committee.

14. La Follette deleted from the bill the provision for home rule by the District of Columbia because a similar measure was then pending in Congress.

gressmen could derive little political advantage from approving the reorganization measure. Students of government, of course, recognized its importance, but the whole issue, complex and technical as it was, was hardly calculated to excite the public's imagination. The average voter, if he heard about the bill at all, probably could not understand how the number of congressional committees or a legislative budget could affect his life one way or the other. If anything, the bill, with its provision for salary increases and retirement benefits, might actually hurt incumbents in their reelection campaigns. Most congressmen vividly remembered the uproar that had greeted their last attempt to vote themselves pensions.[15]

La Follette, too, faced reelection, beginning with the 13 August primary. And therein lay the probable reason for his seemingly unwise insistence on forcing the issue before adjournment. La Follette expected to lose the primary, or so he confided to some friends. The thought of defeat did not much bother him, but he did want to end his career on a high note. He considered the reorganization bill as important as any he had ever proposed. If he succeeded in getting it passed, it would be the capstone of his career. It would also compensate for some of the bitter disappointments of the past.[16]

The Senate debate got underway on Thursday, 6 June. La Follette put on a masterful performance. He deftly fielded all questions and patiently explained the bill's complex provisions. He approved or rejected various amendments, and his supporters dutifully followed. By the end of the first day it was apparent that he had broad bipartisan support for the bill. On the Republican side, endorsements came from Wallace White, the minority leader, and Robert A. Taft, the Republican's unofficial commander; and on the Democratic side, from Barkley and the liberals' spokesman, Robert F. Wagner.[17]

Leading the opposition was a group of conservative Southern Democrats, including Kenneth D. McKellar of Tennessee, John H. Overton of Louisiana, Tom Connally of Texas, and John L. McClellan of Arkansas. Because of the seniority system and because many Southern states tended to return their representatives to office again and again, Southern Democrats had traditionally dominated the committee system. In 1946, for example, they chaired twelve of the Senate's thirty-three standing committees.[18] Thus, the Southerners

15. Doan, *Wisconsin Idea*, p. 275; *New York Times*, 7 June 1946.
16. Frank C. Hanighen to RML, 16 August 1946, box 24-C, Family Papers; Roger T. Johnson, *La Follette, Jr. and the Decline of the Progressive Party in Wisconsin* (Madison, 1964), pp. 153–54.
17. *CR* 79:2, 1946, vol. 92, pt. 5, pp. 6365–75, 6390–98.
18. Galloway, *Legislative Process*, pp. 366–67; *Congressional Directory*

probably feared that a reduction in the number of committees would weaken their hold on the system.

Opponents, however, chose to focus their attack not on the committee-reorganization section but on another provision. The offending provision established an office of personnel, headed by a personnel director, to regulate hiring and firing practices in Congress. At the time most congressional employees, from committee staff members to elevator operators, were patronage appointees. The proposed office of personnel would replace patronage with the merit system. For example, committee chairmen, in staffing their committees, would have to appoint persons whom the personnel director deemed qualified for the job. No longer would a chairman be able to place his nephew or the unqualified son of a campaign contributor on the public payroll.

Opponents variously described the proposed personnel director as "czar," "generalissimo," "dictator," and "superlord" of the Senate. McKellar offered the dire prediction that enactment of the bill "would virtually turn over the Senate of the United States and all its prerogatives to the Director of Congressional Personnel." If the founding fathers had wanted a personnel director, the Tennessee senator intoned, they would have provided for one.[19]

As the debate wound into its third day, La Follette made a concession. He accepted an amendment allowing each standing committee, by majority vote, to appoint staff members without having to go through the personnel director. Not appeased, opponents continued the attack. At the end of the day La Follette informed reporters that he had the votes to pass the measure if only he could shut off debate.[20]

Monday, 10 June, was the final day allotted for debate. Unless La Follette secured a roll call, reorganization would probably be dead for the session. The opposition launched a filibuster. John L. McClellan of Arkansas led off with a leisurely review of his objections, the major one being that the personnel director would deprive McClellan and his colleagues of the power of appointing worthy youngsters as Senate pages. At about three o'clock in the afternoon, with prospects for a roll call dim, La Follette made a dramatic announcement. If he could get unanimous consent to end debate by five o'clock, he said, he was prepared to eliminate from the bill all references to the

(Washington, D.C., 1946), pp. 179–85. Not all Southern Democrats opposed the measure. Claude Pepper of Florida, Lister Hill of Alabama, and J. William Fulbright of Arkansas were vigorous supporters.

19. CR 79:2, 1946, vol. 92, pt. 5, pp. 6452–53, 6460.
20. Ibid., pp. 6517–18; New York Times, 9 June 1946.

personnel office. Having undercut the main argument of the bill's foes, La Follette received both unanimous consent to limit debate and acceptance of his amendment. The rest was mere formality. Shortly after five o'clock, the roll was called and the Senate passed the reorganization bill, 49 to 16. Southern Democrats cast 9 of the 16 dissenting votes.[21]

As one of La Follette's former aides, Norman Clapp, later told it, from the outset the senator had regarded the personnel-office provision as desirable, but easily expendable if it became necessary to save the bill. Yet, he had carefully concealed this fact. By vigorously defending the provision for four days, he had encouraged opponents to attack it all the more, to the neglect of more important sections of the bill. According to Clapp, the provision had served as a lightning rod, drawing off attack and leaving the main structure of the bill undamaged.[22]

The reorganization bill next moved to the House, where it faced an even stiffer test. There Democrat Monroney, the bill's cosponsor, and Republican Everett M. Dirksen of Illinois led the fight. But Speaker of the House Sam Rayburn opposed the measure and threatened to keep it bottled up in the Rules Committee for the session. Finally, on 25 July, a week before adjournment, Monroney and Dirksen managed to pry the measure out of committee and onto the floor, where the House approved it by the lopsided margin of 229 to 61. But the House version was flawed. Missing from it were three important provisions: the one providing an administrative assistant for each congressman; the section establishing a legislative-executive council; and most important, the mandatory features of the legislative budget, which required the president to reduce expenditures when Congress exceeded its self-imposed budget ceiling. The next day La Follette, claiming that the House bill gave him 80 percent of what he had wanted, decided against a conference committee and persuaded the Senate to adopt the House version.[23]

Despite the limitations of the final product, La Follette and Monroney had reason to be satisfied. They had upset the predictions of almost all observers, who from the beginning had declared reorganization a lost cause. La Follette especially could take pride in the fact that Congress had adopted almost all the proposals he had originally outlined three years earlier. As President Truman signed the legislative-reorganization bill into law, he hailed it as "one of the most

21. *New York Times*, 11 June 1946; *Washington Post*, 11 June 1946.
22. Interview, Norman M. Clapp.
23. Doan, *Wisconsin Idea*, p. 277; *New York Times*, 27 July 1946.

significant advances in organization of Congress . . . since the establishment of that body." At the time most interested observers readily agreed with the president's assessment.[24]

In the long run the La Follette–Monroney Act produced mixed results. It never fulfilled the hopes of its sponsors, but neither did it bear out the dire warnings of its opponents. It became clear that both supporters and opponents had overestimated the possible effects of reorganization.

As intended, the act strengthened the committee system. With their numbers reduced, their jurisdictions clarified, and their staffs expanded, standing committees probably operated more efficiently than before. The measure also strengthened Congress's ability to oversee the executive branch. Heeding the law's mandate to "exercise continuous watchfulness," in the years immediately following 1946 the committees policed as never before the activities of executive agencies, though they did not always do so in the positive, constructive manner that La Follette had wanted. One unexpected result of committee reorganization was the proliferation of subcommittees after 1946; by the 1960s over 250 subcommittees had come into existence. This development partially offset the positive effects of reorganization.[25]

Some provisions of the La Follette–Monroney Act failed to work. The most conspicuous example was the provision calling for a legislative budget and coordination of congressional spending and revenue policies. The first two years that the law was in effect, Congress unsuccessfully tried to comply with the budget provision. In 1947 the appropriations and revenue committees, meeting as the Joint Committee on the Budget, drew up a budget and submitted it to Congress for approval. But the House and Senate disagreed over certain details and never put the budget into effect. In 1948 Congress did approve a budget but then promptly exceeded the spending ceiling. In 1949 Congress abandoned the experiment.[26] But the idea lived on, and twenty years later Congress launched another experiment in budgeting.

It became apparent that in some areas the Reorganization Act

24. New York Times, 3 August 1946; Washington Post, 3, 4 August 1946.
25. Important assessments of the act include: Galloway, Legislative Process, pp. 591–669; George B. Galloway, Congressional Reorganization Revisited (College Park, Md., 1956); A. S. Mike Monroney et al., The Strengthening of American Political Institutions (Ithaca, N.Y., 1949); Samuel P. Huntington, "Congressional Response to the Twentieth Century," in David B. Truman, ed., The Congress and America's Future (Englewood Cliffs, N.J., 1965), pp. 20–21.
26. Galloway, Legislative Process, pp. 657–58.

failed to go far enough. For example, the section regulating lobbying did force many lobbyists to register with, and submit regular financial reports to, Congress. But due to sloppy draftsmanship this provision contained gaping loopholes allowing many other lobbyists to avoid compliance.[27] It became clear also that La Follette and Monroney had been remiss in not dealing with such problems as the seniority system that governed the selection of committee chairmen, the filibuster rule in the Senate, and the near dictatorial powers of the House Rules Committee, all of which were impediments to the effective and responsible functioning of Congress.

All in all, the act failed to achieve its broadest objectives. It did not reverse the flow of power and prestige from the legislative branch to the executive branch. Nor did it restore to Congress its traditional legislative function. After 1946 presidents continued to initiate legislation, and Congress continued in the subordinate role of approving or rejecting presidential programs. Had it not been for reorganization, however, Congress might possibly have fallen even further behind the executive branch. Despite all the limitations of his handiwork, La Follette could take pride in the knowledge that without his initiative, persistence, and skillful handling of the measure, there probably would have been no congressional reforms at all.

27. Ibid., pp. 620–22. For La Follette's assessment of the measure see U.S. Congress, Senate, Committee on Expenditures in Executive Departments, *Hearings on Evaluation of Legislative Reorganization Act of 1946*, 80th Cong., 2d sess., 1948, pp. 59–79.

CHAPTER 16

Defeat

As soon as President Truman signed the reorganization bill into law on 2 August 1946, La Follette left for Wisconsin, where he was long overdue. The Republican primary, in which he was entered, was only eleven days away. For months his aides in the state had been pleading with him to return home and campaign. They were quite confident about the outcome of the primary, for the senator had the good fortune, or so they thought, of running against a relatively unknown circuit court judge named Joseph R. McCarthy. Still, it seemed foolish to take chances. But La Follette's answer had always been the same. No, he said, he could not leave Washington just yet; he had to see the reorganization bill through to the end. Finally he did return home and campaign for about a week. But it proved to be too little too late. On 13 August La Follette lost to McCarthy by a slim five-thousand-vote margin. Paradoxically, during the primary campaign and the ensuing general-election campaign La Follette placed far more emphasis on the so-called communist menace than did Mc-Carthy, whose name would later become synonymous with that whole issue.

It was sometime in the summer or fall of 1945, after months of doubt, that La Follette decided to stand for reelection. He then had to decide whether to run as a Progressive, a Democrat, or a Republican. Progressive party members were undecided on the question. A small band of loyalists, including Phil La Follette, who had recently returned from the South Pacific, wanted to keep the party alive. A second group, labor oriented and from the industrial southeastern part of the state, urged affiliation with the Democrats. This course had several advantages. Most state and national Democratic leaders were enthusiastic about the prospect of having their ranks swelled by La Follette and his Progressive followers. If La Follette ran as a Democrat, he would have the support of the administration, he would probably run unopposed in the primary, and he would be assured of strong labor support. On the other hand, the state Democratic party was weak and ineffective; and if the 1944 elections were any indication, the tide nationally was moving against the Democrats. The vast majority of Progressive leaders rejected these first two alternatives and wanted instead to return to the party of Lincoln and Fighting Bob. The GOP dominated the state, and most Progressives saw it as their only hope of regaining power.[1]

After several more months of doubt, La Follette picked the Republican party. Expediency undoubtedly played a part. The Progressive party was hopeless, the Democratic party seemed risky, the GOP looked like a winner. But two other considerations probably figured as much, or more, in his decision. As Wilbur R. Voigt, the senator's chief aide, remembered it, La Follette had come to believe that the Democratic party was a bit too beholden to organized labor. He still considered himself a champion of labor, but if he ran and won as a Democrat he might owe his election to labor. If he won on the Republican ticket he would have more freedom to support labor when it was right and oppose it when it was wrong. La Follette was also critical of the Roosevelt-Truman foreign policy, especially as it concerned the Soviet Union. As his Madison friend and adviser Gordon Sinykin later put it, the senator felt that the Democrats were playing "footsy" with Russia. On domestic issues La Follette was clearly closer to the Democratic party than to the GOP. But foreign policy seemed uppermost in his mind in 1945 and early 1946.[2]

La Follette announced his decision on 17 March 1946 at Portage, Wisconsin, where upward of four hundred Progressives had assembled to consider their party's future. Following the senator's speech the delegates voted 284 to 128 to return to the GOP. Of the dissenting votes, 77 were for maintaining the party, 51 for joining the Democrats, and 3 for joining the Socialist party. Conspicuously absent from the convention was Phil La Follette. The night before, Bob, fearing that his brother's presence might touch off a movement to keep the party going, had directed their mutual friend Gordon Sinykin to phone Phil and tell him to stay away. Phil, Sinykin recalled, was deeply hurt.[3]

1. Philip F. La Follette, *Adventure in Politics: The Memoirs of Philip La Follette* (New York, 1970), p. 275; Roger T. Johnson, *Robert M. La Follette, Jr. and the Decline of the Progressive Party in Wisconsin* (Madison, 1964), pp. 109–10, 119; Charles H. Backstrom, "The Progressive Party of Wisconsin, 1934–1946" (Ph.D. diss., University of Wisconsin, 1956), p. 276; *Eau Claire Leader*, 15 March 1946, clipping, box 667-C, Glenn D. Roberts to RML, 6 June, 14 November 1945, box 23-C, Dick Lund to RML, 23 September 1945, box 54-C, Family Papers (see list of abbreviations p. x).

2. Interviews, Wilbur Voigt, 9 July 1973; Gordon Sinykin, August 1972.

3. Johnson, *La Follette, Jr.*, pp. 113–17; interview, Gordon Sinykin. For organized labor's view of the convention, see Elmer Beck, "Henry Wallace Booed," *Capital Times*, 25 March 1946, clipping, box 668-C, Family Papers.

The Republican hierarchy in Wisconsin, with the exception of the incumbent governor, Walter S. Goodland, a Progressive at heart, bitterly opposed the Progressive invasion. Leading the assult was the chairman of the state GOP, Thomas E. Coleman, a fifty-three-year-old manufacturer from Madison, a normally soft-spoken man whose face flushed and voice rose in anger only when he talked about the La Follettes. In 1945 Coleman had gone so far as to direct his men in the legislature to sponsor a bill prohibiting La Follette and the Progressives from switching parties in time for the 1946 elections. Only Governor Goodland's veto had prevented the bill from becoming law. After the Portage convention, Coleman and other GOP leaders vowed to defeat La Follette in the Republican primary.[4]

To accomplish that formidable feat they wanted to put forth a candidate of stature and proven ability. Instead they got Joseph R. McCarthy. Born and raised on a small farm near Appleton, the thirty-seven-year-old McCarthy was a graduate of the Marquette University Law School, a circuit court judge, and a marine captain during World War II. In 1944, while still in the service, he ran in the Republican primary against the state's conservative junior senator, Alexander Wiley. McCarthy lost to Wiley but finished a surprisingly strong second. Over the years McCarthy had shown an interest in the La Follettes. In late 1941 he paid a visit to the senator's Washington office and before leaving signed up for a subscription to the *Progressive*. In 1944, while stationed in the South Pacific, he looked up Phil La Follette. "We had a nice talk," Phil wrote afterward, "but it was hard to convince him that I knew so little about politics at home."[5]

There was nothing in McCarthy's undistinguished background to suggest that he would fare any better against La Follette than had past opponents. So when he announced his candidacy, Coleman continued his talent search as though nothing had happened. But McCarthy persisted, saying that he would run with or without the blessings of the party organization. Finally, to avoid the risk of splitting the anti-La Follette vote in the primary, Coleman gave his support to McCarthy.[6]

The Democrats, meanwhile, were having no such difficulty finding their candidate for the Senate. He was Howard J. McMurray, forty-six years old, a former one-term congressman from the Milwaukee

4. Johnson, *La Follette, Jr.*, pp. 104–6.
5. Robert Griffith, *The Politics of Fear: Joseph R. McCarthy and the Senate* (Lexington, Ky., 1970), pp. 2–7; Norman M. Clapp to Morris H. Rubin, 3 December 1941, box 19-C, Family Papers; PFL to Mrs. PFL, 15 June 1944, box 142-2, PFL Papers.
6. Johnson, *La Follette, Jr.*, pp. 124–27.

district, and in 1946 a political science instructor at the University of Wisconsin. McMurray was liberal on domestic issues and internationalist in foreign affairs. Like most Democrats he had urged the Progressives to join his party. He also had promised to back La Follette if La Follette ran as a Democrat.[7] Running unopposed for his party's nomination, McMurray was the wild card in the primary; no one could predict how many voters might support him. But one thing was certain: every vote he received would be one less vote for La Follette.

As the campaign got underway, McCarthy emerged as the star attraction. Sensitive to the widespread belief that he was a political lightweight, he waged a campaign the likes of which, in sheer energy at least, Wisconsinites had not seen since the early days of Phil La Follette or the last days of Fighting Bob. McCarthy crisscrossed the state, handshaking his way through every barbershop, beauty parlor, and tavern he could find. Behind him was the well-financed regular Republican organization, which took out full-page newspaper advertisements and blanketed the state with political fliers. From the start McCarthy and his supporters outhustled La Follette and his supporters.[8]

McCarthy's strategy, the *Nation* observed, was the "simple one of taking any position that La Follette opposed" and opposing every position that La Follette took. He attacked the senator for supporting the New Deal, for supporting price controls, and for contributing to that bloated, self-perpetuating bureaucracy in Washington. He criticized La Follette's conduct of the civil-liberties investigation. And he denounced the pending La Follette–Monroney bill, singling out the provision that increased congressmen's salaries.[9]

But the campaign revolved more around personalities than issues. The McCarthy organization portrayed their man as Joe, a regular fellow, who when war broke out had given up his "soft job" as a judge to do his duty. One advertisement gave a highly exaggerated account of Joe's wartime record and concluded, "Yes folks. Congress NEEDS A TAILGUNNER." La Follette by contrast was the "gentleman from Virginia" who had "sat out" the war amidst the splendor of his Virginia estate. In truth, La Follette had never lived in Virginia and had sold his property there in 1944.[10]

7. Ibid., pp. 110, 115.
8. Griffith, *Politics of Fear*, p. 9.
9. "La Follette's Folly," *Nation* 163(24 August 1946):200–201.
10. McCarthy advertisement quoted in Jack Anderson and Ronald W. May, *McCarthy: The Man, the Senator, the "Ism"* (Boston, 1952), pp. 83–85; RML

The most serious charge the McCarthy forces leveled against La Follette concerned his part ownership of Milwaukee radio station WEMP. In 1942 La Follette, worried as always about his financial status and looking for a good investment, bought stock in the WEMP Broadcasting Company, which his Madison friend and adviser Glenn Roberts had helped organize in 1935.[11] Late in 1945 La Follette's opponents learned that he had made a profit of close to fifty thousand dollars over a two-year period, this in addition to his annual income of approximately eleven thousand dollars. Thomas E. Coleman, with a curious twist of reasoning, promptly accused La Follette of "political hypocrisy" for advocating excess-profits taxation while at the same time making so much money off the radio station.[12]

Taking his cue from Coleman, McCarthy implied that the senator was guilty of something far worse than hypocrisy: conflict of interest. Lacking proof and doubtless hoping to avoid a lawsuit, McCarthy made no direct accusation. Rather he couched the charge in a series of statements and questions. "How did La Follette get that money?" one of his newspaper advertisements asked. So as not to leave too much to the imagination, McCarthy pointed out that the Federal Communications Commission licensed WEMP and that La Follette voted on appropriations for the FCC.[13] La Follette, apparently considering the charge unworthy of reply, remained silent.

If La Follette had laid out the facts about his relationship with WEMP he might have suffered some embarrassment but probably could have cleared himself of charges of wrongdoing. In 1935 Glenn Roberts and a group of Milwaukee businessmen organized the radio station and then applied to the FCC for a license. At Roberts's request, La Follette apparently put in a good word for the station with FCC commissioner Eugene O. Sykes. The FCC granted the license, and Roberts thanked La Follette for "all you did for me in the Milwaukee Radio situation." La Follette's help in this matter probably fell under the classification of constituent service. He, like all senators, frequently aided constituents in their dealings with federal agencies. The difference in this case was that the constituent was also a friend and political associate. There was no evidence that La Follette interceded

to Rachel, 5 September 1942, box 48-A, Rachel to PFL, October 1944, box 142-2, PFL Papers.

11. For details of the transaction, see RML-Roberts correspondence, box 21-C, Family Papers.

12. RML income tax records, boxes 640-C–642-C, Family Papers; *Milwaukee Sentinel*, 5 December 1944, clipping, box 666-C, Family Papers.

13. Anderson and May, *McCarthy*, pp. 84, 98; unidentified clippings, n.d., box 666-C, Family Papers.

with the FCC on WEMP's behalf after he became a part owner of the station, except perhaps to request speedy consideration of WEMP matters.[14]

Although La Follette was not guilty of wrongdoing, he was, as when he had purchased his Virginia property, guilty of poor political judgment. He seemed not to realize, or not to care, that in public life appearances were as important as realities. He had bought and sold a house and some property in Virginia, and it remained a symbol of his neglect of his constituents. In the controversy about the radio station, what probably most harmed La Follette's chances for reelection was not the charge of conflict of interest but rather the damage done to La Follette's image as a man of the people. Thomas Amlie, a Progressive turned Democrat, probably expressed a widespread opinion when after the election he wrote a friend, "Bob had no business with that ownership of WEMP. Coleman was right. Bob and his friends made almost $200,000 a year on that station. That is not only monopoly but . . . also big business. No man can get involved in that way and still be with the common man." When Isen La Follette, who sometimes displayed more political savvy than her brother-in-law, had first heard about Bob's purchase of the radio stock, she commented to Phil, "Personally I think it has angles of dynamite."[15]

As McCarthy burrowed in from the Right, Democrat Howard J. McMurray burrowed in from the Left. Though running unopposed for his party's nomination, he waged a vigorous campaign, trying to convince liberals that they should vote for him in the Democratic primary rather than waste their votes on either of the Republican contenders. McMurray, who just a few months before had been urging La Follette to run as a Democrat, was now telling voters that La Follette had lost his passion for liberal causes. He played up the fact that Sen. Robert A. Taft of Ohio, a conservative, had endorsed La Follette.[16]

McMurray concentrated his attack on La Follette's foreign-policy

14. Glenn D. Roberts to RML, 12 February 1935, box 13-C, Family Papers. See also RML-Roberts correspondence, boxes 13-C, 16-C, 21-C, Family Papers.

15. Thomas R. Amlie to H. C. Holdridge, 10 October 1947, box 51, Thomas R. Amlie Papers, State Historical Society of Wisconsin, Madison; Mrs. PFL to PFL, 20 April 1943, box 140-2, PFL Papers.

16. Johnson, *La Follette, Jr.*, pp. 134–36. According to Glenn D. Roberts, La Follette's campaign manager in 1946, and John Clifford Folger, a friend of La Follette and of Senator Taft, Taft also secretly contributed one thousand dollars to La Follette's campaign. The money, according to Roberts, was not spent and was returned to Taft after the election. Interviews, Glenn D. Roberts, 3 July 1973; John Clifford Folger, 5 June 1973.

views. Trying to pin the label of *isolationist* on him, McMurray reminded the voters of the senator's anti-interventionist posture before Pearl Harbor and of his criticisms of the Soviet Union, Great Britain, and the United Nations. He also made personal attacks on La Follette exceeding anything said by McCarthy. "La Follette spent five years before the war voting for Hitler," McMurray said, adding, "If a man had to sell out his civilization to get votes he should not represent a free people in a democratic society."[17]

Organized labor played an active role in the campaign. Leaders of the Wisconsin CIO supported McMurray and battered at La Follette. The local Political Action Committee of the CIO issued a political guide purporting to summarize the positions of the candidates on labor related issues. In La Follette's case, the guide contained several misleading or false statements about his voting record. In April the *Wisconsin CIO News* ran a story that also falsified the senator's stands on key issues. When the story appeared, Nathan Cowan, a legislative representative of the national CIO, issued a statement repudiating the article and setting the record straight. But the *CIO News* refused to print Cowan's statement, even though the national organization had directed that it do so.[18] The state American Federation of Labor refused to endorse any candidate. La Follette still managed to garner endorsements from a few union locals and a few labor leaders, but for the first time in his career he did not enjoy the full support of organized labor.[19]

Even though labor refused to support him, La Follette continued to support labor. Between the end of the war in September 1945 and the August primary, a huge wave of labor unrest swept the country. In rapid succession workers in the auto, steel, coal-mining, and railroad industries went out on strike, all demanding wage increases so that they could cope with anticipated inflation. Each new strike brought cries for the government to clamp down on labor. La Follette sided with the unions. Early in 1946 he joined, and contributed money to, the National Committee to Aid Families of General Motors Strik-

17. *Wisconsin State Journal*, 2 May 1946. Professor McMurray employed some of the techniques that later would be associated with McCarthyism.

18. Backstrom, "Progressive Party," pp. 171–72; Nathan Feinsinger to RML, 20 April 1946, RML to Lloyd Garrison, 26 April 1946, Garrison to RML, n.d., box 59-C, Family Papers; Robert M. La Follette, Jr., "Turn the Light on Communism," *Colliers* 119 (8 February 1947): 73.

19. Johnson, *La Follette, Jr.*, p. 143. For a thorough discussion of organized labor's role in the 1946 campaign, see David M. Oshinsky, *Senator Joseph McCarthy and the American Labor Movement* (Columbia, Mo., 1976), chaps. 1–3.

ers. In February, in New York City, he addressed a jointly sponsored AFL-CIO fund raiser for the GM strikers. He told the cheering throng that a powerful minority of industrialists was trying to "foment hysteria and thus secure passage of legislation that will hamstring labor and give them free reign."[20] By May antiunion hysteria had gripped Washington. That month Congress passed the Case bill, which imposed numerous restrictions on organized labor. President Truman vetoed the measure, but then offered a far more drastic proposal of his own. He told Congress that when a strike hit a vital national industry, the government should have the power to operate that industry and to draft into the armed services any strikers who refused to return to work. Without hesitation La Follette voted against both the Case bill and the more extreme Truman antistrike proposal.[21]

Similarly, La Follette took labor's side on most economic and social-welfare issues. During the 1946 session he voted for public housing; for continuation of the Fair Employment Practices Commission; for a higher minimum wage, although not one as high as labor wanted; for extension of price controls; and for the Employment Act of 1946, which for the first time acknowledged the federal government's ultimate responsibility for maintaining full employment. La Follette did not sponsor the Employment Act; nevertheless it represented a significant victory, for it enunciated a principle that he had been advocating since the early years of the depression. The act also established a Council of Economic Advisors, which in form and function resembled the national economic council La Follette proposed in 1931.[22]

La Follette's strong labor record put him in a strangely awkward position. Wisconsin labor leaders either opposed or were noncommittal to his candidacy. But antiunion constituents, and there were many

20. Eliot Janeway to RML, 1 February 1946, Elizabeth Janeway to RML, 5 March 1946, RML to Llewellyn G. Ross, 12 February 1946, box 24-C, RML speech, box 565-C, *New York Post*, 26 February 1946, clipping, box 667-C, Family Papers.

21. Joseph G. Rayback, *A History of American Labor* (New York, 1966), pp. 389–95; James T. Patterson, *Mr. Republican: A Biography of Robert A. Taft* (Boston, 1972), pp. 305–7; RML to William T. Evjue, 3 July 1946, box 591-C, Family Papers.

22. William Green to RML, 17 April 1946, RML to William T. Evjue, 3 July 1946, box 59-C, correspondence on Employment Act, box 328-C, RML radio address, 25 July 1946, box 565-C, Family Papers. The similarity between RML's national economic council and the Council of Economic Advisors is discussed in R. Alan Lawson, *The Failure of Independent Liberalism, 1930–1941* (New York, 1971), pp. 62–63.

of them, angrily lashed out at him for "selling out" to labor. One constituent's reaction to the senator's opposition to the Truman anti-strike bill was typical: "If you expect to return to Washington I suggest you get behind President Truman's Emergency Labor Bill, as the people you are supposed to represent are fed up on politicians playing up to labor for their votes and creating a hardship on the whole nation." A Baptist minister from La Crosse asked, "Mr. La Follette, what have you done to get the antistrike law before the Senate? . . . What have you done to help put John L. Lewis in his place and keep him there?"[23] It was precisely this "damned if you do and damned if you don't" situation that had driven La Follette to the brink of retirement in 1945 and that in 1946 made him regard the prospects of reelection with mixed emotions.

In view of La Follette's record, labor's refusal to support him was difficult to understand. For La Follette and many of his supporters, however, there was no mystery. For several years they had suspected that communists were gaining control of the labor movement, particularly the state CIO, and now they were convinced of it. According to their theory, the communists wanted to punish La Follette for his frequent and harsh criticisms of the Soviet Union.[24] In all probability, communists did hold positions of influence in the state CIO and affiliated organizations, although the evidence of communist infiltration was not quite as clear-cut as some people at the time and some scholars later made it out to be.[25]

But this theory did not explain the obvious lack of enthusiasm for the senator among AFL leaders, whom no one accused of being communist. They were disturbed not by La Follette's stand on the issues but by his reentry into the GOP. Labor had long since decided that the Democratic party was more responsive to its needs. Moreover, by 1946 organized labor was moving away from its traditional policy of voluntarism, whereby it rewarded its friends and punished its enemies without taking into account their political affiliations. Instead, labor was looking for a permanent, reliable vehicle for its political influence, and that vehicle was the Democratic party. La Follette

23. Z. W. Miller to RML, 4 June 1946, box 331-C, Rev. M. Vanderbeck to RML, 25 May 1946, box 62-C, similar letters, boxes 331–32-C, Family Papers.
24. Interviews, Morris H. Rubin, 1, 8 August 1972; Glenn D. Roberts.
25. For a discussion of communist infiltration into the Wisconsin labor movement, see Thomas W. Gavett, *The Development of the Labor Movement in Milwaukee* (Madison, 1965), pp. 176–97, and Robert Willard Ozanne, "The Effects of Communist Leadership on American Trade Unions" (Ph.D. diss., University of Wisconsin, 1954).

had thus forced a difficult choice upon labor. Under Wisconsin law, on primary day voters had to select either a Republican or a Democratic ballot, but not both. So laborers and liberal Democrats had to decide whether to select the Democratic ballot, on which most of their candidates were listed, or the Republican ballot, containing La Follette's name.[26]

From March to early August, as McCarthy and McMurray attacked, La Follette remained in Washington, steering the reorganization bill through Congress. In his absence his supporters, under the direction of Glenn Roberts, did what they could. With a campaign fund of approximately thirteen thousand dollars, one-fourth of which came out of La Follette's own pocket, they bought newspaper space and radio time. One radio spot featured "soldiers" talking about how much La Follette had done for veterans. La Follette also delivered weekly speeches over the radio. In one broadcast he explained that although he would naturally prefer to be in Wisconsin, the business of the country required his presence in Washington.[27]

Campaign aides realized that media presentations were a poor substitute for the candidate himself, and they urged him to return home. In March, Roberts, perhaps sensing trouble in the industrial region of the state, advised La Follette to spend a week in Milwaukee with sidetrips to Racine and Kenosha. La Follette declined, but no one was particularly upset. It was still early, and his aides knew him well enough to know that this was normal behavior for him at this stage of the campaign. But weeks stretched into months, and still he remained in Washington. On one occasion he agreed to attend an important meeting in Stevens Point. But then at the last moment he canceled out. When they heard the news, Morris Rubin and Glenn Roberts called him long distance, and according to Rubin, "we hammered him as hard as we could but he refused. He said he had to see his reorganization bill through."[28]

By May, Roberts was pleading with him. "Frankly, Bob," he wrote,

26. Oshinsky, *Senator Joseph McCarthy and the American Labor Movement*, esp. chaps. 2–3; on labor's commitment to the Democratic party see James C. Foster, *The Union Politic: The Political Action Committee* (Columbia, Mo., 1976) and J. David Greenstone, *Labor in American Politics* (New York, 1969).

27. Statement of campaign contributions, box 143-2, PFL Papers; radio script, enclosed in RML to Glenn D. Roberts, 8 March 1946, box 24-C, RML radio speech, June 1946, box 565-C, Family Papers.

28. Glenn D. Roberts to RML, 20 March 1946, box 24-C, Family Papers; interview, Morris H. Rubin.

"our leaders have a feeling that perhaps you do not care too much for them. Perhaps I do not put this well, but they long to shake your hand and to have you slap them on the back and say hello. . . . They are for you, and they are going to put on a terrific fight, but their effectiveness will increase 100% if they just can have a word with you." Roberts urged La Follette to come out for a week and spend three days in Milwaukee and one day each in Racine, Kenosha, and Sheboygan. To make the offer as attractive as possible, Roberts assured him that he would not have to make any speeches but only meet informally with labor leaders, religious groups, and others. Roberts concluded, "I beg of you . . . to leave some [voting] pairs in Washington and get out here to do this job. There are thousands upon thousands of votes that can be tipped our way now merely through a handshake. Later they may be harder to get."[29]

When the Senate passed the La Follette–Monroney bill on 10 June, La Follette's supporters breathed a sigh of relief. At last, they thought, he was free to campaign. Not quite yet, he promptly informed them, for the Senate was now taking up the all-important price-control bill. Congress did not dispose of the price-control matter until late July, at which time the House began consideration of the reorganization bill. La Follette of course had to be on hand to guide the bill through the final stages.[30] But these were merely excuses. Between 10 June, when the Senate passed the reorganization bill, and late July, when the House took it up, La Follette could have gone to Wisconsin without in any way jeopardizing the outcome. The simple fact was that he did not want to campaign.

His campaign leaders were disturbed but not alarmed. From start to finish they were confident of victory. And even as they pleaded with La Follette to return home, they gave him optimistic reports, as evidenced by those of campaign manager Glenn Roberts: 6 April, "Things continue to look good"; 24 June, "We continue to receive good reports on your standing"; 26 July, "I think the line is holding well." On 31 July, two weeks before the primary, Rep. Alvin E. O'Konski told La Follette that the senator would sweep, by a two-to-one margin, the Tenth District in the northwestern part of the state.[31]

29. Roberts to RML, 16 May 1946, box 24-C, Family Papers.

30. RML radio address, June 1946, box 565-C, Family Papers; interviews, Morris H. Rubin, Gordon Sinykin, Glenn D. Roberts.

31. Roberts to RML, 6 April, 24 June, 26 July 1946, box 24-C, telegram, A. E. O'Konski to RML, 31 July 1946, box 61-C, Family Papers. See also PFL to Robert La Follette III, 22 May 1946, box 143-2, PFL Papers.

How La Follette himself assessed his chances was uncertain. Despite all the favorable reports he privately told at least three persons, two reporters and a Senate colleague, that he thought he would lose. But this may only have been his pessimistic nature speaking, preparing himself and others for the worst.[32]

Nor was it even certain that La Follette really wanted to be reelected. His campaign manager, Roberts, remembered having the impression that the senator did not care whether he won or lost. Another friend, Gordon Sinykin, recalled hearing La Follette say that very thing. But other persons, also in a position to know, believed that he definitely did want to return to the Senate.[33] It is likely that La Follette himself did not know what he wanted. At times the prospect of defeat, of relief at long last from the pressures and frustrations of public life, might have seemed appealing. Yet at other times the prospect of forced retirement from the only life he had ever known must have seemed most unappealing. But one thing was clear. La Follette did not want reelection if it meant waging more than a token campaign.

On 2 August, when Truman signed the reorganization bill and Congress adjourned, La Follette had no more excuses. He returned to Wisconsin and waged a six-day campaign. In a series of public appearances and radio addresses he portrayed himself as a political moderate and his opponents as extremists. "The Communists," he declared on election eve in obvious reference to the state CIO, "want Bob La Follette's scalp because I am not far enough to the left to suit them. The Colemanites have been attacking Bob La Follette because I am not far enough to the right to suit them." Then, with an uncharacteristic burst of patriotic sloganeering, he concluded, "We can steer clear of foreign ideologies on the one hand and a do-nothing reactionary policy on the other hand by driving down the Middle Way, the American Way, with a vigorous progressive program directed toward the social and economic betterment of all people, regardless of race, color, creed, or social origins." Phil, unhappily confined to the sidelines at his brother's request, captured the essence of the campaign. "Bob's whole strategy," he wrote his son, "is to refrain from any controversial issue—and keep re-election on the basis that he has been a good representative of the various interests in the

32. Johnson, *La Follette, Jr.*, pp. 153–54; Frank C. Hanighen to RML, 16 August 1946, box 24-C, Family Papers.

33. Interviews, Glenn D. Roberts; Gordon Sinykin; John Clifford Folger; Mary La Follette, 22 February 1973.

state—as his campaign literature puts it—'he is neither radical nor reactionary' but 'middle of the road.'" He added, "For this reason he does not want my face or voice stirring up controversy—so I shall keep out of it."[34]

As primary day approached, almost everyone predicted a La Follette victory. McCarthy had waged an aggressive campaign, no one doubted that. Still, seasoned political observers, especially those from out of state, had a hard time taking him seriously. He was an upstart, with no experience or qualifications to speak of, who presumed to challenge the famous La Follette, a veteran of twenty years with a record that was impressive by any standards and made even more impressive by his recent success with the Reorganization Act.[35]

On election night La Follette, his family, and his friends gathered to await the results. As the returns started to come in, it was clear that the outcome would be closer than almost anyone had expected. Early on, La Follette took a narrow lead based on returns from rural counties. Later in the evening, as the industrial counties began to report, McCarthy narrowed the gap and by midnight was trailing by only fifty-seven votes. By early morning it was evident that, just as in 1940, Milwaukee would decide the outcome. The La Follette camp was still hopeful, however. All the senator had to do to win was stay even with McCarthy in Milwaukee. Then came the shock. Milwaukee County reported 48,614 for McCarthy, 38,437 for La Follette, and 31,816 for McMurray. It was over. McCarthy had won the primary by five thousand votes. The final totals gave McCarthy 207,935, or 41 percent; La Follette 202,557, or 40 percent; and McMurray 62,361, or 12 percent. La Follette "didn't seem to take it hard that night," recalled Morris Rubin. "In fact he was cheering me up."[36]

La Follette's defeat sent shock waves throughout the country. As far back as most people could remember a La Follette had been in the Senate. "The fall of the La Follette dynasty," said one magazine, "reverberated far outside the boundaries of that green and pleasant

34. RML radio speech over WIBA, 12 August 1946, box 565-C, Family Papers; PFL to Robert La Follette III, 31 July 1946, box 143-2, PFL Papers.

35. Johnson, *La Follette, Jr.*, pp. 149–50. Perhaps the only political observer who sensed a close race and possible defeat for La Follette was John Wyngaard, whose column appeared in many newspapers across the state. Not coincidentally, Wyngaard's columns probably contained the most objective and most perceptive reporting of the campaign. See for example, Wyngaard, "La Follette Safe, But Trouble Brews," *Eau Claire Leader*, and other clippings, box 673-C, Family Papers.

36. *New York Times*, 14, 15 August 1946; *Wisconsin Blue Book, 1948* (Madison, 1948), p. 604; interview, Morris H. Rubin.

land. In Washington many a congressman trembled with nervous wonder; if the voters were tired of Bob they could be tired of anybody."[37]

Embarrassed political reporters had some explaining to do. They not only had to dig up some information on McCarthy but also had to explain to their readers why their predictions had been so wrong. For one thing, they agreed, there had been an exceptionally low turnout at the polls, a situation that usually hurts the incumbent. It was an off-year election, the primary came unusually early in the year, the campaign had generated little excitement, and as a result only a third of all registered voters had bothered to vote.[38] For another thing, 1946 was a bad year to be an incumbent. Angry about high prices, shortages of housing and consumer goods, labor unrest, and all the other postwar problems, many people blamed Congress. Before the year was out, other veteran incumbents fell, including such notables as Sen. Burton K. Wheeler of Montana, Sen. Henrik Shipstead of Minnesota, and the highly respected Rep. Jerry Voorhis of California.

In retrospect it also appeared that La Follette had made a costly blunder during the campaign. Contesting for the Republican nomination for governor were Ralph M. Immel, a longtime La Follette friend and political associate, and the popular incumbent, Walter S. Goodland. As governor, Goodland had frequently sided with the Progressives, and he had warmly welcomed them into the GOP. But just before the primary, La Follette had endorsed his friend Immel. To many people his endorsement smacked of cronyism, and it probably cost him the votes of many Goodland supporters.[39]

Another and more important cause of La Follette's defeat, everyone agreed, was his poor showing in the industrial counties of Kenosha, Racine, and especially Milwaukee. In 1940 he had gained almost a majority of the votes in each of those counties, while his opponents had trailed far behind. In 1946 he finished third behind McMurray and McCarthy in Kenosha and second behind McCarthy in Racine and Milwaukee. The difference between 1940 and 1946 was McMurray, whom most observers had overlooked when they sat down to write their predictions. McMurray had attracted enough labor-Democrat votes to cost La Follette the election.[40]

Why had so many workers abandoned La Follette? The senator, his

37. "La Follette's Defeat," n.d., clipping, box 666-C, Family Papers. See also Amlie to "Howard," 10 October 1947, box 51, Amlie Papers.

38. *New York Times*, 14, 15 August 1946.

39. Johnson, *La Follette, Jr.*, pp. 155–56.

40. *Wisconsin Blue Book*, 1948, p. 604.

supporters, and even some labor leaders blamed the communists. "I'm still convinced," Morris Rubin said many years later, "that the Communists did him in—that CIO crowd in Milwaukee, Racine, and Kenosha."[41]

But by focusing on communist activities, La Follette partisans ignored a more important cause of labor dissatisfaction: the senator's affiliation with the GOP. Had he joined the Democrats, as many party and labor leaders had urged, he probably would have faced no opposion in the primary and would have enjoyed substantial labor support. The *Nation* expressed a widely held opinion when it said editorially that La Follette "needlessly brought about his own downfall. The simple political truth is that he had no business running in the Republican primary at all."[42]

But above all, La Follette lost because he had fallen out of touch with his constituents and because he had failed to wage more than a token campaign. Had he made a fight of it he might very well have drawn more people to the polls, and he might have offset the effects of his endorsement of Immel. Had he gone into the Milwaukee area, taken his case directly to the workers, and cleared up the misunderstandings about certain aspects of his voting record, he might have overcome the opposition and apathy of union leaders. But La Follette did none of these things. He sat out the campaign by staying in Washington, thereby reinforcing the image that McCarthy was building of him as the aloof "gentleman from Virginia." In retrospect the surprising thing was not that La Follette lost but that he came so close to winning. Few, if any, other senators, no matter how impressive their records, would have been able to briefly visit their states two or three times a year, return home a week or ten days before their election, and still pull within a percentage point of victory.

In the general election campaign between McCarthy and McMurray, La Follette played an indirect role on McCarthy's behalf. He played no direct role, he told his close friend Sen. Robert A. Taft, not because he did not want to, but because no one in the McCarthy camp asked him to. And, he explained, "under the circumstances, and especially in view of the type of campaign which McCarthy and the Republican organization had conducted against me in the primary,

41. Marquis Childs, "Washington Calling," *Washington Post*, 2 August 1946; Harvey Kitzman to PFL, 31 January 1952, box 147-2, PFL Papers; interview, Morris H. Rubin. See also, David M. Oshinsky, "Wisconsin Labor and the Campaign of 1952," *Wisconsin Magazine of History* 56 (Winter 1972–1973): 109.
42. "La Follette's Folly," pp. 200–201.

I did not feel I should barge into the campaign unsolicited." So he did what he considered the next best thing in the way of helping Mc-Carthy, and that was to "write a couple of pieces for the *Progressive* which were widely carried in Wisconsin papers, attacking the left-wing Wallace-Pepper axis in the Democratic Party and the infiltration of Commies and fellow-travelers."[43]

One of the articles to which La Follette referred was a slashing attack on Commerce Secretary Henry A. Wallace and Sen. Claude Pepper of Florida, who, in a joint appearance at Madison Square Garden in September, had criticized the increasingly "get tough" attitude of the Truman administration toward the Soviet Union. Wallace and Pepper, La Follette charged, had "urged on America and proclaimed to the world doctrines for which we professed to have fought World War II."[44] By attacking Wallace, La Follette was taking an indirect jab at Howard J. McMurray, who was a friend of Wallace's and who generally agreed with Wallace's views on foreign policy.[45]

In a second article La Follette elaborated on a theme that he had only hinted at in the past: communist infiltration of American society. "Some subversive elements, in league with political charlatans," he charged, "are prostituting liberalism for their own devious purposes. Like vermin, they are infesting and polluting liberal thought, while undermining the structure of democratic organizations and even that of government itself." La Follette went on to describe a vast communist conspiracy. Communists and their fellow travelers, he claimed, had infiltrated labor unions and other "respectable" liberal organizations. Without providing any examples, he charged that there were "vigorous exponents of the communist party line in the motion picture industry, printing and publishing, radio, and other media for influencing public opinion." The communists' influence, he added, was "further augmented by the political yes-men who cater to the party line in order to bask in the support which can be signed, sealed, and delivered by this aggressive minority."

At one point La Follette came perilously close to identifying as a communist or fellow traveler anyone who urged that the United States follow a more conciliatory policy toward the Soviet Union. He wrote: "The acid test is foreign policy. The determining factor is placement of loyalty. Is it with America and democracy, or is it with the Soviet Union and totalitarianism? Does it follow the flip-flops of

43. RML to Robert A. Taft, 7 November 1946, box 62-C, Family Papers.
44. Quoted in *Appleton Post-Crescent*, 2 November 1946, clipping, box 668-C, Family Papers.
45. Ibid.

Soviet doctrine?"[46] Curiously, before Pearl Harbor it was precisely this type of reasoning that many interventionists had employed to attack La Follette and the noninterventionists.

Nowhere in the article did La Follette mention either the Wisconsin CIO or McMurray by name. But it was clear that he had both of them in mind. And it was no accident that pro-McCarthy newspapers, like the *Wisconsin State Journal* of Madison, reprinted La Follette's article shortly before the election. McCarthy, the candidate, devoted less time to the communist issue than did La Follette, a noncandidate.

This strident anticommunism was for La Follette a new and puzzeling departure. He had always been opposed to communism, of course; but he also had always avoided anything that smacked of Red-baiting. True, there had been times in his career when he had yielded to the passions of the moment and had said things for which he had no proof. In 1937, during the battle over Roosevelt's Court-reorganization plan, he had implied that foes of reorganization were involved in a sinister conspiracy. But instances like this were rare. Indeed, he, like his father, prided himself on the reasonableness of his arguments and the thoroughness of his documentation.

Rather than being a tendency latent in the La Follette "style," his anticommunist zeal probably was a reaction to the personal and political frustrations he experienced during the mid-1940s, which culminated in his defeat. Especially frustrating for him had been the emergence of interest-based politics, the chief feature of which was a self-conscious and aggressive labor movement. Because the concept of the general interest was so deeply ingrained in him, and because he had fallen out of touch with his blue-collar constituents, he did not understand and therefore could not adapt to that development. Moreover, he failed to realize that labor's defection during the 1946 campaign was not so much a rejection of him as a positive commitment to the Democratic party. Instead he blamed his troubles with labor on communists.

La Follette was not alone in seizing upon this explanation. In the postwar years, increasing numbers of Americans were finding in communism an explanation for the nation's frustrations, at home and abroad.

In the November election McCarthy overwhelmed McMurray by a better than two-to-one margin. "Naturally," La Follette wrote Senator Taft, "I supported the Republican ticket with my personal vote." Elsewhere the GOP picked up enough seats to gain control of Con-

46. Robert M. La Follette, Jr., "Look Out Liberals," *Wisconsin State Journal*, 3 November 1946, clipping, box 668-C, Family Papers.

gress for the first time in eighteen years. Had La Follette been re-elected he might have been more powerful than ever, for according to the rules of seniority, he would have had his choice of three of the most powerful committee chairmanships in the Senate: Finance, Education and Labor, or Foreign Relations.[47]

Yet, initially at least, La Follette did not outwardly appear to be brooding over the "what might have beens." He was disappointed; but he probably also felt relief. After a lifetime in or on the fringes of public life he was free—free to devote more time to his family, to travel, to pursuing his business interests. And at age fifty-one he was free to enjoy his new status as a retired elder statesman.

47. RML to Robert A. Taft, 7 November 1946, box 62-C, Family Papers.

CHAPTER 17

The Last Years, 1947–1953

In the months before the 1946 primary La Follette had at times seemed not to care whether he won or lost. Then when he did lose he seemed to react with a mixture of regret and relief. In the years following his defeat, La Follette sadly found that private life was worse than public life. But just how unhappy life had become for him no one realized until 24 February 1953, when at age fifty-eight he committed suicide.

In 1947 La Follette, at age fifty-two, embarked upon a new career as a business consultant. He opened up an office in Washington and kept on two persons from his Senate staff, Wilbur and Rosemary Voigt. Apparently at Phil's urging, Robert E. Wood, chairman of the board of Sears, Roebuck and Company and, before Pearl Harbor, chairman of the noninterventionist America First Committee, hired La Follette as a consultant to Sears. La Follette eventually sat on the board of directors and became vice-president of the Sears Foundation, which administered various philanthropic projects. La Follette also served as a consultant for two other firms, Hawaiian Steamship Company and, oddly, United Fruit Company, which for decades had symbolized the type of economic imperialism the La Follettes had so often criticized.[1]

La Follette plunged into his new job with the same energy that had characterized his Senate work. But it was not clear whether or not he really enjoyed it. According to the Voigts, who saw him nearly every day, he did like the business life. He was able to travel, to spend more time with his family, and to finally satisfy his need for financial security. By 1952 he and Rachel had built up their combined net worth to almost $160,000.[2] Other close friends, however, had a different impression. They sensed that he missed the Senate far more than he had ever imagined he would and that he found business life

1. Mrs. PFL, "Isen's Political Diary," 16 March 1952, p. 93, box 16-3, PFL Papers (see list of abbreviations p. x); *Washington Post*, 24, 25 February 1953; *New York Times*, 25 February 1953.

2. Interview, Wilbur and Rosemary Voigt, 9 July 1973; RML financial statement, enclosed in RML to Glenn D. Roberts, 15 February 1952, box 26-C, Family Papers.

boring and unfulfilling. Even the Voigts admitted that he did not always have enough work to occupy his time. On occasion, when La Follette seemed bored and in low spirits, Wilbur Voigt would go into his office and purposely try to engage him in a discussion about politics, a subject that usually perked him up.[3]

From time to time La Follette seriously considered making a political comeback. The first opportunity presented itself shortly after his defeat. Late in 1946 Congressman Robert K. Henry of Wisconsin died. La Follette received over thirty letters urging him to run in the special election scheduled for the spring of 1947. One person even sent him a campaign contribution. His sister-in-law, Isen, wrote him, "The idea has drama and appeal—your father's old seat, easy to campaign geographically, . . . and a traditionally Progressive Republican area with practically no Commie infiltration." Isen added that if he won the House seat he would be in a good position to challenge Sen. Alexander Wiley, a Republican, for his seat in 1950. After giving the matter "serious consideration from every aspect," he decided against it.[4] Norman Clapp, a close friend and a former aide, remembered La Follette saying, pathetically, "If the people of Wisconsin would be content to let me come to Washington and serve as a Congressman, I would be happy. But they won't let me. They would make me go out and rebuild the Progressive movement. I am not as young as I was. I don't have it in me." To Isen he added that if he were elected to the House he would have to start at the bottom and rebuild his seniority and influence. Moreover, he said, in Isen's words, "that our kind of campaigning days were over; that now it was the money which spoke; that he would not stoop to [the] methods used, etc." Still, La Follette never completely ruled out the possibility of running for elective office, and as late as 1950 he was telling friends that he might yet make a comeback.[5]

La Follette had numerous opportunities to serve in the executive branch. In 1947, when John Winet resigned as the United States representative to the United Nations Economic and Social Council,

3. Interviews, Morris H. Rubin, 1, 8 August 1972; Gordon Sinykin, August 1972; Glenn D. Roberts, 3 July 1973; Maurice B. Pasch, 25 July 1972; Wilbur and Rosemary Voigt.

4. Letters concerning Robert Henry's congressional seat, box 63-C, Family Papers; Mrs. PFL to RML, 21 November 1946, box 143-2, PFL Papers; RML to Paul S. Taylor, 4 February 1947, box 63-C, Family Papers.

5. Interview, Norman M. Clapp, 1961, quoted in Roger T. Johnson, *Robert M. La Follette, Jr. and the Decline of the Progressive Party in Wisconsin* (Madison, 1964), p. 160; Mrs. PFL, "Isen's Political Diary," 16 March 1952, pp. 92–93, box 161-3, PFL Papers; RML to Morris H. Rubin, 8 November 1950, box 26-C, Family Papers.

President Truman offered the position to La Follette, but he turned it down. Later that year it was widely rumored that Truman was considering him to head the European Recovery Program, otherwise known as the Marshall Plan. According to Phil, Truman offered La Follette so many positions that La Follette finally had to tell the president that he was not interested in returning to public service. However, from time to time he did serve on government-sponsored commissions, like the Hoover Commission on Executive Reorganization.[6]

Despite his disinclination to return to public life, La Follette never lost his keen interest in public affairs. And on occasion, especially in the first two years after his defeat, he felt compelled to speak out on certain issues. The one issue that concerned him most, almost to the point of becoming an obsession, was communism.

Early in 1947 he wrote a widely publicized article for *Collier's* entitled "Turn the Light on Communism." "In my opinion," he began, "Communist and fellow-traveler activities in America have become a serious menace to our democracy." He went on to level charges against numerous persons and organizations, most of them connected with organized labor. In the 1946 elections, he said, the Political Action Committee of the CIO "in many communities . . . became the purveyor of the Communist line." He singled out eight CIO national unions with leaders who were "sympathetic to the communist party line." He also accused the *Wisconsin CIO News*, which had attacked him and distorted his record during the 1946 campaign, of being "Communist dominated."

La Follette's most startling allegation was his claim to know "from firsthand experience that Communist sympathizers have infiltrated into committee staffs on Capitol Hill in Washington." He directly implicated the staffs of two Senate committees: his own Civil Liberties Committee and the Education and Labor Committee's Subcommittee on Wartime Health and Education, under the chairmanship of Claude Pepper. La Follette indirectly implicated the staffs of two other committees. "Similarly," he wrote, "the Kilgore Subcommittee on War Mobilization (of the Military Affairs Committee) and the Murray Special Committee on Small Business had staffs that many senators believed had been infiltrated by fellow travelers." As one example of communist activities, La Follette cited their practice of

6. RML to Milo Perkins, 21 October 1947, box 25-C, RML to Dr. George M. Saunders, 24 February 1947, box 64-C, RML to family, 24 June 1947, box 50-C, Family Papers; PFL to Lyon L. Brinsmade, 5 January 1948, box 146-2, PFL interview with Alan P. Kent, 1956, box 148-2, PFL Papers.

selectively leaking to the press confidential committee documents and information. He also claimed that in 1946 communists among the staff of a Senate committee considering minimum-wage legislation had rigged the hearings in such a way as to reduce the influence of anticommunists. La Follette presented no concrete evidence to support his allegations. Nor did he name the individual staff members he suspected of being communists.

Throughout the article La Follette warned that in fighting communism, Americans must not resort to totalitarian methods. The problem as he defined it was "how to take intelligent action to combat the menace without at the same time impairing civil liberties." Among the remedial steps he recommended were strengthening security checks on government employees, minimizing "the superficial appeal of Communism by improving the status of the under-privileged," and above all turning the "spotlight of publicity" on communists and fellow travelers.[7]

La Follette's article caused a minor sensation. According to Wilbur Voigt, who actually drafted the article for his boss, a Milwaukee labor union, which La Follette had indirectly implicated, threatened a libel suit against La Follette and *Collier's*. Several persons who had worked on one or more of the committee staffs that La Follette had implicated, justifiably complained that La Follette, by not naming names, had cast a shadow over everyone connected with the committees.[8] Thus La Follette had fallen into the trap he had warned against. In his eagerness to expose the communist menace he had not shown enough sensitivity for the reputations of innocent persons.

In 1950, Joseph R. McCarthy, who until that time had been known only as the man who beat La Follette, launched his reckless, wrenching crusade against communists in government. It was not entirely clear what La Follette's attitude toward his successor really was. He had no personal liking for the man, that much was certain. He still resented the type of campaign McCarthy had waged against him. And on top of that, according to one story, he once had an unpleasant personal encounter with McCarthy. Sometime in 1948 or 1949, not long after he had been hospitalized for treatment of a heart problem, La Follette attended the annual Gridiron dinner in Washington. To his surprise Joe McCarthy was seated across the table from him. They shook hands, exchanged pleasantries, and then McCarthy, with

7. Robert M. La Follette, Jr., "Turn the Light on Communism," *Collier's* 119 (8 February 1947):22, 73–74.
8. Interview, Wilbur and Rosemary Voigt.

characteristic grace, said, "I hear you've had a heart attack. That means you can't run against me in 1952."[9] As for McCarthy the communist hunter, many La Follette intimates later claimed that La Follette considered him a ruthless demagogue. La Follette's close friend Gordon Sinykin said that McCarthy's tactics sickened La Follette. Yet, another friend, the editor of the *Progressive* and an outspoken foe of McCarthy, Morris Rubin, recalled having "a feeling that Bob didn't take it as heavily as I did." La Follette, Rubin explained, "had some residue of some experiences which were never quite clear to me that I think made him quite mistrustful of some people in Washington who became targets of McCarthy's attacks, . . . if not by name . . . then perhaps by the general classification of that type of person."[10]

In any event La Follette said little about McCarthy in private and nothing about him in public. In September 1951 Vance Packard, editor of *American Magazine*, asked La Follette if he would be interested in writing "a hard-hitting piece about Senator Joseph McCarthy." La Follette declined, citing "inability to secure sufficient time for research and writing," even though Packard had offered to help prepare the manuscript.[11]

It was not clear why La Follette, the champion of civil liberties, never spoke out against his ruthless successor. Initially perhaps, given his own warnings of communist infiltration, he may have felt that McCarthy was only doing what had to be done. Later, when it should have been clear to him that McCarthy was swinging wildly, he may have thought that people would dismiss as sour grapes any criticism he might make of the man who had defeated him. The most likely reason for his silence, however, was that by the time McCarthy launched his crusade, La Follette had become so absorbed in his personal problems that he lacked the energy and the will to inject himself into the public spotlight.

As usual ill health led the list of problems. La Follette's case history read like a medical glossary. He suffered from diverticulitis; bursitis; mild diabetes; and chronic neck, shoulder, and hip pains. In July 1948 he entered Georgetown University Hospital complaining of recurrent chest pains. His doctors, as always, had difficulty diagnosing the prob-

9. Interview, John Clifford Folger, 5 June 1973. Folger related the story as he remembered hearing it from La Follette.

10. Interviews, John Clifford Folger; Bronson C. La Follette, 5 July 1973; Glenn D. Roberts; Morris H. Rubin; Wilbur and Rosemary Voigt.

11. Vance Packard to RML, 12 September 1951, memorandum by RML, 17 September 1951, box 26-C, Family Papers. Philip La Follette did, however, publically criticize McCarthy. See *Madison Capital Times*, 2 January 1952.

lem. They found no conclusive evidence of a heart attack; but they did find strong indication that the chest pains were brought on by poor circulation, which in turn was probably due to coronary heart disease. La Follette spent close to two months in the hospital, a fact he tried to conceal from the press and his business associates, probably for fear that his associates would consider him unable to handle his business responsibilities. For the rest of his life he remained in generally poor health. His son Bronson later estimated that he was laid up as much as one week out of every month.[12]

By 1952 La Follette had been retired from public life for five years; but although out of the public spotlight, he was not completely forgotten. He rarely visited Capitol Hill, probably because he wanted to avoid using, and to avoid even the appearance of using, his still considerable influence there to secure favors for his business clients. Never much of a party goer, he rarely attended social functions.

Still, he was not completely forgotten. From time to time former colleagues called on him or he called on them. Occasionally friends from the media dropped by his office to chat about current events.[13] Early in 1952 several Wisconsin Democrats, possibly at the urging of the Truman administration, approached La Follette to ask him whether he would run as a Democrat against McCarthy in November. Citing personal reasons, La Follette declined.[14] Later that year, supporters of both the Democratic presidential candidate, Adlai Stevenson, and the Republican, Dwight D. Eisenhower, sought La Follette's help in the presidential campaign. He made no public endorsement but he did contribute two hundred fifty dollars to the Citizens for Eisenhower-Nixon Committee and an additional fifteen hundred dollars to the Republican National Committee.[15]

On 6 February 1953, La Follette celebrated his fifty-eighth birthday; his hair was now almost completely gray, and the appellation *Young Bob* was no longer appropriate. It was at about this time that his family and a few close friends began to worry about his emotional well-being. He frequently experienced anxiety attacks, especially

12. RML medical history, "Summary in the Case of Robert La Follette," June 1949, box 26-C, Wilbur Voigt to Morris H. Rubin, 30 July, 25 August 1948, box 25-C, Family Papers; interview, Bronson C. La Follette.
13. Interviews, Wilbur and Rosemary Voigt, Bronson C. La Follette.
14. Michael O'Brien, "The Anti-McCarthy Campaign in Wisconsin, 1951–1952," *Wisconsin Magazine of History* 56(Winter 1972–1973):95.
15. Telegram, Estes Kefauver et al. to RML, 13 October 1952, Walter Williams et al. to RML, 28 October 1952, box 26-C, RML's contributions mentioned in RML to Sidney J. Weinberg, 3 October 1952, Sidney J. Weinberg to RML, 7 October 1952, R. Douglas Stuart to RML, 10 October 1952, box 34-C, Family Papers.

when at home. His son Bronson, sixteen years old at the time, later described one such attack. While eating breakfast one morning, Bronson looked into the next room where his father was sitting alone. For no apparent reason La Follette had a worried expression on his face. Then he began to fidget nervously, and finally he broke out into a cold sweat. When Bronson entered the room, his father, in an uncharacteristic display of affection, hugged him and told him that he loved him.[16]

Wilbur and Rosemary Voigt, who saw La Follette at his office, also noticed that he was a bit more depressed than usual. For one thing he was complaining about a loss of memory. This especially concerned him because he had once possessed an exceptional memory. During his Senate career he had been able to read over a lengthy speech once or twice and then recite it almost verbatim. But now, he complained to the Voigts, he was unable to remember names and other things that he thought he should be able to remember.[17]

According to the Voigts, in February, La Follette also became obsessed with the fear that McCarthy would summon him to testify before his Senate committee. In the 1947 *Collier's* article, La Follette had written, without going into detail, that as chairman of the Civil Liberties Committee he had been "forced to stamp out [communist] influence within my own committee staff." Now, six years later, La Follette expressed to the Voigts his fear that McCarthy might put him on the stand and ask him to describe specifically what steps he had taken to stamp out communist influence. In fact he had quietly fired suspected communists from the committee staff. But in 1953 La Follette told the Voigts that he probably should have taken stronger action. Perhaps, he said, he should have called in the Federal Bureau of Investigation. And he was worried that he would have to admit to McCarthy that he had been remiss in dealing with the communists. Apparently La Follette's fears were groundless. There was no evidence that McCarthy had contacted La Follette or that McCarthy intended to summon him to testify.[18]

On Tuesday, 24 February 1953, La Follette committed suicide. The day began routinely. At breakfast with Rachel and Bronson he seemed perfectly normal, showing no trace of depression or anxiety.[19] At approximately nine-thirty Rachel, on her way to a Red Cross meet-

16. Interview, Bronson C. La Follette.
17. Interview, Wilbur and Rosemary Voigt.
18. RML, "Turn the Light on Communism," p. 22; interview, Wilbur and Rosemary Voigt.
19. Interview, Bronson C. La Follette. RML's other son, Joseph, nineteen, was a sophomore at Cornell University and was away at school.

ing on Capitol Hill, dropped him off at his office in the National Press Building. A little after eleven o'clock he emerged from his inner office carrying a briefcase and saying to his secretary, Rosemary Voigt, "I'm going out. I'll call you later." Mrs. Voigt was mildly surprised because she was not aware that he had an appointment anywhere and because he normally said where he was going when he left the office during the day.

Sometime before noon Rachel was summoned from her meeting to the telephone. Bob was on the other end. "Would you come home and meet me there," he asked in a calm voice and without explanation. At about eleven-thirty La Follette arrived at his home on Manning Place in northeast Washington. He greeted the maid, Mrs. Henrietta Lewis, went up to his bedroom on the second floor, and closed the door. Mrs. Lewis went down into the basement to work. She heard nothing until Rachel arrived at twelve-thirty.

Not finding her husband on the ground floor, Rachel went upstairs to the bedroom. On the bed she saw an empty pistol holster. She then went into the bathroom off the bedroom. There, sprawled on the floor, was Bob. He was lying face up, his shoulder across the step up to the shower stall, one hand by his side, and the other hand, clutching a 22-caliber Woodsman target pistol, lying across his chest. He was dead, a bullet had passed through the roof of his mouth and lodged in his brain.

In a state of shock Rachel telephoned Wilbur Voigt at the office. When he arrived and saw what had happened, he summoned Doctor Worth Daniels, La Follette's longtime physician. Daniels pronounced La Follette dead at one-fifteen in the afternoon. After a routine investigation and without an inquest, the authorities ruled it a suicide.

La Follette's body was transported to Madison. He had had no religious affiliation, but at Rachel's request a brief service was held at Grace Episcopal Church on Friday, 27 February. He was then buried alongside his parents in Madison's Forest Hill Cemetery. On 2 March the United States Senate held an emotional memorial service, one of the few times it so honored a member who died after leaving office.[20]

In the aftermath of LaFollette's death, his family and friends tortured themselves with the obvious questions: Why had he done it? Could anyone have averted the tragedy? In retrospect, they recalled that during the last weeks, or maybe even months, of his life La Fol-

20. Interview, Wilbur and Rosemary Voigt; *New York Times*, 25, 28 February 1953; *Washington Post*, 25, 26 February 1953; *Washington Star*, 25 February 1953; *CR* 83:1, 1953, vol. 83, pt. 2, pp. 1497–1506.

lette had showed signs of severe mental distress: his anxiety attacks at home, his obsessive and apparently groundless fear of being summoned before McCarthy's committee, and his complaints about losing his memory. Yet he had experienced periods of depression and anxiety throughout his life, and he had always managed to snap out of them. There had been no real reason to think that this time would be different. Moreover, La Follette had a tendency, more pronounced in him than in most people, of showing different aspects of himself to different people and never showing his whole self to any one person. Thus one acquaintance could describe him as the "least introverted, least depressed man" he ever knew, while another friend could call him a "gloomy Gus."[21]

Because he left no suicide note and had never submitted himself to psychiatric examination, all anyone could do was speculate as to why he had killed himself. The first thought that occurred to some people was that he must have learned that he had a terminal illness. But according to Wilbur Voigt, La Follette's doctor rejected that theory.[22] The official explanation released by the family and reported by the press was that he had been despondent for some time over ill health.[23] True, he was in poor health. But there was nothing to indicate that his physical condition was significantly worse in February 1953 than it had been for several years. Still, ill health probably played a part. A lifetime of poor health must have taken an enormous toll, physically and emotionally. Moreover, if he had had coronary artery disease as the doctors had suspected, it was possible that by 1953 it had progressed to the stage where it impeded the flow of blood to the brain, thereby impairing his memory and in other ways distorting his perceptions.

Some people linked his death to his defeat in 1946. That defeat, they said, ate away at him like a cancer and, coupled with an unrewarding job as a business consultant and with the destructive activities of his successor, McCarthy, heavily contributed to his depressed state of mind. In a somewhat similar vein, columnist Drew Pearson suggested that La Follette committed suicide because he felt that he had failed his father. Without giving the source of his information, Pearson said that La Follette, attending a social function shortly

21. Francis Biddle, *In Brief Authority* (New York, 1962), p. 133; interview, Rosemary Voigt.

22. Interview, Wilbur Voigt.

23. *New York Times*, 25 February 1953; *Washington Post*, 25, 26 February 1953.

before his death, had expressed to friends his concern about McCarthy and had "told how he never should have let McCarthy beat him, how he had let his father down."[24]

In trying to explain the seemingly unexplainable, grieving relatives and friends focused on La Follette's last years. But surely another part of the explanation rested deep in his past: in the child and young adult for whom parental affection and approval were intimately tied to incredibly high standards of performance; in the young senator who found himself pursuing a career that, except for circumstance and loyalty to his father, he would never have chosen for himself; and in the slightly older senator who seemed unable to take satisfaction from his considerable accomplishments and who strained heavily under the burdens of public life.

24. Interview, Gordon Sinykin; Doris Fleeson, "Bob La Follette's Despondency," *Washington Star*, 26 February 1953; Drew Pearson, " 'Young Bob' Felt He'd Failed Dad," *Washington Post*, 4 March 1953.

Bibliographical Note

Manuscript Collections

By far the most important source for this biography was the voluminous collection of La Follette Family Papers in the Manuscripts Division of the Library of Congress. Fortunately for historians, the La Follettes were a letter-writing and a letter-saving family. Closed to researchers until 1970, the collection includes the papers of La Follette, Jr. (701 boxes), La Follette, Sr. (323 boxes), Belle Case La Follette (73 boxes), and Fola La Follette (174 boxes). The collection also contains fifty-three boxes of intimate correspondence among family members. Included in the La Follette, Jr., papers are speeches, voting records, press releases, constituent correspondence, newspaper clippings, and items of a personal nature, such as financial and health records. This excellent collection is generally well organized, although every now and then the diligent researcher will find an item of real importance in an unexpected place.

Other collections at the Library of Congress that yielded useful information were the Felix Frankfurter Papers and the papers of La Follette's progressive colleagues in the Senate, William E. Borah, Bronson Cutting, and George W. Norris. The papers of the senators, however, provided little information on the inner workings of the progressive bloc.

After the La Follette Family Papers, the most important source was the Philip F. La Follette Papers at the State Historical Society of Wisconsin in Madison. This collection contains important letters by and to La Follette, Jr., that are not in the La Follette Family Papers. Especially revealing is the extensive correspondence between Phil and his wife, Isen. The collection also contains several drafts of Isen's combination diary-memoirs. Gossipy but filled with insights, her writings must be used with caution, for she interpreted events from her husband's perspective. I have quoted Isen frequently, but usually to express strong impressions I had gathered from other sources.

Also at the State Historical Society of Wisconsin are the Thomas R. Amlie Papers, which are invaluable on the founding of the Progressive party and which shed light on the La Follette brothers as political leaders; the Herman L. Ekern Papers, which illuminate La Follette's activities as his father's secretary; the Orland S. Loomis Papers; and the Edwin E. Witte Papers.

At the Franklin D. Roosevelt Library in Hyde Park, New York, the Roosevelt Papers provided some important materials but were generally disappointing. The diaries of Secretary of the Treasury Henry Morgenthau, Jr., also at the Roosevelt Library, were especially helpful on taxation matters.

The manuscript collections that relate to the Senate Civil Liberties Committee are the committee papers in the National Archives (Record Group 46) and the Heber Blankenhorn Papers in the Archives of Labor History and Urban Affairs, Wayne State University. They are discussed below.

Interviews

Conversations with persons who knew La Follette disclosed facets of his personality that did not come through in his personal papers. Interviews also filled gaps left by other sources and suggested leads for further investigation. Without exception, the persons whom I interviewed talked freely and frankly about La Follette. The following is a list of persons interviewed; it includes the places and dates of the interviews and, where applicable, an explanation of each person's relationship to La Follette: Marquis Childs, political columnist, 9 March 1977, Washington, D. C.; Norman M. Clapp, Senate aide, 1935–1937 and 1939–1944, Madison, Wisconsin, 3 August 1972; John Clifford Folger, close personal friend, 1915–1953, Washington, D. C., 5 June 1973; Frank W. Kuehl, political associate and friend, 1923–1953, Washington, D. C., 1 December 1971; Bronson C. La Follette, son, Madison, 5 July 1973; Isabel B. "Isen" La Follette, sister-in-law, Madison, 5 July 1973; Mary La Follette, sister, Washington, D. C., 22 February 1973 and numerous other conversations between 1973 and 1977; Miles McMillin, Wisconsin political reporter, late 1930s to 1953, Madison, 2 August 1972; Maurice B. Pasch, Senate aide, 1930–1935, friend, 1930–1953, Madison, 25 July 1972; Roderick H. Riley, Senate office staff member, 1933–1934, Washington, D. C., 11 June 1973; Glenn D. Roberts, close personal friend and political associate, 1934–1953, Norwalk, Wisconsin, 3 July 1973; Morris H. Rubin, *Progressive* editor after 1940 and close personal friend and political adviser, 1940–1953, Madison, 1, 8 August 1972; Robert E. Sher, friend and political associate, 1930–1953, Washington, D. C., 30 May 1973; Gordon Sinykin, close personal friend and political adviser, 1934–1953, Madison, August 1972; Rosemary McCormick Voigt, Senate office secretary, 1940–1946, and secretary and close personal friend, 1947–1953, Chicago, 9 July 1973; Wilbur Voigt, chief aide, intermittently from 1939 to 1946 and assistant and close personal friend, 1947–1953, Chicago, 9 July 1973; and Burton K. Wheeler, Senate colleague, 1925–1947, Washington, D. C., 4 December 1973.

Government Publications

The most important government publication for this study was the *U.S. Congressional Record*, 1925–1947, 1953. As a member of a generation that took speechmaking seriously, La Follette was careful with what went into the *Record*. Consequently, his Senate speeches, lengthy and fact filled, provided the best guide to his political thought.

Relevant congressional committee hearings and reports include U.S. Congress, Senate, Subcommittee of the Committee on Manufactures, *Hearings on S. 174 and S. 262, 72d Cong.*, 1st sess., 1931–1932, which documented the inability of state and local governments to cope with relief needs during the depression; the ninety-five volumes of hearings and reports of the Senate Civil Liberties Committee, specific volumes of which are cited in the footnotes; and, on the Legislative Reorganization Act of 1946, U.S. Congress, Joint Committee on the Organization of Congress, *Organization of Congress: Hearings Pursuant to H. Cong. Res. 18*, 79th Cong., 1st sess., 1945; and ibid., *Report Pursuant to H. Cong. Res. 18*, 79th Cong., 2d sess., 1946.

The U.S. Congress, *Congressional Directory*, 1925–1946, provided a wealth of useful information on the Senate. The *Wisconsin Blue Book* (Madison), published yearly to 1940 and biennially thereafter, contains election results, population statistics, party platforms, biographical sketches of state politicians, and other useful facts.

Newspapers and Periodicals

The huge collection of newspaper and magazine clippings in the La Follette Family Papers facilitated the research effort. Included in the collection are thousands of newspaper clippings, many of them from Wisconsin publications, and most of the feature articles written about La Follette. I followed La Follette's career in *La Follette's Magazine*, 1917–1929, and the *Progressive*, 1929–1946. The *New York Times* was also essential, although its anti–La Follette bias lessened its reliability for Wisconsin politics, especially during the late 1920s and early 1930s. For distorted coverage of La Follette by a major newspaper, however, the *Chicago Tribune* was probably unrivaled. During the heyday of the Progressive party, the *Tribune*, instead of affixing "Prog., Wis." after La Follette's name, designated him as "Rad., Wis." Also helpful for selected topics was the *Baltimore Sun*, especially the columns of H. L. Mencken and Frank Kent. Among periodicals, The *Nation* and *New Republic* were perceptive La Follette watchers.

Secondary Sources and Reminiscences

About La Follette

Although numerous studies deal with aspects of La Follette's career, no biography has previously been published. Historians neglected him not by choice but because the La Follette papers were unavailable for so many years.

The only previously published account of La Follette's Senate career is

Edward N. Doan, *The La Follettes and the Wisconsin Idea* (New York, 1947). A former college teacher who campaigned for La Follette in 1946, Doan devoted half of his book to the younger La Follette and half to the elder La Follette. Although laudatory and superficial and based primarily on newspaper accounts and speeches, Doan's book does demonstrate the range of La Follette's interests and ideas. Roger T. Johnson, *Robert M. La Follette, Jr. and the Decline of the Progressive Party in Wisconsin* (Madison, 1964) discusses La Follette's involvement in state politics and points out his weakness as a political leader. Generally sympathetic to his subject, Johnson made good use of then-existing sources to produce a study broader than the title suggests. A good critical analysis of La Follette's thought is Theodore Rosenof, " 'Young Bob' La Follette on American Capitalism," *Wisconsin Magazine of History* 55 (Winter 1971–1972):130–39, which points out inconsistencies in La Follette's ideas and criticizes him for failing to subject the tenets of capitalism to searching examination. A more detailed discussion along these lines is Rosenof, "The Ideology of Senator Robert M. La Follette, Jr." (M.A. thesis, University of Wisconsin, 1966). Rosenof's arguments are weakened somewhat by an occasional tendency to wrench La Follette's ideas out of the context of the times. Informative on La Follette's foreign policy views is Alan Edmond Kent, "Portrait in Isolationism: The La Follettes and Foreign Policy" (Ph.D. dissertation, University of Wisconsin, 1956).

Perceptive sketches of La Follette by contemporaries are Mauritz A. Hallgren, "Young Bob La Follette," *Nation* 132 (4 March 1931):235–37; and Oswald Garrison Villard, "Pillars of Government: Robert M. La Follette, Jr.," *Forum* 96(August 1936):87–90. Also perceptive, and sympathetic, are the sections on La Follette in John Franklin Carter [The Unofficial Observer], *American Messiahs* (New York, 1935); Stanley High, *Roosevelt—And Then?* (New York, 1937); [Drew Pearson and Robert S. Allen], *Washington Merry-Go-Round* (New York, 1931); and Ray Tucker and Frederick R. Barkley, *Sons of the Wild Jackass* (Boston, 1932). The entry on La Follette in *Current Biography* (1944), pp. 368–72, also contains useful information.

Numerous memoirs, diaries, and related works shed light on La Follette. Francis Biddle, *In Brief Authority* (New York, 1962) contains a brief but interesting assessment of La Follette's personality. Lincoln Steffens, *The Autobiography of Lincoln Steffens*, vol. 2 (New York, 1931) describes the La Follette family's reaction to Russia and communism during their trip in 1923. Ella Winter and Granville Hicks, eds., *The Letters of Lincoln Steffens*, vol. 2 (New York, 1938) contains several letters about La Follette. On La Follette's relationship to Franklin D. Roosevelt and the New Deal, Harold L. Ickes, *The Secret Diary of Harold L. Ickes*, 3 vols. (New York, 1953–1954) is extremely helpful, as is Rexford G. Tugwell, *The Democratic Roosevelt: A Biography of Franklin D. Roosevelt* (Baltimore, 1969 [1957]). La Follette's stature in the Senate is discussed in several entries in Allen

Drury, *A Senate Journal, 1943–1945* (New York, 1963). Drury's best-selling novel, *Advise and Consent* (New York, 1959), also merits attention. One of the books main characters, Sen. Brigham Anderson, besides being a product of the novelist's imagination, is obviously a composite of many persons Drury observed as a political reporter; in some respects Anderson also bears a marked resemblance to La Follette. Philip F. La Follette, *Adventures in Politics: The Memoirs of Philip La Follette,* edited by Donald Young (New York, 1970) contains some useful information but on the whole is a surprisingly bland memoir that reveals little about the author or La Follette, Jr.

La Follette, Sr.

The starting point for studying the career of the elder La Follette is Robert M. La Follette, *La Follette's Autobiography: A Personal Narrative of Political Experiences* (Madison, 1960 [1911, 1913]), a revealing political document. Belle Case La Follette and Fola La Follette, *Robert M. La Follette,* 2 vols. (New York, 1953) remains the best biography. Although uncritical and lacking perspective, this book, which was nearly thirty years in the writing, makes excellent use of La Follette's personal papers and is factually accurate. It also contains much information about La Follette, Jr., as he was growing up. Unfortunately the book is out of print. For La Follette, Sr.'s, early life and rise to power, see David P. Thelen, *The Early Life of Robert M. La Follette, 1855–1884* (Chicago, 1966), which successfully challenges parts of La Follette's autobiographical account; and Thelen, *The New Citizenship: Origins of Progressivism in Wisconsin, 1885–1900* (Columbia, Mo., 1972). The basic works on La Follette's years as governor are Robert S. Maxwell, *La Follette and the Rise of the Progressives in Wisconsin, 1890–1928* (Madison, 1956); and Herbert F. Margulies, *The Decline of the Progressive Movement in Wisconsin, 1890–1920* (Madison, 1968), excellent for its discussion of the shifting coalitions that composed the progressive movement. The most recent work is Thelen, *Robert La Follette and the Insurgent Spirit* (Boston, 1976), which is less a biography than a provocative interpretation of the progressive movement. My research indicated that Thelen's discussion of consumer-taxpayer insurgents and job-oriented modernizers may, in slightly different terms, be applicable to later decades as well as to the Progressive Era.

Progressivism

Among the many books that guided my thinking on progressivism in the 1920s and early 1930s were Lawrence W. Levine, *Defender of the Faith, William Jennings Bryan: The Last Decade, 1915–1925* (London, 1965), a superb study; LeRoy Ashby, *Spearless Leader: William E. Borah and the Progressive Movement in the 1920's* (Urbana, 1972), which skillfully exposes the internal weaknesses and contradictions that rendered Senate progressives largely ineffective; William E. Leuchtenburg, *The Perils of Prosperity, 1914–1932* (Chicago, 1958), esp. chap. 7; Paul Carter, *The Twenties in America* (New York, 1968); Wayne S. Cole, *Senator Gerald*

P. Nye and American Foreign Relations (Minneapolis, 1962), which emphasizes the agrarian orientation of Nye and other progressives; and Otis L. Graham, Jr., *An Encore for Reform: The Old Progressives and the New Deal* (New York, 1967), an excellent study that stresses the discontinuity between the progressive movement and the New Deal. In one way or another, all these studies emphasize the limitations of progressivism and the inability of progressives to adapt to an urban-industrial society.

An important study that discusses the positive side of progressivism is Richard Lowitt, *George W. Norris: The Persistence of a Progressive, 1913–1933* (Urbana, Ill., 1971). See also in this regard, Hugh J. Savage, "Political Independents of the Hoover Era: The Progressive Insurgents of the Senate" (Ph. D. dissertation, University of Illinois, 1961). Informative biographical sketches of the Senate progressives are contained in [Pearson and Allen], *Washington Merry-Go-Round*, and Tucker and Barkley, *Sons of the Wild Jackass*, both previously cited.

Hoover Administration

There is as yet no comprehensive biography of Herbert Hoover. Albert U. Romasco, *The Poverty of Abundance: Hoover, the Nation, the Depression* (New York, 1965) is a fine critical examination of the Hoover administration's response to the depression. Also helpful are Harris Gaylord Warren, *Herbert Hoover and the Great Depression* (New York, 1967) and especially Arthur M. Schlesinger, Jr., *The Age of Roosevelt: The Crisis of the Old Order, 1919–1933* (Boston, 1957). An excellent collection of essays on Hoover is Martin L. Fausold and George T. Mazuzan, eds., *The Hoover Presidency: A Reappraisal* (Albany, 1974).

The congressional debates over relief and public works during the Hoover administration are detailed in Fred Greenbaum, *Fighting Progressive: A Biography of Edward P. Costigan* (Washington, D.C., 1971); J. Joseph Huthmacher, *Senator Robert F. Wagner and the Rise of Urban Liberalism* (New York, 1971); and Jordan A. Schwarz, *The Interregnum of Despair: Hoover, Congress, and the Depression* (Urbana, Ill., 1970). All of these studies mention La Follette, but none accords him the prominence in the relief debates that this biography does.

The New Deal, 1933–1938

For background material on Roosevelt and the New Deal, I relied heavily on James MacGregor Burns, *Roosevelt: The Lion and the Fox* (New York, 1956); Frank Freidel, *Franklin D. Roosevelt: Launching the New Deal* (Boston, 1973); William E. Leuchtenburg, *Franklin D. Roosevelt and the New Deal, 1932–1940* (New York, 1963); Ellis W. Hawley, *The New Deal and the Problem of Monopoly, 1933–39* (Princeton, 1966); Raymond Moley, *After Seven Years* (Lincoln, Nebr., 1971 [1939]; and Arthur M. Schlesinger, Jr., *The Age of Roosevelt: The Coming of the New Deal* (Boston, 1959) and *The Age of Roosevelt: The Politics of Upheaval* (Boston,

1960). Essential, too, were the previously cited works by Ickes, Tugwell, and Huthmacher. Among these, Tugwell, Ickes, and Schlesinger devote the most attention to La Follette.

To my mind, the most stimulating and suggestive interpretation of the New Deal is Paul K. Conkin's essay, *The New Deal* (New York, 1967). A study of La Follette, I think, lends support to many of Conkin's conclusions.

One aspect of the New Deal that has been sorely neglected is taxation policy. Roy G. Blakey and Gladys C. Blakey, *The Federal Income Tax* (London, 1940) and Sidney Ratner, *American Taxation: Its History as a Social Force in Democracy* (New York, 1942) contain much information but little analysis. Helpful for the political context were John Morton Blum, *From the Morgenthau Diaries: Years of Urgency, 1938–1941* (Boston, 1965) and Randolph E. Paul, *Taxation for Prosperity* (Indianapolis, 1947). The Morgenthau diaries at the Roosevelt Library yielded additional materials.

Wisconsin Politics and the Progressive Party

The best general survey of Wisconsin history is Robert C. Nesbit, *Wisconsin: A History* (Madison, 1973), which incorporates much of the recent scholarship on the state. Still useful for selected topics are William F. Raney, *Wisconsin: A Story of Progress* (New York, 1940) and Leon Epstein, *Politics in Wisconsin* (Madison, 1958). An excellent article that touches on the plight of dairy farmers in the state during the depression is A. William Hoglund, "Wisconsin Dairy Farmers on Strike," *Agricultural History* 35 (1961).24–34.

On the Progressive party, the best published work is Johnson, *La Follette, Jr.* Two unpublished studies are also important: Charles H. Backstrom, "The Progressive Party of Wisconsin, 1934–1946" (Ph.D. dissertation, University of Wisconsin, 1956) and John E. Miller, "Governor Philip F. La Follette, the Wisconsin Progressives, and the New Deal, 1930–1939" (Ph.D. dissertation, University of Wisconsin, 1973), which is based on extensive research in the Philip La Follette Papers. All studies of the Progressive party probably overemphasize the leadership and neglect the grass-roots level. Much needed is a study that is firmly grounded in manuscript, newspaper, and related sources but that also analyzes demographic data to determine the ethnic, religious, occupational, and class characteristics of the party's supporters. Michael Paul Rogin, *The Intellectuals and McCarthy: The Radical Specter* (Cambridge, Mass., 1967), pp. 59–103, contains some information along these lines, but much more needs to be done.

On Philip La Follette's three terms as governor, the most recent and most detailed study is Miller's dissertation, previously cited. No historian, however, has yet managed to reconcile the many contradictions in La Follette's career. On the ill-fated National Progressives of America, see Miller's work and Donald R. McCoy, *Angry Voices: Left-of-Center Politics in the New Deal Era* (Lawrence, Kans., 1958). A perceptive contemporary judgment of the NPA is Elmer Davis, "The Wisconsin Brothers," *Harper's Magazine* 178 (February 1939):268–77.

Civil Liberties Investigation, 1936–1940

By far the best account of the investigation is Jerold S. Auerbach, *Labor and Liberty: The La Follette Committee and the New Deal* (Indianapolis, 1966), a superb study. I cited Auerbach's work frequently, but not before covering much the same ground and thus assuring myself of the thoroughness of his research and the accuracy of his documentation. My account takes issue with Auerbach only on relatively minor points. I accorded La Follette a somewhat greater role in determining the course of the investigation, and I found less evidence of communist influence on the committee.

Unfortunately, neither the papers of the committee in the National Archives nor the La Follette papers contain many items to or by La Follette about the committee's activities. A memorandum in the La Follette papers discloses that some of the senator's office files on the investigation were accidentally destroyed. The Heber Blankenhorn Papers in the Archives of Labor History and Urban Affairs at Wayne State University provided several pertinent materials.

An interesting account of the first phase of the investigation is Clinch Calkins, *Spy Overhead: The Story of Industrial Espionage* (New York, 1937). Other contemporary accounts include Meyer Levin, *Citizens* (New York, 1940), a thinly veiled fictional treatment of the Memorial Day incident; Kenneth G. Crawford, *The Pressure Boys: The Inside Story of Lobbying in America* (New York, 1939); and Benjamin C. Marsh, *Lobbyist For the People: A Record of Fifty Years* (Washington, D.C., 1953), which contains a perceptive though incidental remark about the limited scope of the committee's investigation.

On the labor scene in general during the 1930s, two books by Irving Bernstein are excellent: *The Lean Years: A History of the American Worker, 1920–1933* (Boston, 1960) and *Turbulent Years: A History of the American Worker, 1933–1941* (Boston, 1969). A brief survey is Joseph G. Rayback, *A History of American Labor* (New York, 1966).

Foreign Affairs

The most detailed description of La Follette's views on foreign affairs is the previously cited dissertation by Kent. Useful for the period immediately preceding the attack on Pearl Harbor are James MacGregor Burns, *Roosevelt: The Soldier of Freedom* (New York, 1970); Robert A. Divine, *The Reluctant Belligerent: American Entry into World War II* (New York, 1965); and William L. Langer and S. Everett Gleason, *The Challenge to Isolation, 1937–1940* (New York, 1952) and *The Undeclared War, 1940–1941* (New York, 1953). Excellent on the debate between the isolationists and the interventionists are three studies by Wayne S. Cole: *America First: The Battle Against Intervention, 1940–1941* (Madison, 1953); *Charles A. Lindbergh and the Battle Against American Intervention in World War II* (New York, 1974); and the previously cited *Senator Gerald P. Nye and American Foreign Relations*. With commendable detachment, Cole documents the excesses by both sides that marred the so-called Great Debate.

Most historians have been critical of the isolationists. Recently, however, some historians, doubtless influenced by the foreign and domestic events of the 1960s and early 1970s, have begun to cast the isolationists in a more favorable light. See for example James T. Patterson, *Mr. Republican: A Biography of Robert A. Taft* (Boston, 1972), a model biography; Ronald Radosh, *Prophets on the Right: Profiles of Conservative Critics of American Globalism* (New York, 1975), and Joan Hoff Wilson, *Herbert Hoover: Forgotten Progressive* (Boston, 1975). My treatment of La Follette's foreign policy would also seem to fit into this category.

Congressional Reorganization

Significant assessments of the Legislative Reorganization Act of 1946 include George B. Galloway, *The Legislative Process in Congress* (New York, 1953) and *Congressional Reorganization Revisited* (College Park, Md., 1956); A. S. Mike Monroney et al., *The Strengthening of American Political Institutions* (Ithaca, N. Y., 1949); and La Follette's testimony in U.S. Congress, Senate, Committee on Expenditures in the Executive Departments, *Hearings on Evaluation of Legislative Reorganization Act of 1946*, 80th Cong., 2d sess., 1948, pp. 59–79. Conflicting assessments by political scientists are scattered throughout David P. Truman, ed., *The Congress and America's Future* (Englewood Cliffs, N.J., 1965).

On the growth of presidential power during World War II that prompted calls for congressional reform, no adequate study has been published. The general outline, however, is given in Roland Young, *Congressional Politics in the Second World War* (New York, 1956) and Arthur M. Schlesinger, Jr., *The Imperial Presidency* (New York, 1973).

1946 Wisconsin Primary

Generally balanced accounts of the 1946 primary are contained in Johnson, *La Follette, Jr.*; Michael J. O'Brien, "Senator Joseph McCarthy and Wisconsin, 1946–1957" (Ph.D. dissertation, University of Wisconsin, 1971); and the most detailed account, David M. Oshinsky, *Senator Joseph McCarthy and the American Labor Movement* (Columbia, Mo., 1976), which emphasizes the role of organized labor. Less useful is Karl Meyer, "The Politics of Loyalty: From La Follette to McCarthy in Wisconsin, 1918–1952" (Ph.D. dissertation, Princeton University, 1956). Richard Rovere, *Senator Joe McCarthy* (Cleveland, 1960) contains penetrating insights into McCarthy, but Rovere allowed McCarthy's career as a senator to distort his account of the 1946 primary. The worst offender in this regard was

Jack Anderson and Ronald W. May, *McCarthy: the Man, the Senator, the "Ism"* (Boston, 1952) in which the authors employed some of McCarthy's methods in an attempt to discredit him.

On the role of organized labor in the campaign, Oshinsky's is the most thorough treatment, but Johnson's study is also helpful. Two works that do not deal with the Wisconsin situation directly but help explain organized labor's failure to support La Follette are J. David Greenstone, *Labor in American Politics* (New York, 1969) and James C. Foster, *The Union Politic: The CIO Political Action Committee* (Columbia, Mo., 1975).

The subject of communist influence in the Wisconsin labor movement and on the 1946 primary election is in need of thorough reexamination. In generalizing on the subject most historians have relied too heavily on only two accounts, Thomas W. Gavett, *The Development of the Labor Movement in Milwaukee* (Madison, 1965) and especially Robert Willard Ozanne, "The Effects of Communist Leadership on American Trade Unions" (Ph.D. dissertation, University of Wisconsin, 1954).

Index